A Topical Guide to the STRATEGIES Boxes

GENERAL SKILLS

Global Technical Communication	13
Analyzing Your Audience	50
Persuasion	55
Proofreading	62
Avoiding Ethical Abuses	72
Outlining	82

TEAMWORK

Organizing a Team Project	14
Running a Meeting	17
Managing Team Conflicts	18
Peer Review and Editing	19

DOING RESEARCH

Thinking Critically about Research	26
Researching Online	29
Informational Interviews	38
Surveys	40

STYLE

Deciding about Tone	105
Nonsexist Usage	106
Unbiased Usage	107

VISUALS AND DOCUMENT DESIGN

Creating Tables	116
Creating Graphs	118
Creating Charts	121
Illustrations, Diagrams, Photographs, Videos, Icons, and Symbols	125
Designing: Consistency and Cohesiveness	139
Designing: Navigation and Emphasis	144

GETTING A JOB

Creating a Résumé	158
Application Letters	161
Digital Job Application Materials	162
Dossiers, Portfolios, and E-portfolios	165
Interviews and Follow-up Letters	170

MEMOS AND LETTERS

Memos	185
Letters in General	192
Inquiry Letters	195
Claim	198
Sales	200
Adju	201

REPORTS AND PROPOSALS

Progress Reports	284
Periodic Activity Reports	287
Trip Reports	289
Meeting Minutes	292
Feasibility Reports	294
Recommendation Reports	296
Peer Review Reports	298
Formal Reports	312
Proposals	335

OTHER PRINT DOCUMENTS

Definitions	217
Descriptions	235
Specifications	238
Achieving Readability	255
Creating an Accessible Design	258
Instructions and Procedures	263
Summaries	278

DIGITAL MEDIA AND PRESENTATIONS

Email	356
Text Messages	358
Blogs, Wikis, and Web Pages	371
Social Media	383
Preparing Oral Presentations	398
Using Presentation Software and Video Conferencing	400
Delivering Oral Presentations	402

AVOIDING PLAGIARISM

Taking Notes	407
Quoting the Work of Others	409
Paraphrasing the Work of Others	410
Summarizing the Work of Others	411

A Guide to the
CHECKLISTS

CHECKLIST for Effective Technical Communication   22

CHECKLIST for Doing Research   41

CHECKLIST for Usability   63

CHECKLIST for Ethical Communication   72

CHECKLIST for Structuring Information   90

CHECKLIST for Style   107

CHECKLIST for Using Audience-Centered Visuals   128

CHECKLIST for Document Design   145

CHECKLIST for Résumés   171

CHECKLIST for Job Application Letters   172

CHECKLIST for Supporting Materials   172

CHECKLIST for Memos and Letters   203

CHECKLIST for Definitions   218

CHECKLIST for Descriptions and Specifications   239

CHECKLIST for Instructions and Procedures   265

CHECKLIST for Summaries   279

CHECKLIST for Informal Reports   300

CHECKLIST for Formal Reports   324

CHECKLIST for Proposals   347

CHECKLIST for Email and Text Messages   360

CHECKLIST for Blogs, Wikis, and Web Pages   373

CHECKLIST for Social Media   384

CHECKLIST for Oral Presentations   402

STRATEGIES FOR
Technical Communication in the Workplace

THIRD EDITION

Laura J. Gurak
University of Minnesota

John M. Lannon
University of Massachusetts-Dartmouth

New!
2016
MLA
Updates

PEARSON

Boston   Columbus   Hoboken   Indianapolis   New York   San Francisco
Amsterdam   Cape Town   Dubai   London   Madrid   Milan Munich   Paris   Montréal   Toronto
Delhi   Mexico City   São Paulo   Sydney   Hong Kong   Seoul   Singapore   Taipei   Tokyo

Senior Acquisitions Editor: Brad Potthoff
Editorial Assistant: Amanda Norelli
Program Manager: Katharine Glynn
Development Editor: Bruce Cantley
Product Marketing Manager: Jennifer Edwards
Field Marketing Manager: Joyce Nilsen
Supplements Editor: Teresa Ward
Executive Digital Producer: Stefanie A. Snajder
Digital Editor: Sara Gordus
Digital Content Specialist: Erin Reilly

Product Manager: Ellen MacElree
Project Coordination, Text Design, and Electronic Page Makeup: Integra
Design Lead: Barbara Atkinson
Cover Designer: Joel Gendron, Lumina Datamatics
Cover Photos: © mubus7/Shutterstock
Senior Manufacturing Buyer: Roy L. Pickering, Jr.
Printer/Binder: LSC Communications / Crawfordsville
Cover Printer: Phoenix Color/Hagerstown

Acknowledgments of third-party content appears on page 462, which constitute an extension of this copyright page.

Pearson, Always Learning, and MyWritingLab are exclusive trademarks in the United States and/or other countries owned by Pearson Education, Inc., or its affiliates

Library of Congress Cataloging-in-Publication Data

Gurak, Laura J.
Strategies for technical communication in the workplace / Laura J.
Gurak, John M. Lannon.—Third edition.
    pages cm
Includes bibliographical references and index.
  ISBN 978-0-321-99589-6 (student edition)
  1. Business communication.   2. Communication of technical information.
  3. Technical writing.   I. Lannon, John M.   II. Title.
HF5718.G87 2015
658.4'5—dc23

2014023880

5 17

www.pearsonhighered.com

Student ISBN-13: 978-0-13-458637-3
Student ISBN-10:   0-13-458637-9

A la Carte ISBN-13: 978-0-13-458246-7
A la Carte ISBN-10:   0-13-458246-2

BRIEF CONTENTS

Detailed Contents   vii
Preface   xvi

PART 1 Foundations   1

1   Technical Communication: Global, Collaborative, and Digital   2
2   The Research Process in Technical Communication   25
3   Providing Audiences with Usable Information   44
4   Recognizing Ethical Issues in Technical Communication   66

PART 2 Blueprints   75

5   Structuring Information for Your Readers   76
6   Writing with a Readable Style   93
7   Using Audience-Centered Visuals   111
8   Designing User-Friendly Documents   131

PART 3 Documents   149

9   Résumés and Other Employment Materials   150
10   Memos and Letters   175
11   Definitions   205
12   Descriptions   220
13   Instructions and Procedures   242
14   Summaries   267
15   Informal Reports   281
16   Formal Reports   302
17   Proposals   326

PART 4 Digital Media and Presentations   349

18   Email and Text Messages   350
19   Blogs, Wikis, and Web Pages   362
20   Social Media   375
21   Oral Presentations and Video Conferencing   386

Appendices

A   Documenting Sources   405
B   A Brief Handbook   439

Works Cited   462
Photo Credits   462
Index   463

DETAILED CONTENTS

Preface   xvi

PART 1 — Foundations 1

1 Technical Communication: Global, Collaborative, and Digital 2

What Is Technical Communication?   3

Main Features of Technical Communication   4
Focus Is on the Reader, Not the Writer   4
Document Design Is Efficient and Accessible   5
Writing Style Is Clear and Relevant   5
Information Is Persuasive, Truthful, and Based on Research   5

Three Primary Purposes of Technical Communication   6
Informational Purpose   6
Instructional Purpose   6
Persuasive Purpose   9

Common Types of Technical Documents   9

Technical Communication Is Global, Collaborative, and Digital   12
Technical Communication Is Global   12
STRATEGIES for Global Technical Communication   13
Technical Communication Is Collaborative   14
STRATEGIES for Organizing a Team Project   14
Running Successful Meetings   15
Identifying and Managing Group Conflicts   15
STRATEGIES for Running a Meeting   17
STRATEGIES for Managing Team Conflicts   18
Reviewing and Editing the Work of Others   19

STRATEGIES for Peer Review and Editing   19
Technical Communication Is Digital   20
CHECKLIST for Effective Technical Communication   22
APPLICATIONS   23

2 The Research Process in Technical Communication 25

Thinking Critically about Research   26
STRATEGIES for Thinking Critically about Research   26

Primary versus Secondary Sources   27

Exploring Secondary Sources   28
Online Secondary Sources   28
STRATEGIES for Researching Online   29
Hard-Copy Secondary Sources   34

Exploring Primary Sources   37
Unsolicited Inquiries   37
Informational Interviews   38
STRATEGIES for Informational Interviews   38
Surveys   39
STRATEGIES for Surveys   40
Observations and Experiments   41
CHECKLIST for Doing Research   41
APPLICATIONS   42

3 Providing Audiences with Usable Information 44

Analyze the Document's Audience   45
Primary and Secondary Audiences   45
Relationship with Audience   46

Audience's Technical Background   47
Audience's Cultural Background   47
STRATEGIES for Analyzing Your Audience   50

Determine the Document's Purpose   50
Primary and Secondary Purposes   51
Intended Use of the Document   51

Know How to Be Persuasive   51
Using Claims as a Basis for Persuasion   52
Connecting with Your Audience   52
STRATEGIES for Persuasion   55

Create a Task Analysis for the Document   56

Consider Other Related Usability Factors   57
Setting   57
Potential Problems   58
Length   59
Format   59
Timing   59
Budget   59

Develop an Information Plan for the Document   59

Write, Test, Revise, and Proofread the Document   61
STRATEGIES for Proofreading   62
CHECKLIST for Usability   63
APPLICATIONS   64

4 Recognizing Ethical Issues in Technical Communication   66

Ethics, Technology, and Communication   67
Types of Ethical Choices   67
How Workplace Pressures Affect Ethical Values   69
Recognizing and Avoiding Ethical Abuses   69
STRATEGIES for Avoiding Ethical Abuses   72
CHECKLIST for Ethical Communication   72
APPLICATIONS   73

PART 2 Blueprints   75

5 Structuring Information for Your Readers   76

The Importance of an Understandable Structure   77

Outlining   80
STRATEGIES for Outlining   82

Chunking   83

Sequencing   83

Paragraphing   84
The Topic Sentence   84
Paragraph Unity   85
Paragraph Coherence   85

Clarifying Headings   86

Providing an Overview   87
CHECKLIST for Structuring Information   90
APPLICATIONS   92

6 Writing with a Readable Style   93

The Importance of a Readable Style   94

Writing Clearly   95
Avoiding Ambiguous Pronoun References   95
Avoiding Ambiguous Modifiers   96
Using Active Voice Whenever Possible   96
Using Passive Voice Selectively   97
Avoiding Nominalizations   98
Unstack Modifying Nouns   99
Avoiding Unnecessary Jargon   100

Writing Concisely   100
Avoiding Wordiness   100
Eliminating Redundancy and Repetition   102

Writing Fluently   102
Combining Related Ideas   103
Varying Sentence Construction and Length   103
Using Parallel Structure   104

Writing Personally 105
Adjusting Your Tone 105
STRATEGIES for Deciding about Tone 105
Avoiding Sexist and Biased Language 106
STRATEGIES for Nonsexist Usage 106
STRATEGIES for Unbiased Usage 107

CHECKLIST for Style 107

APPLICATIONS 108

7 Using Audience-Centered Visuals 111

The Importance of Using Audience-Centered Visuals 112

When to Use Visuals 113
Using Visuals to Support Text 113
Using Visuals on Their Own 115

Types of Visuals 115
Tables 115
STRATEGIES for Creating Tables 116
Graphs 116
STRATEGIES for Creating Graphs 118
Charts 119
STRATEGIES for Creating Charts 121
Illustrations and Diagrams 122
Photographs 123
Videos 124
Icons and Symbols 124
STRATEGIES for Illustrations, Diagrams, Photographs, Videos, Icons, and Symbols 125

Special Considerations When Using Visuals 126
Selecting Appropriate Visuals 126
Placing, Cross-Referencing, and Presenting Visuals 127
Using Color in Visuals 127
Using Visuals Ethically 128

CHECKLIST for Using Audience-Centered Visuals 128

APPLICATIONS 129

8 Designing User-Friendly Documents 131

The Importance of User-Friendly Document Design 132

Characteristics of Well-Designed Documents 133

Specific Design Elements 135
Designing for Consistency and Cohesiveness 136
STRATEGIES for Designing: Consistency and Cohesiveness 139
Designing for Navigation and Emphasis 140
STRATEGIES for Designing: Navigation and Emphasis 144

CHECKLIST for Document Design 145

APPLICATIONS 146

PART 3 Documents 149

9 Résumés and Other Employment Materials 150

LET'S GET STARTED Résumés and Application Letters 151

Assessing Your Skills and Aptitudes 152

Researching the Job Market 153

Résumés 154
Parts of a Résumé 154
Organizing Your Résumé 156
STRATEGIES for Creating a Résumé 158

Application Letters 158
Solicited Application Letters 159
Unsolicited Application Letters 159
STRATEGIES for Application Letters 161

Digital versus Print Job Application Materials 161
STRATEGIES for Digital Job Application Materials 162

Dossiers, Portfolios, and E-portfolios   163
   Dossiers   163
   Portfolios and E-portfolios   165
   STRATEGIES for Dossiers, Portfolios, and
      E-portfolios   165

Interviews and Follow-up Letters   167
   Interviews   167
   Follow-up Letters   168
   STRATEGIES for Interviews and Follow-up
      Letters   170

CHECKLIST for Résumés   171
CHECKLIST for Job Application Letters   172
CHECKLIST for Supporting Materials   172
APPLICATIONS   173

10   Memos and Letters   175

LET'S GET STARTED Memos   176
LET'S GET STARTED Letters   176

Memo Basics   177
Memo Parts and Format   178
Memo Tone   178
Types of Memos   181
   Transmittal Memo   181
   Summary or Follow-up Memo   181
   Informational Memo   182
   STRATEGIES for Memos   185

Letter Basics   185
Letter Parts and Formats   185
   Parts of a Letter   185
   Formats for Letters   188
Letter Tone   188
   Establishing and Maintaining a "You"
      Perspective   188
   Being Polite and Tactful   191
   Using Plain English   191
   Considering the Needs of International Readers   192
   Being Direct or Indirect   192

STRATEGIES for Letters in General   192
Types of Letters   193
   Inquiry Letters   193
   STRATEGIES for Inquiry Letters   195
   Claim Letters   195
   STRATEGIES for Claim Letters   198
   Sales Letters   198
   STRATEGIES for Sales Letters   200
   Adjustment Letters   200
   STRATEGIES for Adjustment Letters   201

CHECKLIST for Memos and Letters   203
APPLICATIONS   203

11   Definitions   205

LET'S GET STARTED Definitions   206
Audience and Purpose of Definitions   207
**Legal, Ethical, and Societal Implications
   of Definitions**   208
Types of Definitions   209
   Parenthetical Definitions   209
   Sentence Definitions   209
   Expanded Definitions   210
Methods for Expanding Definitions   210
   Etymology   211
   History   211
   Negation   212
   Operating Principle   212
   Analysis of Parts   212
   Visuals   213
   Comparison and Contrast   213
   Required Conditions   214
   Examples   214
Using Multiple Expansion Methods   214
Placement of Definitions   216
   STRATEGIES for Definitions   217
CHECKLIST for Definitions   218
APPLICATIONS   218

12 Descriptions 220

LET'S GET STARTED Descriptions   221

Audience and Purpose of Descriptions   222

Objectivity in Descriptions   222

Elements of Descriptions   223
Title   223
Introduction   223
Sequence of Topics   224
Visuals   224
Conclusion   224

Product and Process Descriptions   225

A Complex Product Description   228

A Complex Process Description   232
STRATEGIES for Descriptions   235

Specifications   236
STRATEGIES for Specifications   238

CHECKLIST for Descriptions and Specifications   239

APPLICATIONS   240

13 Instructions and Procedures 242

LET'S GET STARTED Instructions   243

Audience and Purpose of Instructions   244

Types of Instructional Formats   245
Instructional Brochures   245
User Manuals   246
Quick Reference Materials   246
Web-based Instructions   247
Online Instructions   250

Ethical and Legal Implications   251

Elements of Effective Instructions   251
Title   251
Overview or Introduction   252
Body   252
Conclusion   252

Visuals   252
Notes, Cautions, Warnings, and Danger
Notices   252

Content, Style, and Design Considerations   254
Detail and Technicality   254
Style   255
STRATEGIES for Achieving Readability   255
Design   256
STRATEGIES for Creating an Accessible
Design   258

Procedures   261
Audience and Purpose Considerations   261
Types of Procedures   261

Usability Testing   263
STRATEGIES for Instructions and Procedures   263

CHECKLIST for Instructions and Procedures   265

APPLICATIONS   265

14 Summaries 267

LET'S GET STARTED Summaries   268

Audience and Purpose of Summaries   268

Elements of Effective Summaries   269
Accuracy   270
Completeness   270
Conciseness   270
Nontechnical Style   270

Writing Summaries Step by Step   270
Step 1: Read the Original Document   271
Step 2: Reread and Mark Essential Material   271
Step 3: Cut and Paste the Key Information   271
Step 4: Redraft the Information into Your Own
Organizational Pattern and Words   271
Step 5: Edit Your Draft   271
Step 6: Compare Your Version with the Original
Document   271

Special Types of Summaries   273
Closing Summaries   275
Informative Abstracts   275

Descriptive Abstracts   275
Executive Summaries   276

Ethical Considerations in Summarizing Information   276
STRATEGIES for Summaries   278

CHECKLIST for Summaries   279

APPLICATIONS   279

15   Informal Reports   281

LET'S GET STARTED Informal Reports   282

Two Categories of Reports: Informational and Analytical   283

Progress Reports (Informational)   283
STRATEGIES for Progress Reports   284

Periodic Activity Reports (Informational)   287
STRATEGIES for Periodic Activity Reports   287

Trip Reports (Informational)   287
STRATEGIES for Trip Reports   289

Meeting Minutes (Informational)   292
STRATEGIES for Meeting Minutes   292

Feasibility Reports (Analytical)   293
STRATEGIES for Feasibility Reports   294

Recommendation Reports (Analytical)   296
STRATEGIES for Recommendation Reports   296

Peer Review Reports (Analytical)   298
STRATEGIES for Peer Review Reports   298

CHECKLIST for Informal Reports   300

APPLICATIONS   300

16   Formal Reports   302

LET'S GET STARTED Formal Reports   303

Audience and Purpose of Formal Reports   304
Comparative Analysis   305
Causal Analysis   305

Feasibility Analysis   306

Elements of Effective Formal Reports   306
Accurate, Appropriate, and Clearly Interpreted Data   307
Clearly Identified Purpose Statement   307
Understandable Structure   308
Readable Style   308
Audience-centered Visuals   308
User-friendly Design   308

Parts of Formal Reports   309
Letter of Transmittal   309
Front Matter   310
Text of the Report   311
End Matter   311
STRATEGIES for Formal Reports   312

A Sample Formal Report   313

CHECKLIST for Formal Reports   324

APPLICATIONS   325

17   Proposals   326

LET'S GET STARTED Proposals   327

Audience and Purpose of Proposals   328

Types of Proposals   328
Planning Proposals   329
Research Proposals   329
Sales Proposals   332

Organization of Informal and Formal Proposals   332
Clear Title or Subject Line   332
Background Information   334
Statement of Problem or Situation   334
Description of Solution or Resolution   334
Costs, Timing, and Qualifications   334
Conclusion   334
STRATEGIES for Proposals   335

A Sample Formal Proposal   336

CHECKLIST for Proposals   347

APPLICATIONS   347

PART 4 Digital Media and Presentations 349

18 Email and Text Messages 350

LET'S GET STARTED Email and Text Messages 351

Email 351
Audience and Purpose of Email 352
Components and Organization of Email 353
Appropriate Style for Workplace Email 353
STRATEGIES for Email 356

Text Messages 357
Audience and Purpose of Workplace Text Messages 357
STRATEGIES for Text Messages 358

Comparing Email and Text Messaging 358

Copyright and Privacy in Digital Communication 358

Be Prepared for Technology to Fail 360

CHECKLIST for Email and Text Messages 360

APPLICATIONS 361

19 Blogs, Wikis, and Web Pages 362

LET'S GET STARTED Blogs, Wikis, and Web Pages 363

Internal Blogs 363

External Blogs 364

Internal Wikis 365

External Wikis 365

Web Pages 365

Audience and Purpose of Web Pages 366

Elements of Effective Web Pages 367
Structure 367
Style 370
Visuals 370
Design 370

Ethical Considerations 371
STRATEGIES for Blogs, Wikis, and Web Pages 371

CHECKLIST for Blogs, Wikis, and Web Pages 373

APPLICATIONS 374

20 Social Media 375

LET'S GET STARTED Social Media 376

Considering Audience and Purpose 377
Audience as Contributor 379

Social Media in Technical and Workplace Communication 379
Customer Review Sites 379
Facebook 380
Google+ 380
LinkedIn and Other Job Sites 380
Twitter 381
YouTube 382

Ethical and Legal Issues 382
STRATEGIES for Social Media 383

CHECKLIST for Social Media 384

APPLICATIONS 384

21 Oral Presentations and Video Conferencing 386

LET'S GET STARTED Oral Presentations 387

Audience and Purpose of Oral Presentations 388

Types of Oral Presentations 388
Informative Presentations 388
Training Presentations 390
Persuasive Presentations 390
Action Plan Presentations 390
Sales Presentations 391

Parts of Oral Presentations 391
Introduction 391
Body 392
Conclusion 392

Preparing Oral Presentations 392
Research and Connect the Topic to Your
Audience 392
Create an Outline or Storyboard 393
Determine a Delivery Style 394
Choose Your Technology 396
Plan the Use of Visuals 396
Practice the Presentation 398
STRATEGIES for Preparing Oral
Presentations 398

Using Presentation Software 399

Video Conferencing 400
STRATEGIES for Using Presentation Software
and Video Conferencing 400

Delivering Oral Presentations 401
STRATEGIES for Delivering Oral
Presentations 402

CHECKLIST for Oral Presentations 402

APPLICATIONS 403

Appendices 405

A Documenting Sources 405

What Is Plagiarism? 405

**Identifying Sources and Information to Be
Documented** 406

Taking Effective and Accurate Notes 406
STRATEGIES for Taking Notes 407

**Quoting, Paraphrasing, and Summarizing
Properly** 408
Quoting the Work of Others 408
STRATEGIES for Quoting the Work of Others 409
Paraphrasing the Work of Others 409

STRATEGIES for Paraphrasing the Work of
Others 410
Summarizing the Work of Others 410
STRATEGIES for Summarizing the Work
of Others 411

**Documentation: The Key to Avoiding
Plagiarism** 411
Why You Should Document 411
What You Should Document 412
How You Should Document 412

MLA Documentation Style 413
MLA Parenthetical References 413
MLA Works Cited Entries 414

APA Documentation Style 425
APA Parenthetical References 425
APA Reference Entries 426

Other Documentation Styles 436

Recognizing Copyright Issues 436
Works in the Public Domain 437
Fair Use 437
The Difference between Plagiarism and Copyright
Infringement 438

B A Brief Handbook 439

Grammar 440
Sentence Fragments 440
Run-on Sentences 441
Comma Splices 441
Faulty Agreement—Subject and Verb 442
Faulty Agreement—Pronoun and
Referent 443
Faulty Coordination and
Subordination 443
Faulty Pronoun Case 445

Punctuation 445
Period 446
Question Mark 446
Exclamation Point 446
Semicolon 446
Colon 447
Comma 447

Apostrophe   450
Quotation Marks   451
Ellipses   452
Brackets   452
Italics   452
Parentheses   453
Dashes   453

Mechanics   453
Abbreviation   453
Hyphenation   454
Capitalization   454
Numbers and Numerals   455
Spelling   456

Usage   456

Transitions   456
Use Transitional Expressions   456
Repeat Key Words and Phrases   459
Use Forecasting Statements   459

Lists   460
Embedded Lists   460
Vertical Lists   460

Works Cited   462
Photo Credits   462
Index   463

OVERVIEW

In today's workplace, professionals in all fields are expected to adapt to a variety of communication situations. Virtually everyone must be able to write routine workplace documents such as memos, emails, letters, and informal reports. In addition, employees must create more complex forms of communication such as formal reports and proposals, instructions, definitions and descriptions, Web pages, oral presentations, video presentations, and more. All the while, these professionals must also negotiate technological innovations, communicate in a global marketplace, work in teams, write persuasively, research effectively, and understand the ethical implications of the documents they produce.

We wrote *Strategies for Technical Communication in the Workplace* as a medium-length textbook that covers all the preceding topics thoroughly and concisely. Like the first two editions, this third edition text draws on the strengths of our other two technical communication books: the best-selling *Technical Communication*, 13th edition, and *Concise Guide to Technical Communication*, 3rd edition. We hope that students and faculty alike will appreciate the new edition of this distinctive textbook.

NEW TO THE THIRD EDITION

In addition to streamlining the text and thoroughly revising the model documents and pedagogical features throughout, we have made the following key changes for the third edition of *Strategies*:

Thoroughly Revised Introductory Chapter

Chapter 1 (now re-titled as "Technical Communication: Global, Collaborative, and Digital") continues to provide a clear definition of technical communication, an introduction to its main features, and an exploration of the three main purposes of technical communication. In addition, the chapter incorporates Chapter 2 from the second edition and has been reorganized to place special emphasis on the global, collaborative, and digital nature of technical communication.

Updated Coverage of Using Digital Writing and Presentation Technologies

We have kept current with changing technologies by revising our coverage throughout the book. Changes include a new section on digital versus print job application materials, with a revised section on e-portfolios (Chapter 9); updated coverage on memos and letters, including using PDF attachments in relation to email (Chapter 10); the latest on writing Web-based and online instructions (Chapter 13); up-to-date coverage of documenting electronic sources in both MLA and APA styles (Appendix A); and new Digital and Social Media Applications at the end of every chapter. In addition, Part IV of the book, "Digital Media and Presentations," has been thoroughly revised to include updated coverage of email and text messages in the workplace, including discussion of appropriate style (Chapter 18); a new section on using external wikis and streamlined coverage of writing and designing Web pages (Chapter 19); a new chapter on social media in workplace communication (Chapter 20—more information below); and updated material on oral presentations, with a new section on video conferencing (Chapter 21).

New Stand-Alone Chapter on Using Social Media in the Workplace

Now its own chapter with thoroughly expanded coverage, Chapter 20 covers a wide variety of social media being used in the workplace. Social media sites explored in depth include customer review sites such as Yelp and TripAdvisor, Facebook, Google+, LinkedIn and other job sites, Twitter, and YouTube. The chapter also includes advice on audience and purpose considerations when using social media on the job as well as ethical and legal issues.

KEY FEATURES

To help you get a better idea how *Strategies* works as a whole, following is a point-by-point discussion of the key features of this book.

Complete but Streamlined Coverage

Strategies includes all topics essential for an undergraduate technical communication course in a compact yet thorough format. The book covers everything technical communicators need to know—from writing basic letters and memos, to writing complex proposals and formal reports, to delivering oral presentations and writing for the Web—in roughly 500 pages. In addition, *Strategies* offers innovative coverage of emerging technologies used in the workplace, including text messages, social networks, and online videos.

Emphasis on Student Practice

This book is guided by the idea of providing students with practical, accessible concepts that are easy to follow and that get students writing and designing documents immediately. One key feature, as the title suggests, is the Strategies box, which provides step-by-step advice to follow in writing and discussing a given document. In addition, chapters in Parts 3 and 4 emphasize the importance of "doing" immediately via the Let's Get Started feature; students are asked to draft their best version of each chapter's document type or communication situation before they read the chapter. Then, as they work through the chapter content, students are encouraged to review and revise their original work. Finally, every chapter, including the foundational and "blueprints" chapters in Parts 1 and 2, includes Applications exercises, grouped into general, collaborative, global, digital, and social media categories.

Clear Explanations and Straightforward Organization

As we wrote and organized this book, we kept in mind five essential questions students most frequently ask: "What needs to be done?", "What should it look like?", "How do I do it?", "What should be avoided?", and "How well have I done it?" The features described previously focus on these questions. Also, marginal notes summarize and reinforce main points in each chapter.

The chapter sequence in *Strategies* proceeds from general foundational concepts and blueprints in Parts 1 and 2 to cumulatively more complex writing and communicating situations in Parts 3 and 4.

Practical Pedagogical Features

Strategies includes several practical, easy-to-access pedagogical tools. These features include:

- **Chapter Outlines and Learning Objectives.** On the opening page of each chapter, the outlines provide a quick orientation to the chapter topics and sequence, and the learning objectives emphasize the practical skills students can expect to acquire.

- **Let's Get Started boxes.** At the beginning of each chapter in Parts 3 and 4, the Let's Get Started boxes encourage students to begin "doing" immediately by producing the type of draft document or communication product discussed in each chapter based on their prior knowledge. Then, as they work through the chapter, students can refine their draft.

- **Strategies boxes.** Featured in every chapter, the Strategies boxes summarize key strategies discussed in the text and provide additional pointers for approaching each communication situation.

- **Checklists.** End-of-chapter Checklists summarize each chapter, and more importantly, they emphasize "doing" by asking students to check off each item as they review their work.

- **Applications.** Called "applications" rather than "exercises" to emphasize applied learning, the end-of-chapter Applications fall into four categories: General Applications (for individual practice), Team Applications (for pair or group practice), Global Applications (for highlighting global issues in workplace communication), and Digital and Social Media Applications (for highlighting the use of technology in workplace communication).

Realistic and Accessible Annotated Model Documents

Model documents resemble the kinds of documents students will write in the workplace. Accessible, engaging, and easy to emulate, most of these documents are fully annotated.

Consistent Focus on Audience and Purpose

Technical communication in the workplace is more than a mere exercise in "information transfer"; it is also a social transaction involving individuals, teams, companies, and organizations that are national and international in scope. In the contemporary workplace, a one-size-fits-all approach to technical communication doesn't work. Effective communication must be tailored for different audiences and different purposes. Today's communicator must be smart about researching, summarizing, and customizing information to meet many different situations. *Strategies* has therefore been designed to provide much more than a "cookie cutter" approach to creating typical workplace documents and making presentations by focusing on key rhetorical principles of audience and purpose.

The Latest Technology and Global Issues Coverage

With the Internet and digital technology at our fingertips and with companies and teams spread across the world, communication reaches a wide audience and often is transmitted instantly. We receive or convey professional information in a variety of ways—handwritten, in word-processed documents, via email or text messaging; in video format; as a Web page; via blogs, wikis, or social networks; or as live presentations—and each medium and potential audience brings with it unique challenges about how to best present the information. *Strategies* incorporates relevant technology coverage and stresses the importance of thinking about global audiences wherever relevant.

ORGANIZATION OF THE BOOK

Strategies begins with foundational concepts, then moves to "blueprints," and then applies the foundations and blueprints to increasingly complex documents and communication situations.

- **Part 1 ("Foundations")** introduces the underlying concepts for creating effective technical communication. This section provides a definition of technical communication (Chapter 1); coverage of research as a pivotal part of technical communication (Chapter 2); an introduction to the analysis of audience, purpose, and other factors (Chapter 3), and in-depth coverage of workplace ethics (Chapter4).

- **Part 2 ("Blueprints")** builds upon Part 1 by discussing four basic considerations for approaching each type of workplace document or communication situation: understandable structure (Chapter 5), readable style (Chapter 6), audience-centered visuals (Chapter 7), and user-friendly design (Chapter 8).

- **Part 3 ("Documents")** applies the previous foundations and blueprints, presenting increasingly complex types of print documents. This section begins with the types of documents students need to get hired and concludes with the two most complex types of documents: formal reports and proposals. Specific documents covered in Part 3 include résumés and other employment materials (Chapter 9), memos and letters (Chapter 10), definitions (Chapter 11), descriptions (Chapter 12), instructions and procedures (Chapter 13), summaries (Chapter 14), informal reports (Chapter 15), formal reports (Chapter 16), and proposals (Chapter 17).

- **Part 4 ("Digital Media and Presentations")** provides guidance for creating documents for digital media and for giving oral presentations. Included are chapters on email and text messages (Chapter 18); blogs, wikis, and Web pages (Chapter 19); social media (Chapter 20); and oral presentations and video conferencing (Chapter 21).

- **Appendices A ("Documenting Sources") and B ("A Brief Handbook")** offer guidance on citations and grammar. Appendix A includes guidelines for avoiding plagiarism and documenting sources completely and accurately. Appendix B provides a brief handbook of grammar, punctuation, mechanics, and usage. This appendix also includes useful advice on formatting lists and using transitions in written work.

RESOURCES FOR STUDENTS AND INSTRUCTORS

Accompanying *Strategies* is a wide array of instructor and student supplements, most of which are available packaged with this book at a nominal cost.

MyWritingLab™

- **MyWritingLab for Technical Communication <www.mywritinglab.com/>.** In addition to MyWritingLab's extensive writing, research, and grammar coverage, the new technical communication section offers topics such as: defining technical communication; audience analysis; ethics; collaboration; document design; creating visuals; and each of the major genres of technical communication, ranging from basic correspondence and job search materials to more complex genres like reports, instructions, proposals, Web pages, social media, and oral presentations. Each topic includes a thorough overview, an animated introduction, glossary terms, recall and post-test quizzes, model-based and case-based activities, and writing prompts.

- **Pearson eText** gives students access to *Strategies for Technical Communication in the Workplace,* Third Edition, whenever and wherever they can access the Internet. The eText pages look exactly like the printed text, and include powerful interactive and customization functions. Users can create notes, highlight text in different colors, create bookmarks, zoom, click hyperlinked words and phrases to view definitions, and view as a single page or as two pages. Pearson eText also links students to associated media files, enabling them to view videos as they read the text, and offers a full-text search and the ability to save and export notes. The Pearson eText also includes embedded URLs in the chapter text with active links to the Internet.

  The Pearson eText app is a great companion to Pearson's eText browser-based book reader. It allows existing subscribers who view their Pearson eText titles on a Mac or PC to additionally access their titles in a bookshelf on the iPad or an Android tablet either online or via download.

- **Instructor's Manual, by Lee Scholder, University of Minnesota, and Daun Daemon, North Carolina State University.** Available in digital format, the Instructor's Manual includes general and chapter-by-chapter teaching tips, sample syllabi, and additional chapter exercises and quizzes.

- **PowerPoint slides.** Fully revised to accompany the third edition, the PowerPoint presentations provide a wealth of chapter-by-chapter slides that can be projected or printed to enhance in-class instruction or simply used for review and class planning.

- **MyTest.** Pearson MyTest is a powerful assessment generation program that helps instructors easily create and print quizzes, study guides, and exams. Questions and tests are authored online, allowing instructors ultimate flexibility and the ability to efficiently manage assessments anytime, anywhere. To access MyTest, go to <www.pearsonhighered.com/mytest/>, log on, and follow the instructions. You must first be registered.

ACKNOWLEDGMENTS

We appreciate the valuable advice from our reviewers, who helped us determine the direction of this revision: Teresa Foxworthy Cook, University of Cincinnati; Beata Peterson, Fayetteville Technical Community College; Rebecca Joy Ritzel, University of Maryland; Lisa Stanley-Smith, Forsyth Technical Community College; and Scott Temple, Cleveland Community College.

In addition, we thank the reviewers who helped shape the first and second editions of this book: Michael Avery, Jefferson Community College; Carol Ann Britt, San Antonio College; Sherry A. Cisler, Arizona State University at the West Campus; Teresa Foxworthy Cook, University of Cincinnati; Michael Creeden, Florida International University; Laura H. Davis, Cleveland Community College; Michael-John DePalma, University of New Hampshire; Carolyn Kusbit Dunn, East Carolina University; Sean Flannery, Immaculata University; Terri Gordon, Lake Michigan College; Leslie Janac, Blinn College-Bryan Campus; Michael F. Johanyak, The University of Akron; Barbara Rau Kyle, University of Central Florida; Christine Laursen, Red Rocks Community College; Nancy R. MacKenzie, Minnesota State University, Mankato; Lisa Meloncon, University of Cincinnati; Traci Nathans-Kelly, University of Wisconsin–Madison; Julianne Newmark, New Mexico Tech; Lynnette Porter, Embry-Riddle Aeronautical University; Erin M. Price, Bismarck State College; Anne Regan, California Polytechnic State University; Kelly Sassi, North Dakota State University; Clay Kinchen Smith, Santa Fe College; Carey E. Smitherman, Worcester State College; Betty H. Stack, Rowan Cabarrus Community College; Karina Stokes, University of Houston–Downtown; Suba Subbarao, Oakland Community College; Barry Thatcher, New Mexico State University; Ronald J. Tulley, The University of Findlay; Candace A. Welhausen, The Georgia Institute of Technology; and Miriam F. Williams, Texas State University.

A special thanks to our students who allowed us to reproduce versions of their work and who are named in the text. From Brad Potthoff, Mary Ellen Curley, Ellen MacElree, and Amanda Norelli we received outstanding editorial guidance and support. Thank you to Lee Scholder for her work preparing the first edition of the Instructor's Manual and to Daun Daemon for her work revising the Instructor's Manual for its second and third editions. Many thanks to Bruce Cantley for his generous and unflagging development help and invaluable ideas and to Martha Beyerlein for expertly managing production.

—Laura J. Gurak and John M. Lannon

PART **1**

Foundations

1 Technical Communication: Global, Collaborative, and Digital

2 The Research Process in Technical Communication

3 Providing Audiences with Usable Information

4 Recognizing Ethical Issues in Technical Communication

1 Technical Communication: Global, Collaborative, and Digital

CHAPTER OUTLINE

What Is Technical Communication? *3*

Main Features of Technical Communication *4*

Three Primary Purposes of Technical Communication *6*

Common Types of Technical Documents *9*

Technical Communication Is Global, Collaborative, and Digital *12*

> **STRATEGIES** for Global Technical Communication *13*
>
> **STRATEGIES** for Organizing a Team Project *14*
>
> **STRATEGIES** for Running a Meeting *17*
>
> **STRATEGIES** for Managing Team Conflicts *18*
>
> **STRATEGIES** for Peer Review and Editing *19*
>
> **CHECKLIST** for Effective Technical Communication *22*

Applications *23*

LEARNING OBJECTIVES FOR THIS CHAPTER

▶ Define technical communication

▶ Envision how people at work create technical communication

▶ Describe the key characteristics of effective technical communication

▶ List the primary purposes of technical documents

▶ Recognize typical technical documents

▶ Understand the global nature of technical communication

▶ Organize and manage a team project

▶ Run a successful meeting

▶ Identify and manage team conflicts

▶ Consider the use of digital technologies in technical communication

WHAT IS TECHNICAL COMMUNICATION?

Technical communication is the exchange of information that helps people interact with technology, advance workplace goals, and solve complex problems.

We live in a world where many of our everyday actions depend on complex but usable information. For example, when you purchase or install a new device, such as a DVD player or Wi-Fi router, you need clear, easy-to-use instructions. From banking systems to online courses to business negotiations, countless aspects of daily life are affected by technology, and we rely on usable technical information to answer questions such as these:

- How do I access my online bank statement?
- Which cable do I use to connect my computer to a new monitor?
- How do I paste a digital photo into a document and resize the image?

Technical information is also used in more specialized settings. For example, a physician performing heart surgery must have clear information about how to install a pacemaker. A government research scientist must have accurate instructions about how to write a grant or how to perform a particular experiment. An engineer must have access to the correct specifications for designing a bridge or configuring a software application. In specialized settings, technical communication answers questions such as these:

- Do the benefits of the Lyme disease vaccine outweigh its risks?
- What are the technical limits to wind energy?
- How effectively will the new heating system circulate in the top floors of the new office complex?

In the workplace, we are not only consumers of technical communication but also producers. Virtually all professionals, at some point, function as technical communicators. Experts are often required to present their knowledge to nonexpert audiences. For instance, a nuclear engineer testifying before Congress would need to write a report explaining nuclear science in nonscientific language to policy makers and the general public. Nurses and other medical professionals are often required to explain complex medical concepts to patients and families. Writers of instructions for uploading new software need to be sure that a wide range of readers can perform the task without having to call customer service.

In today's networked world, technical communication is global, collaborative, and digital. Technical documents including user manuals, online help, online instructions, and other such materials are accessible by people around the globe, created by teams from different countries and time zones, and available via Web sites, blogs, and wikis and in formats suitable for computers as well as mobile devices. See the last section of this chapter (page 12) and Chapters 18–21 for more on these important topics.

Definition of technical communication

Technical communication helps us interact with technology in our daily lives

Technical communication helps specialists solve complex problems

Specialized questions

Technical communication helps advance workplace goals

Technical communication is global, collaborative, and digital

MAIN FEATURES OF TECHNICAL COMMUNICATION

Technical communication differs from most academic writing

Technical communication differs from other communication and writing courses you take in college. In first-year writing (freshman composition) or expository writing, the emphasis typically is on one type of document, the traditional college essay. As you work on the assignments for this course, the skills you learned in previous writing classes will remain important, but the writing will often be different. Technical documents typically exhibit the following characteristics.

Focus Is on the Reader, Not the Writer

Produce user-centered documents

Unlike poetry, fiction, or essays, technical documents rarely focus on the author's personal thoughts and feelings. This doesn't mean that technical documents should have no personality (or voice), but it does mean that the needs of your readers must come first. Users of technical communication are only interested in you, the communicator, to the extent that they want to know what you have done, what you recommend, or how you speak for your company or organization. This type of communication is called "user-centered communication" (see Figure 1.1). User-centered communication requires a focus on the people who will be *using* the document. What do your readers need to know? What tasks are they trying to perform?

**FIGURE 1.1
User-centered
communication**

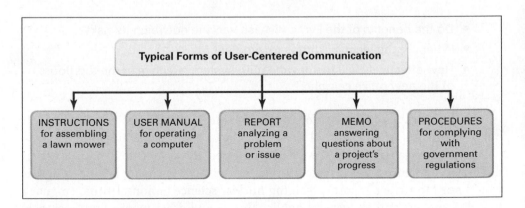

Placing the reader's needs and interests first takes practice because many of us are taught to write from our own perspectives. For instance, assume you've been asked to create a set of instructions that explain how people in the community can bring household hazardous waste (gasoline, paint) for recycling. Assume also that you live in the neighborhood near the recycling center and often visit that location. In this instance, you could easily forget to include a map and directions to the center, unless you focus consistently on your actual readers—people who are new in town, people who don't live close to the facility, and so on.

Learn to put yourself in the reader's place

Document Design Is Efficient and Accessible

Unlike college essays, which take essentially one shape (paragraphs of text), technical documents may take the form of a brochure, a memo, a report with different sections, a numbered set of instructions, a Web site, online help, a blog, a wiki, or an email with a PDF attachment. Regardless of format and media, the design must be efficient and accessible, making it easy for readers to find what they are looking for and use the content to perform a task or answer a question.

Produce documents that are easy for readers to use and navigate

Writing Style Is Clear and Relevant

Technical communication uses clear language. For example, the instructions for using a fire extinguisher (Figure 1.4, page 8) are written for a wide range of readers. Likewise, the letter from the company's general manager to a potential client (Figure 1.5, page 10) is another example of clear communication.

Write clearly

Information is relevant if the audience can apply it to the task at hand. Say, for instance, that a person is interested in learning to use Internet service provider (ISP) software to connect to the Internet: In this case, the documentation should explain how to install the software and connect to the ISP instead of digressing into a history of how the Internet developed.

Provide only relevant information

Information Is Persuasive, Truthful, and Based on Research

Persuasion means trying to influence someone's actions, opinions, or decisions. In the workplace, we rely on persuasion daily: to win coworker support, to attract clients and customers, or to request funding. But changing someone's mind is never easy, and sometimes it is impossible. Your success will depend on who you are trying to persuade, what you are requesting, and how entrenched they are in their own views.

All technical documents are persuasive, in some sense. Some documents, such as the letter in Figure 1.5, are explicitly persuasive, in that the writer is trying to convince the reader that the proposed project is the right choice. Other documents, such as the instructions in Figure 1.4, are mainly informative, but they are also implicitly persuasive: The writer is also trying to show readers that the fire extinguisher is easy to use and safe.

All documents are at least in part persuasive

In short, a technical communicator is a problem solver and, as such, must be aware of the best balance between providing readers with the information they need and persuading them to respond as desired, as illustrated in Figure 1.2.

Balance information and persuasion

Be careful, though, to not let your persuasive goal prevent you from writing ethically. Even when you need to be overtly persuasive, as in a sales proposal, honesty is essential. A document that is highly persuasive but in some way dishonest may influence readers in the short term but will lead to long-term problems. You will lose credibility with the client or your boss and could potentially damage a working relationship for life.

All documents must be ethical

FIGURE 1.2
Balancing information and persuasion

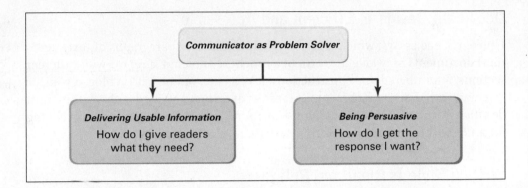

Base your documents on careful research

Even routine technical documents produced on the job are based to some extent on research. For example, though a memo or email may not require extensive searching for data online or at a library, the information must be accurate. Accuracy in this case may only involve double-checking meeting notes or asking a coworker for clarification on some point, but double-checking facts is still research. For more complex documents, the research component of technical communication becomes more obvious.

THREE PRIMARY PURPOSES OF TECHNICAL COMMUNICATION

Three purposes of technical documents: inform, instruct, and persuade

Most technical communication seeks to address one of three primary purposes: to anticipate and answer questions (inform), to enable people to perform a task (instruct), or to influence people's thinking (persuade). Keep in mind that these purposes often overlap (as in the following sample documents). However, most documents have one *primary* purpose: to inform, to instruct, or to persuade.

Informational Purpose

Informational documents anticipate and answer questions

Figure 1.3 displays an *informational* document created by the U.S. Environmental Protection Agency. It is designed for a wide audience of readers who may know little about the topic (bioremediation), but the writer has kept audience diversity in mind by anticipating and answering likely questions.

Instructional Purpose

Instructional documents help people perform a task

Figure 1.4 is an *instructional* document. As we have all experienced, effective instructions can be a pleasure to work with because they help people do what they want to do. But poor instructions can create frustration, often causing people to return the product and to have second thoughts about purchasing that brand in the future.

FIGURE 1.3
An informational document

United States
Environmental Protection
Agency

Office of Solid Waste and
Emergency Response
(5102G)

EPA 542-F-01-001
April 2001
www.epa.gov/superfund/sites
www.cluin.org

♻EPA A Citizen's Guide to Bioremediation

The title is clear and easy to understand

The Citizen's Guide Series

EPA uses many methods to clean up pollution at Superfund and other sites. Some, like bioremediation, are considered new or innovative. Such methods can be quicker and cheaper than more common methods. If you live, work, or go to school near a Superfund site, you may want to learn more about cleanup methods. Perhaps they are being used or are proposed for use at your site. How do they work? Are they safe? This Citizen's Guide is one in a series to help answer your questions.

What is bioremediation?

Bioremediation allows natural processes to clean up harmful chemicals in the environment. Microscopic "bugs" or microbes that live in soil and groundwater like to eat certain harmful chemicals, such as those found in gasoline and oil spills. When microbes completely digest these chemicals, they change them into water and harmless gases such as carbon dioxide.

User-centered headings are phrased as questions that readers would need answered

Microbe eats oil

Microbe digests oil and changes it to water and harmless gases

Microbe releases water and harmless gases into soil or ground

Illustrations combine text and visuals

How does it work?

In order for microbes to clean up harmful chemicals, the right temperature, nutrients (fertilizers), and amount of oxygen must be present in the soil and groundwater. These conditions allow the microbes to grow and multiply—and eat more chemicals. When conditions are not right, microbes grow too slowly or die. Or they can create more harmful chemicals. If conditions are not right at a site, EPA works to improve them. One way they improve conditions is to pump air, nutrients, or other substances (such as molasses) underground. Sometimes microbes are added if enough aren't already there.

The right conditions for bioremediation cannot always be achieved underground. At some sites, the weather is too cold or the soil is too dense. At such sites, EPA might dig up the soil to clean it above ground where heaters and soil mixing help improve conditions. After the soil is dug up, the proper nutrients are added. Oxygen also may be added by stirring the mixture or by forcing air through it. However, some microbes work better without oxygen. With the right temperature and amount of oxygen and nutrients, microbes can do their work to "bioremediate" the harmful chemicals.

Headings and a clean layout make this document easy for readers to navigate

Text provides the most relevant information without being too detailed

Source: U.S. Environmental Protection Agency Web site <www.epa.gov>.

Introduction provides appropriate level of detail for first-time users

How to Operate a Portable Fire Extinguisher

The Occupational Health and Safety Administration (OSHA) requires employers to provide portable fire extinguishers in the workplace. This document illustrates the parts of a fire extinguisher and provides instructions for operating the extinguisher safely and effectively using the P.A.S.S. method: Pull, Aim, Squeeze, and Sweep.

A prominent warning box alerts users before they take action

WARNING: At the first sign of fire, sound the alarm and call the fire department. Before approaching the fire, identify a safe evacuation path. **Never** allow the fire, heat, or smoke to come between you and your evacuation path. **If you have the slightest doubt about your ability to fight a fire...** EVACUATE **IMMEDIATELY!**

Clearly labeled illustration helps readers understand the product

Parts of a Fire Extinguisher

Figure 1 illustrates the parts of a portable fire extinguisher. When the extinguisher handle is compressed, an inner canister of high-pressure gas forces the extinguishing agent from the main cylinder through a siphon and out the nozzle.

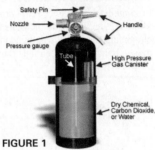

FIGURE 1

Using a Fire Extinguisher with the P.A.S.S. Method

1. **PULL** Pull the pin. This will also break the tamper seal.
2. **AIM** Aim low, pointing the extinguisher nozzle (or its horn or hose) at the base of the fire.
3. **SQUEEZE** Squeeze the handle to release the extinguishing agent.
4. **SWEEP** Sweep from side to side at the base of the fire until it appears to be out. Watch the area. If the fire reignites, repeat steps 2–4.

Numbered steps and a complementary illustration make the instructions easy to navigate and use

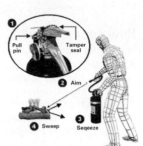

FIGURE 2

FIGURE 1.4 An instructional document
Source: Text and figures from the U.S. Occupational Safety and Health Administration <www.osha.gov>.

Persuasive Purpose

Figure 1.5 shows a *persuasive* document, in the form of a letter from a company that distributes systems for generating electrical power from recycled steam. General Manager William Bullock writes a persuasive answer to a customer's question: "Why should I invest in the system you are proposing for my plant?" As you read the letter, note how the writer focuses on reasons that are important to the reader.

Persuasive documents encourage readers to take a desired action

COMMON TYPES OF TECHNICAL DOCUMENTS

Many of you probably encounter the following types of documents routinely, either through work or school. You may also be asked to produce such documents for a class, an internship, or your job.

The variety of typical technical documents

- **Memos.** Organizations use memos as the primary means of internal written communication. Unlike a conversation, a memo leaves a record for future reference. An employee might write a memo to a manager requesting a pay raise; a team of students might write a memo to an instructor explaining their progress on a term project; or an office manager might write a memo to company employees to outline the new vacation policy.

- **Emails.** In today's workplace, email messages are far more common than paper memos. People use email to communicate with clients, customers, suppliers, and associates worldwide. Email messages are generally written more informally and hastily than paper memos.

- **Letters.** Letters are the most personal form of technical communication, but they also provide written records and often serve as contracts. As a student you might write a letter to request research data or to apply for a summer internship. On the job, you might write to persuade a client to invest in a new technology or to explain the delay in a construction project.

- **Instructions.** Instructions explain the steps or course of action for completing a specific task, such as how to program a DVD player or how to install system software. Instructions come in various formats: online instructions may be built right into a computer application; brief instructions may be written on single-page reference cards; longer instructions may be assembled in magazine format to be mailed or handed out.

- **Procedures.** Procedures are similar to instructions in that they explain how to perform a task step by step; however, procedures are different in that they always deal with matters of company or organizational policy. Many companies maintain standard operating procedures (SOPs) for tasks such as how to test soil samples or how to access corporate databases.

- **Manuals.** Almost every technology product or service comes with a manual. Manuals may include instructions on how to assemble, set up, and use

FIGURE 1.5
A persuasive document

A nicely designed letterhead creates an effective, professional visual appeal

The opening paragraph is written clearly and in a direct but polite manner

Each item in the writer's list of reasons starts out with "first," "second," and "third," making the document easy to navigate

The writer backs up the first reason with evidence

The writer backs up the second reason with an appeal to shared values and goals

Energy Empowerment, Inc.
2568 Sheridan Avenue
Suite 9
St. Paul MN 55106

May 14, 20XX

Mr. Dean Winfield, President
XPressMart, Inc.
1720 St. James Avenue
Minneapolis, MN 55405

Dear Mr. Winfield:

I applaud XPressMart's recent commitment to energy efficiency and sustainability in the retail sector, beginning with your newly-purchased storefront in the Cedar-Riverside area. In our meeting last week, you asked me to follow-up with a detailed explanation as to why we feel energy efficiency is the right decision—both for the environment and your company's bottom line. Below I outline Energy Empowerment's three-point rationale.

First, you and your contractor, Jeff Manko, will find that the process of "going green" is actually quite straightforward, rather than another level of complication to an already complicated renovation process. As you can see from the enclosed chart, we have adapted the guidelines from the EPA's EnergyStar program to make both reconstruction decisions and the purchase of new HVAC systems, insulation, and doors and windows a straightforward process. We will work with Jeff every step of the way to ensure the seamless renovation of the store.

Second, by demonstrating XPressMart's commitment to the environment, you are not only helping reduce your company's carbon footprint, but also attracting today's environmentally-conscious customers. The Cedar-Riverside location, being adjacent to two college campuses, is the perfect place to begin.

1-800-555-3984 www.energyempowerment.com

FIGURE 1.5
(Continued)

 Dean Winfield, May 14, 20XX, page 2

Currently the storefront rates only a 42 on EnergyStar's performance scale. By improving that rating to 75 or above, this location will qualify for an EnergyStar display sticker, which, according to the EPA's Annual Report last year, increases retails sales in urban areas. Between the EnergyStar rating and your focus on sustainable products, expect to attract the interest of all residents of this forward-thinking community.

Finally, and perhaps most importantly, rest assured that the costs you put into reconstruction, systems, and other materials will pay for themselves in less than two years. Jeff and I have assembled a preliminary proposal itemizing costs, to which I will add my estimates regarding cost recuperation. However, know that in Energy Empowerment's 12-year history, every store and office renovation project has paid for itself remarkably quickly. As a recent example, consider our recent small office renovation in Columbia Heights, which recouped its costs in only 14 months.

If I can answer any further questions, please do not hesitate to email me at rgarrido@esi.com or call me (extension 646). Again, we applaud your commitment to the environment and look forward to working with you and Jeff.

Best regards,

Rosemary Garrido

Rosemary Garrido
Executive Manager

cc: Jeff Manko, Manko Construction
Encl. Energy Star's performance chart

The writer provides statistics to reinforce her point

The writer closes with the most important reason and backs it up with an appeal to a common financial goal

The writer closes in a friendly manner but retains a persuasive tone

a product, but they also include background information, such as technical specifications or lists of materials. You have certainly used manuals to perform tasks such as connecting the components of your sound system or setting up the voice mail on your cell phone. Most manuals are also available in electronic form: as help files, on a CD, or as PDF documents on a company's Web site.

- **Brochures.** To market goods or services, companies produce brochures. Brochures from professional organizations such as the American Medical Association may define various medical conditions, explain the causes, and describe available treatments. The government creates brochures to help with issues such as how to obtain student loans or how to start a small business.

- **Proposals.** Proposals offer solutions to problems and make specific recommendations for how to implement those solutions. A proposal's purpose is usually to persuade readers to improve conditions, accept a service or product, or otherwise support a plan of action. Proposals are often written in response to calls for proposals (CFPs) or requests for proposals (RFPs). For example, a nonprofit child-care facility may seek safer playground equipment, or a pharmaceutical company may wish to develop a new online education program for its employees. These organizations would issue RFPs, and each interested vendor would prepare a proposal that examines the problem, presents a solution, and defines the process and associated fees.

- **Reports.** Reports, both short and long, are generally based on the study of a specific problem or issue. Some reports are strictly informative ("Why Laptop Computer Batteries Can Explode"); other reports recommend solutions to urgent problems ("Recommended Security Measures for Airline Safety"); and still others have an overtly persuasive goal, advocating a particular course of action ("Why Voters Should Reject the Nuclear Waste Storage Facility Proposed for Our County").

TECHNICAL COMMUNICATION IS GLOBAL, COLLABORATIVE, AND DIGITAL

In the workplace, the documents we create have global implications, are typically written not by one individual but in teams, and are created using digital technologies and distributed electronically. These concepts are described here and apply across all chapters and assignments in this book.

Technical Communication Is Global

Why global issues are important in today's workplace

Employees who work across different continents, countries, and cultures must pay special attention to various customs and values. Key to this practice is "face saving." No one wants to be embarrassed in public, have his or her traditions or values criticized, or be treated with disrespect. All these situations represent a loss of "face." But people in different cultures have different views about what is embarrassing or insulting. For example, in some cultures a "tell it like it is" approach is considered rude, while in others body language such as leaning back in your chair and crossing your arms signals disrespect.

If you are working on a team project and the team spans different countries and cultures, do some research to learn about your team members, to appreciate their frame of reference, and to establish common ground. You may find, for example, that your team members in another country value a slower, more patient approach or put a value on oral communication (by phone or video conference) rather than written communication at certain stages of the project.

Do your research on international business culture

Any document can reach across the globe. For example, the instructions you write for a new cell phone may well end up on a Web site, where they will be used by customers worldwide. Some international readers of your instructions may be offended by commands in strongly worded imperative forms, such as "STOP: Do not insert the storage card until you reach Step 3." Or they may be baffled by icons and other visuals that have no meaning in their culture.

Remember that any document may be transmitted globally

Documents may originate in English but then be translated into other languages. In these cases, writers must be careful to use English that is easy to translate. Idioms, humor, and analogies are often difficult for translators. One famous example of translation difficulty is the case of the Chevrolet Nova, a car that was successful in the United States but met resistance in Latin America. When translated into Spanish, Nova means "Does Not Go"!

For more advice on global communication, see the following Strategies as well as advice throughout this book.

STRATEGIES
for Global Technical Communication

▸ **Learn as much as possible about the culture and background of your team members or customers.** Use the Internet or find books that can help you understand the communication norms for the countries or cultures with which you will be working.

▸ **Be respectful and considerate.** Do nothing that will cause anyone to lose face.

▸ **Avoid the use of humor, slang, and idioms.** These items are culturally specific, do not translate well, and could be misunderstood by nonnative audiences.

▸ **Avoid stereotyping.** Violating a person's cultural frame of reference is offensive, but so is reducing individual complexity to a laundry list of cultural stereotypes. Any generalization about a culture is just that—a generalization. People are still individuals and should be respected as such.

Technical Communication Is Collaborative

Teamwork is a frequent part of technical communication

Complex technical documents (especially long reports, proposals, and manuals) are rarely created by one person working alone. In the workplace, such documents are typically produced by teams of writers, engineers, scientists, graphic artists, editors, reviewers, marketing personnel, lawyers, and other professionals.

Characteristics of effective in-person and virtual teams

Teams can work in person or virtually. Usually, though, teamwork involves a combination of face-to-face meetings and technology-facilitated exchanges, such as those via the phone, email, or the Web. Whether the team shares information in person or virtually, members have to find ways of openly sharing their ideas, expressing their views persuasively, giving and accepting constructive criticism, and reaching agreement with others who hold different views. Teamwork is successful only when there is strong cooperation, a recognized team structure, and clear communication. The following Strategies explain how to work on a team project systematically.

STRATEGIES
for Organizing a Team Project

- **Appoint a group manager.** The manager assigns tasks, enforces deadlines, conducts meetings, consults with supervisors, and "runs the show."

- **Define a clear and definite goal.** Compose a purpose statement that spells out the project's goal and the plan for achieving the goal. Be sure each team member understands the goal.

- **Identify the type of document required.** Is this a report, a proposal, a manual, or a brochure? Are visuals and supplements (abstract, appendices, and so on) needed? Will the document be in hard copy, digital form, or both?

- **Divide the tasks.** Who will be responsible for which parts of the document or which phases of the project? Who is best at doing what (writing, editing, layout and graphics, oral presentation)? Which tasks will be done individually and which collectively? Spell out—in writing—clear expectations for each team member. Also keep in mind that the final version should display a consistent style throughout, as if written by one person only.

- **Establish a timetable.** A timetable will help the team visualize the whole project, each part of the project, and completion dates for each phase.

- **Decide on a meeting schedule.** How often, where, and for how long will the group meet?

- **Establish a procedure for responding to each other's work.** Will reviewing and editing be done in writing, face to face, as a group, one on one, or online?

▶ **Develop a file-naming system for various drafts.** Be careful about saving documents. It's too easy to save over a previous version and lose something important.

▶ **Establish procedures for dealing with interpersonal problems.** How will disputes be discussed and resolved (by vote, by the manager, or by other means)? How will irrelevant discussion be curtailed?

▶ **Select a group decision-making style.** Will decisions be made by the group manager alone, by group input, or by majority vote?

▶ **Decide how to evaluate each member's contribution.** Will the manager assess each member's performance and in turn be evaluated by each member? Will members evaluate each other? What are the criteria?

▶ **Prepare a project planning form.** Figure 1.6 shows a sample form. Distribute completed copies to members.

▶ **Submit regular progress reports.** These reports (see pages 283–286) track activities, problems, and rate of progress.

Running Successful Meetings

Despite the many digital tools available for collaboration (see page 21), face-to-face meetings provide vital personal contact. Meetings are usually scheduled for one of two purposes: to convey or exchange information or to make decisions. Informational meetings tend to run smoothly because there is less cause for disagreement. But decision-based meetings often fail to reach clear resolution because the meeting leader fails to take charge. Running a meeting doesn't mean imposing one's views or stifling opposing views, but it does mean keeping the discussion moving and centered on the issue, as explained in the Strategies on page 17.

Face-to-face meetings are either informational or decision based

Identifying and Managing Group Conflicts

Even when all team members have good working relationships and positive attitudes, conflicts still can arise, usually because of the following differences:

● **Interpersonal differences.** People might clash because of differences in personality, working style, standards, or ability to take criticism. Some might disagree about exactly what or how much the group should accomplish, who should do what, or who should have the final say. Some might feel intimidated or hesitant to speak out. These interpersonal conflicts can actually worsen when the group interacts exclusively online; lack of personal contact makes it hard for trust to develop.

Differences that may lead to group conflict

FIGURE 1.6
Project planning form

Project Planning Form

Project title:
Audience:
Project manager:
Team members:
Purpose of the project:
Type of document required:

Specific Assignments

Research:	**Due Dates**
Planning:	Research due:
Drafting:	Plan and outline due:
Revising:	First draft due:
Preparing final document:	Reviews due:
Presenting oral briefing:	Revision due:
	Progress report(s) due:
	Final document due:

Work Schedule

Team meetings:	Date	Place	Time	Note-taker
#1				
#2				
#3				
etc.				
Mtgs. w/instructor				
#1				
#2				
etc.				

Miscellaneous

How will disputes and grievances be resolved?
How will performances be evaluated?
Other matters (online searches, email routing, online conferences, etc.)?

- **Gender differences.** Research on the ways women and men communicate in meetings indicates a definite gender gap: Women tend to be more hesitant to speak up, and when they do, they are often seen as overbearing. In contrast, men tend to speak up and sometimes dominate discussions, and when they do, they are typically considered strong and leadership oriented. People of either gender can be soft-spoken and reflective, but such traits most often are attributed to the "feminine" stereotype.

STRATEGIES
for Running a Meeting

- **Set an agenda.** Distribute copies of the agenda to participants beforehand: "Our 10 A.M. Monday meeting will cover the following items:…" Spell out each item, set a strict time limit for discussion of each item, and stick to this plan.

- **Ask each person to prepare as needed.** A meeting works best when each participant makes a specific contribution. Appoint someone to take notes or minutes, and appoint others to other roles, such as doing background research on a particular topic that will be discussed.

- **Appoint a different "observer" for each meeting.** This person's job is to take notes on what aspects of the meeting did or did not work well.

- **Begin by summarizing the minutes of the last meeting.** This process will ensure that the conversation in this meeting moves beyond what was concluded previously. (For preparing meeting minutes, see pages 292–293.)

- **Give all members a chance to speak.** Don't allow anyone to monopolize. At the same time, encourage quiet members to contribute.

- **Stick to the issue.** Curb irrelevant discussion. When the conversation strays, politely nudge members back on track.

- **Keep things moving.** Don't get hung up on a single issue. Work toward a consensus by highlighting points of agreement and pushing for a resolution.

- **Observe, guide, and listen.** As the meeting leader, don't lecture or dictate. Instead, take charge by steering the group discussion.

- **Summarize major points before calling for a vote.** Paraphrase what has been discussed to be sure that everyone has understood the major points and so that clarifications or corrections can be made before the vote.

- **End the meeting on schedule.** This is not a hard-and-fast rule. If you feel the issue is about to be resolved at the meeting's end time, continue. Understand, however, that some participants may need to leave for other appointments.

- **Cultural differences.** International business expert David A. Victor writes about cultural codes that influence interaction in group settings. According to Victor, some cultures value intuition and ambiguity more than hard evidence or data, or they prioritize politeness and personal relationships more than business relationships. Cultures also differ in their perceptions of time. Some are "all business" and like to get directly to the point; others take as long as they feel is needed to weigh the issues and come to carefully considered conclusions (233). Finally, cultures differ in their accepted methods of communication, varying in their willingness to express disagreement, question or be questioned, leave things unstated, or use nonverbal language (shaking hands, kissing, hugging, making eye contact, using facial expressions) (206).

When group conflicts do arise, deal with them directly and openly by using the following Strategies.

STRATEGIES
for Managing Team Conflicts

► **Listen actively.** Perhaps the most constructive way to manage team conflict is to avoid it by *really* listening to others. Listening actively means focusing your attention when people speak, keeping your mind open to what they say, letting them finish before you interject, using direct eye contact and body language that communicates interest, and asking for clarification when genuinely needed. In short, observe the 90/10 rule: listen 90 percent of the time, and speak only 10 percent of the time. As President Calvin Coolidge once said, "Nobody ever listened himself out of a job." Some historians would argue that "Silent Cal" listened himself right into the White House.

► **Avoid gender and cultural bias.** Respect the fact that men and women must be treated equally as team members, and understand that assertiveness and reserve are qualities of both genders. Also, do not assume that one culture's approach to business, time, or communication is better than that of another.

► **Research cultures other than your own.** Apply what you learn to situations in which you collaborate with members of multiple cultures.

► **Give everyone a chance to be heard.** Encourage quieter members to speak up, and curtail dominating members from speaking excessively.

► **Take everyone's feelings and opinions seriously.** Don't play favorites. Every team member has something valid to contribute.

► **Don't be afraid to disagree.** Politely let other team members know if you don't agree with their ideas or opinions. Your point of view is as important as anyone else's.

► **Offer and accept constructive criticism.** Criticism focused on helping reach the team's goal, as opposed to seeming like a personal attack, creates an atmosphere of open communication.

► **Find points of agreement with others who hold different views.** Although you might not agree with everyone in the group, find those points on which you do agree.

► **When the group does make a decision, support it fully.** At some point, decisions must be made. If you are outvoted, accept the fact that a vote is binding and that you represent the group as a whole, even if you disagree with the final decision.

Reviewing and Editing the Work of Others

Documents produced in teams must be reviewed and edited extensively. *Reviewing* means evaluating how well a document connects with its audience and meets its purpose. When reviewing, you explain to the writer how you respond as a reader; you point out what works or doesn't work. This commentary helps the writer think about ways of revising. Reviewers typically examine a document to make sure it includes these features:

The process of reviewing a document

- accurate, appropriate, useful, and legal content
- material organized for the reader's understanding
- clear, easy-to-read, and engaging style
- effective visuals and page design

Qualities reviewers look for

Editing means polishing a document by making it more precise and readable at the sentence and word level. Editing may happen simultaneously with reviewing, but usually it comes after a document has been reviewed and revised—when the more global considerations of content, organization, style, and design have already been resolved and the editor can focus on more particular details. Editors typically suggest improvements such as these:

The process of editing a document

- rephrasing or reorganizing sentences
- clarifying a topic sentence
- choosing a better word or phrase
- correcting spelling, usage, punctuation, and so on

Types of "fixing" that editors do

For a team project, at work or at school, you can each take turns reviewing and editing drafts of the document by using the following Strategies.

STRATEGIES
for Peer Review and Editing

▶ **Read the entire piece at least twice before you comment.** Develop a clear sense of the document's purpose and audience. Try to visualize the document as a whole before you evaluate specific parts.

▶ **Focus first on the big picture.** Begin with the document's content and organization. Is the document appropriate for its audience and purpose? Is the supporting material relevant and convincing? Is the discussion easy to follow? Does each paragraph do its job? Do all the visuals serve a distinct and appropriate purpose? Is the design appropriate for this document?

STRATEGIES *continued*

▶ **Be honest but diplomatic.** Say what you think, but don't merely offer negative comments. Begin with something positive before moving to suggested improvements. Maintain a supportive tone.

▶ **Explain why something doesn't work.** Instead of "this paragraph is confusing," say "because this paragraph lacks a clear topic sentence, I had trouble discovering the main idea." Instead of "I don't like this visual," say "this visual doesn't work, not only because it is a little blurry, but also because it doesn't add to the discussion."

▶ **Make specific recommendations for improvements.** Write out suggestions in enough detail for the writer to know what to do. Don't just say "I think you should add a chart here." Instead offer "I think you should add a new chart here to show all the numerical information you've provided in an easy-to-understand visual way."

▶ **Don't expect everyone to agree with your suggestions.** Even professional editors can disagree. Offer your best advice but don't dictate—others may have better suggestions. If different readers offer conflicting opinions of what needs to be revised, seek your team leader's opinion or take it to a vote.

▶ **Understand the acceptable limits of editing.** Don't simply rewrite an entire document in your own words. Although changes can range from making a few suggestions and additions to closely editing every paragraph, always preserve the author's original vision and style.

▶ **Focus next on the particulars.** Once the document has been reviewed and revised for content, organization, style, and design, refine the sentences and word choice— and proofread several times.

Technical Communication Is Digital

Use the media that suit your purpose

Say you are writing a report for a team at work, and team members are situated in three different countries; in this situation, paper is probably not the best medium for delivering the document. Instead, a PDF version, available on the Web or via the company's intranet, would be more effective.

Use an appropriate combination of text, visuals, and sound

Effective use of media also requires an appropriate combination of words, pictures or other visuals, and sounds (as in videos and podcasts). Some documents, such as formal letters, rely heavily or solely on words; other documents, such as instructions, blend words and pictures or diagrams.

Teams are increasingly distributed across different job sites, time zones, and countries. Even for a school project, you and the other team members may have very different work schedules and may need to meet virtually. The Internet—via email, streamed video, instant messaging, blogs, and other communication tools—offers the primary means for virtual teams to interact. In addition, tools such as computer-supported cooperative work (CSCW) software and project management software (such as Microsoft Project) can be helpful.

Digital technology can help virtual teams collaborate

For personal contact, face-to-face meetings are essential. But virtual collaboration may allow some people to feel more secure about saying what they really think because they eliminate public speaking fears as well as "status cues" such as age, gender, appearance, or ethnicity (Wojahn 747–48).

Advantages of virtual collaboration

Various technologies enable virtual teams to work together:

Virtual collaboration technologies

- **Teleconferencing.** The oldest form of virtual collaboration—still very much in use—occurs when multiple callers hold a conference via the telephone.

- **Email.** The most popular tool today, email is great for keeping track of discussions among multiple recipients.

- **Instant messaging (IM).** IM is a fast and easy way to hold a real-time conversation among multiple people, as long as they are all logged in.

- **Project management software.** Most large organizations use dedicated software, such as Microsoft Project, to manage complex team projects.

- **Editing software.** Editing tools allow multiple users to see each other's edits (which are tagged by the user's initials) and to accept or reject those changes. An example is Microsoft Word's "track changes" feature.

- **Digital whiteboards.** These tools provide a large screen that allows participants to write, sketch, and erase from their own computers in real time.

- **Web conferencing.** A password-protected Web site provides the medium for this more contemporary version of teleconferencing.

- **Blogs.** Short for "Web logs," blogs allow readers to create postings or add comments to previous postings as a way for teams to share and refine ideas.

- **Intranets.** Intranets are sites set up for internal company use only. Readers can access files, blogs, and other information.

- **Wikis.** These Web sites can be set up to allow access only to those directly involved in the project. When a team member edits a document, a new version is created and old versions saved.

For more on digital communication, see Chapters 18–21 on email, text messaging, blogs and wikis, Web pages, and related topics.

✓ **CHECKLIST**
for Effective Technical Communication

My**Writing**Lab™

☐ Does my document focus on the reader not the writer?

☐ Is the document efficient and accessible?

☐ Is the document clear and easy to understand?

☐ Does the document give readers what they need?

☐ Have I used the appropriate media to convey my message?

☐ Have I created the document to address a global audience as needed?

☐ Am I able to work as part of a team?

☐ Is the document sufficiently persuasive to get the response I want?

☐ Is the document ethically acceptable?

☐ Is the document based on careful research?

☐ Does the document achieve its primary purpose (i.e., inform, instruct, persuade)—or a combination of purposes?

GLOBAL CONSIDERATIONS

☐ Do I understand the communication customs of the international audience for my document?

☐ Is my writing clear and direct, so that it is easy to translate?

☐ Have I avoided idioms, humor, and slang?

☐ Have I avoided stereotyping of different cultures and groups of people?

☐ Does my document enable everyone to save face?

COLLABORATIVE CONSIDERATIONS

☐ Has our team appointed a team manager?

☐ Does the team agree on the type of document required?

☐ Do we have a plan for how to divide the tasks?

☐ Have we established a timetable and decided on a meeting schedule?

☐ Do we have an agenda for our first meeting?

☐ Are we using the project planning form (page 16) to help us get organized?

→

CHECKLIST *continued*

DIGITAL CONSIDERATIONS

- ☐ Do we have a clear understanding of how we will share drafts of the document and how we will name the files?

- ☐ Have we decided what technology we should use for our collaboration (e.g., track changes; a wiki; a blog)?

APPLICATIONS

GENERAL APPLICATIONS

MyWritingLab™

1. Write an email to your boss, requesting that the company pay your tuition for this class. Explain how the class will help you be more effective on the job. Proofread your email: Is it too long or too short? Is the tone professional or demanding? Did you write from your perspective or the reader's (your boss)?

2. Find an example of an informational document or a set of instructions or a persuasive letter. Identify in your document the features of effective technical writing discussed in this chapter. Discuss your findings in class.

TEAM APPLICATIONS

1. Class members will work together often this semester. So that everyone becomes acquainted, your task is to introduce to the class the person seated next to you. (That person, in turn, will introduce you.) Follow this procedure:

    a. Exchange with your neighbor whatever personal information you think the class needs: background, major, career plans, communication needs of your intended profession, and so on. Each person gets five minutes to tell her or his story.

    b. Take careful notes; ask questions if you need to.

    c. Take your notes home and select only what you think the class will find useful.

    d. Prepare a one-page memo telling your classmates who this person is. (See pages 178–179 for memo elements and format.)

    e. Ask your neighbor to review the memo for accuracy; revise as needed.

    f. Present the class with a two-minute oral paraphrase of your memo and submit a copy of the memo to your instructor.

2. Write a short memo to your instructor describing the role of teams in a company, organization, or campus group where you have worked or volunteered. Your memo should address questions such as what type of projects your team worked on, how the teams were organized, what worked, and what did not work.

GLOBAL APPLICATION   MyWritingLab™

Technical documents are often read by international audiences. Some companies handle this issue by translating their documentation into multiple languages; other companies use a combination of words and pictures or just pictures. Find an example of technical communication written for an international audience. You might look at the instructions that came with your computer, cell phone, unassembled bookshelves, or other products. Write a short memo explaining what techniques the writer used to make the information useful for people who may not speak English or who speak English as a second language.

DIGITAL AND SOCIAL MEDIA APPLICATION   MyWritingLab™

Use the Internet to research examples of technical communication that are common in your profession or major. For example, if you are studying electrical engineering, what are the typical types of reports or studies you might need to write when you get a job? Using the Checklist for Effective Technical Communication at the end of this chapter, evaluate whether a selected document appears to be effective. Write a memo to your instructor explaining your findings. Include the Web address or other location (Facebook page, LinkedIn, Google site, other) for the document you found.

MyWritingLab™   Visit Chapter 1, *Technical Communication: Global, Collaborative, and Digital*, in MyWritingLab to complete this chapter's applications, to explore this chapter's overview, checklist, and flashcards, and to test your understanding of the chapter objectives.

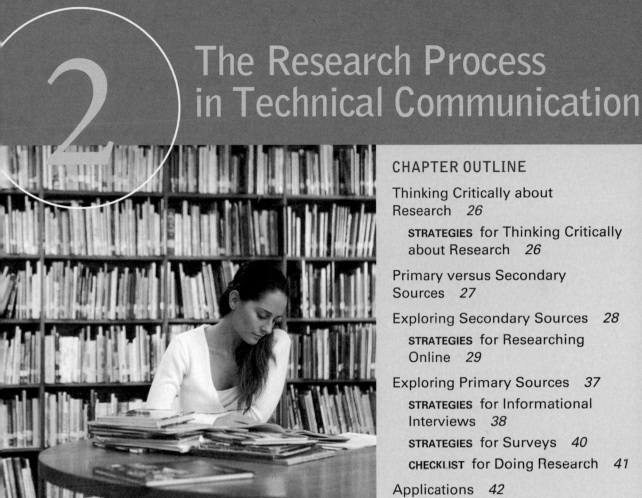

2 The Research Process in Technical Communication

CHAPTER OUTLINE

Thinking Critically about Research *26*

   STRATEGIES for Thinking Critically about Research *26*

Primary versus Secondary Sources *27*

Exploring Secondary Sources *28*

   STRATEGIES for Researching Online *29*

Exploring Primary Sources *37*

   STRATEGIES for Informational Interviews *38*

   STRATEGIES for Surveys *40*

   CHECKLIST for Doing Research *41*

Applications *42*

LEARNING OBJECTIVES FOR THIS CHAPTER

- ▸ Apply critical thinking to your research
- ▸ Understand the difference between primary and secondary research
- ▸ Locate the online and hard-copy secondary sources you need
- ▸ Consult primary sources via inquiries, informational interviews and surveys, observations, and experiments

All technical communication requires some degree of research, even if that research merely entails checking a fact or consulting a colleague before writing a memo, letter, or email. This chapter explains how to conduct more complex research for such technical documents as long reports and proposals. As you read, consider how research in technical communication often differs from research conducted in an academic setting.

THINKING CRITICALLY ABOUT RESEARCH

Research is a vital part of technical communication

Most major decisions in the workplace are based on careful research, often with the findings recorded in a written report, in a long memo, on a Web site, or in some combination of documents. The types of research you will perform as a technical communicator depend largely on your workplace assignment.

Not all findings will be of equal value. For instance, if you really want to know how well the latest invention in robotic surgery works, you need to check with sources other than the inventor (from whom you could expect an overly optimistic or insufficiently critical assessment). Likewise, if you only consult books published before 2000 and don't consult any online sources, you are not likely to get a current and balanced view. Further, if you interpret your findings inaccurately—say, by ignoring a study that contradicts your viewpoint or claim—your research will be invalid.

Why critical thinking is essential in research

Whether you work with your own findings or the findings of other researchers, you need to decide if the information is reliable. Then you need to decide what your information means. *Critical thinking* means that you test the quality of your information and the accuracy of your interpretations. Instead of accepting information at face value, you examine, evaluate, verify, analyze, and weigh alternatives during every stage of your research. You use critical thinking to examine your evidence and your reasoning to discover new connections and new possibilities and to test the soundness of your conclusions. The following Strategies provide specific guidelines.

STRATEGIES
for Thinking Critically about Research

▶ **Ask the right questions.** To get the right answers, start by asking the right questions. Instead of researching an overly general topic that will lead to an enormous variety of information, such as "genetically modified foods," ask a specific, narrowed question, such as "What are the positive and negative effects of genetically modified foods on human health?"

▸ **Explore a balance of views.** Consider your research topic from a variety of angles. Don't just consult one expert because experts may disagree. Instead find out what multiple experts say and examine the points on which the experts agree and disagree.

▸ **Explore your topic in sufficient depth.** Different sources of information represent different levels of detail and dependability. At the surface layer is information from the popular press (newspapers, commercial Web sites, TV shows). This surface information may be useful and valid, but you should also go further and explore deeper levels, such as trade and business publications and Web sites or specialized literature (journals and Web sites from professional associations and government sources).

▸ **Evaluate your sources.** The information you find may be incomplete or misleading. While you can't always verify that a source is trustworthy, you can weed out unreliable sources by looking for common ground among sources, by determining if any of them are driven by an agenda, and by checking the source's credentials.

▸ **Interpret your findings objectively.** Examine what you've uncovered from multiple angles. Do your findings support only one viewpoint, or are there several ways to interpret them? If your research yields indefinite findings, don't try to force a definite conclusion. A wrong conclusion is worse than an indefinite one.

PRIMARY VERSUS SECONDARY SOURCES

Primary research means getting information directly from the source by conducting interviews and surveys and by observing people, events, or processes in action. *Secondary research* means getting information secondhand by reading what other researchers have compiled in books and articles in print or online. Most information found online would be considered a secondary source. Some Web-based information is more accurate than others; for instance, a Web page created by a high school student might be interesting but not overly reliable, whereas a Web site that is the equivalent of a traditional secondary source (encyclopedia, research index, newspaper, journal) would be more reliable for your research.

How primary and secondary research differ

Whenever possible, combine primary and secondary research. Typically, you would start by using secondary sources because they are readily available and can help you get a full background understanding of your topic. However, don't neglect to add your own findings to existing ones by doing primary research. Working with primary sources can help you expand on what other people have already learned and add considerable credibility to your work. For instance, assume that your boss asks you to write a report about how successfully your

Why you should combine primary and secondary research

company's new product is being received in the marketplace: you might consult sales reports and published print and online reviews of the product (secondary research), but you might also survey product users and interview some of them individually (primary research).

EXPLORING SECONDARY SOURCES

Types of secondary sources

Secondary sources include Web sites; online news outlets and magazines; blogs and wikis; books in the library; journal, magazine, and newspaper articles; government publications; and other public records. Research assignments begin more effectively when you first uncover and sort through what is already known about your topic before adding to that knowledge yourself.

Pros and cons of using hard-copy versus online secondary sources

Although online searches are becoming the norm, thorough research may require careful examination of hard-copy sources as well. The advantages and drawbacks of each search medium, listed in Table 2.1, provide good reason for exploring both.

TABLE 2.1
Hard-copy versus online sources: benefits and drawbacks

	Benefits	Drawbacks
Hard-copy sources	• Available on library shelves, where you might also find related material	• Time-consuming and inefficient to search
	• Easy to determine author, publication date, and page number	• Offer only text and images
	• Easier to preserve and keep secure	• Content may not be up to date
Online sources	• More current, efficient, and accessible	• Older content that has not been scanned may not be available.
	• Searches can be narrowed or broadened	• Some Web sites may be unreliable
	• Can offer material that has no hard-copy equivalent	• Researcher might get confused by too many choices

Online Secondary Sources

Locate online secondary sources by using subject directories and search engines

Information in virtually any format—journals, newspapers, and magazines; government documents and research reports; corporate Web sites; library databases—can be accessed online. To find various online sources, use two basic tools: *subject directories* and *search engines*.

- **Subject directories.** Subject directories are indexes compiled by editors who sift through Web sites and sort the most useful links. Popular general subject directories include *Yahoo! Directory, About.com* and *Internet Public Library (ipl2)*. Specialized directories focus on a single topic such as software, health, or employment. See *Beaucoup!*, a "directory of directories" for listings of specialized directories organized by category.

> Subject directories are maintained by editors

- **Search engines.** Search engines, such as *Google, Yahoo!*, and *Bing* scan for Web sites containing key words. Even though search engines yield a lot more information than subject directories, much of it can be irrelevant. Some search engines, however, are more selective than others, and some focus on specialized topics.

> Most search engines are maintained by computers not people

To research online, use the following Strategies. To locate any of the Web sites or online resources mentioned in this or other chapters, just do a Google or other search on the resource name. For instance, to locate the electronic version of a digital newspaper, search on the newspaper name.

STRATEGIES
for Researching Online

▸ **Expect limited results from any one search engine or subject directory.** No single search engine, not even a popular one like Google, can index more than a fraction of material available on the Web. No subject directory will list the same Web sites as another.

▸ **When using a search engine, select keywords or search phrases that are varied and technical rather than general.** Some search terms generate more useful hits than others. In addition to "electromagnetic radiation," for example, try "electromagnetic fields," "power lines and health," or "electrical fields." Specialized terms (say, "vertigo" versus "dizziness") offer the best access to reliable sites. However, if you are not able to locate much by using a specialized term, widen your search somewhat.

▸ **When using a subject directory, drill down to an appropriate level of specificity.** Don't rely on finding what you need at the top, or most general, topic level (e.g., "business" or "education"). The best subject directories will be organized into multiple levels of specificity. Keep digging until you either find what you want or discover that the subject directory doesn't list topics relevant to your research.

▸ **Consider the domain type (where the site originates).** Standard domain types in the United States include .com (commercial organization), .edu (educational institution), .gov or .mil (government or military organization), .net (general usage), and .org (organization). While a .com site or a .net site may contain reliable information, you may be better off with a .gov or .mil site that provides official government information, an .edu site that is written by discipline-specific experts, or an .org site that is written by parties who specialize in a particular area.

► **Identify the site's purpose and sponsor.** Is the intent merely to relay information, to sell something, or to promote an ideology or agenda? The domain type might alert you to bias or a hidden agenda. A .com site might provide accurate information but also some type of sales pitch. An .org site might reflect a political or ideological bias. Looking for a site's sponsor can also help you evaluate its postings. For example, a Web site about genetically modified organisms (GMOs) by an organization called the Non-GMO Project (Figure 2.1) may contain useful information but may also be biased toward one point of view.

► **Look beyond the style of a site.** Sometimes the most reliable material resides in less attractive, text-only sites. A flashy site does not necessarily indicate reliable content.

► **Assess the currency of the site and its materials.** When was the material created, posted, and updated? Many sites have not been updated in months or years.

► **Assess the author's credentials and assertions.** Check the author's reputation, expertise, and institutional affiliation (university, company, environmental group). Do not confuse the *author* (the person who wrote the material) with the *Webmaster* (the person who created and maintains the site). Follow links to other sites that mention the author. Where, on the spectrum of expert opinion and accepted theory, does this author fall? Is each assertion supported by solid evidence? Verify any extreme claim through other sources, such as a professor or expert in the field. Consider whether your own biases might predispose you to accept certain ideas.

► **Use bookmarks and hotlists for quick access to favorite Web sites.** It is always frustrating when you can't find a helpful Web site that you accessed previously but didn't bookmark.

► **Save or print what you need before it changes or disappears.** Web sites often change their content or "go dead." Always record the Web address and your access date.

► **Download only what you need; use it ethically; obtain permission; and credit your sources.** Unless they are crucial to your research, omit graphics, sound, and video files. Do not use material created by others in a way that disrespects or otherwise harms the material's creator. For any type of commercial use of material from the Web, obtain written permission from the source's owner and credit the source exactly as directed by its owner. For more information on copyright, see Chapter 18 and Appendix A.

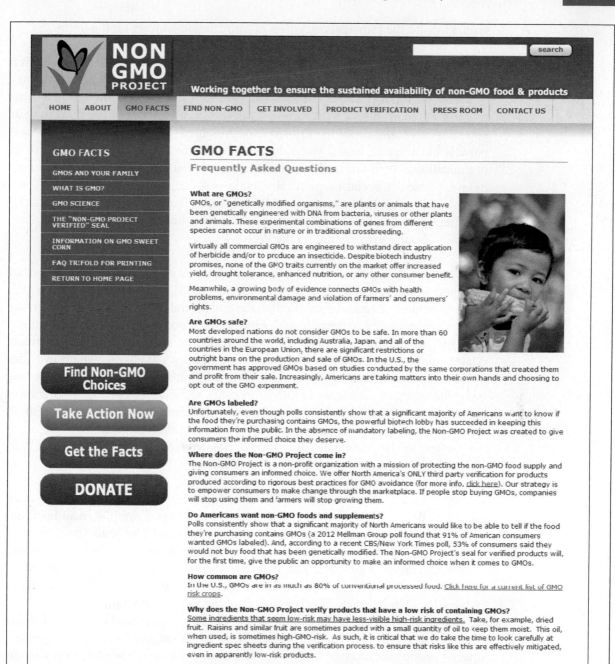

FIGURE 2.1 A Web site that advocates a particular viewpoint
Source: Courtesy of the Non-GMO Project.

Following are the principal categories of information sources on the online.

General Commercial, Organizational, and Academic Web Sites.

Search engines pull up a wide variety of hits, most of which will be commercial (.com), organizational (.org), and academic (.edu) Web sites. If the content within a commercial site looks directly relevant to your search, by all means use it, as long as you think critically about the information presented. Does the fact that the company is likely trying to sell you something affect the content? Be careful also of organizational Web sites, which are likely to be well researched but which may have a particular social or political agenda. Are the opinions expressed by the organization designed to sway you to their agenda? Academic Web sites tend to be credible. However, some academics may also have biases, so never stop thinking critically about what you find on the Web.

Government Web Sites.

Search engines will also pull up government Web sites, but your best way to access them is by going through the U.S. government's Web portal. Most government organizations (local, state, and federal) have a Web site and online access to research and reports. Examples include the Food and Drug Administration's Web site, which offers information on food recalls, clinical drug trials, and countless related items; and the Federal Bureau of Investigation's Web site, which provides information about the most wanted fugitives in the United States, tips on how to avoid being the victim of a crime, and much more. State and local sites provide information on auto licenses, state tax laws, and local property and land issues. From some of these sites you can link to specific government-sponsored research projects.

Be sure to check the dates of reports or data you locate on a government Web site, and find out how often the site is updated.

Online News Outlets and Magazines.

Most major news organizations offer online versions of their broadcast and print publications. Examples include online versions of newspapers such as *The New York Times* and The *Wall Street Journal*, CNN, and National Public Radio. Major magazines, such as *Time*, *Newsweek*, *Forbes*, and other more specialized magazines also offer Web versions. Some news is available online only, as in the online magazines *Slate* and *Salon*. To locate these publications, do a Google or other search on the publication name.

Make sure you understand how the publication obtains and reviews information. Is it a major news site, such as CNN, or is it a smaller site run by a special-interest group? Each can be useful, but you must evaluate the source. Also keep in mind that many online magazines have a particular political bias. Is the magazine conservative or liberal in its point of view?

Blogs.

Blogs are Web sites on which the blog's author posts ideas. Readers are able to post comments and replies. Postings and replies are displayed in reverse chronological order, with the newest topic first. Older posts can usually be viewed via an index or link. Links that the owner has hand chosen also supply ways to connect to other blogs on the same or similar topics. Blogs are great for finding current information from individuals, companies, and nonprofit organizations that are knowledgeable about particular topics. You will find more blogs than you can use, so you need to evaluate the information on individual blogs carefully and decide which ones are most relevant and reliable.

Keep in mind that blogs nearly always represent the particular views of the blog author (whether an individual, company, organization, or academic institution) and of those who reply to the blog postings. Check any information you find on a blog against a professionally edited or peer-reviewed source.

Wikis. *Wikis* are community encyclopedias that allow anyone to add to or edit the content of a listing. The most popular wiki is *Wikipedia*. The theory of a wiki is that if the information from one posting is wrong, someone else will correct it, and over time the site will reach a high level of accuracy and reliability.

Always keep in mind that many wikis have no oversight. Aside from a few people who determine whether to delete articles based on requests from users, the content on a wiki is not checked by editors for accuracy. Always check information you find on a wiki against several other peer-reviewed or traditional sources. Remember that most of what is posted on a wiki has not been evaluated objectively. See Chapter 19 for more on blogs and wikis.

Online Forums and Electronic Mailing Lists. For almost any topic imaginable, you will find a Web forum, or discussion group. Major technology companies like Apple and Microsoft offer discussion forums to help customers solve technical problems. One way to locate relevant forums is to search through one of the major online forum providers. For instance, if you are researching a health-related issue such as stress among college students, you might want to visit *Google Groups* or *Yahoo! Groups* and join a group related directly to that issue. As with blogs, you will find more online forums than you could ever possibly use, so choose them with care.

Electronic mailing lists, or e-lists, are essentially the same as online forums. Most online forums offer two options: either subscribing to and visiting the forum via the Web or subscribing to and receiving messages and responses from participants directly into your email inbox. Messages may be sent to the entire group, or you may reply to participants individually.

Material you find on online forums or receive via e-lists may be insightful but may not represent an adequate range of responses. Visit a variety of forums or subscribe to multiple e-lists to get a broad perspective on the issue. Information posted on online forums or sent out to e-list subscribers may or may not be moderated (approved by a reviewer prior to being posted). Unmoderated material is usually less reliable.

E-Libraries. Entirely searchable online, e-libraries are excellent research tools. Aside from the online sites sponsored by most public libraries, the most notable e-library is the Internet Public Library, an online-only, noncommercial, and academically reliable virtual library founded by the University of Michigan's School of Information. Like other e-libraries, the Internet Public Library (ipl2) includes links to online books, magazines, and newspapers, along with online ready references (almanacs, dictionaries, encyclopedias, etc.), links to periodical databases, online exhibits, links to special collections organized by subject area, and even "live" librarians.

Although e-libraries can be extremely useful stand-ins for traditional, physical libraries, they can never entirely take the place of traditional libraries. They are limited to resources available in electronic form, which will not include current books under copyright or a wide range of magazine and newspaper articles and other resources. Supplement what you discover at an e-library with hard-copy materials from a traditional library.

Periodical Databases. Virtually all libraries have their own Web site where, if you are a library cardholder or a student, you can access a wide variety of periodical databases. Periodical databases are electronic collections of articles from newspapers, magazines, journals, and other publications. You can search these databases by title, author, keyword, and so on.

When searching a periodical database, follow the same keyword guidelines you would use when searching online (pages 29–30); for instance, narrow your search when you get too many hits or expand your search if you don't find enough relevant material. Once you have typed in your keyword(s), you will be presented with a citation page that includes some or all of the following information: author(s), title, source, subject area, abstract (a brief summary of the article), ISSN (International Standard Serial Number—an identifier for the article much like a book's ISBN), and DOI (or Digital Object Identifier—where the article can be found on the Web if it is available online).

Some of the most popular general periodical databases include *InfoTrac*, *NewsBank*, *ProQuest*, and *EBSCOHost*, but there are also many specialized periodical databases in a variety of subjects areas to which your library may also subscribe.

Before initiating a periodical database search, try to meet with your local reference librarian for a tour of the various databases and the instructions for searching them effectively. Also be aware that some databases may not be accessible from school or home—you may need to visit your library in person.

Hard-Copy Secondary Sources

As noted previously, traditional printed secondary research tools are still of great value. Unlike much of what you may find on the Web, most hard-copy secondary sources are carefully reviewed and edited before they are published.

Although it may take more time to go to the library and look through a printed book or other hard-copy source, it's often a better way to get solid information. Also, even though the digitizing of hard-copy materials continues to grow, many of these printed sources are not available on the Web, particularly the full texts of books.

Hard-copy secondary sources can be located in your library by using the "card catalog," or, to use a more contemporary term (because cards are no longer used in most libraries), your library's online public access catalog (OPAC). This catalog can be accessed online or at terminals in the library. You can search a library's holdings by subject, author, title, or keyword in that library's OPAC. Visit the library's Web site, or ask a librarian for help. To search catalogs from libraries worldwide, go to the *Library of Congress Gateway* or *LibrarySpot*.

The following are the principal categories of hard-copy information sources found at libraries and one type of source material (gray literature) that you will need to track down on your own.

> Locate hard-copy secondary sources using your library's "card catalog," or OPAC

Books and Periodicals. Most obviously, any library will be well stocked with books as well as numerous hard-copy magazines, journals, and newspapers. The smaller and more general the library you visit, the less likely you are to find highly specialized print sources, and the larger or more specialized the library, the more likely you are to find books by specialist publishers and periodicals that delve into more specific subject areas.

Although not technically in hard-copy format, some older publications may be available on CD-ROMs and microfiche. However, many publications in these formats have now been converted to digital texts, available online.

When consulting books and periodicals, be sure to check the copyright date and supplement the source with additional information from more recent sources, if necessary.

Reference Works. Reference works are general information sources that provide background and can lead to more specific information.

- **Bibliographies.** Bibliographies are lists of books or articles by subject field. To locate bibliographies in your field, begin by consulting the *Bibliographic Index Plus*, a list (by subject) of major bibliographies, which indexes more than 500,000 bibliographies worldwide. You can also consult such general bibliographies as *Books in Print* or the *Reader's Guide to Periodical Literature*. Or consult subject area bibliographies, such as *Bibliography of World War II History*, or highly focused bibliographies, such as *Health Hazards of Video Display Terminals: An Annotated Bibliography*.

- **Indexes.** Book and article bibliographies may also be referred to as indexes. However, other types of indexes collect information not likely to be found in standard bibliographies, such as indexes to conference proceedings (e.g., the *Index to Scientific and Technical Proceedings* and *Engineering Meetings*), which collect the most current information in various fields not yet published in book or periodical form; patent indexes (e.g., the *Index of Patents Issued from the United States Patent and Trademark Office* and the *World Patents Index*), which collect cutting-edge technological descriptions not yet widely available to the public; and technical report indexes (e.g., *Scientific and Technical Aerospace Reports* and the *Government Reports Announcements and Index*), which also collect highly current information unavailable elsewhere.

- **Encyclopedias.** Encyclopedias are alphabetically arranged collections of articles (written by the encyclopedia's editors and contributors). You may want to start by consulting a general encyclopedia, such as *Encyclopedia Britannica* or the *Columbia Encyclopedia*, but then consult more specific subject-focused encyclopedias, such as *Encyclopedia of Nutritional Supplements, American Jurisprudence, Encyclopedia of Business and Finance,* or *Illustrated Encyclopedia of Aircraft.*

- **Dictionaries.** Dictionaries are alphabetically arranged lists of words, including definitions, pronunciations, and word origins. If you can't locate a particular word in a general dictionary (e.g., a highly specialized term or jargon specific to a certain field), consult a specialized dictionary, such as *Dictionary of Engineering and Technology, Dictionary of Psychology,* or *Dictionary of Media and Communication Studies.*

- **Handbooks.** Handbooks are books that offer condensed facts (formulas, tables, advice, examples) about particular fields. Examples include the *Civil Engineering Handbook* and *The McGraw-Hill Computer Handbook.*

- **Almanacs.** Almanacs are collections of factual and statistical data, usually arranged by subject area and published annually. Examples include general almanacs, such as the *World Almanac and Book of Facts,* or subject-specific almanacs, like the *Almanac for Computers* or *Baer's Agricultural Almanac.*

- **Directories.** Directories are books that provide updated information about organizations, companies, people, products, services, or careers, often listing addresses and phone numbers. Examples include *The Career Guide: Dun's Employment Opportunities Directory* and the *Directory of American Firms Operating in Foreign Countries.* For electronic versions, ask your librarian about *Hoover's Company Capsules* (for basic information on thousands of companies) and *Hoover's Company Profiles* (for detailed information).

- **Abstracts.** Abstracts are collections of summaries of books or articles, as you might find when searching a periodical database, but collected in one place. Abstracts can save you from having to track down a journal before deciding whether to read or skip the article. Abstracts usually are titled by discipline: *Biological Abstracts, Computer Abstracts,* and so on. For some current research, you might consult abstracts of doctoral dissertations in *Dissertation Abstracts International.*

Many of the reference works mentioned here are accessible free via the Internet Public Library or other sites. When using a reference work, check the copyright date to make sure you are accessing the most current information available.

Gray Literature. Some useful printed information may not be available at any library. This is known as "gray literature," or materials that are unpublished or not typically catalogued. Examples include such helpful documents as pamphlets published by organizations or companies (such as medical pamphlets or company marketing materials), unpublished government documents (available under the Freedom of Information Act, with the exception of classified documents), dissertations by graduate students, papers presented at professional conferences, or self-published works.

The only way to track down gray literature is to contact organizations, companies, or individuals who may produce such literature and ask them if they have anything available in your subject area. For instance, you could contact a professional organization asking for papers on your topic delivered at its recent annual conference or contact a specific government agency for statistics reports directly relevant to your topic. Before doing so, know your research topic well and know specifically whom to contact and why, in case you should be asked. Don't contact potential gray literature providers with vague, general requests for information.

Keep in mind that gray literature, like much material found on the Web, is often not carefully scrutinized for content by editors. Therefore, the material may not be reliable and should be backed up by information from other sources.

EXPLORING PRIMARY SOURCES

Once you have explored your research topic in depth by finding out what others have already uncovered, supplement that knowledge with information you uncover yourself by doing primary research. Primary sources include unsolicited inquiries, informational interviews, surveys, and observations or experiments.

Types of primary sources

Unsolicited Inquiries

The most basic form of primary research is making simple unsolicited inquiries. Letters, phone calls, or email inquiries to experts listed in Web pages or to people you find out about in other ways can yield information that adds to, clarifies, or supplements information you already have. When making an unsolicited inquiry, make sure you contact the right individual or individuals. Don't just contact a company or department. Also, ask exactly what you need to know, rather than vague, general questions, and be sure what you ask is not confidential or otherwise sensitive.

Unsolicited inquiries uncover basic but important information

Note that unsolicited inquiries, especially by phone or email, can be intrusive or even offensive. Therefore, limit yourself to one or two questions that don't require extensive research or thought on the part of the person or persons you contact.

Informational Interviews

Informational interviews lead to original, unpublished material

An excellent primary source of information is the informational interview, a solicited and extended form of inquiry. Much of what an expert knows may never be published. Therefore, you can uncover highly original information by spending time with someone and asking pertinent questions. In addition, an interviewee might refer you to other experts or sources of information.

Expert opinion is not always reliable

Of course, an expert's opinion can be just as mistaken or biased as anyone else's. Like patients who seek second opinions about serious medical conditions, researchers seek a balanced range of expert opinions about complex problems or controversial issues—not only from a company engineer and environmentalist, for example, but also from independent and presumably more objective third parties such as a professor or journalist who has studied the issue. See the following Strategies for advice on effective interviews.

STRATEGIES
for Informational Interviews

- **Know exactly what you're seeking.** Write out a purpose statement. For example, "The purpose of my interview with Leslie Brown, clinical nutritionist, is to ask about her latest research on the possible links between certain genetically modified foods and childhood attention deficit disorder."

- **Do your homework.** Learn all you can about the topic beforehand. If the interviewee has published anything relevant, read it. Be sure the information this person might provide is unavailable in print.

- **Request the interview at your respondent's convenience.** Ask whether the person objects to being quoted or taped. If possible, submit your questions beforehand.

- **Make each question clear, specific, and open-ended.** Don't ask vague or general questions, and avoid questions that can be answered with a mere *yes* or *no*. Get the benefit of the interviewee's elaboration.

- **Avoid loaded questions.** A loaded question invites or promotes a particular bias. For example, don't ask, "In what ways do you think the hazards of genetically modified foods have been overstated?" Ask impartial questions instead, such as "In your opinion, have the hazards associated with genetically modified food been accurately stated, overstated, or understated?"

- **Save the most difficult, complex, or sensitive questions for last.** Leading off with your toughest questions might annoy interviewees, making them uncooperative for the remainder of the interview.

- ▸ **Be polite and professional.** Arrive on time, express your gratitude, and explain why you believe the interviewee can be helpful and how you will use the information.

- ▸ **Let your interviewee do most of the talking.** Be a good listener. This courtesy ensures that the interviewee will provide the most information with the least interruption or leading from you.

- ▸ **Ask for clarification if needed, but do not put words in the respondent's mouth.** Questions such as "Could you go over that again?" or "What did you mean by that word?" are fine, but do not impose erroneous conclusions. Instead, paraphrase what the interviewee said so that she or he can verify your interpretation.

- ▸ **Stick to your interview plan.** If the interviewee wanders off topic, politely nudge him or her back on track (unless the information is useful).

- ▸ **Ask for closing comments.** Questions such as "Would you care to add anything?" or "Do you feel you've said what you wanted to say?" give the interviewee a chance to elaborate and clarify, and you may end up with useful additional information.

- ▸ **Ask for permission to follow up.** Additional questions may come to mind later, so find out if your interviewee would be willing to help with those new questions.

- ▸ **Invite the interviewee to read your version of the interview.** If the interview is to be published, this prevents possible misquotation or misinterpretation.

- ▸ **End on time and thank the interviewee.** Don't drag the interview on longer than the interviewee expected. Be sure to thank the interviewee for his or her time.

- ▸ **As soon as possible, transcribe your notes or recordings.** Get the interview down in writing before you forget important details.

Surveys

Surveys help you form impressions of the concerns, preferences, attitudes, beliefs, or perceptions of a large, identifiable group (a *target population*) by studying representatives of that group (a *sample*). While interviews allow for greater clarity and depth, surveys offer an inexpensive way to get the viewpoints of a large group. Respondents can answer privately and anonymously—and often more candidly than in an interview.

Surveys provide multiple fresh viewpoints on a topic

The tool for conducting surveys is the questionnaire. Use the following Strategies to plan a survey and to develop a questionnaire.

▸ **Define the survey's purpose and target population.** Ask yourself, "Why is this survey being performed?" "What, exactly, is it measuring?" "How much background research do I need?" "How will the survey findings be used?" and "Who is the exact population being studied?"

▸ **Identify the sample group.** Determine how many respondents you need. Generally, the larger the sample surveyed the more dependable the results (assuming a well-chosen and representative sample). Also determine how the sample will be chosen. Will participants be randomly chosen? In the statistical sense, *random* does not mean "haphazard." A random sample means that each member of the target population stands an equal chance of being in the sample group.

▸ **Define the survey method.** Decide how the survey will be administered—by phone, by mail, or online. Each has its benefits and drawbacks. Phone surveys yield fast results and high response rates; however, they take longer than written surveys, many respondents find them annoying, and respondents tend to be less candid when speaking with someone in person. Mail surveys are less expensive than phone surveys and promote candid responses, but many people won't bother taking a trip to the mailbox or post office to return the survey, and results can be slow to arrive. Online surveys, conducted via a Web form or an email, are the least expensive and yield quick results, but computer connections can fail, and (in the case of Web surveys) you have less control over how many times the same person responds to the survey.

▸ **Decide on the types of questions.** Questions can be open-ended or closed-ended. Open-ended questions ("How much do you know about genetically modified food products?") allow respondents to answer in any way they choose. Data gathered from open-ended questions are time-consuming to measure, but they provide rich information. Closed-ended questions ("Are you concerned about genetically modified food products? Yes/No.") do not allow respondents to elaborate on their responses. Data from closed-ended questions are easily measured but more limited in value.

▸ **Develop an engaging and informative introduction.** Thank the respondents; persuade them that the questionnaire relates to their concerns and that their answers matter; provide directions for completing the survey; and ensure the anonymity of respondents. For example: "Thank you for helping us with our survey. Your responses will help determine the public's view regarding genetically modified foods. Please answer each question by filling in one reply only in black ink and return the completed questionnaire in the enclosed postage-paid return envelope. All responses will be kept confidential. Again, thank you for your input."

▶ **Phrase questions precisely.** Vague phrasing will only lead to inaccurate answers and findings. Avoid combining questions or asking the same basic question more than once.

▶ **Avoid loaded questions.** Do not invite or advocate a particular point of view or bias.

▶ **Make the survey brief, simple, and inviting.** Respondents don't mind giving up some time to help, but long and difficult-to-read questionnaires usually get few replies.

▶ **Have an expert review your questionnaire whenever possible.** A survey expert or an expert on the topic can help you ask just the right questions.

Observations and Experiments

Observations or experiments should be your final step because you now know exactly what to look for.

Observations are firsthand examinations of people, processes, places, and so on, using only your senses. When you make observations, have a plan in place. Know how, where, and when to look, and jot down your observations immediately. You might even take photos or draw sketches of what you observe.

Experiments are controlled forms of observations designed to verify assumptions (e.g., the role of fish oil in preventing heart disease) or to test something untried (e.g., the relationship between background music and productivity). Each field has its own guidelines for conducting experiments (e.g., you must use certain equipment, scrutinize your results in a certain way), and you must follow those guidelines to the letter when you conduct your own experiments.

Remember that observations and experiments are not foolproof. When making an observation or performing an experiment, you may be biased about what you see (focusing on the wrong events, ignoring something important). In addition, if you are observing people or experimenting using people as subjects, they may be conscious of being observed and may alter their normal behaviors.

Observations and experiments offer proof to back up assumptions about a topic

CHECKLIST
for Doing Research

MyWritingLab™

☐ Have I maintained a high level of critical thinking while researching?
☐ Have I asked the right questions?
☐ Have I considered a balance of views?

CHECKLIST *continued*

- ☐ Have I explored my topic in sufficient depth?
- ☐ Have I evaluated each source for reliability?
- ☐ Have I interpreted my sources objectively?
- ☐ Have I effectively used search engines and subject directories to consult online secondary sources?
- ☐ Have I used critical thinking to assess online secondary sources?
- ☐ Have I consulted hard-copy secondary sources (including gray literature) as needed?
- ☐ Have I supplemented findings from secondary sources with primary research whenever possible?
- ☐ Have I added my own findings to existing findings whenever possible?
- ☐ Have I kept careful and precise track of each source I am using?

APPLICATIONS

GENERAL APPLICATIONS

MyWritingLab™

1. Locate an expert in your field or your major for an upcoming project (such as a long report). Contact that person and arrange for an interview. Follow the Strategies on pages 38–39. Discuss your interview experiences and your findings with classmates.

2. Identify two major indexes to locate research articles for your field or topic. One source should be a traditional periodical index, and the other should be an online search engine. Find a recent article on a specific topic (e.g., privacy laws in your state), and write a short summary.

TEAM APPLICATION

Divide into small groups, and prepare a comparative evaluation of literature search media. Each group member should select one of the resources listed here and create an individual bibliography of at least 12 recent and relevant works on a specific topic of interest selected by the group.

- Conventional print media
- Electronic catalogs

- Online sources (Web pages, digital publications)
- An electronic consortium of libraries, if applicable

After recording the findings and keeping track of the time spent in each search, compare the ease of searching and quality of results obtained from each type of search on your group's selected topic. Which medium yielded the most current sources? Which provided abstracts and full texts as well as bibliographic data? Which consumed the most time? Which provided the most dependable sources? Which provided the most diverse or varied sources? Which cost the most to use? Finally, which yielded the greatest depth of resources? Prepare a report, and present your findings to the class.

GLOBAL APPLICATION   MyWritingLab™

The International Space Station (ISS) is undoubtedly the largest and most complex international scientific project in history. The project requires the collaboration, expertise, and technological resources of 16 nations.

Use the Internet to do some preliminary research on the project. Start with the U.S.-based NASA site; look for links to the European, Japanese, Canadian, and other space agencies. How do those sites differ from the U.S.-based NASA site? Do you find any differences in the way the mission of the ISS is described?

Imagine that you have been assigned to produce a campaign to reenergize public support around the world for the ISS project. What information would you use to persuade citizens of the participating nations that it is worth their nation's time and money to support continued development of an international space station? Would you use different strategies to persuade people in different countries? Why?

Develop a one-page proposal that outlines the key features of your campaign, detailing how you would customize the style and argument of your campaign to persuade public audiences in the diverse nations involved in the ISS initiative.

DIGITAL AND SOCIAL MEDIA APPLICATION   MyWritingLab™

Researchers often have difficulty judging the validity of information found on a Web site. Working in small groups of three or four develop a set of criteria that can be used when evaluating a Web site for research purposes.

Select two to three Web sites related to a research project for this or another class. Compile a working list of criteria based on these sites; then work as a group to expand your list. For example, do you consider good design to be an indicator of credibility? What else do you look at when you are assessing the relevance, currency, and validity of information on a particular site? How do you know if a site is commercially or politically biased? Present your results in class and compare the findings of the different small groups.

MyWritingLab™   Visit Chapter 2, *The Research Process in Technical Communication*, in MyWritingLab to complete this chapter's applications, to explore this chapter's overview, checklist, and flashcards, and to test your understanding of the chapter objectives.

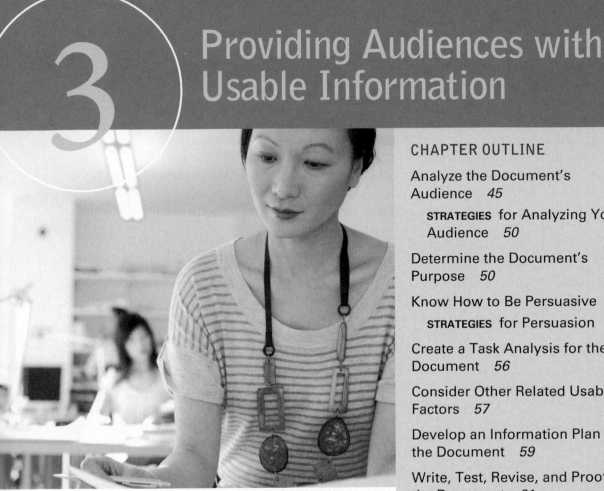

3 Providing Audiences with Usable Information

CHAPTER OUTLINE

Analyze the Document's Audience *45*

   STRATEGIES for Analyzing Your Audience *50*

Determine the Document's Purpose *50*

Know How to Be Persuasive *51*

   STRATEGIES for Persuasion *55*

Create a Task Analysis for the Document *56*

Consider Other Related Usability Factors *57*

Develop an Information Plan for the Document *59*

Write, Test, Revise, and Proofread the Document *61*

   STRATEGIES for Proofreading *62*

   CHECKLIST for Usability *63*

Applications *64*

LEARNING OBJECTIVES FOR THIS CHAPTER

► Analyze a document's audience (primary and secondary, relationship to you, technical and cultural background)

► Determine a document's purpose (primary and secondary, intended use)

► Identify the persuasive elements involved

► Create a task analysis for a document (main task and subtasks)

► Consider a document's setting, potential problems, length, format, timing, and budget

► Develop an information plan for a document

► Understand the stages in writing, testing, revising, and proofreading a document

A document's *usability* is a measure of how well that document fulfills the information needs of its audience. Whatever their specific goals and concerns in using a particular document, readers must be able to do at least three things (Coe, *Human Factors* 193; Spencer 74):

Definition of usability

- Locate the information they need easily.
- Understand the information immediately.
- Use the information safely and successfully.

What a usable document enables readers to do

To assess the usability of a manual that comes with your new gas grill, for instance, you would ask: "How well do these instructions enable me to assemble, operate, and maintain the grill safely and effectively?" To prepare a usable document, follow these six steps:

1. Analyze the document's audience.
2. Determine the document's purpose.
3. Create a task analysis for the document.
4. Consider the setting, potential problems, length, format, timing, and budget.
5. Develop an information plan for the document.
6. Write, test, and revise the document.

Steps in preparing a usable document

ANALYZE THE DOCUMENT'S AUDIENCE

You cannot create an effective document until you first explore all you can about *who* will use your document. In other words, understand your audience. Ask these questions:

- Who is the main audience for this document?
- Who else is likely to read it?
- What is your relationship with the audience? Are there multiple types of relationships involved?
- How familiar might the audience be with technical details?
- What culture or cultures does your audience represent?

Questions to ask to analyze a document's audience

Answer these questions by considering the suggestions in the sections that follow, and by filling in the audience portion of the Audience and Purpose Profile Sheet shown in Figure 3.1 before writing any technical documents. Also, have a look at the Strategies for Analyzing Your Audience on page 50.

Primary and Secondary Audiences

When writing a technical document, keep two audiences in mind. Most documents are geared to an immediate audience. This is your *primary audience*. For instance, a set of instructions for installing new email software for an office

Determine the primary and secondary audiences

FIGURE 3.1
Audience and purpose profile sheet

Audience

Primary audience: _____ (*name, title*)

Secondary audience(s): _____

Relationship with audience members: _____

_____ (*client, employer, other*)

Technical background of audience: _____

_____ (*layperson, expert, other*)

Cultural background of audience: _____

Purpose

Primary purpose: _____ (*inform, instruct, persuade*)

Secondary purpose(s): _____

Intended use of document: _____

_____ (*master concepts, follow directions, other*)

might be directed primarily at the computer support staff who would be doing the installing. But most documents also have a *secondary audience* as well, those people outside the immediate circle of people who will be needing the information directly. For example, a secondary audience for software instructions might be managers, who will check to see if the instructions comply with company policy, or lawyers, who will make sure the instructions meet legal standards.

Relationship with Audience

Determine your relationship with the audience or audiences

Besides identifying the primary and secondary audiences in a general way, you also need to understand your relationship with everyone involved. In your situation, are the primary readers of your document going to be superiors, colleagues, or subordinates? Determining which will help you decide the level of formality and authority to use in the document. Are they going to be from inside or outside your organization? Answering this question will help you to decide how confidential you need to be. Do you know your readers personally? This information can help you decide if you can adopt a more informal tone. Are they likely to welcome or reject your information? Knowing the answer will help you decide how persuasive you need to be. Are they a combination of people from various levels, both inside and outside the company? This knowledge will help you to determine how evenhanded your writing needs to be. Also, how might you speak to the needs of secondary audience members, who may be interested in or affected by your document?

Audience's Technical Background

Any message can be conveyed in numerous ways, depending on how it is written and designed for different audiences. For example, information about a new cancer treatment may appear in a medical journal for health care professionals, in a textbook for nursing or medical students, or in a newspaper article for the general public. Always keep in mind the technical background of your audience.

Be aware of your audience's technical background

A document's technical level needs to target the intended audience. For example, an audience of medical professionals will understand technical terms readily; an audience of medical and nursing students will have some familiarity with such terms but will be in the process of learning; and the general public may not understand technical terminology at all. Thus, articles for each of these audiences will differ in language, content, organization, illustrations, and overall design.

Consider the technical level of your general target audience

The larger the audience the more you must consider the various levels of expertise and language differences. For example, medical professionals can be divided into subgroups of specialists and general practitioners; medical and nursing students can be divided into subgroups based on years of training; and the general public can be divided into subgroups who read popular medical journals and those who have little or no familiarity with medical information.

Consider the technical level of your specific target audience

To illustrate the importance of these audience differences, Figures 3.2 and 3.3 show two pieces of information, both about the over-the-counter medication Bayer aspirin. Both items address the same topic, but each document is designed and written for a different audience. The Web page in Figure 3.2 is designed for a general audience. It uses straightforward, nontechnical language and color visuals. Note, however, that the page is written not for just any general audience but more specifically for a subgroup: readers who have some awareness of the medical uses of aspirin (for pain; for the heart) and want to learn more. The page from the *Physicians' Desk Reference* (PDR) in Figure 3.3, on the other hand, is designed for an audience of health care professionals, not patients. It uses highly technical language and a molecular diagram as its one visual. Yet it, too, targets a specific audience within the larger group: not all health care professionals, but physicians, nurses, and pharmacists who will understand the complex statistics, terminology, and visuals.

Audience's Cultural Background

Information needs and preferences often are culturally determined. German audiences, for example, often value thoroughness and complexity with detail included and explained in a businesslike tone. Japanese audiences generally prefer multiple

Consider the audience's cultural background

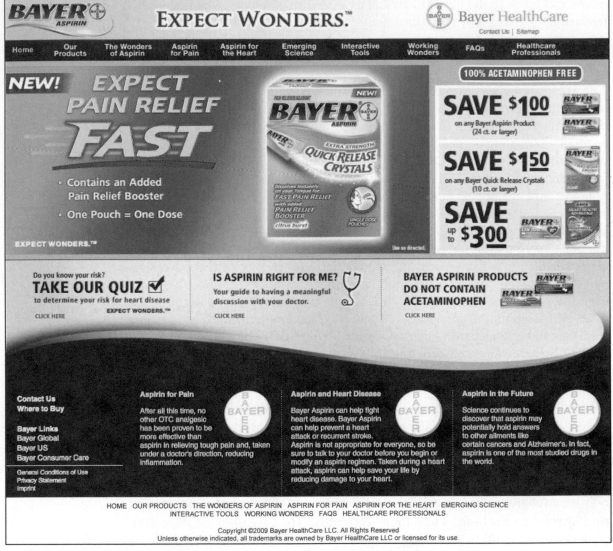

FIGURE 3.2 Bayer aspirin Web page written and designed for a general audience
Source: Copyright © 2009 BayerHealthCare LLC. All rights reserved. Reproduced by permission.

perspectives on the material, plenty of graphics, and a friendly, encouraging tone (Hein 125–26).Western business culture generally values plain talk that gets right to the point, but Eastern cultures consider this rude, preferring indirect, more ambiguous messages that leave interpretation up to the reader. Consider how cultural differences might create misunderstanding in your situation, and seek an approach that bridges these differences.

The Strategies on page 50 will help you analyze your audience.

Bayer HealthCare LLC

Consumer Care

36 COLUMBIA ROAD
P.O. BOX 1910
MORRISTOWN, NJ 07962-1910

Direct Inquiries to:
Consumer Relations
(800) 331-4536
www.BayerAspirin.com

BAYER® ASPIRIN   OTC
Comprehensive Prescribing Information

DESCRIPTION
Aspirin for Oral Administration
Regular Strength 325 mg and Low Strength 81 mg Tablets
Antiplatelet, Antiarthritic

Aspirin

COOH
CH₃
O

$C_9H_8O_4$
Mol. Wt.: 180.16
C 60.00 %; H 4.48 %; O 35.52%

Aspirin is an odorless, white, needle-like crystalline or powdery substance. When exposed to moisture, aspirin hydrolyzes into salicylic and acetic acids, and gives off a vinegary-odor. It is highly lipid soluble and slightly soluble in water.

CLINICAL PHARMACOLOGY
Mechanism of Action
Aspirin is a more potent inhibitor of both prostaglandin synthesis and platelet aggregation than other salicylic acid derivatives. The differences in activity between aspirin and salicylic acid are thought to be due to the acetyl group on the aspirin molecule. This acetyl group is responsible for the inactivation of cyclo-oxygenase via acetylation.

Pharmacokinetics

Absorption: In general, immediate release aspirin is well and completely absorbed from the gastrointestinal (GI) tract. Following absorption, aspirin is hydrolyzed to salicylic acid with peak plasma levels of salicylic acid occurring within 1–2 hours of dosing (see Pharmacokinetics—Metabolism). The rate of absorption from the GI tract is dependent upon the dosage form, the presence or absence of food, gastric pH (the presence or absence of GI antacids or buffering agents), and other physiologic factors. Enteric coated aspirin products are erratically absorbed from the GI tract.

Distribution: Salicylic acid is widely distributed to all tissues and fluids in the body including the central nervous system (CNS), breast milk, and fetal tissues. The highest concentrations are found in the plasma, liver, renal cortex, heart, and lungs. The protein binding of salicylate is concentration-dependent. i.e., non-linear. At low concentrations (< 100 micrograms/milliliter (mcg/mL)), approximately 90 percent of plasma salicylate is bound to albumin while at higher concentrations (>400 mcg/mL), only about 75 percent is bound. The early signs of salicylic overdose (salicylism), including tinnitus (ringing in the ears), occur at plasma concentrations approximating 200 mcg/mL. Severe toxic effects are associated with levels >400 mcg/mL. (See **ADVERSE REACTIONS** and **OVER DOSAGE**.)

Metabolism: Aspirin is rapidly hydrolyzed in the plasma to salicylic acid such that plasma levels of aspirin are essentially undetectable 1–2 hours after dosing. Salicylic acid is primarily conjugated in the liver to form salicyluric acid, a phenolic glucuronide, an acyl glucuronide, and a number of minor metabolites. Salicylic acid has a plasma half-life of approximately 6 hours. Salicylate metabolism is saturable and total body clearance decreases at higher serum concentrations due to the limited ability of the liver to form both salicyluric acid and phenolic glucuronide. Following toxic doses (10–20 grams (g)), the plasma half-life may be increased over 20 hours.

Elimination: The elimination of salicylic acid follows zero order pharmacokinetics; (i.e., the rate of drug elimination is constant in relation to plasma concentration). Renal excretion of unchanged drug depends upon urine pH. As urinary pH rises above 6.5, the renal clearance of free salicylate increases from < 5 percent to >80 percent. Alkalinization of the urine is a key concept in the management of salicylate overdose. (See **OVERDOSAGE**.) Following therapeutic doses, approximately 10 percent is found excreted in the urine as salicylic acid, 75 percent as salicyluric acid, 10 percent phenolic and 5 percent acyl glucuronides of salicylic acid.

Pharmacodynamics
Aspirin affects platelet aggregation by irreversibly inhibiting prostaglandin cyclo-oxygenase. This effect lasts for the life of the platelet and prevents the formation of the platelet aggregating factor thromboxane A2. Non-acetylated salicylates do not inhibit this enzyme and have no effect on platelet aggregation. At somewhat higher doses, aspirin reversibly inhibits the formation of prostaglandin I2 (prostacyclin), which is an arterial vasodilator and inhibits platelet aggregation. At higher doses aspirin is an effective anti-inflammatory agent, partially due to inhibition of inflammatory mediators via cyclo-oxygenase inhibition in peripheral tissues. In vitro studies suggest that other mediators of inflammation may also be suppressed by aspirin administration, although the precise mechanism of action has not been elucidated. It is this nonspecific suppression of cyclo-oxygenase activity in peripheral tissues following large doses that leads to its primary side effect of gastric irritation. (See **ADVERSE REACTIONS**.)

CLINICAL STUDIES
Ischemic Stroke and Transient Ischemic Attack (TIA):
In clinical trials of subjects with TIA's due to fibrin platelet emboli or ischemic stroke, aspirin has been shown to significantly reduce the risk of the combined endpoint of stroke or death and the combined endpoint of TIA, stroke, or death by about 13–18 percent.

Suspected Acute Myocardial Infarction (MI):
In a large, multi-center study of aspirin, streptokinase, and the combination of aspirin and streptokinase in 17,187 patients with suspected MI, aspirin treatment produced a 23-percent reduction in the risk of vascular mortality. Aspirin was also shown to have an additional benefit in patients given a thrombolytic agent.

Prevention of Recurrent MI and Unstable Angina Pectoris:
These indications are supported by the results of six large, randomized, multi-center, placebo-controlled trials of

Continued on next page

FIGURE 3.3
Bayer aspirin entry from the *Physicians' Desk Reference*, written and designed for a technical audience

STRATEGIES
for Analyzing Your Audience

▸ **Picture your readers and exactly what they need and expect.** Whether your audience is the company president or the person next to you in class, that person has specific concerns and information needs. Your readers may need to complete a task, solve a problem, make a decision, evaluate your performance, or take a stand on an issue.

▸ **Identify the primary and secondary audiences, your relationship to them, and their technical and cultural background.**

▸ **When you don't know exactly who will be reading your document, picture the "general reader."** General readers are impatient with abstract theories yet expect enough background to help them grasp your message. They are bored or confused by excessive detail and frustrated by raw facts left unexplained or not interpreted. Instead of trying to show readers how smart you are, make *them* feel smart. Whoever they are, readers need enough material to understand your position and to react appropriately.

▸ **Anticipate readers' questions.** Based on their needs and concerns, readers have questions: What is it? What does it mean? What happened? Who was involved? When, where, and why did it happen? What might happen? How do I do it? How did you do it? Why is X better than Y? Can you give examples? Says who? So what? Give readers what they need to know.

▸ **Recognize that audiences are not merely passive recipients of information.** Technical communicators and their audiences should overlap and interact. Therefore, as you analyze and learn about your audience, remember that the communication process works both ways.

DETERMINE THE DOCUMENT'S PURPOSE

To create an effective technical document you need to understand *how* readers will use it. In other words, determine your purpose. Ask these questions:

Questions to ask to determine a document's purpose

- What is the main purpose of the document?
- What other purpose or purposes does the document serve?
- What will readers do with this information?

Answer these questions by considering the suggestions in the sections that follow and by filling in the purpose portion of the Audience and Purpose Profile Sheet shown in Figure 3.1 before writing any technical document.

Primary and Secondary Purposes

All forms of technical communication are intended to fulfill a specific *primary purpose*. As discussed in Chapter 1, the primary purpose (to inform, to instruct, or to persuade) will affect the document's overall shape and substance.

Many documents have a primary purpose and one or more *secondary purposes*. For example, the primary purpose in most instruction manuals is to instruct, that is, to teach an audience how to assemble or use the product. But for ethical and legal reasons, companies also want people to use the product safely. A manual for a power tool or a lawnmower, for instance, typically begins with a page that spells out safety hazards, before instructing readers how to assemble and use the mechanism.

In planning a document, work from a clear statement of purpose that takes into account both the primary and secondary purposes. For example, "The purpose of my document is to inform my readers of the new absentee policy and to instruct them on how to follow the procedures properly," or "The purpose of my document is to inform my readers about the new antivirus software, as well as to instruct them on how to install the software and to persuade them of the importance of running weekly virus scans."

Decide if the primary purpose of the document is to inform, instruct, or persuade

Determine if the document serves any secondary purposes

Always write a comprehensive purpose statement

Intended Use of the Document

In addition to determining purposes of a document from your own perspective, also consider how and why it will be used by others. Answer a variety of questions: Do my readers simply want to learn facts or understand concepts? Will they use my information in making some decision? Will people act immediately on the information? Do they need step-by-step instructions? In my audience's view, what is most important about this document? In addition to asking yourself these questions, try asking members of your audience directly, so you can verify what they want to know.

Determine how the document will be used

KNOW HOW TO BE PERSUASIVE

In the workplace, we rely on persuasion daily: to win coworker support, to attract clients and customers, to request funding. An email, a memo, a product description, or a set of instructions can be an implicitly persuasive document. Even the most complex report, which at first glance may appear to be "all facts," can be persuasive because the writer probably shaped the report to favor a particular interpretation of the data.

Changing someone's mind is never easy—in fact, sometimes it is impossible. Your success will depend on what you are requesting, who you are trying to persuade, and how entrenched those people are in their own views.

Why persuasion is difficult

Using Claims as a Basis for Persuasion

Explicit persuasion is required whenever you tackle an issue about which people disagree. Assume, for example, that you are Manager of Employee Relations at Softbyte, a software developer whose recent sales have plunged. To avoid layoffs, the company is trying to persuade employees to accept a temporary cut in salary. As you plan your various memos and presentations on this volatile issue, you must first identify your major claim or claims (a claim is a statement of the point you are trying to prove).

For example, in the Softbyte case, you might first want employees to recognize and acknowledge facts about which they may have been unaware or have ignored:

> Because of the global recession, our software sales in two recent quarters have fallen nearly 30 percent, and earnings should remain flat all year.

Even when a fact is obvious, people often disagree about what it means or what should be done about it. And so you might want to influence their interpretation of the facts:

> Reduced earnings mean temporary layoffs for roughly 25 percent of our staff. But we could avoid layoffs entirely if each of us at Softbyte would accept a 10 percent salary cut until the market improves.

And eventually you might want to ask for direct action:

> Our labor contract stipulates that such an across-the-board salary cut would require a two-thirds majority vote. Once you've had time to examine the facts, we hope you'll vote "yes" on next Tuesday's secret ballot.

As you present your case, you will offer support for your claims before you finally ask readers to take the action you favor.

Whenever people disagree about what the facts are or what the facts mean or what should be done, you need to make the best case for your own view by presenting an argument that is not only well supported but that also connects with your audience.

Connecting with Your Audience

Determine how best to connect with your audience. Persuasive people know when to simply declare what they want (get the reader to *comply* with what you say), when to reach out and create a relationship (get the reader to *identify* with what you say), when to appeal to reason and common sense (get the reader to *internalize* what you say), and when to employ some combination of these approaches (Kipnis and Schmidt 40–46). These three approaches, respectively, can be labeled the *power*

Claims set the stage for a persuasive appeal

A claim about what the facts are

A claim about what the facts mean

A claim about what should be done

connection, the *relationship connection*, and the *rational connection*, as illustrated in Figure 3.4.

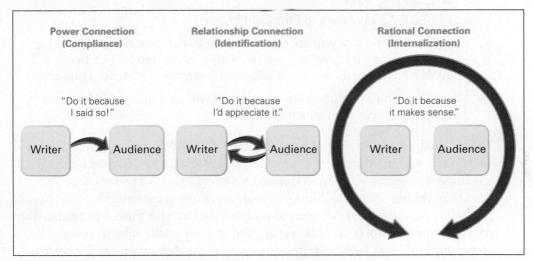

FIGURE 3.4 Three approaches for connecting with an audience

To get a better understanding of these three different approaches, consider the following scenario: Your Company, XYZ Engineering, has just developed a fitness program based on findings that healthy employees work better, take fewer sick days, and cost less to insure. This program offers clinics for smoking cessation, stress reduction, and weight loss, along with group exercise. **Choosing the best connection(s)**

In your second month on the job you read this notice in your email:

> TO: Employees at XYZ.com
>
> FROM: GMaximus@XYZ.com
>
> DATE: June 6, 20xx
>
> SUBJECT: Physical Fitness
>
> On Monday, June 10, all employees will report to the company gymnasium at 8:00 A.M. for the purpose of choosing a walking or jogging group. Each group will meet for 30 minutes three times weekly during lunch time.

Power connection

How would you react to the previous notice? Despite the reference to "choosing," the recipients of this memo are given no real choice. They are simply ordered to show up at the company gymnasium. Typically used by bosses and other authority figures, this type of approach does get people to comply, but it almost always alienates them as well.

Suppose, instead, that you receive this next version of the memo. How would you react in this instance?

TO: Employees at XYZ.com
FROM: GMaximus@XYZ.com
DATE: June 6, 20xx
SUBJECT: An Invitation to Physical Fitness

I realize that most of you spend lunch hour playing cards, reading, or just enjoying a bit of well-earned relaxation in the middle of a hectic day. But I'd like to invite you to join our lunchtime walking/jogging club.

We're starting this club in the hope that it will be a great way for us all to feel better. Why not give it a try?

Relationship connection

This second version conveys the sense that "we're all in this together." Instead of being commanded, readers are invited to participate in the exercise program. Someone who seems likable and considerate offers readers a real choice.

Often the biggest variable in a persuasive message is the reader's perception of the writer. Readers are more open to people they like and trust. The relationship connection often works for this reason, and it is especially vital in cross-cultural communication—as long as it does not sound too "chummy" and informal to carry any real authority.

Of course, you would be unethical using a relationship connection merely to hide the fact that you have no evidence to support your claim (R. Ross 28). People need to find the claim believable ("Exercise will help me feel better") and relevant ("I personally need this kind of exercise").

Here is a third version of the memo. As you read, think about the ways in which its approach differs from the first two examples.

TO: Employees at XYZ.com
FROM: GMaximus@XYZ.com
DATE: June 6, 20xx
SUBJECT: Invitation to Join One of Our Jogging or Walking Groups

Rational connection

I want to share a recent study from the *New England Journal of Medicine*, which reports that adults who walk two miles a day could increase their life expectancy by as much as three years.

Other research shows that 30 minutes of moderate aerobic exercise, at least three times weekly, has a significant and long-term effect in reducing stress, lowering blood pressure, and improving job performance.

As a first step in our exercise program, XYZ Engineering is offering a variety of daily jogging groups: The One-Milers, Three-Milers, and Five-Milers. All groups will meet at designated times on our brand-new quarter-mile, rubberized clay track.

For beginners or skeptics, we're offering daily two-mile walking groups. For the truly resistant, we offer the option of a Monday–Wednesday–Friday two-mile walk.

> Coffee and lunch breaks can be rearranged to accommodate whichever group you select.
>
> Why not take advantage of our hot new track? As small incentives, XYZ will reimburse anyone who signs up as much as $100 for running or walking shoes and will even throw in an extra fifteen minutes for lunch breaks. And with a consistent turnout of 90 percent or better, our company insurer may be able to eliminate everyone's $200 yearly deductible in medical costs.

This version conveys respect for the reader's intelligence and for the relationship. With any reasonable audience, the rational connection stands the best chance of success.

For more on persuasion see the Strategies that follow.

STRATEGIES
for Persuasion

- **Identify your specific goal.** What exactly do you want readers to do: change their opinion, change their behavior, or take specific action?

- **Anticipate your audience's reaction.** Typically, when you try to change people's minds or get them to do something, they will naturally resist. Try to address their biggest objections beforehand. Will people be surprised, annoyed, or angry at your attempt? Will they agree with you in essence but want to know further details? Be careful to express your arguments ("We could do better") without making people defensive ("It's all your fault"). Also, be prepared to field negative reactions after your message is delivered and to back off if your message is rejected.

- **Don't ask for too much.** No matter how persuasive you are, if you ask for what seems like too much, your argument will fail. Ask for what your audience will consider reasonable, not outlandish. Consider what is achievable in this situation.

- **Allow for give-and-take.** Be flexible in your argument. Indicate you are able to see your argument from the recipient's point of view, and offer possible alternatives or compromises along with what you want to accomplish.

- **Recognize constraints.** For various reasons other than their personal opinions, recipients may be unable to comply with your request. For example, readers may have time constraints, organizational constraints (deadlines, budgets), legal constraints (agreements, laws), ethical constraints (when the request is legal but not necessarily ethical), and social and psychological constraints (shyness, fear of failure, fear of disruption, fear of the unknown).

- **Consider the cultural context.** How people react to your persuasive appeals may be culturally based. Will some audience members feel that your message ignores customs? Will they be offended by too many facts and figures without a relationship connection? Will they be offended by a direct approach? Remember that cultural groups consist not only of racial and ethnic groups but also groups connected by religious or spiritual views, sexual orientation, physical ability, and so on.

▶ **Choose the right time and the right medium.** Consider how the timing of your message (just prior to a vacation, during the busy season, during a period of optimism) and the way in which it is delivered (in person, over email, in a printed memo) will affect how positively it is received.

▶ **Connect with your audience.** Using the power connection may work but will likely alienate your audience; using the relationship connection may appeal to readers but fail to convince them. Whenever possible, use the rational connection or, even better, a rational connection combined with a relationship connection.

CREATE A TASK ANALYSIS FOR THE DOCUMENT

Most technical documents entail a series of tasks to be completed, tasks most evident in a set of instructions: If people want to change an oil filter, assemble a new gas grill, or install a new word-processing program, they clearly must follow a step-by-step procedure. Less obvious is that other documents, such as reports, memos, and brochures, also involve a series of tasks. For instance, when reading a report, a manager may need to extract information and write a response. Similarly, a technician may need to make a persuasive argument as to why the company should purchase new equipment. In short, most technical communication is task-oriented. People come to the information wanting to *do* something, and you want to ensure that they achieve their goal; therefore, you need to think through the step-by-step nature of your document before you write it by creating a *task analysis*.

Define main tasks, then subtasks

For your task analysis, you can create a worksheet similar to those shown in Figures 3.5 and 3.6. Begin by defining the main tasks. For example, in planning an instruction manual to accompany a gas grill, you might start your task analysis (Figure 3.5) by defining the main tasks as "assemble the grill," "use the grill," and "maintain the grill" and then divide these larger tasks into several smaller tasks, or subtasks ("locate all parts," "get the required tools," "lay out parts in order," etc.). Note that both the tasks and subtasks should be listed using active verb forms (*assemble, locate, get*, and so on).

Similarly, planning a short report to management arguing for change in a company policy, you would begin your persuasive task plan (Figure 3.6) with the main task to be accomplished ("get company dress code policy changed") and then plan out the subtasks required to accomplish that main task.

FIGURE 3.5
**Sample task
analysis for a
procedure**

Main task: Assemble the grill.

Subtasks

1. Locate all parts.
2. Get the required tools.
3. Lay out parts in order.
4. Assemble parts into smaller units.
5. Assemble these smaller units into large units.

Main task: Use the grill.

Subtasks

1. Attach the gas canister.
2. Turn on the main gas valve.
3. Turn on the individual burners.
4. Press button to ignite.

Main task: Maintain the grill.

Subtasks

1. Turn off the main gas valve when not in use.
2. Cover to protect from rain.
3. Clean the grate regularly.

You can determine these tasks by interviewing customers and watching them perform each step to complete the project (Figure 3.5) or by just carefully thinking through the approach that will yield the results you want (Figure 3.6). In short, your document will be most useful if you know what your audience needs to *do* in order to produce the desired results.

CONSIDER OTHER RELATED USABILITY FACTORS

Once you've answered questions about audience (*Who*?), purpose (*Why*?), and tasks (*How*?), it's time to consider smaller but no less important factors that influence the usability of your document: setting (*Where*?), potential problems (*What are the hazards*?), length (*How much information*?), format (*How does it look*?), timing (*When*?), and budget (*How much money*?).

Think about setting, potential problems, length, format, timing, and budget

Setting

Will distractions or interruptions make it hard for people to pay attention? Will readers always have the document in front of them? Will they be scanning the

Determine where your document will be used

FIGURE 3.6
**Sample task
analysis
worksheet
for a goal**

Main task:	Persuade management to change company dress code policy.
Subtasks	• Remind management of specifics of current company dress policy.
	• Persuade management to agree to first reason for new policy: employee resentment over too-strict policy.
	• Persuade management to agree to second reason for new policy: changing attitude toward office dress countrywide (e.g., acceptance of "business casual," "casual Fridays").
	• Persuade management to agree to third reason for new policy: flat salaries during recession versus rising cost of business attire.
	• Win management over to new policy by highlighting beneficial results: higher employee morale, less absenteeism, more respect for management.

document, studying it, or memorizing it? Will they read page by page or consult the document randomly?

Potential Problems

Anticipate what might go wrong

How might the document be misinterpreted or misunderstood? Are there potential "trouble spots" (material too complex for this audience, hard to follow, or packed with information)? Are any important points missing? Anticipating problems is important in creating any technical document but especially in a set of instructions; therefore, when preparing instructions plan on background research. In planning the gas grill instruction manual, for example, learn all you can about the typical audience for this information (age, education, and so on). If possible, observe first-time operators using the instructions for a previous model and then ask for their feedback. Also, find out how most injuries occur; check company records for customer complaints; get feedback from dealers; and ask your legal department about prior injury claims by customers.

Length

How much information is enough? This depends on what you can learn about your audience's needs. Were you asked to "keep it short" or to "be comprehensive"? Are people more interested in conclusions and recommendations, or do they want everything spelled out?

Decide on an acceptable length

Format

Does your audience expect a letter, a memo, a short report, or a long, formal report with supplements (title page, table of contents, appendices, and so on—see pages 309–312)? Can visuals and page layout (charts, graphs, drawings, headings, lists) make the material more accessible?

Decide on your document's format

Timing

Does your document have a deadline? Workplace documents almost always do. Is there a best time to submit it? Do you need to break down the deadline into a schedule of milestones? Will any of your information become out of date if you wait too long to complete the document?

Consider due dates and timing

Budget

Does your document have a budget? If so, how much? Where can you save money? How much time can your company afford to allot you for creating the document? How much money can you spend obtaining permission to use materials from other sources? How much can you spend on printing, binding, and distributing your document?

Consider the financial issues

DEVELOP AN INFORMATION PLAN FOR THE DOCUMENT

Once you have a clear picture of the audience, purpose, tasks, and related factors, you can draft an *information plan:* an outline based on all the previous considerations in this chapter. Information plans can be as short as a two- to three-page memo or as long as a multipage report, depending on your project. Begin with a clearly stated purpose statement ("People will be able to assemble a gas grill within 30 minutes") so you can measure when a task has been successfully completed (Rubin 97). Also include information about the audience, tasks, setting, potential problems, length, format, timing, and budget.

Figure 3.7 is a sample information plan created in a short-memo format for the gas grill instructions. Note how this plan takes into account not just audience,

Write out your plan

FIGURE 3.7
Sample information plan

GrillChef Corporation

To: Technical writing design team
From: Erin Green and Geoff Brannigan, team leaders
Date: January 21, 20XX
Re: Information plan for gas grill manual

As you know, our team recently performed an analysis of user needs as we prepare to design and write the new User Manual for the new GrillChef Model 2014 double-burner grill. This memo summarizes our findings and presents a plan for proceeding.

Part One: Analysis

Audience   The audience for this manual is very broad. It consists of consumers who purchase the grill. This purchase may be their first gas grill, or they may be replacing an old grill. Some users are making a switch from charcoal to gas. Our analysis revealed that the primary users are male and female, ranging in age from 25 to 50. From a focus group, we determined that most users are afraid to assemble the grill. But all members expressed enthusiasm about using the grill. Also, according to marketing, this grill is only sold in the United States.

Purpose   The manual has several purposes:
1. Instruct the user in assembling and using the grill.
2. Provide adequate safety instructions. These are to protect the user and to make sure we have complied with our legal requirements.
3. Provide a phone number, Web address, and other contact information if users have questions or need replacement parts.

User tasks Our task analysis revealed three main tasks this manual must address:
1. How to assemble the grill. Users need clear instructions, a list of parts, and diagrams that can assist them in assembling the grill within one hour.
2. How to use the grill. Users need clear instructions for operating the grill safely. Because some users have never used gas for grilling, we need to stress safety.
3. How to maintain the grill. Users need to know how to keep the grill clean, dry, and operational.

Part Two: Design Plans

Based on our analysis, we suggest designing a manual that is simple, easy to use, and contains information users need. We will follow the layout and format of our other manuals.

Rough   Cover with drawing of grill, model number, company name.
outline   Inside front cover: safety warnings (our legal department has indicated that these warnings need to go first).
            First section: Exploded diagram, list of parts, drawings of parts, numbered list of instructions for assembly.
            Second section: Numbered list of steps for using the grill, accompanied by diagrams.
            Third section: Bulleted list of tasks users must perform to maintain the grill.
            Final page: Company address, phone number, and Web address.

Production   Our budget for this project will not allow for color printing or any photographs. We suggest black ink on white paper, 8-1/2 x 11 folded in half vertically. We can use line drawings of the Model 2012 and modify these to the specifications of the Model 2014.

Schedule   The manual must be ready for shipping on April 1, 20XX. We will follow our usual production and writing schedule, briefly summarized here:
            February 21: First draft of manual is complete. Manual is usability tested on sample customers.
            March 1: Manual is revised based on results of usability test.
            March 3: Copyediting, proofreading, and final changes. Manual goes to the printer.
            March 30: Manual is back from printer and sent to the warehouse.
            April 1: Product is shipped.

purpose, and tasks (each get their own section), but also all the related factors (some of which are implied):

- **Setting.** Although not spelled out, it is understood that people will be reading the instructions while assembling their grills, which the authors have accounted for via the document's simple, lightweight design.

- **Potential problems.** Although safety issues are not given their own sub-headed section, the authors have considered safety measures at a number of points.

- **Length.** In the "Rough outline" section, the authors have determined that the instructions will be four pages long.

- **Format.** In the "Rough outline" section, both text and visuals have been carefully considered, page by page.

- **Timing.** In the "Schedule" section, the authors have not only accounted for the due date but also the various milestones to be reached along the way.

- **Budget.** Under the "Production guidelines" section, the authors note that the budget will not allow for color printing or photographs.

WRITE, TEST, REVISE, AND PROOFREAD THE DOCUMENT

When your planning is completed, you will be ready to write, test, revise, and proofread your document. For a gas grill manual, you would write the instructions and design the graphics as you've planned and select a medium (print, CD, Web—or some combination) for distributing the information.

Once you have a workable draft, test the document on potential readers, if possible. Ask people what they find useful and what they find confusing. If you have created a set of instructions, watch people use the document and measure their ability to perform the task based on what you have written. If someone trying to assemble the gas grill, for instance, could not locate a part because of unclear instructions, knowing about this would be valuable as you revise your material. Ask respondents to identify specific difficulties they encountered in reading the instructions and in performing the task:

- **Content.** Are there any inaccuracies? Is the level of technicality appropriate to this audience? Are claims, conclusions, or recommendations supported by evidence? Are all key terms defined? Is the material free of gaps, foggy areas, or needless details?

  Questions for assessing a document's usability

- **Organization.** Is the structure of the document visible at a glance? Is anything out of order or hard to find or follow? Is the material "chunked" into easily digestible parts? Is the material organized in a logical sequence?

- **Style.** Is anything hard to understand, imprecise, too complex, or too wordy? Are sentences put together with enough variety? Is the tone appropriate for the situation? Are words chosen for exactness, not for camouflage?

- **Layout and visuals.** Are there adequate aids to navigation (heads, numbered lists, bullets, type styles)? Are there any excessively long paragraphs, lists, or steps? Are any visuals overly complex or misleading? Could anything be clarified by a visual? Is anything cramped and hard to read?

- **Ethical, legal, and cultural considerations.** Is there any distortion or misrepresentation of facts? Are there any potential legal problems? Does the document respect readers' cultural diversity?

All technical documents should be proofread carefully

Based on feedback, revise your plan and your draft document. Finally, proofread your document carefully. Regardless of how engaging and informative a document is, basic errors distract the reader and make the writer look careless. Proofreading is vital in detecting easily correctable errors such as these:

- Sentence errors, such as fragments, comma splices, or run-ons

- Punctuation errors, such as missing apostrophes or excessive commas

- Usage errors, such as "it's" for "its"; "lay" for "lie"; or "their" for "there"

- Mechanical errors, such as misspelled words, inaccurate dates, or incorrect abbreviations

- Formatting errors, such as missing page numbers, inconsistent spacing, or incorrect form of documenting sources

- Typographical errors (typos), such as repeated or missing words or letters, missing word endings (say, *-s* or *-ed* or *-ing*), or an omitted quotation mark

Follow these Strategies for proofreading and refer to the Brief Handbook (Appendix B) for more information.

STRATEGIES
for Proofreading

▶ **Save it for the final draft.** Proofreading previous drafts might cause writer's block and distract you from the document's rhetorical features (content, organization, style, and design).

▶ **Take a break before proofreading your final document.** Revisit your document with a fresh, rested pair of eyes.

▶ **Work from hard copy.** Research indicates that people read more perceptively (and with less fatigue) from a printed page than from a computer screen.

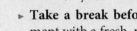

STRATEGIES *continued*

- **Keep it slow.** Read each word—don't skim. Slide a ruler under each line or move backward through the document, sentence by sentence. For a long document, read only small chunks at one time.

- **Be especially alert for problem areas in your writing.** Do you have trouble spelling? Do you get commas confused with semicolons? Do you make a lot of typos? Make one final pass to check on any problem areas like these.

- **Proofread more than once.** The more often you proofread, the more likely you will catch all errors.

- **Never rely only on autocorrect.** A synonym found in an electronic thesaurus may distort your meaning, and a spell checker cannot differentiate among correctly spelled words such as "their," "they're," and "there" or "nope" versus "hope." In the end, nothing can replace your own careful proofreading.

CHECKLIST
For Usability

MyWritingLab™

- ☐ Have I identified my exact audience (primary and secondary)?
- ☐ Have I identified my relationship with this audience?
- ☐ Have I identified this audience's technical background?
- ☐ Have I identified the exact purpose of this document (primary and secondary)?
- ☐ Am I seeking an outcome that is achievable in this situation?
- ☐ Have I anticipated my audience's reaction?
- ☐ Have I stated my claim clearly?
- ☐ Have I supported my claim with convincing evidence?
- ☐ Have I considered the various constraints and the cultural context?
- ☐ Have I chosen the approach most likely to connect with my audience?
- ☐ Have I written a purpose statement?
- ☐ Do I know exactly how this information will be used?
- ☐ By creating a task analysis, have I identified the steps involved?
- ☐ Have I pinpointed the main tasks and the subtasks?
- ☐ Have I considered the document's setting, potential problems, length, format, timing, and budget?

➡

☐ Have I developed an information plan that outlines all the preceding factors?

☐ After drafting the document, have I tested it with potential readers?

☐ Have I identified any problems in terms of content, organization, style, layout and visuals, and ethical/legal/cultural/persuasive considerations?

☐ Did I make needed revisions based on testing?

☐ Have I proofread the document carefully?

APPLICATIONS

GENERAL APPLICATIONS

MyWritingLab™

1. Identify an activity that could require instructions for a novice to complete. Prepare a task analysis for this activity similar to the one in Figure 3.5. Exchange your task analysis with another student in your class, and critique each other's work. With your class, discuss the challenges of doing such an analysis and identify strategies for performing a task analysis effectively.

2. Find a set of instructions or another type of technical document that is easy to use. Identify specific characteristics of the document, including any persuasive elements, that make it usable. (Refer to the usability questions on page 61 to guide your assessment.) Then find a technical document that is hard to use. What characteristics make it unusable? In a memo to your instructor, define specific changes that you would make in revising the document. Submit both examples along with your memo.

TEAM APPLICATION

Bring in some children's connecting blocks, such as TinkerToys or Lego blocks. Form teams of four to six people, and assign two people as technical writers. The technical writers should assemble a few of the pieces into a simple design (don't use more than three or four pieces). Then the technical writers should write up a quick instruction card explaining how to assemble the pieces into the design they've created. For example, the card for Lego blocks might read like this:

1. Select two large red blocks and two small green blocks.
2. Place one red block on its side.
3. Attach one green block to the red block.

…and so on. Then present the "parts" and your instructions to team members. Watch as your team tries to assemble the blocks according to your instructions. Assess the instructions for usability. Were all tasks accounted for? Did any terms or language confuse the readers? Go back and perform a task analysis, and discuss what you could do to improve the usability of your instruction card.

GLOBAL APPLICATION   MyWritingLab™

Astronomy and planetary science have become truly global sciences, and space exploration is now conducted by multinational teams. Knowledge about astronomy belongs to everyone, regardless of nationality or language. Do the Web sites representing these disciplines succeed in making themselves accessible to and useful for a global audience?

Explore Web sites such as the Planetary Society, NASA, and the European Space Agency, and assess their usability for international audiences. Would non-English speakers be able to access the information on these sites? What efforts are made to inform and persuade international readers? Are language and cultural differences accounted for in the design, content, and interface?

Draw up a list of key elements and features of each site that contribute to or detract from usability for international audiences. What changes would you recommend to make each site more accessible, usable, and persuasive for non-English readers? Summarize your assessment in a brief memo, including printed copies of specific pages from each Web site that you discuss.

DIGITAL AND SOCIAL MEDIA APPLICATION   MyWritingLab™

Locate a Web site that accommodates various audiences at various levels of technicality. Sites for government agencies such as the Environmental Protection Agency (EPA), the Nuclear Regulatory Commission (NRC), the National Institutes of Health (NIH), and the Food and Drug Administration (FDA) are good sources of both general and specialized information.

Examine one of these sites and find one example of (a) material aimed at a general audience and (b) material on the same topic aimed at a specialized or expert audience. First, list the features that enabled you to identify each piece's level of technicality. Next, using the Audience and Purpose Profile Sheet, record assumptions about the audience made by the author of the nontechnical version. See if the agency you selected also has a Facebook page; if so, compare the content on Facebook to what you noted for the Web site.

MyWritingLab™   Visit Chapter 3, *Providing Audiences with Usable Information*, in MyWritingLab
to complete this chapter's applications, to explore this chapter's overview, checklist,
and flashcards, and to test your understanding of the chapter objectives.

4 Recognizing Ethical Issues in Technical Communication

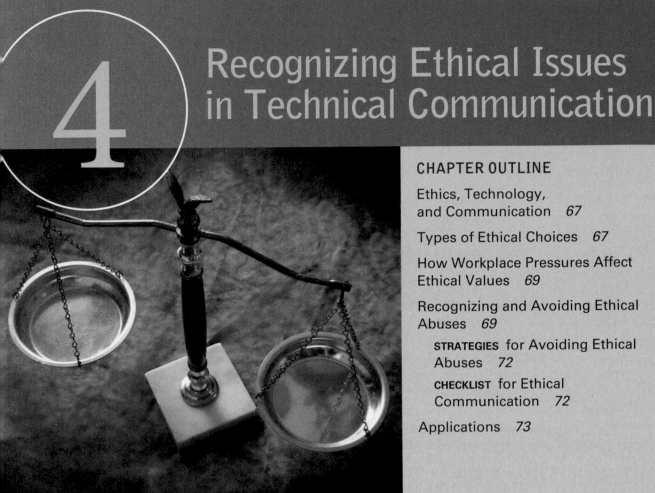

CHAPTER OUTLINE

Ethics, Technology, and Communication *67*

Types of Ethical Choices *67*

How Workplace Pressures Affect Ethical Values *69*

Recognizing and Avoiding Ethical Abuses *69*

STRATEGIES for Avoiding Ethical Abuses *72*

CHECKLIST for Ethical Communication *72*

Applications *73*

LEARNING OBJECTIVES FOR THIS CHAPTER

► Recognize ethical dilemmas and understand that they are not always black and white

► Realize how ethics are often compromised by workplace pressures

► Avoid various types of ethical abuses

Technical communication does not occur in a void. It happens in the world of human beings, politics, and social conditions, a world in which we regularly face ethical dilemmas that balance our sense of what is right against a decision that may be more efficient, profitable, or better for the company.

ETHICS, TECHNOLOGY, AND COMMUNICATION

Ethical questions often revolve around topics related to technology. For example, a new computer chip that secretly collects personal information about a person's Websurfing habits presents a privacy dilemma. Should people be allowed to choose whether to have this information collected? Some would say yes, but in the United States, few laws address personal privacy at this level. So the decision becomes less a legal one than an ethical one. The communication about this product (a press release announcing it or a user's manual that accompanies the computer) plays a central role in this ethical dilemma. Should the technical writer include this information, exclude it altogether, or deemphasize it by using a small font?

Typical ethical dilemmas

These are not simple questions. Taking an ethical stance requires a personal decision on your part as to how to weigh your ethical and moral beliefs against the realities of the job. This stance requires you to consider the effects of your decisions on the people who use your product, on your company, on society at large, and on your job. Sometimes standing your ground on an ethical issue may mean losing your job or suffering retaliation from coworkers.

Ethical decisions are not always "black and white"

TYPES OF ETHICAL CHOICES

Virtually all areas of science and technology are involved in issues of communication and ethics. Here are a few examples:

- *Medical technologies,* such as genetic testing, raise questions about personal privacy and medical insurance.

- *Banking and retail operations,* which increasingly collect personal information on consumers, raise concerns about how this information is used and who has access to it.

- *Environmental pollutants,* such as pesticides or smokestack output, raise serious questions about the long-term health of the planet.

In your own communication, you will often face ethical decisions—about how much information to include, how much to leave out, how to word an issue, or how to shape the information for your audience. Note how the memo from David Michem in Figure 4.1 sounds completely well-reasoned and persuasive. An employee reading the memo, especially one with an existing medical condition, might go straight to the company Web site and sign up for a Medical History Card. But in his desire to make the card program a success, Michem has provided

FIGURE 4.1
An unethical document

Note the misleading omission of information about employee confidentiality.

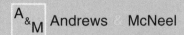
A&M Andrews & McNeel

MEMORANDUM

To: All Employees
From: David Michem, Health Benefits Manager *D.M.*
Date: November 10, 20XX
Subject: *Medical History Card Program*

Last week, you received a brochure about the new Medical History Cards (MHCs) available through the Human Resources Department. I encourage you to enroll in the card program for a variety of reasons:

• **MHCs ensure that all employees receive safe and efficient health care.** Whether you have a serious medical condition, take a prescription medication, have an allergy, or none of the above, MHCs instantly provide medical personnel with personalized medical data during an emergency or routine visit.

• **The cards are free to all Andrews and McNeel employees.** Any employee at Andrews and McNeel—whether full-time, part-time, or contract—may enroll in the program and receive a card free of charge.

• **Enrolling in the MHC program is easy.** Simply go to http://www.andrews-mcneel.com/hr/mhc to enroll in the program and fill out the requested personal and medical information to be uploaded to your card.

• **MHCs contain much more information than standard medical ID bracelets.** While an emergency bracelet may only provide basic information, such as the fact that a person is diabetic, MHCs hold your complete medical data, including emergency contact information, prescription information, and so on.

• **MHCs are easy to update.** If your medical information changes (for example, you are prescribed a new medication or your emergency contact information changes) simply update that information online. You will receive a replacement card within 5 business days.

Please take advantage of this program by re-reading your brochure or simply going to the Human Resources MHC Web page above to learn more. This is an excellent benefit not offered at many companies. We strongly encourage you to participate.

cc: Elizabeth Sanchirico-Edwards, Director of Human Resources

employees with no information about confidentiality in his memo. Will the company have access to personal and medical information when employees sign up via the Andrews and McNeel Web site? Will the information be password-protected? Will third parties have access to this information? By omitting this information from the memo, Michem has been misleading, as reasonable as his memo may sound. In the end, communication is never neutral but instead always carries some type of consequence.

HOW WORKPLACE PRESSURES AFFECT ETHICAL VALUES

Usually, ethical rules are broken not because people are dishonest but because they feel pressure to bend or break the rules. More than 50 percent of managers surveyed nationwide feel "pressure to compromise personal ethics for company goals" (Golen et al. 75). To save face, escape blame, or get ahead, anyone might feel obliged to say what other people want to hear or to suppress or downplay bad news. Figure 4.2 depicts how workplace pressures to "succeed at any cost" can influence ethical values.

Despite outside pressures, however, everyone must maintain ethical standards at all times on the job. Unethical decisions can harm a company's reputation and bottom line.More importantly, unethical decisions can compromise the safety and welfare of workers and customers. When an instruction manual is written and vital safety information is purposely omitted to save on the cost of printing, for example, people can be injured.

Ethics are often compromised by outside pressure

Why ethics matter

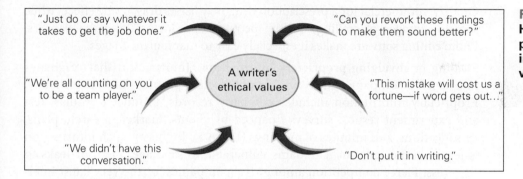

"Just do or say whatever it takes to get the job done."

"Can you rework these findings to make them sound better?"

A writer's ethical values

"We're all counting on you to be a team player."

"This mistake will cost us a fortune—if word gets out..."

"We didn't have this conversation."

"Don't put it in writing."

FIGURE 4.2
How workplace pressures can influence ethical values

RECOGNIZING AND AVOIDING ETHICAL ABUSES

Following are some of the major examples of unethical communication in the workplace.

- **Plagiarizing the work of others.** Technical communicators may feel pressure from upper management to produce results quickly and may be tempted to cut corners. Workplace plagiarism occurs when a person claims the work of someone else as one's own, without citing or even mentioning the original source. Plagiarism may also happen in collaborative work, as when a team leader claims all the credit for the work of team members.

- **Falsifying or fabricating information.** Outside pressure to produce results that others seek may tempt people to distort information. For example, research data might be manipulated or invented by a scientist seeking grant money. Developments in fields such as biotechnology often occur too rapidly to allow

Types of ethical abuses

for adequate peer review of articles before they are published, thereby leading to the release of information that isn't verifiably correct ("Misconduct Scandal" 2).

- **Suppressing or downplaying information.** Withholding information is just as unethical as supplying false information. For example, a report author may purposely fail to mention an important study that contradicts what he or she wants to prove. Or a company may fail to inform the public about a safety hazard in one of its products—or, if the hazard is revealed, may downplay its importance.

- **Exaggerating claims.** Organizations that have a stake in a particular technology (e.g., bioengineered foods) may be especially tempted to exaggerate its benefits, potential, or safety and to downplay its risks. If your organization depends on outside funding (e.g., defense or space industry), you might find yourself pressured to make unrealistic promises.

- **Using visual images that conceal the truth.** Pictures are generally more powerful than words and can easily distort the real meaning of a message through manipulation. For example, an individual might create a pie chart that paints a more optimistic picture than the data indicate by distorting the sizes of the pie pieces. Or a TV commercial for a prescription drug may list its drastic side effects while showing images of smiling, healthy people, thus downplaying the dangers. Photo editing software makes it especially easy to manipulate images.

- **Stealing or divulging proprietary information.** Information that originates in a specific company is the exclusive intellectual property of that company. Proprietary information includes company records, product formulas, test and experiment results, surveys financed by clients, market research, plans, specifications, and minutes of meetings (Lavin 5). In theory, such information is legally protected, but it remains vulnerable to sabotage, theft, or leaks to the press. Fierce competition among rival companies for the very latest intelligence gives rise to theft or unethical divulging of such information.

- **Misusing electronic information.** Ever-increasing amounts of personal information are stored in databases (by schools, governments, credit card companies, insurance companies, pharmacies), and all employers, of course, keep data about their employees. How we combine, use, and share all of this electronic information raises questions about privacy. If you are designing a Web site, for example, should you create a page that asks customers for their name, address, and other personal information without providing information about how your company intends to use that information? Most Web sites have links to privacy policies that allow customers to learn more about the company's approach to privacy. The lack of such a policy could be considered an ethical breach.

- **Exploiting cultural differences.** Both individuals and organizations can exploit the vulnerabilities of various cultural groups through manipulation or deception. For instance, one employee of a company might exploit another's English-language limitations for personal gain. So too, an organization might exploit clients for whom the culture places greater emphasis on interpersonal trust than on lawyers or legal wording.

To avoid ethical abuses, follow the guidelines provided by professional organizations in your field (e.g., see the American Medical Writers Association Code of Ethics in Figure 4.3), and use the Strategies on page 72.

FIGURE 4.3
A code of ethics from a professional organization

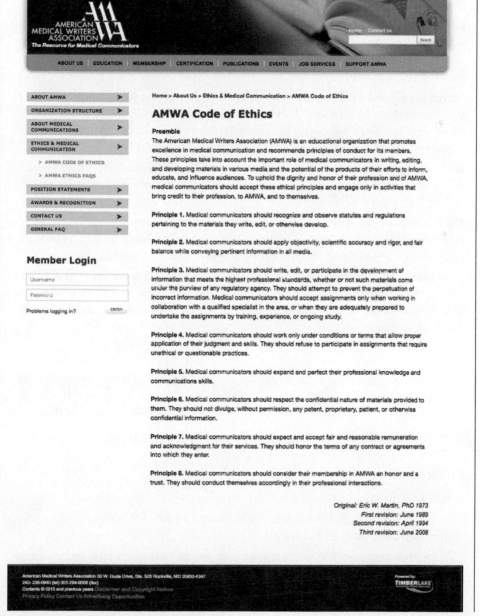

Source: American Medical Writers Association

STRATEGIES
for Avoiding Ethical Abuses

▶ **Always cite your sources if the information or data are not your own.** For specific advice on avoiding plagiarism and citing outside sources, see Appendix A.

▶ **Give the audience everything it needs to know.** To accurately see things as you do, people need more than just a partial view. Don't bury readers in needless details, but do make sure they get all the facts and get them straight.

▶ **Give people a clear understanding of what the information means.** Even when all the facts are known, they can be misinterpreted. Try to ensure that readers understand the facts as you do. If you are not certain about your own understanding, say so.

▶ **Never manipulate information or data in your writing or in your visuals.** If you encounter data that contradict what you want to say, include and interpret those data honestly. Likewise, do not make your case via exaggeration, understatement, sugarcoating, or any other distortion or omission.

▶ **Use common sense or follow your company's confidentiality guidelines.** If you suspect that information may be confidential, assume that it is or ask the appropriate personnel to clarify.

▶ **Do not exploit cultural inequalities or manipulate international readers.** Try to be fair. When producing a document for an international audience, be especially careful about using simple and honest language and visuals.

▶ **Constantly ask yourself, "Would I stand behind what I have created if I were held publicly accountable for it?"** If you would not, then chances are what you have written is unethical to some degree. It may be not entirely honest, fair, confidential, or safe.

CHECKLIST
for Ethical Communication

MyWritingLab™

Use this checklist for any document you prepare or for which you are responsible.

ACCURACY

☐ Have I explored all sides of the issue and all possible alternatives?

☐ Do I provide enough information and interpretation for recipients to understand the facts as I know them?

☐ Do I avoid exaggeration, understatement, sugarcoating, or any distortion or omission that leaves recipients at a disadvantage?

➡

CHECKLIST *continued*

HONESTY

☐ Do I make a clear distinction between what is certain and what is probable?

☐ Are my information sources valid, reliable, and relatively unbiased?

☐ Do I actually believe what I'm saying instead of advancing some hidden agenda?

☐ Would I still advocate this position if I were held publicly accountable for it?

☐ Do I inform people of the consequences or risks (as I am able to predict) of what I am advocating?

☐ Do I give candid feedback or criticism, if it is warranted?

FAIRNESS

☐ Am I reasonably sure this document will not harm innocent persons or damage their reputations?

☐ Am I respecting all legitimate rights to privacy and confidentiality?

☐ Am I distributing copies of this document to every person who has the right to know about it?

☐ Do I credit all contributors and sources of ideas and information?

Sources: Brownell and Fitzgerald (1992), p. 18; Bryan (1992), p. 87; Johannesen (1983), pp. 21–22; Larson (1995), p. 39; Unger (1982), pp. 39–46; Yoos (1979), pp. 50–55.

APPLICATIONS

GENERAL APPLICATION

MyWritingLab™

Find the professional code of ethics for your major or career. Divide into groups of three or four students, each of whom has a different major. Compare your professional codes, noting similarities and differences. Discuss why each code seems appropriate for that profession.

TEAM APPLICATION

In groups of two or three, locate a piece of technical communication (or use one provided by your instructor), and evaluate its ethical stance. Is the information presented in such a way that ideas or facts are exaggerated or suppressed? Are any cultural issues exploited? Share your thoughts in class, and explain how your team would redo the information.

GLOBAL APPLICATION   MyWritingLab™

Counterfeiting, sometimes known as "intellectual property piracy," has become a major point of tension between the United States and many developing nations. Counterfeit products ranging from computer chips and pharmaceuticals to cigarettes and cell phones now flood markets in Asia and South America, and many may even be found on the streets of New York and other U.S. cities.

Use your library and the Internet to do some preliminary reading about the problems of counterfeit products. What are the advantages and disadvantages, both economically and politically, of trying to crack down on unauthorized copycat products? Why do some countries do little to police such piracy while others, including the United States, view it as a major priority?

Write a brief report analyzing the ethical, economic, and political issues that influence the global debate on counterfeiting, and present your findings in a brief oral presentation to your class.

DIGITAL AND SOCIAL MEDIA APPLICATION   MyWritingLab™

Social media has created new ethical challenges in the workplace. For example, people use Facebook to post about personal activities and assume that this information is only viewable by friends. But during a job interview, a person may be surprised to discover that a posting intended for friends was also discovered by the potential employer. Should the employer have looked at a person's social media postings? Also, the use of content from Twitter or blogs as the basis for workplace decisions could result in unintended consequences if that information turns out to be inaccurate.

Do an online search on "ethics and social media." Select two or three articles or sources that are highly credible (e.g., published in a journal or magazine or as part of an organization's code of ethics). Meet with two other students in class and share your findings. Give a brief presentation in class describing the main points made in these sources.

MyWritingLab™   Visit Chapter 4, *Recognizing Ethical Issues in Technical Communication*, in MyWritingLab to complete this chapter's applications, to explore this chapter's overview, checklist, and flashcards, and to test your understanding of the chapter objectives.

PART 2

Blueprints

(5) Structuring Information for Your Readers

(6) Writing with a Readable Style

(7) Using Audience-Centered Visuals

(8) Designing User-Friendly Documents

5 Structuring Information for Your Readers

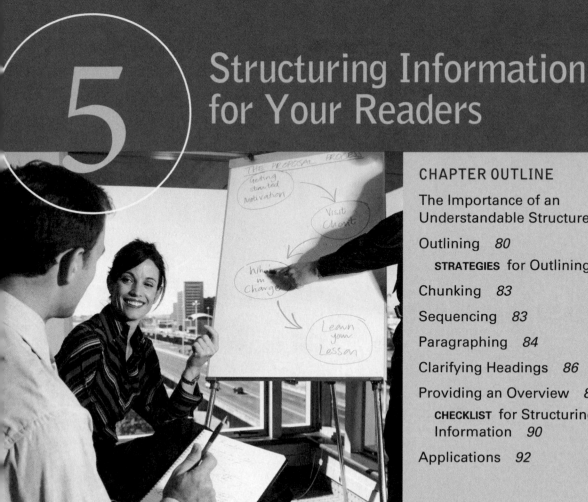

CHAPTER OUTLINE

The Importance of an
Understandable Structure *77*

Outlining *80*

   STRATEGIES for Outlining *82*

Chunking *83*

Sequencing *83*

Paragraphing *84*

Clarifying Headings *86*

Providing an Overview *87*

   CHECKLIST for Structuring
   Information *90*

Applications *92*

LEARNING OBJECTIVES FOR THIS CHAPTER

- ▸ Use a standard or varied introduction/body/
  conclusion structure

- ▸ Create a brief or formal outline

- ▸ Chunk information into discrete units

- ▸ Determine the best sequence for your material

- ▸ Shape each paragraph for effectiveness

- ▸ Create clear headings

- ▸ Provide overviews of longer documents

To use a familiar architectural metaphor, Part I of this book has focused on the *foundations* of technical communication—the underlying supports upon which the technical communication "building" stands. To review, these foundations include: 1) a definition of technical communication; 2) teamwork, ethics, persuasion, and global issues as cornerstones; 3) research as a vital part of the technical communication process; and 4) usability as a key feature of technical communication.

Before producing specific technical documents, you need a set of *blueprints*. This section, Part II, discusses the four components of technical communication blueprints: an understandable *structure* (Chapter 5), a readable *style* (Chapter 6), audience-centered *visuals* (Chapter 7), and a user-friendly *design* (Chapter 8).

Structure, style, visuals, and design as technical communication blueprints

This chapter focuses on the first of these blueprint components, structure.

THE IMPORTANCE OF AN UNDERSTANDABLE STRUCTURE

Structure your information in a way that readers can easily grasp. To follow your thinking, readers need a clear path from point *a* to point *b*. This path needs to be obvious as readers scan through your document, looking for its overall structure.

Your audience comes first

Unfortunately, information rarely materializes—and thinking rarely occurs—in neat, predictable sequences. As you look over your collected information and begin to think about how you will structure it for your readers, you will face questions such as these:

Getting started: questions to ask yourself when structuring for readers

- What relationships do the collected data suggest?
- What should I emphasize?
- In which sequence will readers approach this material?
- What belongs where?
- What do I say first? Why?
- What comes next?
- How do I end?

Although a great deal of thinking goes into the process of answering these types of questions, the result will be worth the effort, as Figures 5.1 and 5.2 illustrate.

The end result: two examples of well-organized writing

Figure 5.1 depicts the standard structure of a technical document, one that readers will instantly recognize: introduction, body, and conclusion. The introduction attracts the reader's attention, announces the writer's viewpoint, and previews what will follow. The body delivers on the promise implied in the introduction. The body explains and supports the writer's viewpoint, achieving *unity* by remaining focused on that viewpoint and *coherence* by carrying a line of thought from sentence to sentence in a logical order. Finally, the conclusion has

Standard introduction/body/ conclusion structure

various purposes: it might reemphasize key points, take a position, predict an out-come, offer a solution, or suggest further study. Good conclusions give readers a clear perspective on what they have just read.

**FIGURE 5.1
Document with a standard introduction/body/conclusion structure**

Introduction announces the topic and provides an overview of what is to follow

Body provides the evidence and data to support the claims made in the introduction

Conclusion summarizes by taking a position and making recommendations

> Powell   Rabkin
>
> ## *MEMORANDUM*
>
> **To:**   Department Managers
> **From:**   Jill McCreary, General Manager *J.M.*
> **Date:**   December 8, 20XX
> **Subject:** *Diversity training initiative*
>
> As part of our ongoing efforts to highlight the company's commitment to diversity, we recently conducted two surveys—one directed to company employees and one to our retail buyers. We have just received the survey results from our outside analysts. The employee survey indicates that the members of all departments appreciate our efforts to create a diverse and comfortable work environment. The customer survey indicates that our company is well regarded for marketing products in ways that appeal to diverse buyers. However, both surveys also illuminate areas in which we could do even better. As a result, we will be initiating a new series of diversity training workshops early next year. Let me explain the survey findings that have led to this initiative.
>
> First, the employee survey indicates that our workforce is rated "highly diverse" in terms of gender, with nearly equal representation of male and female employees in both managerial and nonmanagerial positions; however, we could do better in terms of minority representation at the managerial level. Meanwhile, the customer survey demonstrates that our customers are "very satisfied" with the diversity of our marketing materials, but that we fail to provide enough materials for our native Spanish-speaking buyers.
>
> Those are the survey highlights—see the attached analysis for a more detailed picture. Again, we are doing well, but could do better. We feel that the best solution to address our weaker areas is to conduct a second series of diversity training workshops in the upcoming 12 months. We hope that these workshops—which are often illuminating to both new employees and those who have attended diversity trainings earlier—will help keep the word "diversity" at the forefront of everyone's thoughts when hiring and mentoring employees and creating marketing materials. More information will follow, but for now, please emphasize to your department employees the importance and value of these workshops.

A nonstandard structure that also clarifies data for readers

There are, however, many ways of adapting this standard structure: For exam-ple, Figure 5.2 provides visual features (columns, colors), headings, and an engaging layout. Although organized differently from the previous document, Figure 5.2 does provide an introduction, a body, and a conclusion: The heading "What is arsenic?" represents a form of introduction. The next several headings answer the question posed in the introduction, forming in essence the body of the document. The final heading, asking about EPA standards, represents a form of conclusion, moving beyond data and description to the topic of policy and use.

FIGURE 5.2
Document with a nonstandard but well-organized structure

JUST THE FACTS FOR CONSUMERS

ARSENIC IN YOUR DRINKING WATER

What is arsenic?

Arsenic is a toxic chemical element that is unevenly distributed in the Earth's crust in soil, rocks, and minerals.

Use of visuals, color, and columns makes the organization clear

"What is arsenic?" paragraph is placed above subsequent sections, indicating that it is the introduction

How does arsenic get into my drinking water?

Arsenic occurs naturally in the environment and as a by-product of some agricultural and industrial activities. It can enter drinking water through the ground or as runoff into surface water sources.

How is arsenic in drinking water regulated?

In 1974, Congress passed the Safe Drinking Water Act. This law directs EPA to issue non-enforceable health goals and enforceable drinking water regulations for contaminants that may cause health problems. The goals, which reflect the level at which no adverse health effects are expected, are called maximum contaminant level goals (MCLGs). The MCLG for arsenic is 0 parts per billion (ppb).

The enforceable standard for arsenic is a maximum contaminant level (MCL). MCLs are set as close to the health goals as possible, considering cost, benefits, and the ability of public water systems to detect and remove contaminants using suitable treatment technologies.

Why should I be concerned about arsenic in my drinking water?

Although short-term exposures to high doses (about a thousand times higher than the drinking water standard) cause adverse effects in people, such exposures do not occur from public water supplies in the U.S. that comply with the arsenic MCL.

Some people who drink water containing arsenic in excess of EPA's standard over many years could experience skin damage or problems with their circulatory system, and may have an increased risk of getting cancer. Health effects might include:

- Thickening and discoloration of the skin, stomach pain, nausea, vomiting, diarrhea, and liver effects;

- Cardiovascular, pulmonary, immunological, neurological (e.g., numbness and partial paralysis), reproductive, and endocrine (e.g., diabetes) effects;

- Cancer of the bladder, lungs, skin, kidney, nasal passages, liver, and prostate.

Three lengthier sections—all of equal importance—are balanced in the middle of the page to indicate the body

What is EPA's standard for arsenic in drinking water?

To protect consumers served by public water systems from the health risks of long-term (chronic) arsenic exposure, EPA recently lowered the arsenic MCL from 50 ppb to 10 ppb.

"What is EPA's standard" section is placed at the bottom of the page, indicating that it is the conclusion

Source: U.S. Environmental Protection Agency <www.epa.gov>

Additional ways
of structuring
information

Beyond the introduction/body/conclusion structure and its variations, there are other ways to structure information, as discussed below.

OUTLINING

Outlining is essential

Even basic documents require at least an introduction-body-conclusion outline done in your head and/or a few ideas jotted down in list form. Longer documents require a more detailed outline so that you can visualize your document overall and ensure that ideas flow logically from point to point.

Start by searching through the information you have gathered and creating a random list of key topics your document should include. For instance, in preparing the arsenic document in Figure 5.2, you might start by simply listing all the information you think readers need or expect:

Start by creating
a list of essential
information

- explain what the EPA is doing about arsenic in drinking water
- define what arsenic is
- explain how arsenic gets into drinking water
- list some of the effects of arsenic (stomach, heart, cancer)
- include specific data
- mention/explain the Safe Water Drinking Act
- refer to/define MCLGs

Now you can reorganize this list.

A simple list like the one above usually suffices for organizing a short document like the memo in Figure 5.1. However, for a more complex document, transform your list into a deliberate map that will guide readers from point to point. Create an introduction, body, and conclusion and then decide how you will divide each of these parts into subtopics. An outline for Figure 5.2 might look like this:

Then organize the
information into an
outline

I. INTRODUCTION—Define arsenic.

II. BODY

   A. Explain how arsenic gets into drinking water.

   B. Explain how it is regulated (1974 Safe Drinking Water Act/MCLGs; Maximum Contaminant Levels).

   C. List some of the health effects of arsenic (visible effects; diseases, cancers).

III. CONCLUSION—Describe the EPA's standards.

For a long document,
create a formal
outline

For a long, complex document, you will want a formal outline to keep you organized as you write (Figure 5.3).

FIGURE 5.3
**A formal
outline using
alphanumeric
notation**

Converting ABCD's Office Building from Oil to Gas Heating: A Feasibility Analysis

I. INTRODUCTION
   A. Background
   B. Purpose of the Report
   C. Intended Audience (usually for in-school reports only)
   D. Information Sources
   E. Limitations of the Report
   F. Scope (list of major topics)

II. DATA (BODY)
   A. Description of Our Present Heating System
      1. Physical condition
      2. Required yearly maintenance
      3. Fuel supply problems
         a. Overworked distributor
         b. Varying local supply
      4. Cost of operation
   B. Removal of the Oil Burner and Tank
      1. Data from the oil company
      2. Data from the salvage company
         a. Procedure
         b. Cost
      3. Possibility of private sale
   C. Installation of a Gas Pipe from the Street to the Building
      1. Procedure
      2. Cost of installation
      3. Cost of landscaping

III. CONCLUSION
   A. Summary of Findings
   B. Comprehensive Interpretation of Findings
   C. Recommendations

Notice a few key characteristics of formal outlines:

- Roman numerals indicate the three main sections (introduction/body/conclusion).
- The first level of subtopics under each main section is indented and preceded by capital letters; the next level is further indented and preceded by Arabic numerals; and the third level is again indented three spaces and preceded by lowercase letters. This is known as *alphanumeric notation*.

An alternate system, *decimal notation*, appears in Figure 5.4. The decimal outline makes it easier to refer readers to various sections in your final document. But both systems achieve the same organizing objective.

- Each level of division must yield at least two subtopics—if you cannot divide a larger topic into at least two subtopics, retain only your larger topic.
- A formal outline typically undergoes changes as you write. Expect to adjust it as needed. When the document is complete you can use the formal outline to create a table of contents for the document.

See also the Strategies (below) for more advice.

FIGURE 5.4
Part of a formal outline using decimal notation

```
2.0 Data (Body)
    2.1 Description of Our Present Heating System
        2.1.1 Physical condition
        2.1.2 Required yearly maintenance
        2.1.3 Fuel supply problems
            2.1.3.1 Overworked distributor
            2.1.3.2 Varying local supply
        2.1.4 Cost of operation
    2.2 Removal of the Oil Burner and Tank
        2.2.1 Data from the oil company
        2.2.2 (and so on)
```

STRATEGIES
for Outlining

- ▶ **List key topics and subtopics to be included in your document.** Gather your information, determine what information is important to include, decide what information is superfluous, and make a list of the topics to be included.
- ▶ **Set up a standard outline.** Start with a typical introduction, body, and conclusion structure, even if you plan to vary the structure later.
- ▶ **Place key topics and subtopics where they fit within your standard outline.** Keep your introduction brief, using it to set the stage for the rest of your document. Include your specific data in the body section to back up what you promised in your introduction. Do not introduce new data in the conclusion.
- ▶ **Use alphanumeric or decimal notation consistently throughout the outline.**
- ▶ **Avoid excessive subtopics.** If you find that your outline is getting into multiple levels of detail too often, think of ways to combine information. Do not go to another level unless there are at least two distinct subtopics at that level.
- ▶ **Refine your outline as you write your document.** Continue revising your outline until you complete your document.

CHUNKING

Outlining helps to illustrate the importance of *chunking*: breaking information down into discrete, digestible units, based on the readers' needs and the document's purpose. When you chunk information into smaller portions, you help readers to see which pieces of information belong together and how the various pieces are connected.

Chunking requires careful decisions about exactly how much information is enough for each portion and what constitutes sensible proportions among the parts. For example, note how in the outline in Figure 5.3 the writer plans to break up the information for readers in a variety of ways. First, the planned report is divided into three general sections, or chunks: introduction, data section (body), and conclusion. Then each of those sections is broken into as many smaller chunks as appropriate to help the reader see how this discussion breaks into parts and yet each of these parts fits together to form a whole.

Chunking information is handled differently on the Web than on the printed page. On Web sites, readers expect information in very short chunks because they don't like reading large portions of text on a computer screen and they want the option of zeroing in on various parts of the page and moving from link to link. In printed documents, however, readers expect longer passages of text because the printed page is easier on the eyes and because the expectation of reading a printed page is to read sequentially rather than jump from section to section.

Breaking information down into smaller units

Chunking on the Web versus chunking on a printed page

SEQUENCING

In addition to chunking information, you also need to show readers the logical progression of information. The specific information sequence will depend on the type of document. For instance, a mechanism description usually follows a *spatial sequence* (What are the parts and how do they fit together?); a progress report or set of instructions usually follows a *chronological sequence* (In what order have things happened/should things happen?); a feasibility, recommendation, or justification report would follow a *problem-solution sequence* (What was/is the problem or goal and how was it/can it be fixed or achieved?); and an analytical report describing an incident and the reasons for the incident would follow a *cause and effect sequence* (What caused something to happen or what were the effects of something?). Examples later in this book illustrate these four sequential approaches:

Sequencing: ordering information to follow a logical progression

- Figure 12.2 (page 226) uses a spatial sequence to describe a stethoscope.
- Figure 15.2 (page 286) uses a chronological sequence to provide a progress report on a student's term project.

- Figure 17.4 (pages 337–346) uses a problem-solution sequence to propose a solution to budgetary issues with a college campus newspaper.
- Figure 16.4 (pages 314–323) uses a cause-effect sequence to show a correlation between periodontal disease in mothers and low birth weight babies.

PARAGRAPHING

Paragraphing: the process of shaping information within paragraphs

The preceding three strategies for structuring information (outlining, chunking, and sequencing) enable you and your readers to see the "big picture" of the document. Once you have thought through the document's larger structure you need to consider how smaller-scale but no less important strategies will help readers follow your message. The first of these strategies, *paragraphing*, is the process of shaping your information within paragraphs.

Why paragraphing is important

In most documents, different types of paragraphs have different shapes and purposes. For example, introductory paragraphs set the stage for the discussion that follows; transitional paragraphs (usually brief) help hold the discussion together; concluding paragraphs wrap up the discussion. But the focus here is on standard *support paragraphs*, typically found in the document's body section. Each support paragraph advances one aspect of the main point made in the document's introduction, and each usually can stand alone in meaning.

Readers look for structures they can recognize both in the document as a whole and within individual paragraphs. Just as the document as a whole needs to have an introduction-body-conclusion structure, so must each paragraph. Most of the standard support paragraphs in a technical document begin with a clear *topic sentence*, stating a generalization. Details in the body section support that generalization. These paragraphs also display *unity* (each sentence in the paragraph's body section must relate to and expand upon the topic sentence). Finally, these paragraphs display *coherence* (all sentences form a connected line of thought, leading from the topic sentence to the conclusion).

The Topic Sentence

Readers look to a paragraph's opening sentences for the main idea. Unless you have good reason to place it elsewhere, the topic sentence should appear first (or at least early) in the paragraph; it should focus and forecast what will come in the remainder of the paragraph. In some instances the main idea may require a "topic statement" consisting of two or more sentences, but usually a single sentence will do, as in the following example:

An effective topic sentence

> Solar power offers the most efficient, economical, and safe solution to the Northeast's energy problems.

Note that key words in the topic sentence signal that the paragraph's next sentences (the body section) will describe how solar energy is *efficient*, *economical*, and *safe*.

Paragraph Unity

un

The body of the paragraph must deliver on the topic sentence's promise. A paragraph is unified when all its material belongs there—when each and every sentence directly expands on the topic sentence. Here, for example, is the complete version of the solar energy paragraph, fully unified:

> *Solar power offers an efficient, economical, and safe solution to the Northeast's energy problems.* To begin with, solar power is highly efficient. Solar collectors installed on fewer than 30 percent of roofs in the Northeast would provide for more than 70 percent of the area's heating and air-conditioning needs. Moreover, solar heat collectors are economical, operating for up to 20 years with little or no maintenance. These savings recoup the initial cost of installation within only ten years. Most important, solar power is safe. It can be transformed into electricity through photovoltaic cells (a type of storage battery) in a noiseless process that produces no air pollution—unlike coal, oil, and wood combustion. In contrast to its nuclear counterpart, solar power produces no toxic waste and poses no catastrophic danger of meltdown. Thus, massive conversion to solar power would ensure abundant energy and a safe, clean environment for future generations.

A unified paragraph

Note how the body of the previous paragraph tackles each of the benefits of solar energy introduced in the topic sentence, sometimes devoting two or more sentences to each benefit, but nonetheless staying on track. One way to damage unity in the paragraph above would be to veer from the focus on the key words *efficient*, *economical*, and *safe* into a discussion about the differences between active and passive solar heating or the advantages of solar power over wind power, neither of which was introduced in the topic sentence.

Paragraph Coherence

coh

The body of the paragraph must deliver on the promise of the topic sentence through paragraph unity and also lead to a conclusion via a connected line of thought, like links in a chain. This feature is called paragraph coherence. Paragraph coherence can be damaged by 1) sentences in the wrong order; 2) insufficient transitions and connectors for linking related ideas; or 3) an inaccessible line of reasoning and lack of conclusion. Here is how the solar energy paragraph might become incoherent:

> Solar power offers an efficient, economical, and safe solution to the Northeast's energy problems. Unlike nuclear power, solar power produces no toxic waste and poses no danger of meltdown. Solar power is efficient. Solar collectors could be installed on fewer than 30 percent of roofs in the Northeast. These collectors would provide for more than

An incoherent paragraph

> 70 percent of the area's heating and air-conditioning needs. Solar power is safe. It can be transformed into electricity. This transformation is made possible by photovoltaic cells (a type of storage battery). Solar heat collectors are economical. The photovoltaic process produces no air pollution.

In the above paragraph, the second sentence, about safety, belongs near the end because it was introduced as the third of the three benefits of solar energy. Also, because of insufficient links between ideas, the paragraph reads more like a list than like a flowing discussion. Finally, a concluding sentence is needed to complete the chain of reasoning and to give readers a clear perspective on what they've just read.

Here, in contrast, is the original, coherent paragraph with sentences numbered for later discussion and with transitions and connectors shown in boldface. Notice how this version reveals a clear line of thought:

A coherent paragraph

> [1]Solar power offers an efficient, economical, and safe solution to the Northeast's energy problems. [2]**To begin with,** solar power is highly efficient. [3]Solar collectors installed on fewer than 30 percent of roofs in the Northeast would provide for more than 70 percent of the area's heating and air-conditioning needs. [4]**Moreover,** solar heat collectors are economical, operating for up to 20 years with little or no maintenance. [5]**These savings** recoup the initial cost of installation within only ten years. [6]**Most important,** solar power is safe. [7]It can be transformed into electricity through photovoltaic cells (a type of storage battery) in a noiseless process that produces no air pollution—unlike coal, oil, and wood combustion. [8]**In contrast** to its nuclear counterpart, solar power produces no toxic waste and poses no danger of catastrophic meltdown. [9]**Thus,** massive conversion to solar power would ensure abundant energy and a safe, clean environment for future generations.

We can easily trace the sequence of thoughts in the previous paragraph:

Sentence 1.	The topic sentence establishes a clear direction.
Sentences 2–3.	The first reason is given and then explained.
Sentences 4–5.	The second reason is given and explained.
Sentences 6–8.	The third and major reason is given and explained.
Sentence 9.	The conclusion reemphasizes the main point.

To reinforce the logical sequence, related ideas are combined in individual sentences, and transitions and connectors signal clear relationships between ideas. The whole paragraph sticks together.

CLARIFYING HEADINGS

Create headings as one of the final steps in the structuring process

One of the final steps in structuring information is to make sure you have used clear headings. Use your outline as a guide. Headings may not be appropriate for all documents, such as short documents (e.g., the memo in

Figure 5.1), but most technical material relies on some use of headings as a way to break up long passages of text and give readers guideposts throughout the document.

Headings often follow standard formats, such as "Introduction," "Methods," "Findings," "Conclusion," and so forth. In certain cases, the type of document (a scientific paper, a report for a company that always follows the same format) will dictate the headings you need to use.

Heading format and purpose

You may use single words, phrases, brief statements, or questions as headings, as long as the headings signal to readers exactly what to expect in the section that falls under the heading's umbrella.

When used consistently, questions are often the most helpful way to construct headings. In effect, the question in the heading is answered by the material that falls under that heading. The author of Figure 5.2 has taken this user-friendly approach, anticipating reader questions ("What is arsenic?" "How does arsenic get into my drinking water?" "How is arsenic in drinking water regulated?" "Why should I be concerned about arsenic in my drinking water?" and "What is the EPA's standard for arsenic in drinking water?") and answering each in turn.

Figure 5.5 is an example of a short report that uses clear, concise, and accurate headings to break up the material into logical sections. Because it is a progress report, the introductory heading gets right to the point of progress and the concluding heading gets directly to the topic of work remaining. Meanwhile, the headings in the middle section directly signal the key topics the reader needs to know about.

For more on the use of headings, see pages 140–141 and 144

PROVIDING AN OVERVIEW

The last step in structuring information for your readers is providing an overview. An overview may not be necessary for all technical documents, particularly short documents and reports. However, if you are writing a longer, more complex document, help your readers by providing a brief (usually paragraph-length) preview of what they can expect. This will help readers get the most out of the document by answering several key questions at the outset:

Provide an overview as the last step in the structuring process

- What is the purpose of this document?
- Why should I read it?
- What information can I expect to find here?

Think about it this way: If you were taking a long trip, you would probably use Google Maps or a GPS system to get the big picture of your journey and to know exactly where you were headed. Overviews provide a similar type of road map.

An overview should be placed at the beginning of a document, but you may also want to provide section overviews at the beginning of each section in a long

Four headings
divide the report
into distinct, logical
sections

Information in each
headed section
is brief and does
not stray from the
heading topic

Progress Report: Equipment for New Operations Building

Work Completed

Our training group has met twice since our May 12 report. In our first
meeting, we identified the types of training we anticipate.

Types of Training Anticipated

- Loan Officer Work Experience
- Divisional Systems Training
- Divisional Clerical Training (Continuing)
- Divisional Clerical Training (New Employees)
- Divisional Management Training (Seminars)
- Special/New Equipment Training

In our second meeting, we considered various areas for the training room.

Training Room Assignment and Equipment

The frequency of training requires us to have a training room available daily.
The large training room in the Corporate Education area (10th floor) would
be ideal. Before submitting our next report, we need your confirmation that
this room can be assigned to us.

To support the training programs, we purchased this equipment:

- Audioviewer
- Large flat screen monitor
- Digital video camera and tripod
- Software for computer-assisted instruction

This equipment will allow us to administer training in a variety of modes,
ranging from programmed and learner-controlled instruction to group
seminars and workshops.

FIGURE 5.5 A short report with clear headings

Work Remaining

To support the training, we need to furnish the room appropriately. Because the types of training will vary, the furniture should provide a flexible environment. Outlined here are our anticipated furnishing needs.

- Tables and chairs that can be set up in many configurations. These would allow for individual or group training and large seminars.
- Portable room dividers. These would provide study space for training with programmed instruction and allow for simultaneous training.
- Built-in storage space for audiovisual equipment and training supplies. Ideally, this storage space should be multipurpose, providing work or display surfaces.
- A flexible lighting system for audiovisual presentations and individualized study.

The project is on schedule. As soon as we receive your approval of these specifications, we will send out bids for room dividers and have plans drawn for the built-in storage.

cc.   R. S. Pike, SVP

Final heading clearly signals that this section is the conclusion

document. The following is an example of an overview paragraph that comes at the beginning of a long report on groundwater contamination.

A report overview

> **About This Report**
>
> This report contains five sections. The first section describes the scope and scale of groundwater contamination in Jackson County. The second section offers background on previous legislation related to groundwater. Section Three shows the most recent data from the Jackson County Groundwater Project, and Section Four compares those data to national averages. Section Five offers recommendations and ideas for next steps.

In addition to helping readers negotiate longer reports, overviews are also extremely helpful in longer instruction and user manuals so that readers will know immediately what to expect in the longer document.

Figure 5.6 is an example of an overview page from a user guide designed to help people find and apply for federal grants. This overview (titled "Introduction" in this document) provides a short, simple introductory paragraph explaining the context for this user guide. Additional paragraphs describe what is contained in the guide, and a bulleted list provides a streamlined, easy-to-read visual overview of what is contained in the rest of this 60-page document.

☑ CHECKLIST
for Structuring Information   MyWritingLab™

- ☐ Am I structuring my document with readers in mind?
- ☐ Does my document employ a standard or varied introduction/body/ conclusion structure?
- ☐ Have I created an outline that will allow me to include all the necessary data for my document?
- ☐ Have I organized my outline using alphanumeric or decimal notation?
- ☐ Have I chunked my information into discrete, digestible units and for the proper medium (print or Web)?
- ☐ Am I using the right sequence?
- ☐ Does each of my paragraphs include these features?
  - Topic sentence (introduction)
  - Unity (body that supports the topic sentence)
  - Coherence (connected line of thought leading to a conclusion)
- ☐ Have I used headings that are clear and address the sections or questions readers expect?
- ☐ If appropriate, does my document include an overview, helping readers understand what will follow?

Introduction

Grants.gov has been designed to make it easier for organizations to find and apply for more than $500 billion in federal grants. With electronic access to more than 1,000 grant programs offered by all federal grant-making agencies, Grants.gov leverages the power of the Web to streamline your grant acquisition process.

This user guide has been developed to help you navigate the Grants.gov environment more easily. In it, you'll find detailed instructions for every step of the process – whether you're an applicant or grant-making agency.

From getting started and registration to viewing and tracking completed applications, this user guide offers clarification throughout the entire process.

Provided information in this user guide:
- How To Register Your Organization
- How To Register As An Authorized Organization Representative
- How To Register As An Individual
- Find and Search Grant Opportunities
- Download Application Packages
- Apply For Grants
- Track Your Application
- And How To Stay Connected

Heading lets readers know that this page will give them an overview of the user guide

Introductory paragraph provides background information in brief format

Second paragraph explains the purpose of the user guide

Bulleted list outlines the major sections in the user guide

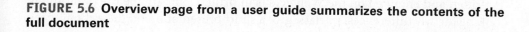

FIGURE 5.6 Overview page from a user guide summarizes the contents of the full document

APPLICATIONS

GENERAL APPLICATION   MyWritingLab™

Locate a set of instructions for something you have purchased. Identify specific features of how this material is organized and written. Are the paragraphs chunked into discrete units? Are headings used, and if so are they in question format? Is the material sequenced in a standard way? Do all of the paragraphs include topic sentences, and are they unified and coherent? Write a brief memo explaining why you think the technical writers who wrote the instructions made the decisions they did.

TEAM APPLICATION

With a team of two to three other students, consider the following documents and discuss the most logical sequence. (For instance, a description of a proposed podcasting computer lab would follow a spatial sequence.)

- a set of instructions for operating a power tool
- a campaign report describing your progress in political fund-raising
- a report analyzing the desirability of a proposed oil refinery in your area
- a detailed breakdown of your monthly budget to trim excess spending
- a report investigating the reasons for student apathy on your campus
- a proposal for a no-grade policy at your college

GLOBAL APPLICATION   MyWritingLab™

Find a document that presents the same information in several languages (assembly instructions, for example). Even without being able to understand all of the languages used, see if you can spot any changes made in the use of headings, the length of paragraphs, or the extent to which information is chunked. Interview a language professor on campus to find out why these choices may have been made.

DIGITAL AND SOCIAL MEDIA APPLICATION   MyWritingLab™

Locate a Web page and a print document (brochure, booklet, user guide) about the same product. Compare these, looking for the different ways in which material is written and chunked on the Web versus in print. Compare the use of headings, looking for any differences. In class, give a short presentation on these differences.

MyWritingLab™   Visit Chapter 5, *Structuring Information for Your Readers*, in MyWritingLab to complete this chapter's applications, to explore this chapter's overview, checklist, and flashcards, and to test your understanding of the chapter objectives.

6 Writing with a Readable Style

CHAPTER OUTLINE

The Importance of
a Readable Style   *94*

Writing Clearly   *95*

Writing Concisely   *100*

Writing Fluently   *102*

Writing Personally   *105*

STRATEGIES for Deciding
about Tone   *105*

STRATEGIES for Nonsexist
Usage   *106*

STRATEGIES for Unbiased
Usage   *107*

CHECKLIST for Style   *107*

Applications   *108*

LEARNING OBJECTIVES FOR THIS CHAPTER

► Recognize that style places your audience's needs first

► Appreciate the importance of style in any document

► Use various strategies to write clearly, concisely, fluently, and personally

Definition of style

W hile *structure* has to do with the reader's ability to understand the document as a whole, including paragraphs, *style* has to do with readability at the sentence and word level.

THE IMPORTANCE OF A READABLE STYLE

Style emphasizes the audience's needs first

No matter how technical your document, your audience won't understand the content unless your sentences are easy to understand and your words are chosen precisely. Your style is a blend of these elements:

What determines your style

- the way in which you construct each sentence
- the length of your sentences
- the way in which you connect sentences
- the words and phrases you choose
- the tone you convey

Whether you are using email, a PDF attachment, or a print document, these elements are always important in creating professional, usable workplace communication. Too often, tone and style in digital communication, email in particular, become sloppy and casual. See Chapter 18 for more on email tone and style.

Style is more than correct grammar, usage, mechanics, and spelling

Readable style, of course, also requires correct grammar, usage, mechanics, and spelling. But correctness alone is no guarantee of readability. For example, the following response to a job application follows the rules of grammar, usage, mechanics, and spelling, but it is hard to read:

Inefficient style

> We are in receipt of your recent correspondence indicating your interest in securing the advertised position. Your correspondence has been duly forwarded for consideration by the personnel office, which has employment candidate selection responsibility. You may expect to hear from us relative to your application as the selection process progresses. Your interest in the position is appreciated.

Notice as a reader how hard you have to work to extract information from the previous paragraph. This information could be expressed clearly and concisely, as in the following paragraph:

Readable style

> Your application for the advertised position has been forwarded to our personnel office. As the selection process moves forward, we will be in touch. Thank you for your interest.

Inefficient style makes readers work harder than they should. Style can be inefficient for many reasons but especially when it does the following:

Ways in which style goes wrong

- makes the writing impossible to interpret
- takes too long to make the point

- reads like a story from primary school
- sounds stuffy and impersonal

Regardless of the cause, inefficient style results in writing that is less informative and less persuasive than it should be. Also, inefficient style can be unethical when it confuses or misleads the audience, whether intentionally or unintentionally. Therefore, take the time to write with a readable style, using the strategies described in the following sections: writing clearly, writing concisely, writing fluently, and writing personably. For advice regarding correct grammar, usage, and mechanics, see Appendix B.

Inefficient style can be uninformative, unpersuasive, and even unethical

WRITING CLEARLY

Clear writing enables people to read each sentence only once in order to fully grasp its meaning. Strategies for writing clearly include avoiding ambiguous pronoun references, avoiding ambiguous modifiers, using active voice whenever possible, using passive voice selectively, avoiding nominalizations, unstacking nouns, and avoiding unnecessary jargon.

Why writing clearly is important

Avoiding Ambiguous Pronoun References

ref

Pronouns (*he, she, it, their,* and so on) must clearly refer to the nouns they replace; otherwise, the sentence will be ambiguous and readers will puzzle over your intended meaning. For example, consider the following sentence, in which the reader is unable to discern whether Jack *or* his assistant is competitive:

Jack resents his assistant because he is competitive.

Unclear referent

Depending on whether the referent for "he" is Jack or his assistant, the sentence can be clarified:

Because his assistant is competitive, Jack resents him.
or
Because Jack is competitive, he resents his assistant.

Clear referent

 EXERCISE 1

Edit each sentence below to eliminate ambiguities in pronoun reference.

a. Bill told Darius that he was working too hard.
b. Janice dislikes working with Magdalena because she's impatient.
c. Our patients enjoy the warm days while they last.

    d. They couldn't start their cars because they were too cold.

    e. Celia can't talk to Betsy because she's still too angry.

Avoiding Ambiguous Modifiers

mod

A *modifier* is a word (usually an adjective or adverb) or a group of words (usually a phrase or clause) that provides information about other words or groups of words. If a modifier is too far from the words it modifies, the message can be ambiguous. For instance, in the following sentence, the reader cannot discern whether "only" modifies "press" or "emergency":

Ambiguous modifier

| Only press the red button in an emergency.

If, however, the writer repositions the modifier, the sentence becomes clear:

Clear modifier

| Press only the red button in an emergency.
| *or*
| Press the red button in an emergency only.

Position modifiers to reflect your meaning.

 EXERCISE 2

Edit each sentence below to clarify ambiguous modifiers.

    a. Just place the dishes back in the cabinets after 8 P.M.

    b. He purchased a ticket for his wife from Carnegie Hall.

    c. I almost sat there waiting for Gino for 45 minutes.

    d. Before she passed away, Philippa told her mother she admired her.

    e. Only use this phone in a red alert.

Using Active Voice Whenever Possible

av

In general, readers understand the meaning more quickly and clearly when the writer uses active voice ("I did it") rather than the passive voice ("It was done by me"). In active voice sentences, a clear agent performs a clear action on a recipient, as in the following example:

Active voice

| Felix lost your report.

Passive voice, by contrast, reverses this pattern, placing the recipient of the action (i.e., *report*, in the previous example) in the subject slot, as in the following sentence:

| Your report was lost by Felix.

Passive voice

Note that passive voice adds a form of the verb "be" ("was") next to the actual verb.

Some writers mistakenly rely on passive voice because they think it sounds more objective and important. But passive voice makes sentences wordier and harder to understand.

In addition, passive voice sometimes obscures the subject of the sentence, as in the following example:

| Your report was lost.

Inappropriate use of passive voice (no subject identified)

Passive voice is unethical if it obscures the person or other agent who performed the action when the person or agent responsible should be identified. In the above example, "Your report was lost" leaves out the responsible party. (Who lost the report?) For these reasons, favor the active voice in most writing situations.

 EXERCISE 3

Convert these passive voice sentences to concise, forceful, and direct expressions in the active voice.

- **a.** The evaluation was performed by us.
- **b.** Unless you pay me within three days, my lawyer will be contacted.
- **c.** Hard hats should be worn at all times.
- **d.** The due date was delayed.
- **e.** Our test results will be sent to you as soon as verification is completed.

Using Passive Voice Selectively

pv

There are times when the passive voice is appropriate: for instance, when the subject is not known or when the object is more important than the subject. For example, if a group of scientists performed an experiment and wanted to explain the results, they might write the following:

| The data were analyzed, and the findings were discussed.

Appropriate use of passive voice

Even here, active voice ("We analyzed the data…") would be preferable. But if it is clear who analyzed the data or truly not important who did the work, passive voice might be acceptable.

Passive voice can also ease the blow a direct sentence might deliver:

Blunt use of active voice

> You have not paid your bill.

To be indirect and less offensive, the writer may choose passive voice instead:

Appropriate (indirect) use of passive voice

> Your bill has not been paid.

Consider this technique when you want to avoid a blunt or hostile tone. But in general, to convey clear, readable technical information, use active voice.

 EXERCISE 4

The sentences below represent blunt uses of active voice. Convert each to passive voice.

    a. Joe's company fired him.
    b. Cecelia's coworkers accused her of being lazy.
    c. You are paying inadequate attention to worker safety.
    d. You are checking temperatures too infrequently.
    e. You did a poor job editing this report.

Avoiding Nominalizations

nom

A nominalization is a noun that would be easier to understand as a verb. Verbs are generally easier to read because they signal action that can be visualized. You can usually spot a nominalization in two ways. First, look for words with *-tion* endings. Second, look for sentences in which the "[noun] of [noun]" formula appears. Following is an example of each type of nominalization:

Unclear (*-tion* ending)

Unclear ("[noun] of [noun]")

> My recommendation is for a larger budget.
>
> The managing of this project is up to me.

To fix the *-tion* problem, strike the ending to find the root verb ("recommend") and rewrite the sentence in a more direct form. To fix the "[noun] of [noun]" problem, identify the root verb form ("manage") and create a more accessible sentence. Following are improved versions of the above sentences:

Clear verb form (*-tion* removed)

Clear verb form ("[noun] of [noun]" removed)

> I recommend a larger budget.
>
> I manage this project.

EXERCISE 5

Make these sentences clearer by eliminating nominalizations.

a. Our acceptance of the offer is a necessity.
b. Your assertion is that we spend too much time in meetings.
c. We ask for the cooperation of all employees.
d. My validation of the report is required.
e. Please provide a description of the problem.

Unstack Modifying Nouns

st mod

Too many nouns in a row can create confusion for readers. One noun can modify another (as in "software development"). But when two or more nouns modify a noun, the string of words becomes "stacked"—in other words, hard to read and ambiguous. For example:

> Be sure to leave enough time for today's training session participant evaluation.

Ambiguous use of stacked nouns

In the previous sentence, the reader is left unsure whether evaluation is of the session or of the participants. With no articles, prepositions, or verbs to unstack the nouns, readers cannot sort out the relationships among the nouns. To fix the problem, separate the stacked nouns by changing some nouns into verb forms where appropriate, as in the following example:

> Be sure to leave enough time for participants to evaluate today's training session.
>
> *or*
>
> Be sure to leave enough time to evaluate the participants in today's training session.

Clear sentence with nouns unstacked

EXERCISE 6

Make these sentences clearer by unstacking the nouns.

a. They developed online editing system documentation.
b. I recommend these management performance improvement incentives.
c. Sarah's job involves fault analysis systems troubleshooting handbook preparation.
d. Constantine read through the strategic implementation status guidelines.
e. You should think about providing employees with memory recall stimulus devices.

Avoiding Unnecessary Jargon

jarg

Every profession has its own shorthand and accepted phrases and terms. Among specialists, these terms are an economical way to communicate. For example, "stat" (from the Latin *statim*, "immediately") is medical jargon for "drop everything and deal with this emergency." Jargon can be useful in communications among specialists. However, to avoid confusion, use jargon only when you know your audience will understand it and not simply to sound important or pretentious. Consider the following sentence:

Needless jargon

| We will bilaterally optimize our efforts on this project.

Clearly that writer meant to sound important, but to most readers, the sentence is simultaneously meaningless and pretentious.

Following is a clear and simple version:

Jargon-free version

| We will coopera te on this project.

 EXERCISE 7

Edit these sentences to eliminate useless jargon.

a. To optimize your financial return, prioritize your investment goals.
b. The use of this product engenders a 50 percent repeat consumer encounter.
c. Unless all parties interface synchronously within given parameters, the project will fail.
d. Acoustically attenuate our company's food consumption area.
e. We need to formulate a workable paradigm for this project.

WRITING CONCISELY

Why writing concisely is important

Concise writing provides readers with all of the information they need but without any needless filler. Strategies for writing concisely include avoiding wordiness as well as eliminating redundancy and repetition.

Avoiding Wordiness

w

Wordiness is often unavoidable in a first draft, when a writer is simply trying to get thoughts down on the page. For your readers, however, wordiness is distracting and detracts from a writer's credibility. When you edit your document, go through each sentence and work to eliminate excess words.

Wordiness has multiple causes: First, some writers habitually use needless phrases that can be reduced to one word:

> at a rapid rate = rapidly
>
> due to the fact that = because
>
> aware of the fact that = know
>
> in close proximity to = near
>
> the majority of = most

Wordy phrases and their one-word substitutes

Second, many writers tend to start sentences with "there is," "there are," and "it is," which can often be eliminated:

> There is a danger of explosion in Number 2 mineshaft. = Number 2 mineshaft is in danger of exploding.
>
> It is necessary to complete both sides of the form. = Please complete both sides of the form.

Needless "there is," "there are," and "it is" sentence openers and their corrections

Third, writers often gravitate to weak verbs, such as all forms of the verb "to be" ("am," "are," "is," etc.), "give," "make," "come," and "take." These verbs need to be combined with other words to express fuller meaning, but they can easily be replaced with stronger verbs that can stand on their own:

> has the ability to = can
>
> make an assumption = assume
>
> come to the conclusion that = conclude
>
> give a summary of = summarize
>
> take action = act

Weak verbs and their replacements

Fourth, writers often overuse prepositional phrases, which can easily be reduced to one or two words:

> with the exception of = except for
>
> in the near future = soon
>
> at the present time = now
>
> in the course of = during
>
> in the process of = during (or in)

Prepositional phrases and their replacements

Finally, many writers pad their writing by using clutter words (such as "very," "quite," "somewhat," "really," "actually"), needless qualifiers ("I think," "in my opinion," "it seems"), and unnecessary prefaces ("As far as I am concerned," "the purpose of this is") that add no meaning to a sentence. Of course, if you are expressing a tentative position on a complex issue, do use a qualifier ("I think," "it seems") as appropriate.

 EXERCISE 8

Eliminate wordiness from the following sentences.

    a. Our lateness was due to the fact that we ran into traffic.
    b. I have come to the realization that I was mistaken.
    c. It seems as if I have just wrecked the company car.
    d. It is essential that we act immediately.
    e. A malfunction occurred during the process of rebooting.

Eliminating Redundancy and Repetition

A redundant expression says the same thing twice, in different words, whereas a repetition says the same thing twice or more in the same words. Following are examples of each, which can be fixed simply through cutting out the bracketed words.

Redundant phrases

[completely] eliminate	[mental] awareness
[end] result	[utter] devastation
enter [into]	[mutual] cooperation
consensus [of opinion]	[fellow] colleagues

Needlessly repetitious sentence

Techniques of artificial respiration include mouth-to-mouth [respiration] and mouth-to-nose [respiration].

 EXERCISE 9

Make these sentences more concise by eliminating redundancy and repetition.

    a. Igor's fellow colleagues are ambitious.
    b. We ask for everyone's mutual cooperation during this busy time.
    c. This report is the most informative report on the project.
    d. The consensus of opinion is that we agree with Tanisha's idea.
    e. Sam agrees, Tanya agrees, and Soon-ye agrees too.

WRITING FLUENTLY

Why writing fluently is important

When you write fluently, you will hold your readers' interest and attention by making clear connections between ideas and by reducing monotony. Strategies for writing fluently include combining related ideas, varying sentence construction and length, and using parallel structure.

Combining Related Ideas

comb

Readers who are forced to trudge through a series of short, choppy sentences will not only lose interest but will also fail to see how ideas are meant to be related or which ideas should receive emphasis. For example, the following string of five short sentences makes for dull reading. In addition, it forces readers to invent transitions between ideas and decide which points are most important:

> Jogging can be healthful. You need the right equipment. Well-fitting shoes are important. You take the chance of injuring your legs. Your knees are especially prone to injury.

Disconnected series of ideas

In contrast, the following two-sentence revision reads more smoothly and places a stronger emphasis on the importance of having the right jogging shoes:

> Jogging can be healthful if you have the right equipment. Shoes that fit well are particularly important because they prevent injury to your legs, especially your knees.

Fluent combination of ideas

 EXERCISE 10

Combine the following sentences three times, each time creating one fluent sentence that places emphasis in a different place. For the first combination, emphasize the negative aspects of the job. For the second combination, emphasize the positive aspects. For the third combination, emphasize the salary.

> The job offers an attractive salary. It demands long work hours. It can be stressful. Promotions are rapid.

Varying Sentence Construction and Length

var

While you should combine short, choppy sentences into longer, more fluid versions, you don't want to create a string of unvaried longer sentences. Readers will find these just as monotonous, and they will also have a hard time determining which points are meant to receive emphasis. For example, the following two longer sentences are unvaried and dull, and at the same time the reader is forced to decide which of the five points made is the most important:

> Two drawbacks of diesel engines are that they are difficult to start in cold weather and cause sulfur dioxide pollution. In addition, they give off noise, emit an unpleasant odor, and cause vibrations.

In contrast, the following two-sentence revision reads less monotonously and incorporates one short sentence to place special emphasis on sulfur dioxide pollution:

> Diesel engines have a number of drawbacks, including cold weather starting difficulties, noisiness, odor, and vibrations. More seriously, they also cause sulfur dioxide pollution.

 EXERCISE 11

Add variety to the following string of similar sentences.

> Because people are busy these days, television DVRs are unsurprisingly popular. Because you can record while you are at work, you don't have to worry about missing your favorite programs. In addition, because you can record programs that show late at night, you don't have to stay up late to catch your favorite programs. Finally, in case you are on vacation, you can set the DVR to record your favorite shows automatically every week.

Using Parallel Structure

 par

Parallel structure is a fancy way of saying that similar items should be expressed in similar grammatical form. Without parallelism, readers will lose attention, being mentally forced to "fix" the grammatical fluency of your sentence. For example, the structure of the following sentence is not parallel:

Not parallel

> She likes many outdoor activities, including running, kayaking, and to design new hiking trails.

This sentence is essentially a list of items. The first two items, "running" and "kayaking," are expressed as gerunds (verbs converted into nouns by using -*ing* endings). The third item, "to design," is not a gerund but a verb followed by an object. To make this sentence parallel and increase its fluency you would revise as follows:

Parallel

> She likes many outdoor activities, including running, kayaking, and designing new hiking trails.

 EXERCISE 12

Make these sentences clearer by eliminating faulty parallelism.

    a. The weather today is going to be cold, rainy, and without much sun.
    b. My television picture is cloudy and I can see pixellation.

c. My car needs a tune-up, an oil change, and the tires should be replaced.
d. The new tutor is enthusiastic, skilled, and you can depend on her.
e. In his new job, Ramon felt lonely and without a friend.

WRITING PERSONABLY

When you write in a personable manner, you connect directly with your readers and avoid inadvertently offending them. Strategies for writing personably include adjusting your tone and avoiding sexist and biased language.

Why writing personably is important

Adjusting Your Tone

`tone`

Your tone is your personal stamp-the personality that takes shape between the lines. The tone you create depends on 1) the distance you impose between yourself and the reader, and 2) the attitude you show toward the subject. To increase the likelihood of bringing readers over to your side, see the Strategies that follow.

STRATEGIES
for Deciding about Tone

▶ **Determine if you want a formal, semiformal, or informal tone.** You may prefer a formal tone when writing to superiors, professionals, or academics (depending on what you think they expect), a semiformal tone for colleagues and subordinates (depending on how close you feel to your readers), or a slightly informal tone when you want your writing to be conversational.

▶ **Remain consistent.** Once you've determined the appropriate overall tone of the document, stay with it throughout.

▶ **Address readers directly.** Prefer the personal pronouns "you" and "your" to connect with readers.

▶ **Use "I" and "we" when appropriate.** Instead of disappearing behind your writing, use "I" and "we" to connect with your readers.

▶ **Prefer the active voice.** Show confidence and directness by using active rather than passive voice.

▶ **Emphasize the positive.** Avoid a negative tone when conveying unpleasant information.

▶ **Always avoid an overly informal tone.** Achieving a conversational tone does not mean relying on substandard usage ("He ain't got none"), profanity ("This idea sucks"), and colloquialisms ("OK," "a lot," "snooze"). Pay special attention to tone when using email (see Chapter 18 for more on email tone and style).

EXERCISE 13

Adjust the tone of the following sentences to improve the connection between the writer and the reader.

    a. The writer of this letter would like a refund.

    b. The requested report will be sent next week.

    c. Students at this college will find the faculty always willing to help.

    d. No way am I going to approve this dog of a proposal.

    e. Because of your division's lagging productivity, a management review may be needed.

sexist ## Avoiding Sexist and Biased Language

bias Language that is offensive or makes unwarranted assumptions will alienate readers. Women, for example, who receive a letter addressed to "Dear Sir" will probably discard the letter without ever reading it. Also, our communication should respect all people regardless of cultural, racial, or national background, sexual or religious orientation, age, or physical condition. See the following Strategies.

 ## STRATEGIES
for Nonsexist Usage

▶ **Use gender-neutral expressions.** Use "chair" or "chairperson" rather than "chairman" and "postal worker" rather than "postman."

▶ **Don't mention gender if it is not relevant.** Don't use "the female police officer" unless you are talking about police officers in the context of gender.

▶ **Avoid sexist pronouns.** You can avoid using a sexist pronoun by revising the sentence ("A writer who revises will succeed" rather than "A writer will succeed if he revises"), by using a plural form ("Writers will succeed if they revise"), or by occasionally using paired pronouns ("A writer will succeed if he or she revises").

▶ **Drop condescending diminutive endings.** Avoid words such as "poetess" and "majorette" and simply use "poet" and "major" instead.

▶ **Use "Ms."** Unless you know that a person prefers a traditional title, avoid "Mrs." and "Miss." Males are not identified by marital status, nor should females have to be.

STRATEGIES
for Unbiased Usage

▸ **Be specific when referring to a person's cultural/national identity.** Instead of "Asian" or "Hispanic," for example, prefer "Korean" or "Cuban American." Use the cultural/national designation preferred by people in that group (e.g., "Native American" rather than "Indian" or "Senegalese" rather than "African").

▸ **Avoid potentially judgmental expressions.** Instead of "Third World" or "underdeveloped" use "newly industrialized" or "developing," and instead of "nonwhite" use "people of color."

▸ **Never use demeaning expressions.** Avoid expressions such as "lame excuse," "the blind leading the blind," or "that's queer."

▸ **Use person-first language for people with disabilities or medical conditions.** Avoid terms that place the disability over the person or that suggest pity. Use "person with a disability" rather than "disabled person" and "person with AIDS" rather than "AIDS victim."

▸ **Use age-appropriate designations.** A "girl" or a "boy" is age 14 or under; a "young person," "young adult," "young woman," or "young man" is of high school age; and a "man" or a "woman" is college-aged or older. Avoid "old" or "elderly" and use "older person" or "senior" instead, if age is relevant.

EXERCISE 14

The sentences below suffer from sexist or biased expressions. Adjust the tone.

a. The group's spokesman demanded salary increases.
b. The explosion left me blind as a bat for nearly two hours.
c. While the girls played football, the men waved pom-poms to cheer them on.
d. The Latino mechanic fixed the problem in under an hour.
e. Lame excuses for late papers will not be tolerated.

CHECKLIST
for Style

MyWritingLab™

CLARITY

☐ Have I ensured that each pronoun clearly refers to the noun it replaces?

☐ Have I placed each modifier close enough to the word(s) it explains?

☐ Have I used active rather than passive voice (unless the agent is immaterial)?

☐ Have I restored nominalizations to their verb forms?

☐ Have I unstacked modifying nouns?

☐ Have I avoided needless jargon?

CONCISENESS

☐ Have I avoided needless sentence openers?

☐ Have I traded weak verbs for verbs that express a definite action?

☐ Have I avoided needless prepositional phrases?

☐ Have I avoided clutter words and needless qualifiers?

☐ Have I eliminated redundancy and needless repetition?

FLUENCY

☐ Have I combined related ideas appropriately?

☐ Have I varied sentence construction and length?

☐ Have I used parallel structure?

☐ Have I used short sentences for special emphasis?

TONE

☐ Is my tone appropriate and consistent for the situation and audience?

☐ Is the level of formality what the intended audience would expect?

☐ Is my writing free of implied bias or offensive language?

☐ Does the piece display sensitivity to cultural differences?

☐ If using email, is my tone professional and polite?

APPLICATIONS

GENERAL APPLICATION   MyWritingLab™

Using the Checklist for Style, revise the following selections. (Hint: Use the example on page 94 as a model for revision.) If available, use the "track changes" or "comments" function in your word processing software to record your suggested revisions and to identify the specific style problems in the original selection.

a. Letter to a local newspaper

In the absence of definitive studies regarding the optimum length of the school day, I can only state my personal opinion based upon observations made by me and upon teacher observations that have been conveyed to me. Considering the length of the present school day, it is my opinion that the day is excessive length-wise for most elementary pupils, certainly for almost all of the primary children.

To find the answer to the problem requires consideration of two ways in which the problem may be viewed. One way focuses upon the needs of the children, while the other focuses upon logistics, transportation, scheduling, and other limits imposed by the educational system. If it is necessary to prioritize these two ideas, it would seem most reasonable to give the first consideration to the primary reason for the very existence of the system, i.e., to meet the educational needs of the children the system is trying to serve.

b. Memo to employees

We are presently awaiting an on-site inspection of the designated professional library location by corporate representatives relative to electrical adaptations necessary for the computer installation. Meanwhile, all staff members are asked to respect the off-limits designation of the aforementioned location, as requested, due to the liability insurance provisions in regard to the computer.

TEAM APPLICATION

Locate a poorly written document. In groups of four, look for problems of style and readability. Each person in the group should be assigned to improve a different stylistic area in the document: The first person should improve clarity; the second, conciseness; the third fluency; and the fourth should make the document more personable. Keep track of the improvements each team member makes, and present your edits and final version to the class. Note how each group will have revised the document differently.

GLOBAL APPLICATION   MyWritingLab™

The style guidelines in this chapter apply specifically to Standard English in North America, but technical communication is a global process. Practices and preferences differ widely. For example, some cultures prefer long sentences and elaborate language to convey an idea's full complexity. Others expect lengthy introductions and expressions of politeness and praise rather than clarity or directness. Certain documents may originate in English but then be translated into other languages or read by audiences for whom English is a second language. In such cases, writers must be careful to use language that is easy to translate. Idioms ("cutthroat competition," "over the top," etc.), cultural references ("the Bronx Bomber," "the Deep South"), and humor ("heads I win; tails you lose") are often difficult to translate. Some words may carry insulting connotations, as in cultures in which the terms "male" and "female" refer only to animals.

Your assignment is to search online using the keywords "international business culture" to learn about the style preferences of one particular culture. Then, in a one-page memo to your instructor and classmates, describe the style preferences of that culture, and give examples of how these preferences differ from the style guidelines (i.e., for North American English) in this chapter.

DIGITAL AND SOCIAL MEDIA APPLICATION   MyWritingLab™

Do an online search for the phrase "writing for social media." Look for Web sites from professional organizations such as major news media, colleges and universities, government agencies, and corporations. Compare the advice given on these Web sites with the strategies offered in this chapter, particularly about audience, tone, and formality. Make a list of items that are important regardless of the delivery medium (print or digital) and another list of style and tone considerations specific to social media. Discuss your findings with two or three other students, then share your findings in a brief in-class presentation.

MyWritingLab™   Visit Chapter 6, *Writing with a Readable Style*, in MyWritingLab to complete this chapter's applications, to explore this chapter's overview, checklist, and flashcards, and to test your understanding of the chapter objectives.

7 Using Audience-Centered Visuals

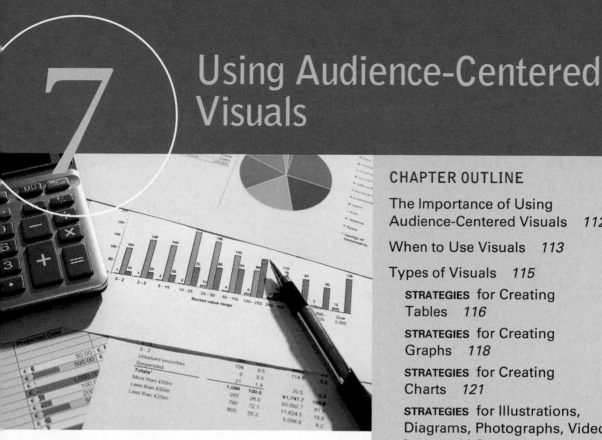

CHAPTER OUTLINE

The Importance of Using
Audience-Centered Visuals   *112*

When to Use Visuals   *113*

Types of Visuals   *115*

   STRATEGIES for Creating
   Tables   *116*

   STRATEGIES for Creating
   Graphs   *118*

   STRATEGIES for Creating
   Charts   *121*

   STRATEGIES for Illustrations,
   Diagrams, Photographs, Videos,
   Icons, and Symbols   *125*

Special Considerations When
Using Visuals   *126*

   CHECKLIST for Using
   Audience-Centered Visuals   *128*

Applications   *129*

LEARNING OBJECTIVES FOR THIS CHAPTER

▸ Appreciate the role of visuals
  in technical communication

▸ Decide when to use visuals on their
  own or with text

▸ Distinguish between different types of visuals

▸ Understand how to choose visuals appropriately
  for your audience and purpose

▸ Place, cross-reference, and present visuals
  appropriately for your readers

▸ Use color in your visuals

▸ Appreciate the importance of using visuals
  in an ethical manner

I n addition to structure and style, the use of audience-centered visuals is one of the four essential elements in technical communication.

THE IMPORTANCE OF USING AUDIENCE-CENTERED VISUALS

Visuals are important in print or digital documents, in oral presentations, and in multimedia programs for several reasons: They help readers interpret and remember complex information; they show how items look or work; and they show how items are organized or actions are performed.

Visuals help readers interpret and remember complex information

Because they focus and organize complex information into more simplified form, visuals make data easier for readers to interpret and remember. Visuals work because readers want more than just raw information; they want the information presented so they can understand it at a glance. Consider, for example, how the following passage might be better presented using a visual:

Technical data in prose form can be hard to interpret

> The time required for the global population to grow from 5 to 6 billion was shorter than the interval between any of the previous billions. It took just 12 years for this to occur, just slightly less than the 13 years between the fourth and fifth billion and the 15 years between the third and fourth billion, but much less time than the 118 years between the first and second billion....

Now consider this same information presented as a graph in Figure 7.1.

FIGURE 7.1
A graph that simplifies complex information

Labels identify key elements (in this case, units of measure)

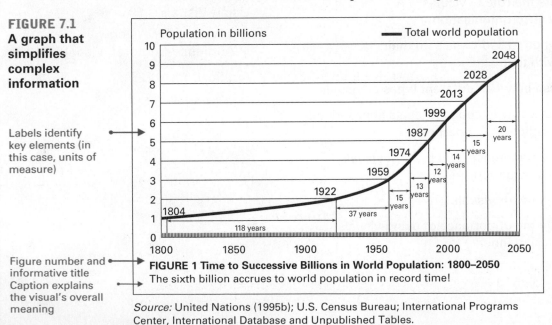

Figure number and informative title
Caption explains the visual's overall meaning

FIGURE 1 Time to Successive Billions in World Population: 1800–2050
The sixth billion accrues to world population in record time!

Source: United Nations (1995b); U.S. Census Bureau; International Programs Center, International Database and Unpublished Tables.

Notice how Figure 7.1 makes it easier to understand and remember the upward population trend and the numerous facts and figures described in the paragraph that precedes it.

Not all visuals are designed to convey numeric or other data. A second reason visuals are important is that they can show readers at a glance what something looks like and/or how it works—as opposed to lengthy descriptions in prose form.

Visuals show readers how items look or work

Visuals that show how items look include illustrations and photographs, while visuals that show how items work include diagrams. For example, the diagram in Figure 7.10 (page 122) illustrates how a safety belt locking mechanism operates. Notice how this diagram is much easier to understand than if the idea were described using text only.

Finally, visuals are important because they can quickly and efficiently show how items are organized or actions are performed, without resorting to long and difficult-to-follow textual explanations. Such visuals include organizational charts and flowcharts. For example, imagine the dense and wordy paragraphs that would be needed to describe the process for helping an adult choking victim, as shown in the flowchart in Figure 7.6 on page 120.

Visuals show readers how items are organized or actions are performed

WHEN TO USE VISUALS

Visuals should be used to enhance your document, not just to decorate it. There may also be organizational reasons for using visuals; for example, some companies may always expect photographs, charts, and graphs as part of an annual report. Certain industries, such as the financial sector, routinely use visuals (such as a line graph showing recent fluctuations in the Dow Jones Industrial Average).

Use visuals to enhance, not decorate

As discussed below, you may choose to use visuals to support the text of your document, or you may choose to use visuals on their own.

Using Visuals to Support Text

Visuals are often an excellent way to support, but not replace, essential discussion in the actual text. For example, you may be writing about an important financial trend, describing features about the world economy, and making a case for financial reforms. A series of graphs or charts would augment, not substitute for, the text. In a situation like that, visuals would add to your discussion.

Use supporting visuals when you want to add to important textual discussion

Be sure to refer to each visual by number ("see Figure 1") in the text. Explain what the visual means; supply a caption for it; and place the visual as close as possible to the text it supports.

For captions, use "Table" for tables; for all other visuals, use "Figure." See, for example, Tables 7.1 and 7.2 versus Figure 7.2 or any of the other figures in this chapter.

TABLE 7.1 A numerical table

Title explains the table's purpose →

Each column has a clear heading →

Numbers are aligned properly for ease of reading →

Where helpful, data are tallied →

Years of Potential Life Lost Before Age 75				
(Per 100,000 population under age 75)				
	Heart Disease		Unintentional Injuries	
Year	Male	Female	Male	Female
1990	2356.0	948.5	1162.1	607.4
2000	1766.0	774.6	1026.5	573.2
2005	1559.0	680.2	1137.2	647.9
2009	1399.2	606.5	1028.2	604.6
2010	1370.8	593.6	1025.2	616.4
% change, 1990–2010	−41.8	−37.4	−11.8	+1.5

A caption explains the numerical relationships →

This table compares years of potential life lost before age 75 due to heart disease and unintentional injury in males and females. In both males and females, years lost due to heart disease decreased between 1990 and 2010. Years lost due to unintentional injury decreased only slightly in males and increased very slightly in females.

Source: Health, United States 2012, from the U.S. National Center on Health Statistics.

TABLE 7.2 A textual table

Title explains the table's purpose →

Each column has a clear heading that leads readers into the information →

Phrases are brief and aligned for ease of reading →

Numbers enhance the verbal information →

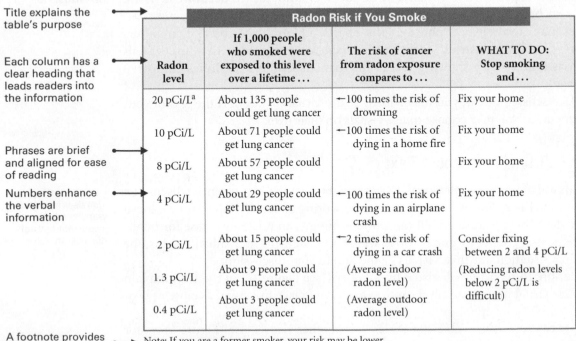

Radon Risk if You Smoke			
Radon level	If 1,000 people who smoked were exposed to this level over a lifetime ...	The risk of cancer from radon exposure compares to ...	WHAT TO DO: Stop smoking and ...
20 pCi/L[a]	About 135 people could get lung cancer	←100 times the risk of drowning	Fix your home
10 pCi/L	About 71 people could get lung cancer	←100 times the risk of dying in a home fire	Fix your home
8 pCi/L	About 57 people could get lung cancer		Fix your home
4 pCi/L	About 29 people could get lung cancer	←100 times the risk of dying in an airplane crash	Fix your home
2 pCi/L	About 15 people could get lung cancer	←2 times the risk of dying in a car crash	Consider fixing between 2 and 4 pCi/L
1.3 pCi/L	About 9 people could get lung cancer	(Average indoor radon level)	(Reducing radon levels below 2 pCi/L is difficult)
0.4 pCi/L	About 3 people could get lung cancer	(Average outdoor radon level)	

A footnote provides more detail →

Note: If you are a former smoker, your risk may be lower.
[a] picocuries per liter

Source: Home Buyer's and Seller's Guide to Radon, by the U.S. Environmental Protection Agency.

Using Visuals on Their Own

In some cases, visuals may work well on their own, as when they make your point more clearly than text can. In situations like these, merely refer to the visuals that show readers what they need to see. For instance, to show how customers who have purchased your company's new plasma televisions break out by age group, don't list the percentages in a lengthy paragraph. Simply supply a chart or graph that conveys these data visually.

Use visuals on their own when textual discussion is not necessary

When you use stand-alone visuals, make sure they tell the whole story you want readers to understand and that you introduce them clearly. If you need to explain how the visual should be interpreted, do so briefly in the figure's caption.

TYPES OF VISUALS

The most commonly used types of visuals are tables, graphs, charts, illustrations, diagrams, photographs, videos, symbols, and icons. The following sections describe each type.

Tables

Tables display organized data or information across columns and rows for easy comparison. Tables can be used to display quantitative information (*numeric tables*) or qualitative information (*textual tables*) or sometimes both. For specific advice on creating tables, see the annotations to Tables 7.1 and 7.2 (page 114) and the Strategies on page 116.

Numeric Tables. Numeric tables simplify complex quantitative information. Although text may be used in headings to organize the table, the primary purpose of the table is to show numbers and their relationships. Note in Table 7.1 how the data are compared in a variety of ways and how a tally of the numbers and an explanatory caption further help readers understand and interpret the data.

Numeric tables focus on quantitative information

Textual Tables. Textual tables simplify complex qualitative information. Numbers may be used to help organize the textual information, but the primary purpose of the textual table is to show written information and relationships. Note how Table 7.2 simplifies written information that would be difficult to explain in paragraph form and uses a footnote to explain a nuance to the reader.

Textual tables focus on qualitative information

▸ **Don't include too much information in a single table.** Overly complex tables are confusing. Limit your table to two or three areas of comparison. Or use multiple tables.

▸ **Provide a brief but descriptive title.** Announce exactly what is being compared.

▸ **Label the rows and columns.**

▸ **Line up data and information clearly.** Use neat columns and rows and plenty of white space between items.

▸ **Keep qualitative information and quantitative data brief.** When including high numbers (more than three digits), abbreviate the numbers and indicate "in thousands," "in millions," and so on. When using text in a table, limit the number of words.

▸ **Provide additional information, if necessary.** Add footnotes or a caption at the bottom of the table to explain anything readers may not understand at first glance.

▸ **Credit your sources.** Unless you collected the data or information yourself, always credit the source (see page 407 for advice on avoiding plagiarism).

Graphs

Graphs translate numbers into shapes, shades, and patterns. At a glance, graphs display the approximate values, the point being made about those values, and the relationship being emphasized. Typically, a graph's horizontal axis shows categories to be compared, such as time periods, while the vertical axis shows the range of values, such as numbers. The most common types of graphs are *bar graphs* (simple or multiple) and *line graphs* (simple or multiple). For specific advice on creating graphs, see the annotations to Figures 7.2 through 7.5 and the Strategies on pages 118–119.

Bar graphs depict changes over time, patterns, and trends

Bar Graphs. Bar graphs present data using colored (or shaded) bars, usually lined up along the horizontal axis. Simple bar graphs depict changes over time, patterns, or trends for a single category. For instance, the simple bar graph in Figure 7.2 shows one trend extracted from Table 7.1, male deaths from heart disease between 1970 and 2006.

Multiple bar graphs, meanwhile, compare two or more categories. For example, the multiple bar graph in Figure 7.3 (also extracted from Table 7.1) shows not only a trend in male deaths from heart disease between 1990 and 2010 but also from cancer during that same period.

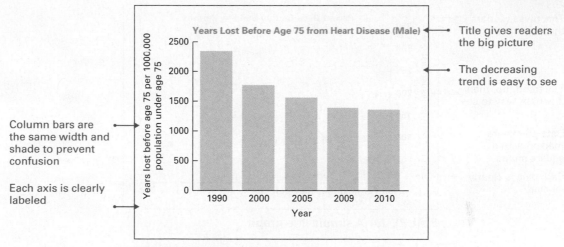

FIGURE 7.2 A simple bar graph

Source: Health, United States 2012, from the U.S. National Center on Health Statistics.

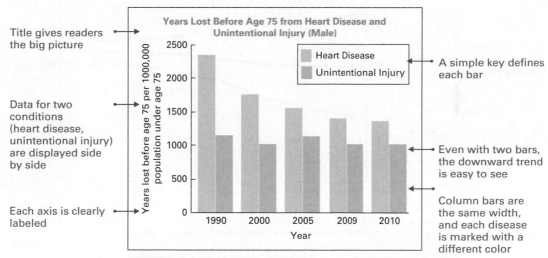

FIGURE 7.3 A multiple bar graph

Source: Health, United States 2012, from the U.S. National Center on Health Statistics.

Line Graphs. Line graphs present data using colored (or shaded) lines, marked at regular intervals so that the data points line up with the items on the horizontal axis. A line graph can accommodate and display more data points than a bar graph. Simple line graphs show changes, patterns, or trends for a single category. In Figure 7.4 the single line tracks the number of building permits issued during the year, showing how permit requests are more common between May and October.

Multiple line graphs display several relationships simultaneously, as in Figure 7.5.

Line graphs can synthesize large quantities of data

Title gives readers the big picture →

The trend (up, then down) is easy to see →

Data points are marked with a square shape →

Each axis is clearly labeled →

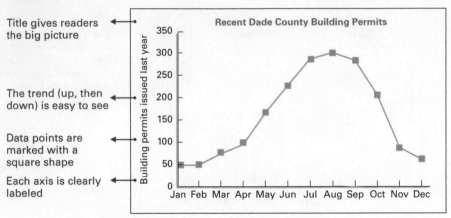

FIGURE 7.4 A simple line graph

Title gives readers the big picture →

The overall trend (moving closer together) is easy to see →

Each axis is clearly labeled →

A short caption helps explain the relationship that the writer wants readers to notice →

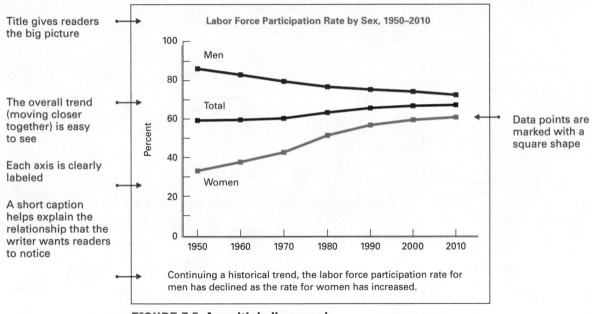

← Data points are marked with a square shape

FIGURE 7.5 A multiple line graph
Source: U.S. Department of Labor.

STRATEGIES
for Creating Graphs

▶ **Use a graph only to compare values that are noticeably different.** A bar graph in which all bars are about the same height or a line graph depicting a single straight line (or overlapping multiple lines) serves no purpose.

▸ **Provide a clear title.** Announce exactly what is being displayed.

▸ **Label both the purpose and divisions of each axis.** Use numbers or gradations that are evenly divided (e.g., multiples of 10, spans of 5 years, months of the year), and add tick marks next to each number/gradation.

▸ **Keep the graph simple and easy to read.** Use no more than three bars (bar graph) or three to four lines (line graph) per graph. Avoid needless details; readers should understand the graph at a glance.

▸ **Make each bar or line distinct.** In multiple bar or line charts, use different colors or shades for each bar or line. Provide a key or label that indicates what each bar or line represents.

▸ **Use consistent format for bars and lines.** In a bar graph, bars should all be of the same width. In a line graph, lines should all be of the same thickness and all data points (those points at which a line intersects with gradations on the horizontal axis) should be marked.

▸ **Credit your sources.** As always, avoid plagiarism by citing the sources of your information or data.

Charts

Charts depict relationships via shapes, arrows, lines, and other design elements. The terms "chart" and "graph" are often used interchangeably; technically, however, a chart displays relationships (quantitative or cause-and-effect) that are not plotted on vertical and horizontal axes. Commonly used charts include *flowcharts, pie charts, and organization charts*. For more specific advice on creating charts, see the annotations to Figures 7.6 through 7.8 and the Strategies on page 121.

Flowcharts. A flowchart traces a process or procedure from beginning to end, moving from top to bottom or from left to right and using connector bars to show relationships, as in Figure 7.6.

Flowcharts show processes and procedures

Pie Charts. Easy for almost anyone to understand, pie charts are circular diagrams that display the status of each "piece" of the "pie"—the percentage of the whole pie (which totals 100%) that each piece represents. Readers can compare the differently colored (or shaded) pieces to each other as well as to the whole. Figure 7.7 shows a basic pie chart comparing major food sources of trans fat for American adults.

Pie charts show proportions among the segments

Organization Charts. An organization chart shows the hierarchy and relationships between different departments and other units in an organization, using a top-down series of boxes connected by arrows, as in Figure 7.8.

Organization charts show relationships between departments or units

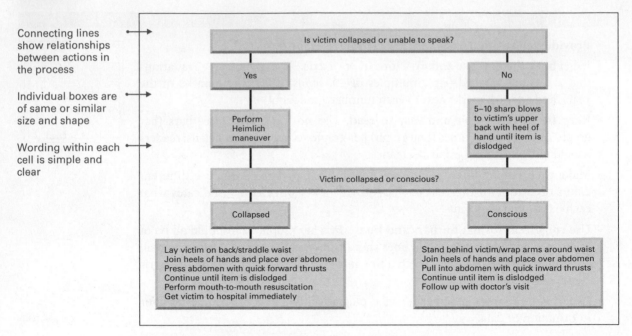

Connecting lines show relationships between actions in the process

Individual boxes are of same or similar size and shape

Wording within each cell is simple and clear

FIGURE 7.6 A flowchart

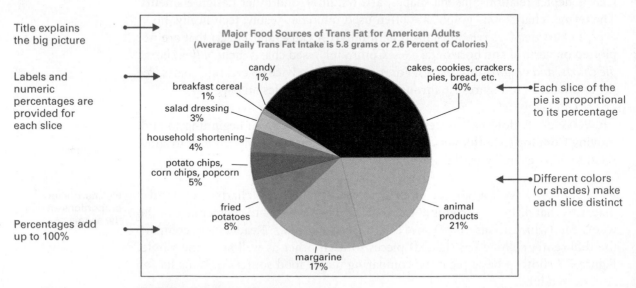

Title explains the big picture

Labels and numeric percentages are provided for each slice

Percentages add up to 100%

FIGURE 7.7 A pie chart
Source: U.S. Food and Drug Administration.

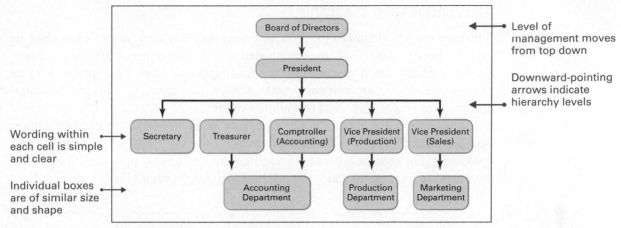

FIGURE 7.8 An organization chart

STRATEGIES
for Creating Charts

For all types of charts, provide a clear title and credit your sources.

► **Flowcharts**

- **Move from top to bottom or left to right.** The process must start at the top (top-to-bottom chart) or left (left-to-right chart).

- **Use connector lines.** Show relationships between parts of the process.

- **Keep boxes uniform and text brief.** See the tips for organization charts below.

► **Pie charts**

- **Make sure the parts of the pie add up to 100%.**

- **Differentiate and label each slice clearly.** Use different colors or shades for each slice, and label the category and percentage of each slice.

- **Keep all labels horizontal.** Make the chart easy to read.

- **Combine very small pie slices.** Group categories with very small percentages under "other."

► **Organization charts**

- **Move from top to bottom or left to right.** Place the highest level of hierarchy at the top (top-to-bottom chart) or at the left (left-to-right chart).

- **Use downward- or rightward-pointing arrows.** Arrows show the flow of hierarchy from highest to lowest.

- **Keep boxes uniform and text brief.** Shape may vary slightly according to how much text is in each box. Maintain a uniform look. Avoid too much text in any box.

Illustrations and Diagrams

Illustrations and diagrams rely on drawings and sketches rather than data or words, though some words may be needed to point out names, parts, or purposes. In some cases, even if you attempt the most accurate prose description, only an illustration or diagram can show what it is you are trying to explain. Technical illustrations accomplish what text alone cannot.

Illustrations and diagrams are especially valuable when you need to convey spatial relationships or help readers visualize what an item or process actually looks like. For specific advice on creating illustrations and diagrams, see the annotations to Figures 7.9 and 7.10 and the Strategies on page 125.

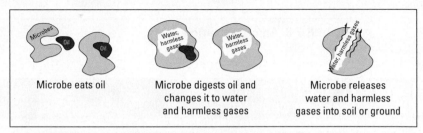

Microbe eats oil   Microbe digests oil and   Microbe releases
                        changes it to water   water and harmless
                        and harmless gases   gases into soil or ground

FIGURE 7.9 An illustration
Source: Environmental Protection Agency. Information available at <www.epa.gov/superfund/sites> or <www.cluin.org>.

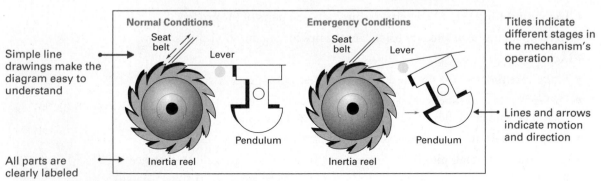

Simple line drawings make the diagram easy to understand

All parts are clearly labeled

Titles indicate different stages in the mechanism's operation

Lines and arrows indicate motion and direction

FIGURE 7.10 A diagram
Source: Department of Transportation.

Illustrations show what something looks like

Illustrations. An illustration shows with accuracy what something looks like. Impressive-looking visuals are easy to create by using electronic drawing programs or by locating clip art and other images online. However, more complex illustrations or those suited to your exact needs generally require the services of graphic artists or technical illustrators. See, for example, how the illustration in Figure 7.9 (taken from the document in Figure 1.3) provides a clear visual picture of the bioremediation process.

If you are unable to locate an illustration that points out just the parts of a product, process, or other item you want to display, you may need a professional illustrator. However, the variety of illustrations available online grows every day.

Diagrams. Unlike illustrations, which simply show what something looks like, diagrams show how parts of an object fit together or how mechanisms operate. For example, the diagram of a safety belt locking mechanism in Figure 7.10 portrays the mechanism in operation by juxtaposing "normal conditions" and "emergency conditions."

Diagrams show how parts fit or operate

Among the many types of diagrams, three of the most common are *exploded diagrams* (which separate parts of an object while showing how the parts fit together), *cutaway diagrams* (which show the interior of an object by "cutting away" the shell), and *maps.*

Photographs

Although photographs are obviously more realistic than illustrations and diagrams (which often highlight certain parts of an object), photographs can provide *too much* detail or fail to emphasize the parts you want viewers to focus on.

Photographs show an ultra-realistic view

Many people take their own digital photographs and then use software to crop the image for proper emphasis. For basic documents circulated to a small group inside a department or organization, this can be fine. But for important documents circulated to high-level audiences inside or outside an organization, use professionally taken photographs.

If you locate photographs online, be sure to credit your sources. You also need to request permission if your document will be printed and circulated. For more advice on taking and altering photographs, see the annotations to Figure 7.11 and the Strategies on page 125.

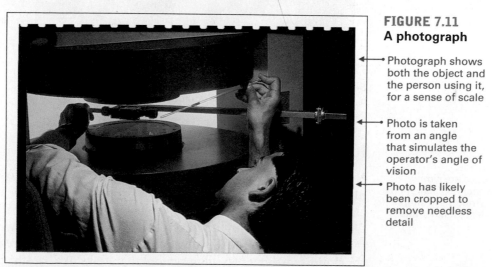

**FIGURE 7.11
A photograph**

- Photograph shows both the object and the person using it, for a sense of scale
- Photo is taken from an angle that simulates the operator's angle of vision
- Photo has likely been cropped to remove needless detail

Source: Charles Orrico/SuperStock.

Videos

Videos show a full-motion view

Until recently, workplace videos were typically used for training and safety purposes only and were filmed by outside professionals. Today, with the advent of YouTube and similar sites, as well as the ease of filming by using a small video camera or even a cell phone, organizations are using videos to supplement traditional documents such as user manuals. For instance, the video frame captured in Figure 7.12 is from a set of video instructions for a product called Dust-Aid (used to clean dust from the camera sensor of a digital SLR camera). The principles for using videos are similar to those for photographs, except that videos are altered via editing rather than cropping. For more advice, see the annotations to Figure 7.12, the Strategies on page 125, and Chapter 20.

Video is taken from an angle that simulates the angle of vision of an in-person learner

Video shows both the object and the person using it, for a sense of scale

Full motion helps people see how to perform a task

FIGURE 7.12 A video frame

Source: From "Dust-Aid: DSLR Camera Sensor Cleaning Video" by Ross Wordhouse from www.youtube.com. Reproduced by permission.

Icons and Symbols

Icons are simple concrete illustrations; symbols are simple abstract illustrations

Icons and symbols use simple illustrations that reduce a concept or item to its most basic, understandable level. The words *icon* and *symbol* are often used interchangeably. But icons resemble the items they represent (for instance, an icon of a file folder on your computer that looks like a real file folder), whereas symbols get the meaning across without resembling the items they represent (for example, a skull-and-crossbones warning symbol that looks like "death" but gets the "do not

Simplicity of the drawings reduces any chance for confusion

The first three images are icons (representative); the last two are symbols (abstract)

FIGURE 7.13 Internationally recognized icons and symbols

ingest/poison" message across or a cross that symbolizes not "cross" but "medical help"). Because these types of illustrations generally do not rely on text, they are more easily understood by international audiences, children, and people who have difficulty reading. For specific advice on using icons and symbols, see the annotations to Figure 7.13 and the Strategies below.

STRATEGIES
for Illustrations, Diagrams, Photographs, Videos, Icons, and Symbols

For all such visuals, always credit the source if not self-created, and seek permission if reproduced and circulated.

▸ **Illustrations**

- **Use illustrations that are easy to interpret.** Avoid illustrations that distort an object's actual appearances.

- **Show only those parts that your viewers need to see.**

- **Label each important part.**

▸ **Diagrams**

- **Provide clear explanations.** Explain how diagram parts fit together or operate.

- **Use lines and arrows to indicate direction and motion.** For diagrams that show action, directional markers help viewers understand the action.

- **Keep diagram illustrations simple.** Merely show viewers what they need to see.

- **Label each important part.**

▸ **Photographs**

- **Provide a sense of scale.** Try to show the object and a person using it, a ruler, or a hand.

- **Simulate the viewer's angle of vision.** Consider how your readers would need to view the item.

→

- **Crop out needless details.**
- **Label key parts.** A simple photograph may not need labels, but a more complicated photograph should have essential parts labeled.

▸ **Videos**

- **Provide a sense of scale.** Try to show the object and a person using it (or a ruler or a hand).
- **Show only what the viewer needs to see.** For example, in a video of a long procedure, focus on just the part of the procedure that's most relevant.
- **Edit out needless detail.** If you have editing software, shorten the video to include only the essentials.
- **Avoid excess outside or office noise when recording sound.**

▸ **Icons and Symbols**

- **Use icons and symbols sparingly.** Use them only when directly appropriate, say, to supplement textual warnings or instructions.
- **Use internationally recognized icons and symbols.** Some icons and symbols may not convey your intended meaning in other cultures.

SPECIAL CONSIDERATIONS WHEN USING VISUALS

Once you are aware of the variety of visuals at your disposal, select those most appropriate for your audience and purpose, and consider how to integrate them within your document.

Selecting Appropriate Visuals

When selecting visuals for any document, first ask yourself this question: Who is my audience, and what do audience members need to know?

Generally speaking, expert audiences tend to prefer numerical tables, complex graphs and charts, and diagrams that they can interpret for themselves. Nonexpert audiences tend to prefer basic tables, graphs, and charts, uncomplicated illustrations and diagrams, and other visuals that direct their focus and interpret key points for them. If your audience is a combination of experts and nonexperts, you should err on the side of the nonexperts.

Also be aware that your audience may include international readers or North American readers from different cultural backgrounds. When choosing icons or symbols, use those that are internationally recognized (when in doubt, check the

Special audience considerations

International Organization for Standardization's Web site). Also keep your visuals (including text within visuals) simple and basic and avoid images and colors that might unintentionally offend people from other cultures. If you are knowingly writing to members of a particular culture or nationality, search online for more background on that audience.

Consider how each visual advances your purpose. For example, don't decide to use a bar chart just because you like its professional appearance; make sure the information or data you want to present are best served via a bar chart. Following are additional suggestions for fitting a visual to its purpose:

- To simplify complex numerical data or textual information, use a table.

- To get your audience to draw conclusions from facts and figures, use a graph or a chart that shows comparisons.

- To show how parts make up the whole, use a pie chart.

- To show hierarchy and relationships in an organization, use an organization chart.

- To show steps in a process from beginning to end, use a flowchart.

- To show what something looks like, use an illustration or photograph.

- To show how parts fit together or operate, use a diagram or a photograph depicting a process.

Consider the purpose of each visual

Placing, Cross-Referencing, and Presenting Visuals

Place your visuals where they best serve the needs of your readers: as close as possible to the related discussion if they are central to that discussion or in an appendix if they are peripheral to your discussion. Introduce your visuals within the text by referring to them by number (Figure 1, Table 4, etc.) and explaining what they mean (e.g., "As Figure 3.4 shows…"), making sure that the figure and table numbers match the cross-references in the text. See the sample formal report on page 320 for an example of a table used as part of a larger document. Make your visuals user-friendly in their presentation by framing them with plenty of white space, eliminating visual "noise" (excessive lines, bars, numbers, and inessential information), and sizing each visual for the right proportion and emphasis on the page.

Place visuals close to their related topic in the text

Using Color in Visuals

Color focuses reader attention and helps readers identify various elements of a visual. Most of the software you will use to create visuals (e.g., Excel, PowerPoint) automatically adds color to charts and graphs. In an illustration or diagram you can highlight particular areas by using color against a more subdued background.

Color helps focus your reader's attention

When color is not available, try using grayscale shades. In some visuals, however, grayscale may not be effective; for example, in a pie chart with numerous "slices" (see Figure 7.7), using slight gradations of gray may cause the slices to blend too closely. Likewise, in a multiple bar chart or multiple line chart (see Figures 7.3 and 7.4) you will want to sharply differentiate bars and lines. For more information on using color, see Chapter 8.

Using Visuals Ethically

Always present the real and complete picture

Although you are perfectly justified in presenting data in its best light, you are responsible for avoiding misrepresentation. The golden rule of using visuals ethically is to always present the real and complete picture.

Some ways in which visuals can be distorted

Following are some of the ways in which visuals can be distorted: using inaccurately sized slices in a pie chart misrepresents the true percentages; leaving out essential information from a table, chart, or graph doesn't give readers the true picture of what's happening; inflating or reducing the size of illustrations or photographs can make items appear more or less important than they actually are. When creating visuals, take care to convey and explain information accurately.

☑ **CHECKLIST** for Using Audience-Centered Visuals   MyWritingLab™

- ☐ Have I looked for parts of the document that contain numeric or other data that would be best conveyed as a visual?
- ☐ Is the visual located near the text and have I referenced the visual within the text (for example, "See Figure 1 on page 9")?
- ☐ Are my visuals easy to understand at a glance?
- ☐ Are my visuals accurate and not distorted in any way?
- ☐ Have I considered each type of visual and determined the most appropriate?

TABLES

- ☐ Am I using a table to compare data or other information?
- ☐ Is the table clear and uncluttered?
- ☐ Can readers make easy comparisons of the data in the table?
- ☐ Are rows and columns clearly labeled?

→

GRAPHS

☐ Am I using a graph to depict patterns, trends, or changes over time?

☐ Will a bar graph or a line graph be more effective for these data?

☐ Am I using color effectively but not overwhelmingly?

☐ Is each bar or line distinct and easy to distinguish?

CHARTS

☐ Am I using a chart to illustrate relationships of parts to a larger whole?

☐ In a flowchart is the flow easy to follow and are all boxes connected?

☐ In an organization chart are the titles/names clear and easy to read?

☐ In a pie chart do the slices of the pie add up to 100%?

ILLUSTRATIONS, DIAGRAMS, AND PHOTOGRAPHS

☐ Are the illustrations sufficiently clear without being too detailed?

☐ Do all illustrations and diagrams have a title or explanation?

☐ Is the quality of my photographs sufficient for viewers to see what I am trying to illustrate?

☐ Am I using any symbols or icons sparingly?

APPLICATIONS

GENERAL APPLICATIONS   MyWritingLab™

1. Display the following information in the visual format most appropriate for a particular audience. Describe that audience and explain why you selected the type of visual as most effective for that audience. Include with the visual a caption that interprets and explains the data.

   Data: Assume that the Department of Energy breaks down energy consumption in the United States (by source) into these percentages: In 1970, coal, 18.5; natural gas, 32.8; hydro and geothermal, 3.1; nuclear, 1.2; oil, 44.4. In 1980, coal, 20.3; natural gas, 26.9; hydro and geothermal, 3.8; nuclear, 4.0; oil, 45.0. In 1990, coal, 23.5; natural gas, 23.8; hydro and geothermal, 7.3; nuclear, 4.1; oil, 41.3. In 2000, coal, 20.3; natural gas, 25.2; hydro and geothermal, 9.6; nuclear, 6.3; oil, 38.6.

2. Find an article in a newspaper, in a journal, or on the Web that lacks the visuals necessary to support the purpose of the article or the needs of its readers. Analyze the article and identify where visuals would be helpful. Make a list of the visuals you would recommend. Pick one visual from your list and create it. Does the article contain all the data or information you need to create the visual?

3. Devise a pie chart to depict your yearly expenses. Title the chart and be prepared to discuss it in class.

TEAM APPLICATIONS

1. As a team, obtain enrollment figures at your college for the past five years by gender, age, race, or any other pertinent category. Construct a bar graph to illustrate one of these relationships over the five years.

2. As a team, decide what would be the most appropriate visual for illustrating this relationship: a comparison of three top brands of skis, according to cost, weight, durability, and edge control. In groups of two, create this visual, then compare approaches. Why did one group choose one type of visual over another?

GLOBAL APPLICATION   MyWritingLab™

The International Organization for Standardization (ISO) is a group devoted to standardizing a range of material, including technical specifications and visual information. If you've ever been in an airport and seen the many international signs directing travelers to the restroom or informing them not to smoke, you have seen ISO signs. Go to the ISO Web site to learn about ISO icons and symbols. Show some of the icons and symbols, and explain why these work for international audiences.

DIGITAL AND SOCIAL MEDIA APPLICATION   MyWritingLab™

Digital communication relies heavily on the use of images. Find the Facebook page for a government agency (such as NASA) or for an organization at your college or university (such as a student club or department). Using the Checklist on pages 128–129 in this chapter, analyze the page's use of visuals. Write a short memo to your instructor presenting your findings.

MyWritingLab™   Visit Chapter 7, *Using Audience-Centered Visuals*, in MyWritingLab to complete this chapter's applications, to explore this chapter's overview, checklist, and flashcards, and to test your understanding of the chapter objectives.

8 Designing User-Friendly Documents

CHAPTER OUTLINE

The Importance of User-Friendly Document Design *132*

Characteristics of Well-Designed Documents *133*

Specific Design Elements *135*

STRATEGIES for Designing: Consistency and Cohesiveness *139*

STRATEGIES for Designing: Navigation and Emphasis *144*

CHECKLIST for Document Design *145*

Applications *146*

LEARNING OBJECTIVES FOR THIS CHAPTER

▶ Understand the importance of document design

▶ Identify and create well-designed documents

▶ Use design elements for consistency and coherence

▶ Use design elements for navigation and emphasis

Design, the layout of words and graphics, determines the look of a document. Whether hard copy or digital, well-designed pages invite readers in, guide them through the material, and help them understand and remember the information.

This chapter provides principles and guidelines that are generally applicable across many media types (print, digital). See Chapter 19 for more on blogs, wikis, and Web pages.

THE IMPORTANCE OF USER-FRIENDLY DOCUMENT DESIGN

Design affects a document's usability

Like all decisions about technical communication, document design consists of a series of informed choices. You need to decide about fonts, typography, white space, and other visual elements, based on the document's audience and purpose. These decisions affect the usability of the document.

Imagine that you are asked to produce a heart surgery brochure for a hospital. The brochure's intended audience consists of patients who have a particular heart condition and may need to undergo a specific type of heart surgery. The brochure's purpose is to explain the procedure, answer frequently asked questions, and review the risks—while reassuring patients.

Begin by analyzing your audience and purpose

Determine your document's usability requirements by doing a task analysis

Before you would even begin to think about what to write or how to design the document, you would need to do an audience and purpose analysis (see Chapter 3). If the brochure also needed to include a list of tasks, such as a checklist of actions patients must take, you might also conduct a task analysis (explained in Chapter 3). Your analysis would yield much important information. For example, you are likely to determine the following as the most important outcomes for the document:

1. To reassure fearful patients that the surgery is safe and that the recovery rate is quicker than that of many other types of heart surgery.

2. To ensure that readers are able to understand what they need to do before, during, and after the surgery.

3. To make certain that older patients—who make up the largest population of candidates for this surgery and who sometimes have poor eyesight—are able to read the document.

Design the document to meet reader needs

To reassure fearful patients, you could choose a comforting typeface, a warm color scheme, and plenty of white space to give the brochure an unimposing look. To ensure that patients understand the steps involved you could use numbered and bulleted lists to break up and simplify the various procedures. To make the document more readable for older patients, you could use a large font size. To make the document accessible to as many readers as possible, you could design print copies for a doctor's waiting room and a PDF version for the Web site.

Document design, like all aspects of technical communication, puts audience and purpose first.

CHARACTERISTICS OF WELL-DESIGNED DOCUMENTS

Readers appreciate documents that are well designed because such documents make it easy and pleasant for people to access and use the information they need. Well-designed documents typically have four characteristics: they are inviting and accessible; they flow well as a single, cohesive unit; they provide a visual hierarchy, displaying information in the right order; they address a diversity of readers. Figure 8.1 does not meet those requirements, while Figure 8.2 (a revision of the same document) does.

Four audience expectations of a document's design

People generally read technical documents only because they have to. They may pick up a document because they need information, as in the heart surgery brochure described above, or they may be presented with a document they

Readers expect an inviting and accessible design

Mold is a public health problem. Molds are simple organisms that are found virtually everywhere, indoors and outdoors. The potential health effects of indoor mold are a growing concern. Mold can cause or worsen certain illnesses (e.g., some allergic and occupation-related diseases and infections in health care settings). There is not conclusive evidence, however, about whether indoor mold is associated with a multitude of other health problems, such as pulmonary hemorrhage, memory loss, and lack of energy.

The Centers for Disease Control has accomplished much on the problem. The CDC has a mold Web site (http://www.cdc.gov/nceh/airpollution/mold) that provides information on molds and health and links to resources. In conjunction with the Council of State and Territorial Epidemiologists, the CDC has created an inventory of state indoor air quality programs which is available at http://www.cdc.gov/nceh.airpollution/indoor_air.htm. The CDC assists states in responding to mold-related issues, including offering technical assistance with assessment, cleanup efforts, and prevention of further mold growth and unnecessary exposure. The CDC is strengthening state, local and tribal capacity to respond to mold-related issues, including: determining the extent to which state programs establish coordinated responses to indoor mold exposures, working with federal and other organizations to coordinate plans related to indoor air and mold, developing a coordinated public response strategy, and identifying resources for developing and implementing responses. The CDC is also developing an agenda for research, service, and education related to mold. As a first step, the CDC contracted with the Institute of Medicine (IOM) to conduct a study on the relationship between damp or moldy indoor environments and the manifestation of adverse health effects and to provide recommendations for future research. The CDC's mold-related agenda is expected to address subjects such as the following: characterizing environmental conditions that allow mold growth indoors and the association between indoor mold and disease or illness; improving the capacity of state, local, and tribal health departments to prevent, investigate, and control mold exposures; and conducting and supporting research to define the association between damp or moldy indoor environments and harmful health effects.

The next steps the CDC will take include assisting states and others in responding to mold issues and developing an agenda for research, service, and education related to mold as described above. For more information, visit http://www.cdc.gov/nceh/airpollution/mold.

Document is untitled and provides no visual hierarchy: everything looks equal

Small margins make the document look crowded

Unbroken paragraph looks dense and intimidating

Inadequate white space makes this version hard on the eye

FIGURE 8.1 Ineffective page design

Even from a distance, readers can see the document as a cohesive, single unit

Title, headings, and bullets provide a visual hierarchy

Ample margins and white space give the document an open, accessible look

Bulleted list breaks up dense paragraph

Document is available in PDF and can be viewed on a screen or printed on paper

Simple use of second color for Web address and headings helps readers focus on essential information

Hyperlink allows readers of a PDF version to navigate to more information

---

CDC ™   **PROGRAM IN BRIEF**

Mold

WHAT IS THE PUBLIC HEALTH PROBLEM?

Molds are simple organisms that are found virtually everywhere, indoors and outdoors. The potential health effects of indoor mold are a growing concern. Mold can cause or worsen certain illnesses (e.g., some allergic and occupation-related diseases and infections in health care settings). There is not conclusive evidence, however, about whether indoor mold is associated with a multitude of other health problems, such as pulmonary hemorrhage, memory loss, and lack of energy.

WHAT HAS CDC ACCOMPLISHED?

- CDC's Mold Web site (http://www.cdc.gov/mold) provides information on molds and health and links to resources. In conjunction with the Council of State and Territorial Epidemiologists, CDC has created an inventory of state indoor air quality programs, which is available at http://www.cdc.gov/nceh/airpollution/indoor_air.htm.
- CDC assists states in responding to mold-related issues, including offering technical assistance with assessment, cleanup efforts, and prevention of further mold growth and unnecessary exposure.
- CDC is strengthening state, local, and tribal capacity to respond to mold-related issues, including (1) determining the extent to which state programs establish coordinated responses to indoor mold exposures; (2) working with federal and other organizations to coordinate plans related to indoor air and mold; (3) developing a coordinated public response strategy; and (4) identifying resources for developing and implementing responses.
- CDC is developing an agenda for research, service, and education related to mold. As a first step, CDC contracted with the Institute of Medicine (IOM) to conduct a study on the relationship between damp or moldy indoor environments and the manifestation of adverse health effects and to provide recommendations for future research. CDC's mold-related agenda is expected to address subjects such as the following:
  - Characterizing environmental conditions that allow mold growth indoors and the association between indoor mold and disease or illness;
  - Improving the capacity of state, local, and tribal health departments to prevent, investigate, and control mold exposures;
  - Conducting and supporting research to define the association between damp or moldy indoor environments and harmful health effects.

WHAT ARE THE NEXT STEPS?

CDC will continue to assist states and others in responding to mold issues and develop an agenda for research, service, and education related to ***mold*** as described above.

For more information, visit http://www.cdc.gov/mold.

DEPARTMENT OF HEALTH AND HUMAN SERVICES
CENTERS FOR DISEASE CONTROL AND PREVENTION
SAFER·HEALTHIER·PEOPLE™

FIGURE 8.2 Effective redesign of Figure 8.1
Source: Centers for Disease Control and Prevention.

are required to read for work. Either way, readers will resist a document that is intimidating or hard to read and will try to get the information in some other way (e.g., going online to find a more straightforward presentation or asking a colleague or the writer for clarification).

Various types of software can help with document design, but all the software in the world won't help unless writers understand basic principles of visual appeal and accessibility.

Notice how Figure 8.1 presents a barrage of information with absolutely no design elements, making the information needlessly intimidating, unappealing, and hard to grasp. In contrast, Figure 8.2 uses a clear title, margins, white space, bullets, headings, and color to present the same information in a much more open, inviting, and accessible manner.

Generally, readers view a document first as a whole unit, scanning the page quickly to get a sense of the overall layout. Even from a distance, without being able to read the text, readers should be able to answer the question "How is this document structured?" Design elements help readers answer that question.

Readers appreciate a design that works as a single, cohesive unit

Consider how Figure 8.1 tells readers nothing about how the document works as a unit—it is simply a page full of text. Figure 8.2, on the other hand, has a purpose (as indicated by a title), moves from point A to point B (as indicated by the headings), and presents a list of specific facts (as indicated by the bullets).

Readers also expect the document to highlight the most important information. In other words, they expect the document's design to help them determine the *visual hierarchy* of the information, displayed primarily through the level and design of the headings and the inclusion of numbered or bulleted lists.

Readers appreciate a design that forms a visual hierarchy

Notice how Figure 8.1 provides no visual hierarchy. It simply offers a series of paragraphs, each seemingly offering information of equal importance. In contrast, Figure 8.2 offers a clear hierarchy of information. All three headed sections are of equal importance, and so the headers are designed identically (same font, font size, and color). The bulleted items fall into two levels of detail: general and specific (the more specific bulleted items are indented further in a different style of bullet).

A document's design can also affect its multicultural appeal. For instance, a certain color might be interpreted differently by different readers. As a rule, use subtle and varied colors, standard fonts and font sizes, and appropriate white space.

Readers appreciate a design that takes a wide range of people into account

SPECIFIC DESIGN ELEMENTS

The elements of document design comprise two categories: those that give a document a consistent and cohesive look and those that aid navigation and add emphasis. No design elements should be merely decorative; all should enhance the reader's orientation and understanding.

Designing for Consistency and Cohesiveness

Elements that provide consistency and cohesiveness include grid patterns, margins, paragraphs, justification, white space, line spacing and indentation, font style, and font size. Each element is described below and summarized in the Strategies on pages 139–140.

Grid Patterns. Grid patterns help readers make sense of a document as a single unit because they create an underlying structure throughout the document. Figure 8.3 shows a sampling of grid patterns.Most documents follow a standard horizontal grid pattern, as, for example, a memo or letter. A vertical grid is commonly used in manuals, brochures, or newsletters. In rare cases, you may want to use a combined grid pattern.

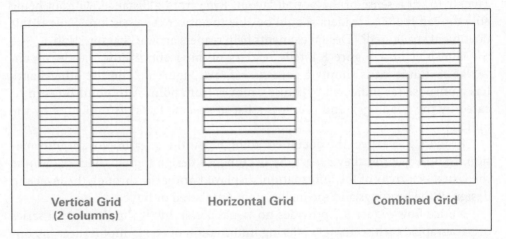

Vertical Grid
(2 columns)   Horizontal Grid   Combined Grid

FIGURE 8.3 Grid patterns

Margins. Consistent margins give the document a unified appearance. Margins must not only be the same width throughout a document but also wide enough. Narrow margins crowd the page and make the material look harder than it probably is. On your 8½-by-11-inch page, provide margins of at least 1 or 1½ inches on each side, as well as at the top and bottom, of every page. If the manuscript is to be bound in a cover, increase the left (inside) margin to 2 inches.

Paragraphs. Whereas ordering information within paragraphs (as discussed in Chapter 5) affects a document's overall structure, the shape of each paragraph serves a design function.Use a long paragraph (but try to keep it to 15 lines or less) for clustering material that is closely related or best understood in one block; use short paragraphs for making complex material more digestible (as in step-by-step instructions or for emphasizing vital information). At the same time, try to vary the lengths of your paragraphs. Readers are likely to resist a document that consists primarily of long or short paragraphs only. Also, avoid "orphans" (one line of a paragraph at the bottom of a page) and "widows" (one line of a paragraph at the top of a page).

Justification. Text is always automatically flush left (lined up evenly along the left margin). However, along the right margin, you have a choice between *justified* text (even right margins) or *unjustified* text (uneven or "ragged" right margins). Each arrangement creates its own feel.

In justified text, blocks of text look clean and even on either side, but spacing varies between words and letters on a line, and you may need to frequently hyphenate words. Justified text is generally used in books, annual reports, and other formal materials. In unjustified text, text is ragged on the right side of text blocks, but spacing between words and letters on a line is even, and you can avoid overuse of hyphenation.Unjustified text is appropriate for more personal forms of communication, such as letters, memos, and in-house reports. Whichever justification you choose be consistent throughout the document. Figure 8.4 illustrates justified and unjustified text.

According to the chart in Figure 3, the population of Queens County, New York, remains the most diverse in the United States. Historically, particular populations have been concentrated in particular areas. For example, Long Island has long been known as a largely Latino area, Woodside as mostly Asian and Middle eastern, and Jamaica as primarily African and Caribbean. However, over the last 15 years, these concentrations have become less cogent.
— Right and left justified text (from a formal report)

In order for this new initiative to be a success, we ask for the support and participation of every employee of the company. Please take a moment to review the enclosed list of training sessions, which will begin on August 24th. We strongly suggest that you sign up for at least one session during the first month to get an overview of the initiative, then take intermediate and advanced sessions in the upcoming months.
— Left-only justified text (from a memo)

FIGURE 8.4 Justified and unjustified text

White Space. Sometimes, it's what's *not* on the page that makes a difference. Whereas margins are the empty spaces along the left, right, top, and bottom of a document, white space is any empty space surrounding figures and tables, between columns, and between paragraphs. Areas of text or visuals surrounded by appropriate white space draw the reader's eye to those areas.Well-designed white space is used evenly throughout an entire document, orienting readers by keeping related elements together, isolating and emphasizing important elements, and providing breathing room between blocks of information, as in Figure 8.5.

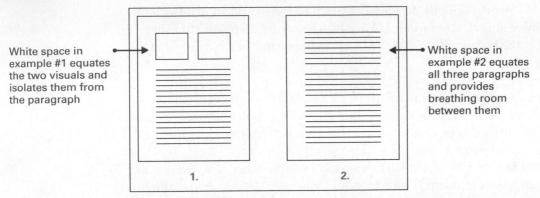

White space in example #1 equates the two visuals and isolates them from the paragraph

White space in example #2 equates all three paragraphs and provides breathing room between them

FIGURE 8.5 White space

Line Spacing and Indentation. Always be consistent about line spacing. In most technical documents, use double spacing for ease of reading. When inserting a long quotation, indent the quotation, use single spacing within the quotation only, then return to double spacing for regular text. Also be consistent about indentation. As a general rule, indent each paragraph unless you insert an extra line space between paragraphs.

Font Style. Font style refers to the typeface used and the personality that each typeface conveys. Fonts fall into several categories: *Serif* fonts (such as Times New Roman and Palatino) include serifs, or fine lines that extend horizontally from the main strokes of a letter. Serif fonts are generally considered more formal. *Sans-serif* fonts (such as Helvetica and Arial) do not include these fine lines ("sans" is French for "without"). They tend to look professional without being quite as formal as serif fonts and are appropriate for most other types of technical documents. *Decorative fonts* are often used in advertising and marketing but should be avoided in technical documents. Figure 8.6 shows the differences between these font styles. Pick an appropriate font and stick with it throughout a document. For headings, you might select a different font (and a larger size), but use those heading fonts consistently as well.

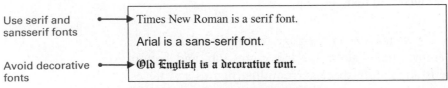

Use serif and sansserif fonts

Times New Roman is a serif font.

Arial is a sans-serif font.

Avoid decorative fonts

Old English is a decorative font.

FIGURE 8.6 Sample font styles

Italics, **boldface**, and ALL CAPS are another element of font style you need to consider. Sometimes people use italics much as they would use a highlighter or marker, to set words apart and draw attention to these words. But excessive use of italics can make it hard for your audience to decide which information is truly important. The same is true for boldface: Too much bold will lose its appeal. Bold is good for headings, subheadings, or terms or concepts in a sentence that you want to emphasize. Within text, use bold selectively. Use all-capital letters for a few words only or when creating short headings. Long strings of capital (upper-case) letters and words are hard to read.

Font Size. Use font sizes that are easy to read. Standard guidelines suggest using between a 10-point and 12-point font size for the text of most documents (usually erring to the side of 12-point). Use a 2-point-larger font for each level of headings (see page 140). Most important, be consistent throughout the document.

STRATEGIES
for Designing: Consistency and Cohesiveness

GRID PATTERNS

► **Select an appropriate grid pattern.** Use a horizontal grid pattern for most basic documents (memos, letters, reports). Use a vertical grid pattern for specialized documents (manuals, brochures, and newsletters).Use a combined pattern rarely.

► **Use the same grid pattern throughout the document.**

MARGINS

► **Use adequate margins.** Use a 1-inch to 1½-inch margin along the top, bottom, left, and right of the page. For bound documents, use a 2-inch inside margin.

► **Use the same margins throughout the document.**

PARAGRAPHS

► **Vary the length of paragraphs.** Use long and short paragraphs as appropriate to keep blocks of related text together.

► **Avoid orphans and widows.** Add extra space to bump orphans to the next page, and reduce space (or shorten paragraph content) to pull widows to the previous page.

JUSTIFICATION

► **Determine if your text will be justified on one or both margins.** Use justified left and right for formal documents, and use left-only justified (ragged right margin) for less formal documents (memos, letters, in-house reports, and so on).

► **Use the same justification throughout the document.**

WHITE SPACE

► **Use plenty of white space.** Use white space between paragraphs and/or columns and around visuals, when appropriate.

▸ **Use white space consistently.** If you include white space between paragraphs or columns, use the same amount throughout the document. Include the same amount of white space around each visual in the document.

LINE SPACING AND INDENTATION

▸ **Decide how you want to use line spacing and indentation.** Use single, double, or other (for instance, 1½) line spacing. Indent all paragraphs or none.

▸ **Stick with your original plan.** Don't vary the line spacing or paragraph indentation. Be consistent.

FONT STYLE

▸ **Use either a serif or sans-serif font.** Prefer a serif font for formal reports and a sans-serif font for most other documents.

▸ **Decide which serif or sans-serif font to use.** Some of the most popular serif fonts are Times New Roman and Times. The most popular sans-serif font is Helvetica.

▸ **Stay with the same font throughout.** You might choose a different font for any headings in your document.

▸ **Use italics, boldface, and ALL CAPS selectively and sparingly.**

FONT SIZE

▸ **Use a standard font size.** Generally, a 10-point to 12-point size (depending on the font style) should be used for text and a slightly larger size for each level of heading.

▸ **Use a consistent font size.** Stay with the font size you've chosen for each element (text, headings, notes) throughout the document.

Designing for Navigation and Emphasis

Elements that aid navigation and add emphasis include headings; color, shading, boldface, italic, and underlining; bulleted and numbered lists; running heads and feet; and tables of contents and indexes.

Headings. Headings not only help chunk information into easily digestible parts (structure, see Chapter 5) but also guide readers through a page and signal the relative importance of topics. Readers often will move back and forth in a document, searching for the sections that seem most relevant, or they will scan only the main headings, skipping the lower-level headings. To help readers navigate, design your headings consistently.

Headings generally break down into A-level (major headings), B-level (secondary headings, which always fall beneath A-level headings), and C-level (minor headings, which always fall beneath B-level headings). Each higher level of heading should encompass at least two heads at the next lower level. Lower levels of headings (D-level, etc.) make a document appear hard to navigate. Use bulleted or numbered lists instead.

Levels and design of headings

Always use the same font style, size, and color at each level. Avoid orphans (headings that stand alone at the bottom of a page without any text beneath them). Notice how the headings are set up in Figure 8.2 (page 134). The A-level heading ("Mold") uses a bold font, larger than the other fonts. B-level heads are in all caps and boldface and italics, set above each paragraph. Instead of using headings, C-level entries use bullets and are indented. These C-level entries could also be set up as actual headings by creating a short title for each and using boldface along with the bullets and indentations.

Color, Shading, Boldface, Italic, and Underlining. Color can help readers move through the text and can draw attention to particular areas. For example, you can use color for headings, tabs, sidebars, callouts (labels that identify parts of a figure), and leader lines (dotted, dashed, or solid lines that connect labels with their objects), as in Figure 8.7. To highlight important information, you can use color for screens, horizontal and vertical rules, type, cross-references, and ruled boxes, as in Figure 8.8.

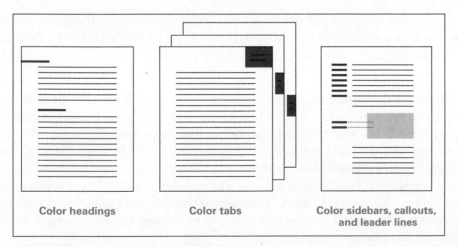

| Color headings | Color tabs | Color sidebars, callouts, and leader lines |

FIGURE 8.7 Using color for navigation

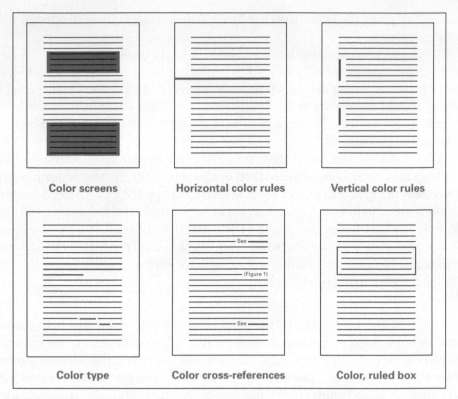

FIGURE 8.8 Using color for emphasis

Use color sparingly and use colors that aren't overly bright, that don't obscure the text they cover, and that contrast well with black print. You may also use shading, bold, italic, or underlining.

Bulleted and Numbered Lists. Whenever you include a series of similar or step-by-step items within a sentence or paragraph, consider using a bulleted or numbered list. Bulleted and numbered lists help readers navigate through dense information and emphasize the information by separating it from the text. However, don't overuse; don't use fancy icons when a plain round dot will do; and don't confuse the functions of bulleted and numbered lists. Bullets separate and highlight equally weighted items. Numbers enumerate the fixed sequence of steps in a process. Figure 8.9 compares in-text lists to bulleted and numbered lists. (For more on using lists, see Appendix B.)

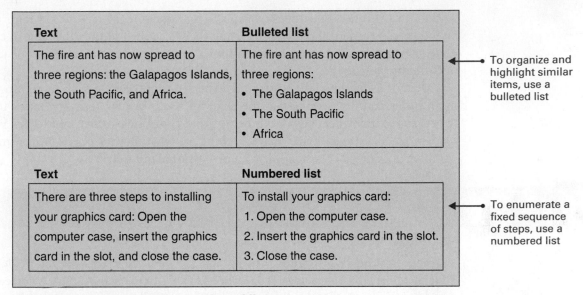

FIGURE 8.9 Bulleted versus numbered lists

Running Headers and Footers. Running heads and feet in longer printed documents help readers find material. They also help readers stay oriented to their location in the document. Typically a running head includes section- or chapter-specific information (as in this book) and running feet are reserved for book titles. However, page numbers may be included either in a running head or running foot. In a document with single-sided pages, running heads or feet should be placed consistently, typically flush right. In a document with double-sided pages, the running heads or feet should appear flush left on left-hand pages and flush right on right-hand pages, as in Figure 8.10.

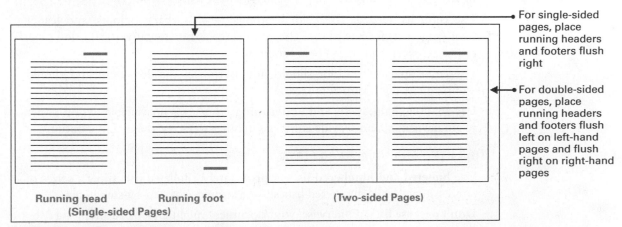

FIGURE 8.10 Running heads and feet

Tables of Contents and Indexes. In a longer document a table of contents and an index help readers find the information they need. In addition, the table of contents signals the relationship between topics and subtopics. Make sure your table of contents matches the heading structure of your document exactly.

Most of us have had the frustrating experience of trying to look something up in an index and discovering that the term we use is not the term the index uses. A successful index depends on knowing what categories, terms, and topics your readers are likely to look up when searching for what they need. For longer, more complex documents, consider hiring a professional indexer.

STRATEGIES
for Designing: Navigation and Emphasis

HEADINGS

- **Design headings consistently.** Always use the same font style, size, and color for the same level of headings. A-level headings are typically in all caps, boldface, and rest above paragraphs; B-level headings are usually in initial caps, boldface, and rest above paragraphs; and C-level heads are typically in initial caps, boldface, and run into paragraphs (whether or not the paragraphs are indented).

- **Divide headings logically.** Make each higher level head yield at least two heads at the next level. B-level headings always fall within A-level headed sections, and C-level headings always fall within B-level headed sections.

- **Avoid excessive headings.** Try to avoid D-level headings and never move to a level beyond that.

- **Avoid orphans.** If a heading stands alone at the bottom of a page, without at least two lines of text beneath, add more space to bump the heading to the next page.

COLOR, SHADING, BOLDFACE, ITALIC, AND UNDERLINING

- **Use color as needed.** Use color headings, tabs, sidebars, callouts, and leader lines (page 141) for navigation. Use color screens, horizontal/vertical rules, type, crossreferences, and ruled boxes for emphasis.

- **Use color sparingly.** Color should not overpower the document and should complement, not obstruct, the text.

- **Use shading, bold, italic, and underlining.** If color is unavailable or you prefer to aid navigation and provide emphasis in other ways, use these design options.

BULLETED AND NUMBERED LISTS

- **Use bulleted and numbered lists appropriately.** Bulleted lists show a series of similar items, while numbered lists show a sequence of step-by-step items.

- **Don't overuse lists.** Otherwise, your document might look like a shopping list.

STRATEGIES *continued*

RUNNING HEADS AND FEET

▸ **Decide if running feet are necessary.** Usually, running feet are used only for full-length books, though you may use them in documents to place page numbers.

▸ **Always include page numbers.** Whether you put them in running heads or running feet, page numbers are essential. For a long document, count your title page as page i, without numbering it, and number all front matter pages, including the table of contents and abstract, with lowercase roman numerals (ii, iii, iv). Number the first and subsequent text pages with arabic numerals (1, 2, 3).

▸ **Include section- or chapter-specific information in running heads.**

▸ **Format running heads and feet correctly.** See Figure 8.10.

TABLES OF CONTENTS AND INDEXES

▸ **Use tables of contents and indexes for longer documents.**

▸ **Make sure tables of contents match document headers exactly.**

▸ **Use standard index categories and topics.** Try to accurately anticipate which terms readers will look up in searching for what they need.

CHECKLIST
for Document Design

MyWritingLab™

CONSISTENCY AND COHESIVENESS

☐ Does my grid structure provide a consistent visual theme?

☐ Are margins ample?

☐ Is each paragraph tailored to suit its purpose?

☐ Is the document's right margin unjustified?

☐ Does the white space create areas of emphasis?

☐ Is the document's line spacing and indentation effective?

☐ Have I chosen readable and appropriate font sizes and styles?

☐ In general, have I used versions of a single typeface throughout?

☐ If different typefaces *are* used, are they used consistently?

☐ Have I used *italics*, **boldface**, and ALL CAPS sparingly?

➡

CHECKLIST *continued*

NAVIGATION AND EMPHASIS

☐ Do headings clearly announce the document's large and small segments?

☐ Are headings sized to reflect their specific level in the document?

☐ Are headings visually consistent and grammatically parallel?

☐ Have I formatted a series of parallel items as a list (numbered or bulleted, as appropriate)?

☐ Do running headers and footers announce sections of the document?

☐ Have I used page numbers appropriately?

☐ Are the table of contents and the index complete and easy to navigate?

APPLICATIONS

GENERAL APPLICATION

MyWritingLab™

With a partner, find two printed documents: one that demonstrates good use of design elements and another that demonstrates confusing or inconsistent use. Imagine that you and your partner are a team of technical communication consultants. Write a memo to the manager of the organization that produced the effective document, explaining its positive features. Write a memo to the manager of the organization that produced the confusing document, making suggestions for improvement.

TEAM APPLICATION

Working in teams of three or four people, find a document that is intended to answer a question—a patient brochure about an illness or medical procedure, a reference guide for new students on campus, or a personnel document from your company, for example. Your team's goal is to redesign the document so that it uses an appropriate grid design, makes effective use of white space, and uses formatting, fonts, headings, and other page design elements consistently and clearly.

Appoint one member of your group to serve as editor. The editor is responsible for making sure the design elements are used consistently throughout the redesigned document. Ask each team member to work on one section of the document. Assemble all the redesigned sections, and ask your editor to review the materials. The editor should check your work against the Checklist for Document Design.

GLOBAL APPLICATION   MyWritingLab™

Find a document that presents the same information in several languages (assembly instructions for various products are often written in two or three languages, for example). Evaluate the design decisions made in these documents. For example, are the different languages presented side by side or in different sections? Write a memo to classmates and your instructor evaluating the document and making recommendations for improvement.

DIGITAL AND SOCIAL MEDIA APPLICATION   MyWritingLab™

Technical documents are often created using preformatted templates, which are readily available in Microsoft Word, Apple Pages, and other word processing programs. Templates allow you to create sophisticated, attractive documents quickly and easily. But this ease of use can restrict your options to change or customize a design for a specific audience and purpose. In groups of two, consider the heart surgery brochure described on the first page of this chapter. Find a few brochure templates and compare your findings to the design principles presented in the Strategies boxes (pages 139–140 and 144). What are the pros and cons of using a template for this situation? How much are you able to manipulate the template's settings? For example, can you change an all caps heading to upper- and lowercase? Can you change the colors?

MyWritingLab™   Visit Chapter 8, *Designing User-Friendly Documents*, in MyWritingLab to complete this chapter's applications, to explore this chapter's overview, checklist, and flashcards, and to test your understanding of the chapter objectives.

PART 3

Documents

9 Résumés and Other Employment Materials

10 Memos and Letters

11 Definitions

12 Descriptions

13 Instructions and Procedures

14 Summaries

15 Informal Reports

16 Formal Reports

17 Proposals

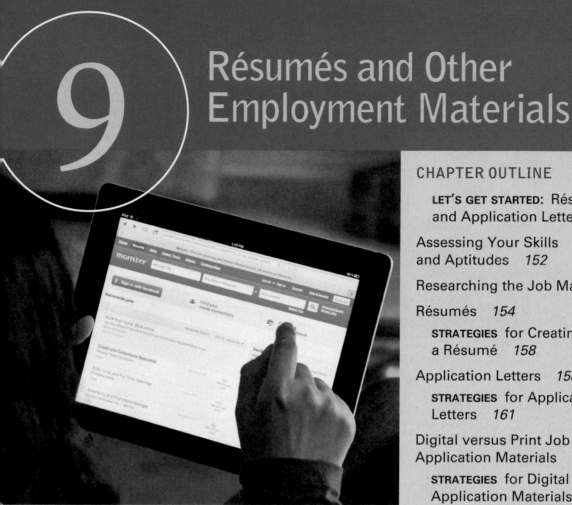

9

Résumés and Other Employment Materials

LEARNING OBJECTIVES FOR THIS CHAPTER

- ▶ Research jobs and narrow your job search
- ▶ Create print and digital résumés
- ▶ Write a persuasive job application letter
- ▶ Compile a dossier and a portfolio (or e-portfolio)
- ▶ Prepare for job interviews
- ▶ Write an appropriate thank you letter
- ▶ Write an appropriate acceptance or refusal letter

CHAPTER OUTLINE

LET'S GET STARTED: Résumés and Application Letters 151

Assessing Your Skills and Aptitudes 152

Researching the Job Market 153

Résumés 154

  STRATEGIES for Creating a Résumé 158

Application Letters 158

  STRATEGIES for Application Letters 161

Digital versus Print Job Application Materials 161

  STRATEGIES for Digital Job Application Materials 162

Dossiers, Portfolios, and E-portfolios 163

  STRATEGIES for Dossiers, Portfolios, and E-portfolios 165

Interviews and Follow-up Letters 167

  STRATEGIES for Interviews and Follow-up Letters 170

  CHECKLIST for Résumés 171

  CHECKLIST for Job Application Letters 172

  CHECKLIST for Supporting Materials 172

Applications 173

LET'S GET STARTED
Résumés and Application Letters

MyWritingLab™

Your friend has told you about a paid internship at a local company, and you would really like to get an interview because you are hoping to get a job related to your college major when you graduate. Also, the location is close to your apartment, so you could walk to and from the internship. Without reading this chapter, create a résumé and write an application letter that is targeted at getting this internship.

Questions to ask about the résumé and application letter you wrote, as you review the material in this chapter:

- Did you research the company?

- Is your résumé brief and to the point?

- Is the material in your résumé described and arranged in the order that makes sense for the company to which you are applying?

- Does your application letter contain the three basic paragraphs (introduction, body, conclusion)?

- Does your application letter get right to the point?

- Does your application letter help highlight specific and relevant items from your résumé?

At the end of this chapter, review your initial Let's Get Started résumé and application with a group of students, and compare what you wrote with what you learned from this chapter. Make a plan to revise or modify your original materials based on what you have learned from the chapter and in class.

This chapter comes first in the documents section of this book for two reasons: to highlight the importance of using the skills you have learned thus far to get hired, and to encourage you to create a portfolio of sample documents as you work through the remainder of the book.

Review the basics of effective communication

Enhance your job search by relying on key principles from earlier chapters. For example, research each specific position for which you apply (see Chapter 2). Show that you communicate persuasively, that you present yourself honestly, and that you understand teamwork (see Chapters 1, 3, and 4). Also, prepare all application materials with a clear sense of audience and purpose (see Chapter 3).

In today's job market, many applicants compete for few openings. Whether you are applying for your first professional job or changing careers, you need to market your skills effectively. At each stage of the job search, you must stand out among the competition.

ASSESSING YOUR SKILLS AND APTITUDES

Identify your assets

Begin your job search by assessing those qualities and skills you can offer a potential employer:

- Do I communicate well, and am I also a good listener?
- Do I work well in groups and with people from different backgrounds?
- Do I have experience or aptitude for a leadership role?
- Can I solve problems and get things done?
- Can I perform well under pressure?
- Can I work independently, with minimal supervision?
- Do I have any special skills (public speaking, working with people, computer or other technical skills, aptitude with words, analytical skills, second or third languages, artistic/musical talent, mathematical aptitude)?

Source: Chris McGrath/Getty Images.

- Do I have any hobbies that could improve my job prospects?
- Would I prefer to work at a large company or a small one? At a for-profit or a nonprofit organization?
- Do I like to travel, or would I prefer working in a single location?

Besides helping you focus your job search, your answers to these questions will come in handy when you write your résumé and prepare for job interviews.

RESEARCHING THE JOB MARKET

Narrowing your search does not mean limiting yourself to one or two types of job, but instead giving yourself a measure of realistic focus. Try to stick to those fields that interest you most and fit you best.

> Search within a reasonable range

Begin your research well in advance of the time you need to have a job lined up. If you've never done job research, the question "Where do I start?" can be daunting: "Do I go to a career counselor first?" "Should I talk with friends and family members?" "Do I go straight to the Help Wanted section—in print or online?" "Should I buy a book on how to find a job?" "Which Web sites are the best?" More than ever, seemingly endless sources of information are available to job seekers. Try to proceed in a step-by-step, logical way, as described below, rather than immediately going online and trying to navigate random Web sites.

> Don't just dive in; work step by step

The human connection is always the best way to start looking for a job. Once you've narrowed down your job search, go to your campus job placement office and meet with a career counselor (either at your school or outside), who will know the job search process inside and out. Also, speak with a reference librarian (in person or online), who can point you to the right library resource. Network with acquaintances who may know someone else you can speak with.

> Start by talking to job experts, librarians, friends, and family

Before you apply for specific jobs, learn more about the industry. There are a number of ways to do this: Consult reference materials (books, magazines, professional journals, Web sites) specific to the industry. Join a professional group related to your industry and either attend meetings or speak with professionals online through sponsored chat groups. Learn about the key companies in your industry of choice—find out who they are, make a list, and research those particular companies. Finally, set up an informational interview with someone at a company in your field. Even busy professionals are often willing to speak with interested job seekers not applying for a specific job. These people can offer general advice about the industry as a whole and about their own company.

> Next, consult industry-specific resources

Job postings can be located in a variety of places: Use nationwide job portals and job networking sites (such as *Monster.com, Careerbuilder.com, Riley Guide*, and *LinkedIn*) to find jobs across the country or specific to your location; consult the print or online Help Wanted sections of your local newspapers; locate industry-specific jobs on professional organization Web sites; or find jobs

> Finally, look for specific job postings or send out unsolicited application letters

advertised only on human resources Web sites of particular companies. You don't have to limit your search options to advertised jobs, however. Another approach is to send an unsolicited application letter to a company that interests you (for more on unsolicited application letters, see page 159).

RÉSUMÉS

Definition and function of a résumé

Of course, before applying for any job, you should create an effective résumé. A *résumé* is essentially an applicant's personal advertisement for employment. It lists (in a standard format) education and employment history, along with other relevant information, providing a snapshot of the person's qualifications.

A résumé is designed to give an employer an instant overview. In fact, employers initially spend only 15 to 45 seconds looking at a résumé; during this scan, they are looking for a persuasive answer to the bottom-line question: "What can you do for us?"

Employers are impressed by a résumé that looks good, reads easily, appears honest, and provides only the relevant information an employer needs to determine if the applicant should be interviewed. Résumés that are mechanically flawed, cluttered, sketchy, hard to follow, or seemingly dishonest simply get discarded.

Parts of a Résumé

What to include—and not include—in a résumé

All résumés contain standard parts. Every résumé must include contact information, career objectives, education, work experience, and references. A résumé is not the place to include such items as your desired salary and benefits or your requirements for time off. In addition, do not include irrelevant personal information, your photograph, or information that employers are not allowed to legally ask (such as your race, age, or marital status). As you read through this section, refer to Figure 9.1, which includes all the required parts.

Contact Information.
Tell prospective employers where they can reach you. If you are between addresses, provide both addresses and check each contact point regularly. Be sure that your email address and phone number are accurate. If you use voice mail, record a message that sounds friendly and professional. If you have your own Web site (professional, not personal, in content), include the Web address. Remember that employers may be able to view your Facebook or other social networking pages, so keep those sites professional in tone and content.

Career Objectives.
Spell out the job you want. Avoid vague statements such as "A position in which I can apply my education and experience." Instead, be specific: "An intensive-care nursing position in a teaching hospital, with the eventual goal of supervising and instructing." Tailor your career objective statement as you apply for different jobs, in order to match yourself with each position.

James David Purdy
203 Elmwood Avenue
San Jose, CA 95139
Phone: (555) 316-2419
Email: jpur@valnet.net

Objective   Customer relations for a hospitality chain, leading to management.

Education   *San Jose City College, San Jose, CA*
2011–2013   Associate of Arts Degree in Hotel and Restaurant Management, May 2009. Grade point average: 3.25 of a possible 4.00. All college expenses financed by scholarship and part-time job (20 hours weekly).

Employment   *Pretalo Lodge and Convention Center, San Jose, CA*
2011–2013   Began as desk clerk, promoted to desk manager (part-time) of this 200-unit resort. Responsible for scheduling custodial and room service staff, planning conventions, and handling customer relations.

2010–2011   *Teo's Restaurant, Pensacola, FL*
Beginning as waiter, advanced to cashier and finally to assistant manager. Responsible for preparing weekly payroll, making banquet arrangements, and supervising dining room and lounge staff.

2009–2010   *Encyclopaedia Britannica, Inc., San Jose, CA*
Sales representative (part-time). Received top bonus twice.

2008–2009   *White Family Inn, San Luis Obispo, CA*
Worked as bus-person, then server (part-time).

Leadership   *Awards*
Captain of basketball team, 2009; Lion's Club Scholarship, 2011.

Languages
Committee chair for student French club; fluent French speaker.

Activities
High school basketball and track team (3 years); college student senate (2 years); Innkeepers' Club—prepared and served monthly dinners at the college (2 years).

References   Available on request.

Contact information includes full name and address, phone, and email address

Career objective is specific and tailored to the job

Education section lists school, location, degree earned, and other relevant information

Work experience section lists most recent jobs first and includes relevant skills applied on the job

Leadership section combines awards, skills, and activities that may be relevant to a job

When no references are included, an "available on request" statement substitutes

FIGURE 9.1 A standard résumé

Education. Begin with your most recent schooling and work backward. Include the name of the school, degree completed, year completed, and your major and minor. Omit high school, unless the high school's prestige or your achievements there warrant its inclusion. List courses that have directly prepared you for the job you seek. If your class rank or grade point average is favorable, list it. Include specialized training during military service. If you finance your education by working, say so, indicating the percentage of your contribution.

Work Experience. If your experience relates to the job, list it before your education. List the most recent job and then earlier jobs. Include employers' names and dates of employment. Indicate whether a job was full-time, part-time (hours weekly), or seasonal. Describe your exact duties for each job, indicating promotions. If it is to your advantage, state why you left each job. Include military experience and relevant volunteer work. If you lack paid experience, emphasize your education, including internships and special projects.

Leadership or Other Activities. By law, you are not required to include a photograph or reveal your sex, religion, race, age, national origin, disability, or marital status. List any awards, skills, activities, and interests that are *relevant* to the given position: say, memberships, demonstrations of leadership, languages, and special skills that may be of interest to the employer.

References. If the employer has requested references, list three to five people who have agreed to provide strong assessments of your qualifications and who can speak on your behalf. Never list as references people who haven't first given you express permission. Your references should not be family members or non-work-related friends; instead, list former employers, professors, and community figures who know you well. If the employer does not request references as part of the initial application, simply state at the end of your résumé, "References available upon request." If you don't list references, prepare a separate reference sheet that you can provide on request. Include each person's job title, company address, and contact information.

Organizing Your Résumé

Organize your résumé to convey the strongest impression of your qualifications, skills, and experience. A standard résumé, like the one in Figure 9.1, is also known as a *reverse chronological résumé*, listing the most recent school and job first. If you have limited experience or education or gaps in your work history (e.g., due to illness, raising children) or if you have frequently switched career paths, create a *functional résumé* (Figure 9.2) to highlight skills relevant to a particular job.

**FIGURE 9.2
A functional
résumé**

Carol R. Chasone
642 Eagle Lane
Eugene, OR 97405
(503-314-5555)
crchasone@eor.edu

OBJECTIVE	Position in marketing/communications with opportunity for advancement

← Includes contact information and objective

**SALES/
MARKETING
SKILLS**
- Wrote recruiting letter currently used by the Eugene Chamber of Commerce
- Designed posters for promotion of industrial development in Central Oregon
- Assisted Chamber President in promoting the organization's activities
- Recruited 7 speakers for Chamber meetings
- Wrote 3 public-relations pieces about a local hospital, for area newspapers

**COMMUNICATION
AND DOCUMENT
DESIGN SKILLS**
- Conducted demographic study of small businesses in Southwestern OR
- Presented study findings to Eugene Chamber of Commerce
- Wrote 15-page report on results of demographic study
- Designed and wrote two brochures to promote the Small Business Institute
- Designed 5 issues of *Patient Care*, 16-page in-house hospital newsletter
- Wrote 8 articles and conducted 3 interviews for the newsletter
- Designed 6 posters for in-service hospital programs

← Emphasizes three skills areas appropriate to the job, with specific accomplishments in bulleted-list format

**ORGANIZATIONAL/
MANAGEMENT
SKILLS**
- Coordinated all weekly Chamber meetings for Feb., March, April, and May
- Attended 2 seminars (Houston, Seattle) for hospital public relations
- Trained and supervised 3 new interns at the Small Business Institute
- Scheduled and chaired weekly intern meetings

EDUCATION
Eastern Oregon University
B.S. in Marketing; Graphic Design minor—May 2012
GPA: 3.3/4.0; Dean's List, 5 semesters
Contract Learning: Eugene Chamber of Commerce, Fall 2011
Internships: EOU's Small Business Institute, Spring 2011; Mercy Hospital, Fall 2011

← Includes but deemphasizes education

EMPLOYMENT
Personal trainer (part-time and summers 2009–2011)—Acme Gym, Eugene
Caddy and Pro Shop salesperson—Eugene Golf Club, summers, 2006–2008

REFERENCES
Available on request

- **Begin your résumé well before your job search.**
- **Tailor your résumé for each job.** Read the advertised job requirements, and adjust your career objective accordingly. Tailor your work experience, personal data, and personal interests to emphasize certain areas for certain jobs. Follow the instructions given on the job application or site.
- **Try to limit the résumé to a single page.** However, if your résumé looks cramped, you might need to go to a second page.
- **Stick to experience relevant to the job.** Don't list everything you've ever done.
- **Use action verbs and key words.** Action verbs (*supervised, developed, built, taught, installed, managed, trained, solved, planned, directed*) stress your ability to produce results. If your résumé is likely to be scanned electronically or if you post it online, list keywords as nouns (*leadership skills, software development, data processing, editing*) below your contact information and your statement of objective (see Figure 9.4).
- **Use bold, italic, underlining, colors, fonts, bullets, and other devices thoughtfully, for emphasis.** Do not use these features to be artsy.
- **Never invent or distort credentials.** Make yourself look as good as the *facts* allow. Companies routinely investigate claims made in résumés, and people who lie will certainly not be hired.
- **Proofread, proofread, proofread.** Don't rely on a computer spell checker. Famous résumé mistakes include winning a "bogus award" instead of a "bonus award" and "ruining" rather than "running" a business.

APPLICATION LETTERS

Definition and function of an application letter

An *application letter*, also known as a *cover letter*, complements your résumé when you apply for a job. The letter's main purpose is to explain how your credentials fit the particular job and to convey a sufficiently informed, professional, and likable persona for the prospective employer to decide that you should be interviewed. Another purpose of the letter is to highlight specific qualifications or skills; for example, you might have listed "Java programming" on your résumé, but for one particular job application you may wish to call attention to this item in your cover letter:

> My résumé notes that I am experienced with Java programming. In fact, I also tutor Java programming students in our school's learning center.

Solicited and unsolicited application letters

Sometimes you will apply for positions advertised in print or by word of mouth or where you have been invited to apply (for example, by a recruiter who visits your campus) (*solicited applications*). At other times you will write prospecting letters to organizations that have not advertised an opening but that might need someone like you (*unsolicited applications*). In either case, tailor your letter to the situation.

Solicited Application Letters

An application letter—whether solicited or unsolicited—consists of an introduction, body, and conclusion as in Figure 9.3.

In your brief introduction (generally, five lines or fewer), do these things: Name the job you're applying for and where you have seen it advertised; identify yourself and your background; and, if possible, establish a connection by naming a mutual acquaintance who encouraged you to apply—but only if that person has given you permission.

Use the introduction to get right to the point

In the body, spell out your case. Without merely repeating your résumé, relate your qualifications specifically to this job. Also, be specific. Instead of referring to "much experience" or "increased sales," stipulate "three years of experience" or "a 35 percent increase in sales between June and October 2013." Support all claims with evidence. Instead of saying, "I have leadership skills," say, "I served as student senate president during my senior year and was captain of the lacrosse team."

Use the body to demonstrate your qualifications

In the conclusion, restate your interest and emphasize your willingness to retrain or relocate if necessary. If the job is nearby, request an interview; otherwise, request a phone call, suggesting a time you can be reached.

Use the conclusion to restate interest

Unsolicited Application Letters

Do not limit your job search to advertised openings. In fact, fewer than 20 percent of all job openings are advertised. Unsolicited application letters are a good way to uncover possibilities. They do have drawbacks, however: You may waste time writing to organizations that have no openings, and you cannot tailor your letter to advertised requirements. But there are also advantages: Even employers with no openings often welcome and file impressive unsolicited applications or pass them on to another employer who has an opening.

Because an unsolicited letter arrives unexpectedly, you need to get the reader's immediate attention. Don't begin, "I am writing to inquire about the possibility of obtaining a position with your company." Instead, open forcefully by establishing a connection with a mutual acquaintance or by making a strong statement or asking a persuasive question as in the following example:

Use the introduction to spark reader interest

Does your hotel chain have a place for a junior manager with a college degree in hospitality management, a proven commitment to quality service, and customer relations experience that extends far beyond textbooks? If so, please consider my application for a position.

A forceful opening

203 Elmwood Avenue
San Jose, CA 10462

April 22, 20XX

Sara Costanza
Personnel Director
Liberty International, Inc.
Lansdowne, PA 24153

Dear Ms. Costanza:

Writer identifies self and purpose → Please consider my application for a junior management position at your Lake Geneva resort, as advertised in the April 19 *Philadephia Inquirer.* I will graduate from San Jose City College on May 30 with an Associate of Arts degree in hotel and restaurant management. Dr. H. V. Garlid, my nutrition professor, described his experience as a consultant for Liberty International and encouraged me to apply.

Establishes a connection →

Relates specific qualifications from his résumé to the job opening → As you can see from my enclosed résumé, for two years I worked as a part-time desk clerk, and I was promoted to manager, at a 200-unit resort. This experience, combined with earlier customer relations work in a variety of situations, has given me a clear and practical understanding of customers' needs and expectations.

Applies relevant personal interests to the job → As an amateur chef, I'm well aware of the effort, attention, and patience required to prepare fine food. Moreover, my skiing and sailing background might be assets to your resort's recreation program.

Expresses confidence and enthusiasm throughout → I have worked hard to hone my hospitality management skills. My experience, education, and personality have prepared me to work well with others and to respond creatively to challenges, crises, and added responsibilities.

Makes follow-up easy for the reader → If my background meets your needs, please phone me any weekday after 4:00 p.m. at (555) 316-2419.

Sincerely,

James D. Purdy

James D. Purdy

FIGURE 9.3 A solicited application letter

STRATEGIES for Application Letters

- ► **Use caution when adapting sample application letters.** There are plenty of free, online sample letters that provide ideas for your own situation. But never borrow them whole. Most employers can spot a "canned" letter immediately.

- ► **Create a dynamic tone with active voice.** Instead of saying, "More and more management responsibilities were steadily given to me," say, "I steadily assumed ever-greater management responsibilities."

- ► **Never be vague.** Paint a clear picture for employers who may not be familiar with what you describe. Instead of saying, "I am familiar with the 1022 interactive database system and RUNOFF processing system," say, "As a lab grader, I kept grading records on the 1022 database management system and composed lab procedures on the RUNOFF text processing system."

- ► **Avoid being overly informal or overly stiff.** Avoid informal terms that sound unprofessional ("Your company sounds like a cool place to work") as well as stuffy language ("Hitherto, I request the honor of your acquaintance").

- ► **Never settle for a first draft—or even a second or third.** The application letter is your one chance to introduce yourself to a prospective employer. Make it perfect by trimming excess wording, double-checking the tone, and making sure that you have connected your qualifications directly to the job. After you are satisfied with the content, proofread repeatedly to spot any factual errors or typos.

Address your letter to the person most likely in charge of hiring. Consult company Web sites for names of company officers. Then call the company to verify the person's name and title.

DIGITAL VERSUS PRINT JOB APPLICATION MATERIALS

Using PDF files for digital résumés

Résumés and cover letters today are typically submitted as PDF or Word documents, uploaded to the online job application site for a particular organization. Social networking sites like *LinkedIn* or *Monster.com* also allow you to upload your résumé and other materials and connect these to your online profile. Some employers may also ask you to submit your materials as email attachments, especially if you were solicited to apply. Whenever possible, use PDF; these files retain the look and feel (fonts, page breaks, line breaks) of the résumé you worked so hard to create. PDF files also make it more difficult for a reader to accidentally insert a stray keystroke or change your formatting while reading your materials.

Print résumés are still important

A printed résumé is also important to have on hand, especially in certain situations. For some jobs, you may still be asked to mail copies of your application materials. Also, if you attend a campus career fair or similar in-person event (for instance, a company holds an information session or comes to campus to recruit), having print copies of your résumé ready to give to recruiters is invaluable. You can point out items of interest on the spot and make a lasting impression. Be sure to use high-quality white stationery paper, available at most copy shops.

Scanned résumés

If you do hand out or mail print copies of your materials, keep in mind that prospective employers will probably end up digitizing your résumé by scanning a copy for their job database systems. Digital résumés, especially at large organizations, become part of a much larger database of applicants (for current or later job openings). Digital résumés are much easier to search via computer, with employers looking for keywords to help them narrow down the application pool.

STRATEGIES
for Digital Job Application Materials

► **Follow the instructions of the job application site.** Employer job sites will tell you what format to use, how large the file size can be, whether to upload just the résumé or the résumé and cover letter, and so forth.

► **Unless otherwise noted, use PDF.** PDF files retain the formatting of the original no matter what computer platform a reader is using.

► **Use a simple font.** Stick with those fonts that are easiest to scan, such as Times New Roman or Helvetica.

► **Use simple formatting.** Especially for print résumés that may be scanned, avoid fancy fonts, tables, and too much formatting. You may substitute ALL CAPS instead of boldface, for example. But even with digital résumés (PDF or Word), keep the design simple and clean (see Figure 9.2 for an example).

► **Use templates carefully.** Word processing templates may not be the best choice for your particular audience and purpose. If you start off using a template, be sure to edit the formatting and layout to fit your needs.

► **Use keywords.** Use words that are likely to get hits if the document is searched. You may want to create a "qualifications" section at the top of your résumé. Include keywords for general skills (conflict management, report and proposal writing), specialized skills (graphic design, XTML), credentials (B.S. in electrical

➤

engineering, Phi Beta Kappa), and job titles (manager, technician, intern). Use nouns for keywords.

▸ **Avoid personal information for job materials that are widely available to the public.** For résumés uploaded to secure job application sites, you will want to use your actual address, phone number, and email address. But for materials you upload to a public space, such as your personal Web page, or even to job networking sites (where you can't predict who will see it), you may wish to avoid the potential for identity theft by leaving off your home address and phone number.

To create a print résumé that can be scanned easily and accurately, keep the formatting as simple as possible. Figure 9.4 provides one example of a résumé suitable for scanning.

LinkedIn and other job networking sites offer templates that help you take your profile and turn it into a résumé. Word processing programs, career advice Web sites, and many other sources also offer résumé templates. Use these templates carefully, always keeping audience and purpose in mind.

Use résumé templates carefully

DOSSIERS, PORTFOLIOS, AND E-PORTFOLIOS

An employer impressed by your résumé and application letter will likely have questions about your credentials and your past work. These questions will be answered, respectively, by your dossier and your portfolio (or e-portfolio).

Definitions and purposes of dossiers and portfolios

Dossiers

Your dossier contains your credentials: college transcript, recommendation letters, and other items (such as a scholarship award or commendation letter) that document your achievements. Prospective employers who decide to follow up on your application may request your dossier. By collecting recommendations in one folder, you spare your references from writing the same letter repeatedly.

What a dossier contains

Your college placement office will keep the dossier (or placement folder) on file and send copies to employers. Always keep your own copy as well, including any nonconfidential recommendation letters. Then, if an employer requests your dossier, you can photocopy and mail it, advising your recipient that the official placement copy is on the way, as sometimes dossiers may not be mailed immediately.

To facilitate online confidentiality, a P.O. box, rather than a street address, is used ●———→

Uses ALL CAPS for emphasis, rather than boldface, italics, etc. ●———→

Uses nouns instead of verb forms ●———→

Chooses a standard, not fancy, font ●———→

All text is flush to the left margin ●———→

KAREN P. GRANGER
P.O. Box 6772
New Bedford, MA 02720
Phone: (555) 864-9318

Email: kgrang@swis.net

OBJECTIVE
A summer internship in software documentation.

QUALIFICATIONS
Software and hardware documentation. Editing. Desktop publishing. Usability testing. Computer science. Internet research. Web collaboration. Networking technology. Instructor-led training. DEC 20 mainframe and VAX 11/780 systems. Adobe *Framemaker, RoboHelp, Webworks Publisher, PowerPoint, Excel*, and *Lotus* software. Logo, Pascal, HTML, and C++ program languages.

EDUCATION
University of Massachusetts at Dartmouth (UMD): B.A. January 2014. English and communications major. Computer science minor. GPA 3.54. Class rank top 7 percent.

EXPERIENCE
Conway Communications, Inc., Marlboro, MA: Intern technical writer. LAN technology. Writing, designing, and testing hardware upgrade manuals. Designing and publishing of installation and maintenance manual. Specifying art and illustrations. Designing a fully linked home page and online help for the company intranet. Summers 2011 and 2012.

Writing and Reading Center, UMD: Tutor. Individual and group instruction in writing and word processing. Training new tutors. Newsletter editing. Scriptwriting and acting in a training video. Designing home page. Fall 2010–present.

The Torch, UMD weekly newspaper: Managing editor. Conducting staff meetings. Generating story ideas. Writing editorials and articles. Supervising page layout, paste-up, and copyediting. Fall 2011–present.

ACHIEVEMENTS AND AWARDS
Writing samples published in Dr. John M. Lannon's and Dr. Laura J. Gurak's Technical Communication, 13th ed. (Pearson/Longman, 2014).

Massachusetts State Honors Scholarship, 2010–2012.

Dean's list each semester.

ACTIVITIES
Student member, Society for Technical Communication and American Society for Training and Development.

Student representative, College Curriculum Committee.

UMD Literary Society.

REFERENCES AND WRITING PORTFOLIO
Available on request.

FIGURE 9.4 A résumé that can be scanned, emailed, or posted online

Portfolios and E-portfolios

Portfolios, whether print or digital (e-portfolios, Figure 9.5), allow you to provide a potential employer with additional information and examples pertinent to your job search, such as copies of documents from your dossier as well as writing samples, more information about honors and awards, and multimedia or visual design projects. Your portfolio or e-portfolio should contain an introduction or mission statement explaining what you've included and why. Do not include items that are unrelated to the job search or your qualifications. An organized, professional portfolio or e-portfolio shows that you can apply your skills and makes you stand out as a candidate. It also gives you concrete material to discuss during job interviews.

What a portfolio contains

As you create your portfolio or e-portfolio, seek advice and feedback from professors in your major and from other people in the field. If you have a portfolio or e-portfolio, indicate this on your résumé, followed by "Available on request." If you have created an e-portfolio, provide the Web address on your résumé, but also bring printed copies of its contents to your interview. Many colleges and universities offer e-portfolio services via their career and student placement centers. You can also find software and templates online; many of these are quite simple to use. *LinkedIn* and other job sites also offer ways to create e-portfolios. Always check the privacy settings when using a social network or online portfolio site.

STRATEGIES
for Dossiers, Portfolios, and E-portfolios

▸ **Always provide an introduction or mission statement.** Place this page at the beginning to introduce and explain the contents.

▸ **Collect relevant materials.** Gather documents or graphics you've prepared in school or on the job, presentations you've given, and projects or experiments you've worked on. Possible items: campus newspaper articles, reports on course projects, papers that earned an "A," examples of persuasive argument, documents from an internship, or visuals you've designed for an oral presentation.

▸ **Include copies of dossier materials.** Although they won't be official unless they go directly from your campus placement office to your prospective employer, have copies of your college transcript and recommendations on hand to give to employers during the waiting period and/or to post on your e-portfolio.

▸ **Assemble your items.** Place your résumé first (after your introduction/mission statement), and use divider pages to separate groups of items. Follow the same structure for an e-portfolio. Position your résumé file immediately below the introduction/mission statement file, and group similar items into appropriate files. In either case, aim for a professional look.

▶ **Omit irrelevant items.** Personal photographs and other items more appropriate for a Facebook page do not belong in your portfolio or e-portfolio.

▶ **Omit your street address or phone number from your e-portfolio.** If your e-portfolio is available to the public, post only your email address to avoid identity theft. If you post your references, include only their names and comments, not their contact information. Always check the privacy settings with any e-portfolio software.

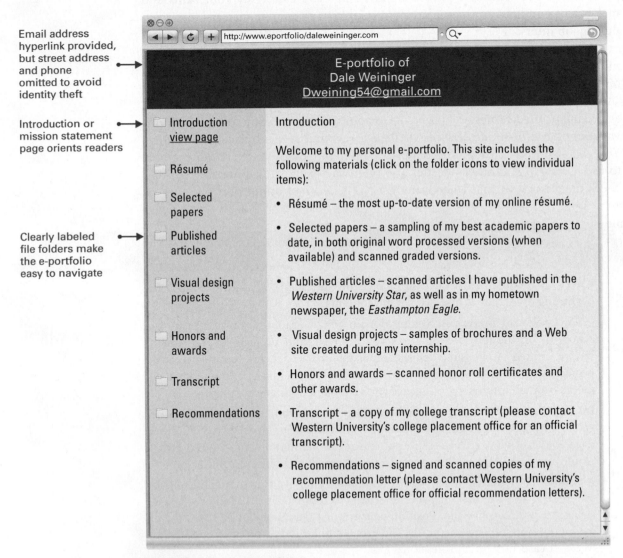

FIGURE 9.5 An e-portfolio

INTERVIEWS AND FOLLOW-UP LETTERS

All of your preparation leads to the last stages of the hiring process: the interview and follow-up to the interview.

Interviews

An employer who is impressed by your credentials will arrange an interview. The interview's purpose is to confirm the employer's impressions from your application letter, résumé, references, and dossier. You will likely be asked to present your portfolio (if you have one) at the interview, rather than beforehand. In addition to your original portfolio or the Web address for your e-portfolio, bring copies/printouts of all relevant documents contained therein. Offer to leave these copies with the interviewer.

Purpose of interviews

Interviews come in various shapes and sizes. They can be face to face or via telephone or video conference. You might meet with a single interviewer, a hiring committee, or several committees in succession. You might be interviewed alone or as part of a group of candidates. Interviews can last an hour or less, a full day, or several days. The interview can range from a pleasant chat to a grueling interrogation. Some interviewers may antagonize you deliberately to observe your reaction.

Types of interview situations

Careful preparation is the key to a productive interview. If you haven't already done so, learn what you can about the company from trade journals, industrial indexes, business magazines (like *Forbes*, *Fortune*, and *Business Week*), and other resources. Request company literature, including the most recent annual report. Speak with people who know about the company, or (well in advance) arrange an informational interview with someone at the company. In addition, visit the company's Web site. Once you've done all this, ask yourself, "Does this job seem like a good fit?"

The importance of preparing for an interview

In addition to knowing about the company, be prepared in other ways. Dress and present yourself appropriately. Be psychologically prepared and confident (but not arrogant). Follow the rules of business etiquette. Unprepared interviewees make mistakes such as the following:

- They know little about the company or what role they would play as an employee in this particular division or department.
- They have inflated ideas about their own worth.
- They have little idea of how their education prepares them for work.
- They dress inappropriately.
- They exhibit little or no self-confidence.
- They have only vague ideas of how they could benefit the employer.
- They inquire only about salary and benefits.
- They speak negatively of former employers or coworkers.

How people fail job interviews

Practice answering
interview questions

Perhaps the most important way to prepare for an interview is to practice answering typical questions. Think about how you would answer the following:

Questions to
expect during a job
interview

- Why does this job appeal to you?
- What do you know about our company? About this division or unit?
- What do you know about our core values (for example, informal management structure, commitment to diversity or to the environment)?
- What do you know about the expectations and demands of this job?
- What are the major issues affecting this industry?
- How would you describe yourself as an employee?
- What do you see as your biggest weakness? Biggest strength?
- Can you describe an instance in which you came up with a new and better way of doing something?
- What are your short-term and long-term career goals?

Prepare your own
questions, too

Don't forget to prepare your own list of well-researched questions about the job and the organization. You will be invited to ask questions, and what you ask can be as revealing as any answers you give.

Be truthful

Finally, tell the truth during the interview—doing so is both ethical and smart. Companies routinely verify an applicant's claims about education, prior employment, positions held, salary, and personal background. Perhaps you have some past infraction (such as a bad credit rating or a brush with the law) or some pressing personal commitment (such as caring for an elderly parent or a disabled child). Experts suggest that it's better to air these issues up front—before the employer finds out from other sources. The employer will appreciate your honesty, and you will know exactly where you stand before accepting the job (Fisher 292).

Follow-up Letters

There are two types of follow-up letters: thank you letters and, if you are offered the job, acceptance or refusal letters. A typed or handwritten thank you, acceptance, or refusal letter is considered the most professional and formal way to follow up after a job interview or job offer. However, if email has been the primary way you and the potential employer have communicated, you may decide to send your follow-up via email. If so, be sure that, just like a print letter, the email is professionally written, checked for spelling and grammar, and formal in tone. (See Chapter 18 for more on this topic.)

Purpose and content
of thank you letters

Thank You Letters. Within a day or so after the interview, send a thank you letter to the person who interviewed you. If you were interviewed by multiple people, send each one an individual thank you letter. Not only is this courteous, but it also reinforces a positive impression. Keep your letter brief, but try to personalize your connection with the reader (Crosby 20).

Open by thanking the interviewer and reemphasizing your interest in the position. Then refer to some details from the interview or some aspect of your visit that would help the interviewer reconnect with the interview experience. If you forgot to mention something important during the interview, include it here—briefly. Finally, close with genuine enthusiasm, and provide your contact information again to make it easy for the interviewer to respond. Following is the text of an effective thank you letter from James Purdy, the entry-level candidate in hotel-restaurant management whose résumé and cover letter appeared earlier:

> Thank you for your hospitality during my Tuesday visit to Lake Geneva Resort. I am very interested in the restaurant-management position and was intrigued by our discussion about developing an eclectic regional cuisine.
>
> Everything about my tour was enjoyable, but I was especially impressed by the friendliness and professionalism of the resort staff. People seem to love working at the Resort, and it's not hard to see why.
>
> I'm convinced I would be a productive employee at Lake Geneva Resort and would welcome the chance to prove my abilities. If you need additional information, please call me at (555) 316-2419.

Acceptance or Refusal Letters. You may receive a job offer by phone or letter. If by phone, request a written offer and respond with a formal letter of acceptance. This letter may serve as part of your contract; spell out the terms you are accepting. Remember also to accept a job offer with enthusiasm. Here is James Purdy's letter of acceptance:

Content and approach of acceptance letters

> I am delighted to accept your offer of a position as assistant recreation supervisor at Liberty International's Lake Geneva Resort, with a starting salary of $44,500.
>
> As you requested, I will phone Bonnie Dunn in Human Resources for instructions on reporting date, physical exam, and employee orientation.
>
> I look forward to a long and satisfying career with Liberty International.

You may also have to refuse a job offer, for example if you receive a preferable offer or decide that the position is not the right fit for you. Even if you refuse by phone, write a prompt and cordial letter of refusal, explaining your reasons and allowing for future possibilities. Remember to be diplomatic when refusing a job.

Content and approach of refusal letters

A courteous refusal and explanation can let the employer know why you have chosen a competing employer or why you have decided against taking the job for other reasons. Purdy handled one job refusal this way:

> Although I thoroughly enjoyed my visit to your company's headquarters, I have to decline your offer of a position as assistant desk manager of your London hotel.
>
> I've decided to accept a position with Liberty International because the company has offered me the chance to participate in its manager-trainee program. Also, Liberty will provide tuition for courses in completing my B.S. degree in hospitality management.
>
> If any future openings should materialize at your Aspen resort, however, I would appreciate your considering me again as a candidate.
>
> Thank you for your confidence in me.

STRATEGIES
for Interviews and Follow-up Letters

- **Confirm the interview's exact time and location.** Arrive early but no more than 10 minutes.
- **Don't show up empty-handed.** Bring a briefcase, pen, and notepad. Have your own questions written out. Bring extra copies of your résumé (unfolded) and a portfolio (if appropriate).
- **Make a positive first impression.** Come dressed as if you already work for the company. Learn the name of your interviewer beforehand so you can greet this person by name—but never by first name unless invited. Extend a firm handshake, smile, and look the interviewer in the eye. Wait to be asked to take a chair. Maintain eye contact much of the time, but don't stare.
- **Don't worry about having all the answers.** When you don't know the answer to a question, say so, and relax. Interviewers typically do most of the talking.
- **Avoid abrupt yes or no answers—as well as life stories.** Just saying yes or no doesn't leave any impression—elaborate on your answers, but also keep them short and to the point.
- **Don't answer questions by merely repeating the material on your résumé.** Instead, explain how specific skills and types of experience could be assets to this particular employer.

➡

STRATEGIES *continued*

- ▶ **Remember to smile often and to be friendly and attentive throughout.** Qualifications are not the only reason a person gets hired. People often hire the candidate they *like* best.

- ▶ **Never criticize a previous employer.** Above all, interviewers like positive attitudes. Complaining about a former employer, whether or not your criticisms are legitimate, only makes you look negative.

- ▶ **Prepare to ask intelligent questions.** When questions are invited, focus on the nature of the job: travel involved, specific responsibilities, typical job assignments, opportunities for further training, types of clients, and so on. Avoid questions that could easily have been answered by your own prior research.

- ▶ **Take a hint.** When your interviewer hints that the meeting is ending (perhaps by checking a watch), restate your interest, ask when a hiring decision is likely to be made, thank the interviewer, and leave.

- ▶ **Follow up as soon as possible.** Send a thank you note to each person with whom you interviewed. Be sure to get the spelling right for each person's name.

CHECKLIST
for Résumés

My WritingLab™

- ☐ Does my résumé's organization (reverse chronological or functional) emphasize my best characteristics?
- ☐ Is my contact information accurate?
- ☐ Does my statement of objective show a clear sense of purpose?
- ☐ Have I included a summary of skills or qualifications, as needed?
- ☐ Is my educational background clear and complete?
- ☐ Have I accurately but briefly described my previous jobs?
- ☐ Have I presented education versus experience in the appropriate sequence?
- ☐ Have I included personal data and interests, as appropriate?
- ☐ Have I listed references or offered to provide them?
- ☐ Have I offered to provide a portfolio, as appropriate?
- ☐ Have I used action verbs and keywords?
- ☐ Have I limited the résumé to a single page, if possible?

➔

CHECKLIST *continued*

☐ Is the résumé uncluttered and tasteful?

☐ For print copies, have I used quality (white) paper?

☐ If I have a scannable résumé, does it use keywords and effective formatting?

☐ Am I being scrupulously honest?

☐ Have I proofread exhaustively?

CHECKLIST
for Job Application Letters

MyWritingLab™

☐ Is my letter addressed to a specifically named person?

☐ If my letter is *solicited*, do I indicate how I heard about the job?

☐ If my letter is *unsolicited*, does it have a forceful opening?

☐ Does my introduction get directly to the point?

☐ Does the body section paint a clear picture of qualifications sketched in the résumé?

☐ Does the conclusion restate my interest and encourage specific action?

☐ Have I made my case without merely repeating the résumé?

☐ Is my letter free of "canned" expressions?

☐ Is my tone confident without being arrogant?

☐ Have I avoided a tone that is overly formal or overly stiff?

☐ Have I avoided flattery and exaggeration?

☐ Have I proofread exhaustively?

☐ Am I being scrupulously honest?

CHECKLIST
for Supporting Materials

MyWritingLab™

☐ Is my dossier complete, with letters of recommendation and other supporting materials?

☐ Is my portfolio or e-portfolio up to date?

☐ If my portfolio has hyperlinks, are they all functioning?

☐ Have I prepared for interviews?

☐ Have I sent the appropriate follow-up correspondence?

APPLICATIONS

GENERAL APPLICATIONS   MyWritingLab™

1. If you have not already prepared a standard print résumé, prepare one following the guidelines in this chapter. If you already have a résumé, revise it not only to follow this chapter's guidelines but also to update your work experience, educational background, and other details. Remember to include persuasive action verbs, to design the résumé in an efficient but attractive way, and to include all relevant experience.

2. Write an application letter applying for a part-time or summer job in response to a specific ad and tailor your résumé for the job. Choose an organization related to your career goals. Identify the exact hours and calendar period during which you are free to work. Submit a copy of the ad along with your letter and résumé.

3. A friend has asked you for help with the following application letter. Read it carefully, evaluate its effectiveness, and rewrite it as needed.

> Dear Ms. Brown,
>
> Please consider my application for the position of assistant in the Engineering Department. I am a second-year student majoring in electrical engineering technology. I am presently an apprentice with your company and would like to continue my employment in the Engineering Department.
>
> I have six years' experience in electronics, including two years of engineering studies. I am confident my background will enable me to assist the engineers, and I would appreciate the chance to improve my skills through their knowledge and experience.
>
> I would appreciate the opportunity to discuss the possibilities and benefits of a position in the Engineering Department at Concord Electric. Please phone me any weekday after 3:00 p.m. at (555) 568-9867. I hope to hear from you soon.
>
> Sincerely,

4. Write an unsolicited application letter to the human resources director of a company that interests you. Go to the company's Web site to research the various positions for which you may be qualified. Select one, and name that position in your letter. Also learn the name of the human resources director and address your letter to that person. Be sure to grab the reader's attention, to remain persuasive throughout, and to conclude with a call to action.

TEAM APPLICATION

Divide into groups and prepare a listing of five Web sites that job seekers should visit for advice about cover letters and résumés. Include a one-paragraph summary of the material found on each site. Compare the findings of your group with others in your class. In addition to sites mentioned in this chapter, see if you can find sites specific to your city, town, or state.

GLOBAL APPLICATION   MyWritingLab™

Assume that you and other students in your major would like to work in a particular country after graduation. Select a country and do some research on the economy, culture, and travel issues. Write a short memo that tells prospective students what they need to know about finding employment abroad.

DIGITAL AND SOCIAL MEDIA APPLICATION   MyWritingLab™

Job networking sites usually provide advice for creating resumes, including samples for different careers. Go to one such site (*LinkedIn* is the largest) and compare the resume samples to the strategies provided in this chapter. Create a draft résumé for one of these sites and review it with your instructor.

MyWritingLab™   Visit Chapter 9, *Résumés and Other Employment Materials*, in MyWritingLab to complete this chapter's applications, to explore this chapter's overview, checklist, and flashcards, and to test your understanding of the chapter objectives.

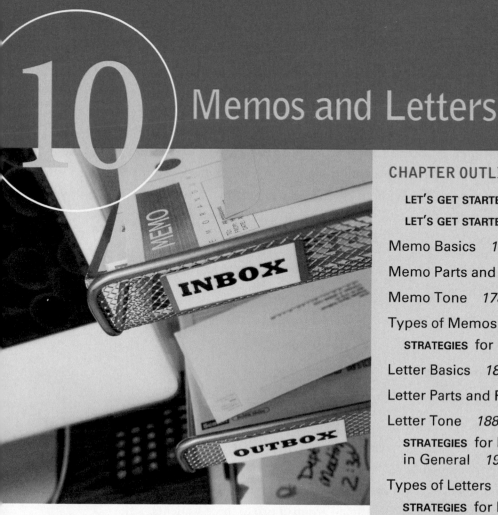

10 Memos and Letters

CHAPTER OUTLINE

LET'S GET STARTED: Memos *176*

LET'S GET STARTED: Letters *176*

Memo Basics *177*

Memo Parts and Format *178*

Memo Tone *178*

Types of Memos *181*

STRATEGIES for Memos *185*

Letter Basics *185*

Letter Parts and Formats *185*

Letter Tone *188*

STRATEGIES for Letters
in General *192*

Types of Letters *193*

STRATEGIES for Inquiry
Letters *195*

STRATEGIES for Claim
Letters *198*

STRATEGIES for Sales
Letters *200*

STRATEGIES for Adjustment
Letters *201*

CHECKLIST for Memos
and Letters *203*

Applications *203*

LEARNING OBJECTIVES FOR THIS CHAPTER

▸ Identify the parts and format of a workplace memo
or letter

▸ Achieve the right tone in a memo or letter

▸ Determine when to take a direct or indirect
approach in a memo or letter

▸ Write an effective memo

▸ Write an effective inquiry, claim, sales,
or adjustment letter

LET'S GET STARTED
Memos

You need to write a memo to your supervisor or professor requesting an extension for a project you are working on. You have decided to use a memo rather than email because a memo is more formal and indicates your professionalism and seriousness. Without reading this chapter, write such a memo. Or, if you have a different situation going on at work or school, write a memo for that situation.

Questions to ask about the memo you wrote as you review the material in this chapter:

► Does the memo contain all of the typical parts?

► Is the memo direct and to the point?

► In the memo professional and respectful in tone?

► Is the memo too long? Too short?

At the end of this chapter, review the memo you wrote for this Let's Get Started exercise. Compare what you wrote with what you learned from this chapter. Revise or modify your memo based on what you have learned from the chapter and what you learn from class. Bring your original and your revision for class, and discuss these with a small group of two to three students.

LET'S GET STARTED
Letters

You have been asked to write a report for a science, history, English, or other class. You would like to request information from a local company, nonprofit, or other organization. Without reading this chapter, write a letter about the topic you are investigating for your report or research assignment. In your letter you might request brochures, pamphlets, or other informative literature, or you might ask specific questions.

Questions to ask about the letter you wrote as you review the material in this chapter:

▶ What type of letter are you writing?

▶ What kind of tone or style did you use (professional, formal, informal)?

▶ How is the content of your letter organized (did you make your request first or provide introductory information first)?

▶ How long is your letter?

▶ What format and layout did you use?

▶ What revisions would you make, based on the material in this chapter and your class discussions?

At the end of this chapter, review the letter you wrote for this Let's Get Started exercise. Compare what you wrote with what you learned from this chapter. In particular, pay attention to the style and tone of your request. Revise or modify your letter based on what you have learned from the chapter and what you learn in class. Bring your original and your revision for class, and discuss these with a small group of two to three students.

The most common forms of everyday workplace communication are memos, letters, and email. Today, memos and letters are often sent via email as attachments, or a short memo might be written directly in the body of an email message. You need to consider audience, purpose, formality, and workplace guidelines when choosing between these forms. This chapter considers memos and letters, discussing these as stand-alone documents that might be delivered in print as well as digital formats.

MEMO BASICS

"Memo" (short for "memorandum") is derived from the same Latin roots as the words "memorize," "remember," and "remind." Memos remind readers about important events, give directives, provide instructions and information, and make requests. Memos are typically distributed to employees within an organization, not to people outside the company. Memos are important in the workplace because they are easy to distribute via email or inter-office mail (print copies) and because they provide written documentation about an event or issue.

Definition and importance of memos

Memos versus email

Informal memos and day-to-day exchanges are typically written as email messages. See Chapter 18 for more on using email for workplace communication. More formal memos should follow the strategies discussed in this chapter. These memos can then be delivered as print documents and/or as PDF attachments via email. (PDF is preferable to Word or other word processing formats because with PDF files the formatting and layout can't change.)

MEMO PARTS AND FORMAT

Standard parts of a memo

A standard memo has the word "Memo" or "Memorandum" centered at the top of the page and includes a heading guide (flush to the left margin) identifying the recipient(s), sender (and sender's initials), date, and subject. If anyone is copied on the memo, use the abbreviation "cc" followed by a colon and the name of each recipient. Because memos are often read rapidly by busy recipients, they should follow this consistent, predictable format. Figure 10.1 shows a standard memo with all parts labeled.

Memo format: introduction, body, conclusion

The body copy (main text portion) of a memo should focus on one topic. Content should be complete yet compact, providing all the information readers need but not going into unnecessary detail. Organize the body of your memo by starting with a short introduction, then writing a paragraph or two to address the main issue, and then concluding by suggesting a course of action or asking your readers to follow up.

MEMO TONE

The importance of memo tone

Memos are typically distributed in-house and circulated among colleagues, subordinates, and superiors. Memo topics often involve evaluations or recommendations about policies, procedures, and, ultimately, the people with whom you work. Because people are sensitive to criticism (even when it is merely implied) and often resistant to change, an ill-conceived memo tone can create problems. So, be particularly careful about your tone.

Achieving the right tone

Achieving the right tone in your memos involves using some common sense. Put yourself in the shoes of your recipients and write accordingly. Be polite and avoid sounding bossy, condescending, and aggressive or deferential and passive. Don't criticize, judge, or blame any individual or department. Don't resort to griping, complaining, and other negative commentary. Try to emphasize the positive. Finally, approach difficult situations reasonably. Instead of taking an extreme stance or suggesting ideas that will never work, be practical and realistic.

Being direct or indirect

The tone of a memo also comes across in the sequence in which you deliver the information. Depending on the sensitivity of your memo's subject matter, you may want to take a direct or indirect approach. A direct approach (as in Figure 10.1) begins with the "bottom line" in the first sentence (as well as

MEMORANDUM

To: All Marketing Assistants, Cincinnati Office Web Marketing Group
From: Marilyn Zito, Purchasing <m.zito@adco.com>*MZ*
Date: October 25, 20XX
Subject: *Your choices for new high-capacity copier*

As you requested at our October 12 meeting, I have gathered all the manufacturer information needed to order a new high-capacity photocopier to replace the inefficient one in your area. As you know, since the MAs typically make the most use of the copy machines, I would appreciate your input as to which copiers from the attached options seem most suitable for your purposes.

Please note that I was required to select from options under $8,500 in order to stay within your department's 20XX purchasing budget, a substantial portion of which was used to purchase your new high-speed fax machine in March. However, I think you will find that the copiers selected are state-of-the art and should more than meet your needs in terms of capacity, speed, quality, precision, and durability—all of which you indicated were important attributes.

Please take a careful look at the models attached, consider your impressions of each model, pick your top three preferences, and email me your lists individually by November 5. I will tabulate your votes, contact you with the results, and order accordingly.

Thank you very much for taking the time to help me make an informed decision that meets your genuine needs.

cc: J. Herrera, Director of Marketing
M. Ziolkowki, Vice President, Purchasing

Annotations (margin callouts):
- "Memo" or "Memorandum" is centered at the top of the page
- Heading guide includes "To" "From" "Date" and "Subject" lines
- Opening paragraph gets right to the point
- Provides necessary background details
- Outlines specific course of action in the conclusion
- Copy notation appears at the bottom

FIGURE 10.1 A properly formatted memo

in the subject line) and then presents the details or analysis that support your case. An indirect approach lays out the details of the case over several sentences (and leaves the subject line vague) before delivering the bottom line later in the paragraph.

Readers generally prefer the direct approach because they want to know the bottom line without being told in advance how to feel about it. Assume, for example, that a company Payroll Manager has to announce to employees that their paychecks will be delayed by two days: This manager should take a direct approach, announcing the unpopular news in the subject line and in the opening sentence and then explaining the causes of the problem:

> MEMO
>
> To: All employees
>
> From: Meredith Rocteau, Payroll Manager *MR*
>
> Date: May 19, 20XX
>
> Subject: *Delay in paychecks*
>
> I regret to inform you that those employees paid by direct deposit will experience a two-day delay in receiving their paychecks.
>
> This delay is due to a virus that infiltrated the primary computer server for our payroll system. Although we hired consultants to identify the virus and clean out the server, the process took nearly 48 hours.
>
> We apologize for the inconvenience.

Direct approach: Subject line gets right to the main point

Opening paragraph starts with the bottom line

However, when you need to convey exceedingly bad news or make an unpopular request or recommendation (as in announcing a strict new policy or employee layoffs), you might consider an indirect approach; this way you can present your case and encourage readers to understand your position before announcing the unpopular bottom line. The danger of the indirect approach, though, is that you may come across as evasive.

> MEMO
>
> To: All employees
>
> From: J. Travis Southfield, Director of Human Resources *JTS*
>
> Date: September 19, 20XX
>
> Subject: *Difficult economic times*
>
> Each employee of the AutoWorld family is a valued member, and each of you has played an important role in our company's expansion over the past 10 years.

Indirect approach: Subject line is not specific about bottom line

Yet as you all know, times are difficult right now for the automobile industry. Sales are down; financing is hard to obtain; and consumers are holding back on major purchases.

In order to keep the company solvent, we must consider all options. Therefore, I have been informed by our company president, John Creaswell, that we must downsize. We will begin with options for retirement packages, but please be prepared for the possibility that layoffs may follow.

We will have more information for you at an all-hands meeting tomorrow.

Opening paragraph starts with an explanation before delivering the bottom line

The bottom line

Finally, a memo's tone comes across in the way you handle its distribution. Use the appropriate delivery medium. If your topic is very short, timely, not overly formal and the message needs to reach everyone quickly, consider sending the memo as an email or email attachment. But if your topic is more formal and more detailed, send out a traditional paper memo. Also, be careful about who receives your memo. Don't send a memo to everyone at work when the content is only appropriate for a few, and don't leave vital people off your distribution list.

Delivering memos in the right medium to the right people

TYPES OF MEMOS

Memo format can also be used for distributing short reports, discussed in Chapter 15. However, for the purposes of this chapter, consider the following common and more basic types of memos.

Transmittal Memo

A transmittal memo accompanies a package of materials, such as a long report, a manuscript, or a proposal. Its purpose is to signal that the information is being sent from one place to another (providing a paper trail), to introduce the material, and to explain what is enclosed. A transmittal memo may be as simple as a sentence or a paragraph with a bulleted list describing the package, as in Figure 10.2.

Summary or Follow-up Memo

A summary or follow-up memo provides a written record of a meeting or conversation or just a topic during the meeting or conversation that was not resolved at the time. In addition to providing documentation that the meeting or conversation took place, summary and follow-up memos also ensure that each recipient

MEMORANDUM

To: D. Spring, Director of Human Resources
From: M. Noll, Head, Biology Division, *M.N.*
Date: January 16, 20XX
Subject: *Hiring of new laboratory manager*

As you know, each unit manager has been asked to prepare a hiring plan
for the coming year. Attached to this memo please find a brief report
outlining the biology division's need for a new laboratory manager.

The attached report includes

• an overview of needs

• a job description

• a budget

Please let me know if you require any additional information. I look
forward to hearing from you.

FIGURE 10.2 A transmittal memo

has the same understanding of what was decided. Figure 10.3 shows a memo that
performs both a summary and follow-up function.

Informational Memo

Informational memos typically contain some type of announcement or update.
For instance, you may receive a memo announcing the closure of a parking
ramp over the holidays for repair or an upcoming awards ceremony on Friday.
Such memos are increasingly sent via email, since email is quick and inexpensive
and has wide reach. But if the memo has a more formal purpose, a traditional
paper version may be preferable, as in Figure 10.4, which reiterates an important
company policy.

Incredible Software
and Graphics, Inc.

MEMO

To: Elaine Lamer and Mitchell Dramson, Software Development Team
From: Christopher Felts, Manager *C.F.*
Date: June 19, 20XX
Subject: *Follow-up to today's meeting*

Thank you for meeting today to discuss next steps to complete the next
version of our animation software package.

As you noted, the original release date of October 1 is probably too
optimistic given the latest hiring freeze. Yet, as I mentioned, we can't afford
to go beyond a date of October 15 if we are to make our fourth-quarter sales
goals. So, let's agree on October 15 as the new due date.

Please communicate this information to the other members of your team.

cc: E. Hearly, Division Chief

FIGURE 10.3 A summary or follow-up memo

MEMORANDUM

To: All employees
From: Jorge Gonsalves, Human Resources *J.G.*
Date: January 12, 20XX
Subject: *401K matching policy*

As the new year begins, we in Human Resources would like to remind you about the company's generous 401K matching policy. We will match your 401K contributions 100% when you roll up to 10% of your salary into your 401K.

Many companies will match only up to 5% of an employee's salary and usually not at a 100% rate, so please take advantage of this program by enrolling now. Enrollment is only open until March 1 and will not be open again until next January.

Please drop by the Human Resources office on the 6th floor to get a handout that provides more detailed information or to speak with an HR representative in person.

Thanks.

cc: Alison Sheffield, Manager, Human Resources

FIGURE 10.4 An informational memo

STRATEGIES
for Memos

▸ **Focus on one topic.** If you need to address more than one topic, consider a format other than a memo (for instance, a report).

▸ **Be brief.** People expect memos that are short and to the point.

▸ **Use the appropriate organizational format (direct or indirect).** Prefer the direct format when you need people to get the point quickly and the indirect format when you have something hard to say that needs to be softened.

▸ **Use white space, headings, and bullets.** These features provide visual structure to your memo.

▸ **Distribute to the right people.** Whether you are sending the memo via email or on paper, be sure it reaches only those who need the information. At the same time, don't leave out anyone who needs to read your message.

▸ **Use PDF for digital delivery.** If your memo will be sent via email or posted to a company internal Web site (intranet), use PDF rather than a word processing format for your attachment.

LETTER BASICS

A well-crafted workplace letter conveys a formal, professional impression. It presents a reasoned, carefully constructed case and represents not only you but also your company or organization. Letters also serve as an official notice or record. Your signature on a letter certifies your approval of the message. Letters often serve as legal documents, and so precision is crucial.

Importance of letters

LETTER PARTS AND FORMATS

All letters contain various parts (date line, return address, signature line), which are formatted in a standard way.

Parts of a Letter

The parts of a letter include the sender's address/heading, date, inside address, salutation, body text, complimentary closing, and signature. In addition, a letter may include such optional parts as a company logo, typist's initials, enclosure notation, and/or copy notation. Figure 10.5 shows a workplace letter with the standard parts (as well as optional typist's initials and enclosure notation) labeled.

Standard and optional parts of a letter

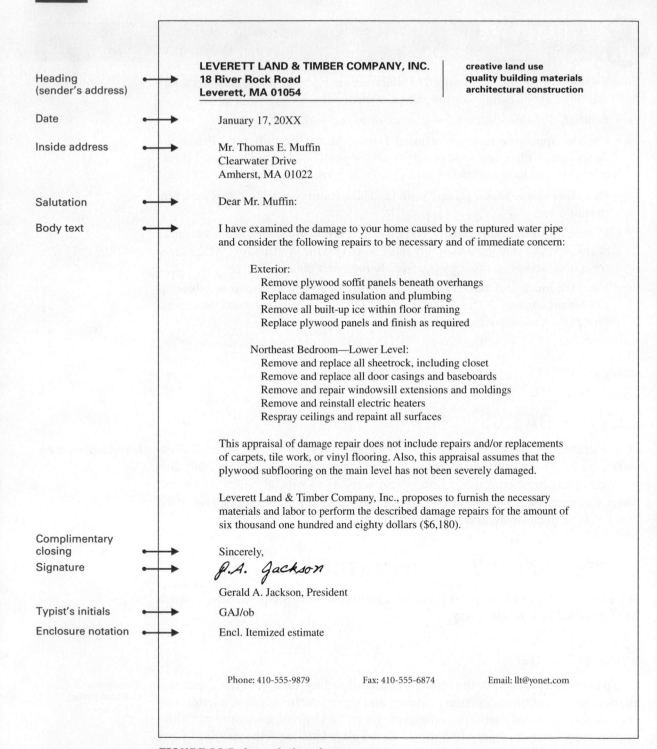

Heading (sender's address)

LEVERETT LAND & TIMBER COMPANY, INC.
18 River Rock Road
Leverett, MA 01054

creative land use
quality building materials
architectural construction

Date

January 17, 20XX

Inside address

Mr. Thomas E. Muffin
Clearwater Drive
Amherst, MA 01022

Salutation

Dear Mr. Muffin:

Body text

I have examined the damage to your home caused by the ruptured water pipe and consider the following repairs to be necessary and of immediate concern:

    Exterior:
      Remove plywood soffit panels beneath overhangs
      Replace damaged insulation and plumbing
      Remove all built-up ice within floor framing
      Replace plywood panels and finish as required

    Northeast Bedroom—Lower Level:
      Remove and replace all sheetrock, including closet
      Remove and replace all door casings and baseboards
      Remove and repair windowsill extensions and moldings
      Remove and reinstall electric heaters
      Respray ceilings and repaint all surfaces

This appraisal of damage repair does not include repairs and/or replacements of carpets, tile work, or vinyl flooring. Also, this appraisal assumes that the plywood subflooring on the main level has not been severely damaged.

Leverett Land & Timber Company, Inc., proposes to furnish the necessary materials and labor to perform the described damage repairs for the amount of six thousand one hundred and eighty dollars ($6,180).

Complimentary closing

Signature

Sincerely,

P.A. Jackson

Gerald A. Jackson, President

Typist's initials

GAJ/ob

Enclosure notation

Encl. Itemized estimate

Phone: 410-555-9879   Fax: 410-555-6874   Email: llt@yonet.com

FIGURE 10.5 A workplace letter

Sender's Address. The sender's address appears at the top of the letter in the form of either a company letterhead or the sender's mailing address. When you use your personal address, omit your name because that will appear below your signature at letter's end. On the first line, include the full street address, and on the next line, include the city, state (abbreviated), country (if applicable), and postal code (ZIP code or other postal code).

Date. The date appears two spaces below the sender's address. Spell out the month completely.

Inside Address. Use between two and four spaces between the date and the inside address (the address of the recipient). Include the courtesy title ("Mr.," "Ms.," "Dr.") and the full name of the recipient on the first line; the person's job title (if applicable) on the second line; the name of the company (if applicable) on the next line; the full street address on the next line; and the city, state, country (if applicable), and postal code on the last line.

Salutation. Double space between the inside address and the salutation. The salutation includes a greeting (usually "Dear"), followed by a courtesy title and the recipient's last name. If you don't know the person's gender, use the full name ("Dear Sandy Martin:"). In a business letter, always use a colon at the end of the salutation, not a comma.

Use an *attention line* when you write to an organization and do not know your recipient's name but are directing the letter to a specific department or position. Place the attention line flush with the left margin two line spaces (returns) below the inside address ("Attention: Director of Research and Development").

Typically, *subject lines* are used with memos, but if the recipient is not expecting your letter, a subject line can be a good way of catching a busy reader's attention ("Subject: *New patent for hybrid wheat crop*"). Place the subject line below the inside address or attention line. You can italicize the subject to make it more prominent.

Body Text. Double space between the salutation and the body text. The introductory paragraph should get right to the point. The middle paragraph(s) should support the introduction without straying off topic. The concluding paragraph should summarize and call for further action.

Complimentary Closing. Double space between the body text and the complimentary closing. Use a standard, businesslike closing such as "Sincerely," "Respectfully," or "Best regards."

Signature. Type your name four lines beneath the complimentary closing and sign in the space between the complimentary closing and typed name.

Optional Parts. Most company letters will feature a preprinted logo at the very top of the page, providing the name and address of the company along with contact information. You may also need a *typist notation*: If not typed by the author, place the author's capitalized initials first, followed by a slash and the typist's lowercase initials. If anything was sent in the same envelope provide an *enclosure notation*: Use the abbreviation "Encl." and briefly describe the contents. If anyone is copied on the letter, provide a *copy notation*. Use the abbreviation "cc" followed by a colon and the name of each recipient. Multiple notations would appear in this order: typist, enclosures, and then copy.

Formats for Letters

Block format

Although several formats are acceptable and your company may have its own, the most popular format for workplace letters is *block format* (Figure 10.6).

LETTER TONE

The importance of a letter's tone

Letters are typically written from one individual to another. But unlike a face-to-face conversation, video chat, or phone call between two people, letters lack important nonverbal cues (smiles, frowns, vocal expressions of agreement or disagreement) that help clarify what's being said. These nonverbal cues allow you to modify your comments and your vocal tone.

When writing a letter, however, you can easily forget that a flesh-and-blood person will be reacting to what you say—or seem to say. You will receive no visual or auditory clues to alter what you write before you send the letter. As a result, the tone of a letter, like that of a memo, is especially important to get right.

To achieve an appropriate tone, consider the factors discussed below that affect the relationship between sender and recipient. As you read through this section, refer to Figure 10.7, which maintains an appropriate tone in conveying bad news.

Establishing and Maintaining a "You" Perspective

Prioritize the readers' needs, wants, and feelings

A letter displaying a "you" perspective puts the reader's interest and feelings first. To convey a "you" perspective, put yourself in the place of the person who will read your correspondence, and ask yourself how this recipient will react to what you have written. Even a single word or sentence, carelessly chosen or phrased, can offend. Consider the following sentence in a letter to a customer:

Offensive

> Our record keeping is very efficient and we have looked into it, so this is obviously your error.

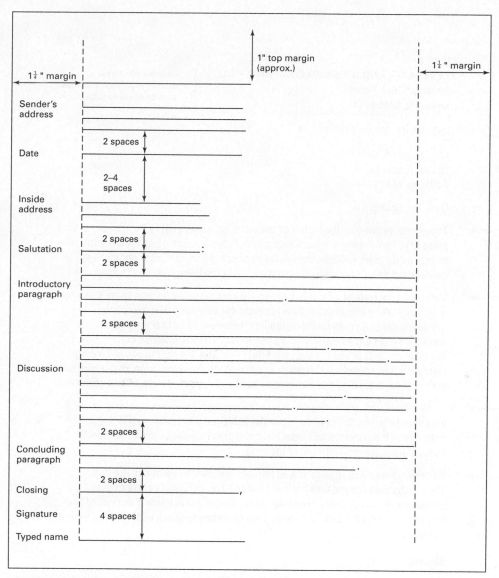

FIGURE 10.6 Block format (without letterhead)

This self-centered tone might be appropriate after numerous investigations into the customer's complaint and failed attempts to communicate your company's perspective to the customer, but in your initial correspondence it would be offensive. The example below shows a more considerate version. Instead of expressing only the writer's point of view, this second version conveys respect for the reader's viewpoint.

Although my paperwork shows that you were charged correctly, I will investigate this matter immediately by checking my files against our computer records.

Considerate and respectful

LEVERETT LAND & TIMBER COMPANY, INC.
18 River Rock Road
Leverett, MA 01054

creative land use
quality building materials
architectural construction

January 17, 20XX

Mr. Thomas E. Shaler
19 Clearwater Drive
Amherst, MA 01022

Dear Mr. Shaler:

Establishes "you" perspective immediately →

Thank you for bringing the matter of the ruptured water pipe to my attention. I was pleased to hear from you again these months after our firm completed construction of your living room addition, though I was of course sorry to hear about the water damage not only to the new construction but to the living room as a whole.

Takes an indirect approach to bad news by easing into it and saving the bad news until end of second paragraph →

Naturally, I understand your desire to receive compensation for your home's damage, especially taking into account how recently the extension was completed. In reviewing the blueprints for the extension, however, I find that the pipes were state-of-the-art and were fully insulated. In fact, it is the practice of Leverett Land & Timber not only to use the best materials available but also to exceed piping insulation requirements by as much as 50 percent. For this reason, we cannot fulfill your request to replace the piping at no cost and repair the water-damaged areas.

Speaks clearly and directly to the reader →

Undoubtedly, your insurance will cover the damage. I suspect that the rupture was caused by insufficient heating of the living room area during this unusually cold winter, but homeowner's insurance will cover damages resulting from cold-ruptured pipes 95 percent of the time.

Remains polite and tactful, despite delivery of bad news →

Maintains the "you" perspective through to the end →

Our policy is to make repairs at a 20 percent discount in situations like this. Though the pipe rupture was not our fault, we feel personally close to every project we do and to every client we serve. Please get in touch if you would like to discuss this matter further. I would also be happy to speak with your insurance company if you wish.

Sincerely,

G.A. Jackson

Gerald A. Jackson

FIGURE 10.7 Appropriate tone in conveying bad news

The "you" perspective is appropriate not only at the beginning of a letter but also throughout. Do not sign and mail the letter until you are certain that the needs, wants, and feelings of your reader consistently get top billing, even when you simultaneously must assert your own perspective.

Being Polite and Tactful

If you must express criticism, do so in a way that conveys good will and trust in the recipient. Avoid the following type of expression:

Be courteous and emphasize good will

> I am shocked that your company lacks the standards to design and manufacture an alarm clock that actually works.

Tactless

Although a company representative would be required to write a polite and thoughtful response to the above complaint, he or she might be inclined to look closely at the clock's warranty, offer only the most basic reimbursement, and not seek the customer's future business via an incentive.

In contrast, a polite and thoughtful letter might yield a full refund, a brand-new replacement, or an attractive incentive:

> Although your clock worked reliably for several months, one of the internal mechanisms recently malfunctioned. I would appreciate your contacting me about an exchange or refund.

Polite

Using Plain English

Avoid the stuffy, puffed-up phrases some writers think they need to make their communications sound important. Even though a letter is more formal than a memo or an email, plain English can still get your point across. For example, consider the following closing section to an inquiry letter asking for help:

Be professional without being stuffy

> Humbly thanking you in anticipation of your kind assistance, I remain
>
> Faithfully yours,

Stuffy

The reader of this letter might feel spoken down to and decide not to respond. However, in this revised version, the reader would likely perceive the writer as a straight-talking equal and be more inclined to follow up:

> I would greatly appreciate any help you could offer me.
>
> Best wishes,

Clear and direct

Here are a few stuffy phrasings, with clearer, more direct translations:

Stuffy, unclear	Clear and direct
As per your request	As you requested
Contingent upon receipt of	As soon as we receive
Due to the fact that	Because

Be natural. Write as you would speak in a classroom or office: professionally and respectfully but clearly and directly.

Considering the Needs of International Readers

Any letter might be read by international readers

In the increasingly global marketplace, you will often find that you need to communicate with readers outside the United States, many of whom do not speak English as a first language. To ensure that your letter is appropriate for an international reader, avoid being overly informal, use plain English, and avoid idiomatic expressions such as "in the ball park" or "under the weather."

Being Direct or Indirect

Determine if the direct or indirect approach is preferable

During your career you will have to write letters that convey bad or unwelcome news. For example, you may have to say no to customers, employees, and job applicants. You may have to make difficult requests, such as asking employees to accept higher medical insurance premiums or seeking an interview with a beleaguered official. You may have to notify consumers or shareholders about accidents or product recalls. You may have to apologize for errors—and so on. In each instance, you will have to decide whether to build your case first (indirect approach) or get right to the point (direct approach).

When to be direct or indirect

Try to anticipate your readers' reaction. Generally speaking, when you have good news use the direct approach; readers will appreciate your getting right to the point. When presenting bad news you may prefer the indirect approach; by presenting your rationale beforehand you give readers the chance to adjust to the bad news.

STRATEGIES
for Letters in General

▶ **Determine whether the situation calls for a letter, memo, or email.** Use a letter to communicate formally with a client or customer (someone not in your organization).

▶ **Use proper letter format and include all the required parts.** Unless your organization has its own guidelines, use block or modified block format and the parts discussed earlier.

➡

▸ **Place the reader's needs first.** Always write from the "you" perspective, putting yourself in your reader's place.

▸ **Decide on the direct or indirect approach.** Generally speaking, take the direct approach for good news and the indirect approach for bad news.

▸ **Maintain a courteous, professional tone.** A professional tone creates goodwill and is more effective in the long run.

▸ **Avoid stuffy language.** Use plain English, no matter how formal or important the letter. Stuffy language only comes across as phony.

▸ **Keep international readers in mind.** Don't assume that every letter you write is directed at a recipient whose first language is English.

▸ **Use PDF for digital delivery.** If your letter will be sent via email, use PDF rather than a word processing format for your attachment.

TYPES OF LETTERS

There are many types of business letters. Among the most common types you can expect to write on the job are inquiry letters, claim letters, sales letters, and adjustment letters.

Inquiry Letters

Inquiry letters ask questions and request a reply. They may be solicited (in response to an advertisement or announcement) or unsolicited (to request some type of information you need for your job). For example, a manager at a computer repair company might write a solicited inquiry to a manufacturer that offers free troubleshooting guides for repair specialists. If there has been no such advertised offer, the manager might write an unsolicited inquiry to the same company asking if any troubleshooting information is available.

Solicited and unsolicited inquiry letters

In a solicited inquiry, be brief and be sure to reference the advertisement or announcement that prompted you to write. In an unsolicited inquiry, you are asking a busy person to read your letter, consider your request, collect the information, and write a response. Therefore, keep your request reasonable and state the purpose clearly and concisely. Express your appreciation. Avoid long, involved inquiries that are unlikely to be answered.

Figure 10.8 is an example of an unsolicited letter requesting information. Research consultant Alan Greene is preparing a report on the feasibility of harnessing solar energy for home heating in Alaska. After learning that a nonprofit research group has been experimenting with solar applications, Alan decides to write for details. Notice how Greene tries to make the respondent's task as easy as possible.

Solar Solutions, Inc.
234 Western Road
Fargo, ND 27116

March 10, 20XX

Rachel Cowans
Director of Energy Systems
The Earth Research Institute
Persham, ME 04619

Dear Ms. Cowans:

States the purpose → As a Research Consultant at Solar Solutions, Inc., I am preparing a report (April 15 deadline) on the feasibility of solar energy for home heating in Arctic regions.

Makes a reasonable and courteous request → While gathering data on home solar heating, I encountered references (in *Scientific American* and elsewhere) to your group's pioneering work in solar energy systems. Would you please allow me to benefit from your experience? Your answers to the following questions would be a great help.

Presents a list of specific questions →
1. At this stage of development, do you consider active or passive heating more practical? (Please explain briefly.)
2. Do you expect to surpass the 60 percent limit of heating needs supplied by the active system? If so, at what level of efficiency and how soon?
3. What is the cost of materials for building your active system, per cubic foot of living space?
4. What metal do you use in collectors to obtain the highest thermal conductivity at the lowest maintenance costs?

Provides complete contact information → Please write your answers on the back of this page and return in the enclosed envelope. If email or phone are more convenient, feel free to contact me at agreene@solarsolutionsND.com or 555-986-6578.

Offers to share findings → I would be glad to send you a copy of the final document. Thank you in advance.

Sincerely,

Alan Greene

Alan Greene
Research Consultant

FIGURE 10.8 An unsolicited inquiry letter

STRATEGIES
for Inquiry Letters

▶ **Don't wait until the last minute.** Provide ample time for a response.

▶ **Whenever possible, write to a specific person.** If you need the name, call the organization and ask to whom you should address your inquiry.

▶ **Do your homework to ask the right questions.** A vague request such as "Please send me your data on..." is likely to be ignored. Don't ask questions for which the answers are readily available elsewhere.

▶ **Explain who you are and how the information will be used.** If you appear to be from a competing company, your request will likely be ignored. But in other situations, you still need to explain what you plan to do with the requested data.

▶ **Write specific questions that are easy to understand and answer.** If you have multiple questions, put them in a numbered list to increase your chances of getting all the information you want.

▶ **Provide alternate contact information.** If you can also be reached by email or phone, provide that information as well.

▶ **Include a stamped, self-addressed envelope.** This courteous gesture will increase the likelihood of a response.

▶ **Say thank you and offer to follow up.** Even if you said it at the beginning, say thank you again at the end. Offer to send a copy of the document in which you plan to use the information, if appropriate.

Claim Letters

In the workplace, things do not always run smoothly. Sometimes people make mistakes, systems break down, or companies make promises that can't be kept. Claim (or complaint) letters request adjustments for defective goods or poor services, or they complain about unfair treatment or the like. Such letters fall into two categories: *routine claims* and *arguable claims*. Each calls for a different approach. Routine claims typically take a direct approach because the customer's claim is not debatable. Arguable claims present more of a persuasive challenge because they convey unwelcome news and are open to interpretation; arguable claims, therefore, typically take an indirect approach.

Figure 10.9 shows a routine claim letter. Writer Jeffrey Ryder does not ask whether the firm will honor his claim; he assumes that it will and asks directly how to return his defective skis for repair. Notice that, in place of a salutation, an attention line directs the claim to the appropriate department, while a subject line (and its reemphasis in the first sentence) makes clear the nature of the claim.

Routine and arguable claim letters

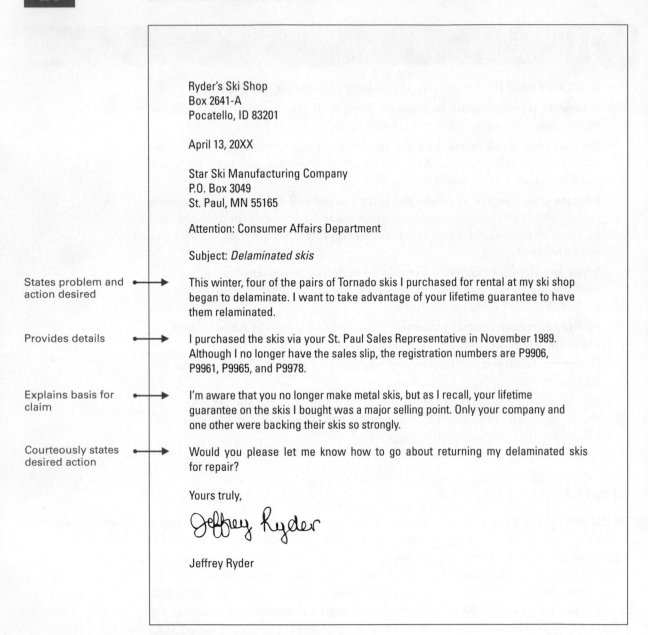

Ryder's Ski Shop
Box 2641-A
Pocatello, ID 83201

April 13, 20XX

Star Ski Manufacturing Company
P.O. Box 3049
St. Paul, MN 55165

Attention: Consumer Affairs Department

Subject: *Delaminated skis*

States problem and action desired →
This winter, four of the pairs of Tornado skis I purchased for rental at my ski shop began to delaminate. I want to take advantage of your lifetime guarantee to have them relaminated.

Provides details →
I purchased the skis via your St. Paul Sales Representative in November 1989. Although I no longer have the sales slip, the registration numbers are P9906, P9961, P9965, and P9978.

Explains basis for claim →
I'm aware that you no longer make metal skis, but as I recall, your lifetime guarantee on the skis I bought was a major selling point. Only your company and one other were backing their skis so strongly.

Courteously states desired action →
Would you please let me know how to go about returning my delaminated skis for repair?

Yours truly,

Jeffrey Ryder

Jeffrey Ryder

FIGURE 10.9 A routine claim letter

Figure 10.10 shows an arguable claim letter. Because the reply may not necessarily be in her favor, writer Sandra Alvarez uses a tactful and reasonable tone and an indirect approach to present her argument. Although she is courteous, she is also somewhat forceful to reflect her insistence on an acceptable adjustment. For example, the attention line creates an immediate businesslike tone.

Office Systems, Inc.
657 High Street
Tulsa, OK 74120

Fax (302) 655-5551 Phone (302) 655-5550 Email osys@sys.com

January 23, 20XX

Consumer Affairs Department
Hightone Office Supplies
93 Cattle Drive
Houston, Texas 77028

Attention: Ms. Dionne Dubree

Dear Ms. Dubree:

Your company has an established reputation as a reliable wholesaler of office
supplies. For eight years we have counted on that reliability, but a recent episode
has left us annoyed and disappointed. ← • Establishes early agreement

On January 29, we ordered 5 cartons of 700 MB "hp" CDs (#A74-866) and 13
cartons of Epson MX 70/80 black cartridges (#A19-556).

On February 5, the order arrived. But instead of the 700 MB "hp" CDs ordered,
we received 650 MB Everlast CDs. And the Epson cartridges were blue, not the
black we had ordered. We returned the order the same day. ← • Presents facts to support claim

Also on the 5th, we called John Fitzsimmons at your company to explain our
problem. He promised delivery of a corrected order by the 12th. Finally, on the 22nd,
we did receive an order—the original incorrect one—with a note claiming that the
packages had been water damaged while in our possession. ← • Offers more support

Our warehouse manager insists the packages were in perfect condition when he
released them to the shipper. Because we had the packages only five hours and had
no rain on the 5th, we are certain the damage did not occur here. ← • Includes all relevant information / ← • Sticks to the facts

Responsibility for damages therefore rests with either the shipper or your
warehouse staff. What bothers us is our outstanding bill from Hightone ($2,049.50) for
the faulty shipment. We insist that the bill be canceled and that we receive a
corrected statement. Until this misunderstanding, our transactions with your
company were excellent. We hope they can be again. ← • Requests a specific adjustment

We would appreciate having this matter resolved before the end of this month. ← • Stipulates a reasonable response time

Yours truly,

Sandra Alvarez

Sandra Alvarez
Manager, Accounting

FIGURE 10.10 An arguable claim letter

STRATEGIES
for Claim Letters

▸ **Routine claim letters**

- **Use a direct approach.** Describe the request or problem; explain the problem clearly; close courteously, restating the action you request.

- **Be polite and reasonable.** Your goal is not to sound off but to achieve results: a refund, a replacement, or an apology. Press your claim objectively yet firmly by explaining it clearly and by stipulating the reasonable action that will satisfy you. Do not insult the reader or revile the company.

- **Provide enough detail to clarify the basis for your claim.** Explain the specific defect. Identify the faulty item clearly, giving serial and model numbers and date and place of purchase.

- **Conclude by expressing goodwill and confidence in the company's integrity.** Do not make threats or create animosity.

▸ **Arguable claim letters**

- **Use an indirect approach.** People are more likely to respond favorably *after* reading your explanation. Begin with a neutral statement both parties can agree to—but that also serves as the basis for your request.

- **Once· you've established agreement, explain and support your claim.** Include enough information for a fair evaluation: date and place of purchase, order number, dates of previous letters or calls, and background.

- **Conclude by requesting a specific action.** Be polite but assertive in how you make your request.

Sales Letters

Purpose and format of sales letters

Sales letters are written to persuade a current or potential customer to buy a company's product or try its services. Because people are bombarded by sales messages—in magazines, on billboards, on television, online—your letter must be genuinely persuasive and must get to the point quickly. First, engage the reader immediately with an attention-grabbing statement or an intriguing question. Next, describe clearly and concisely the product or service you offer and explain its appeal. Finally, conclude by requesting immediate action.

In the letter in Figure 10.11, restaurant owner Jimmy Lekkas opens with an attention-grabbing question that is hard to ignore and has universal appeal: good food, for free, right in the neighborhood. He then makes his case by explaining the history of his restaurant (which provides immediate credibility) and offering vivid descriptions of the food. He closes by asking readers to take action by a specific date.

Jimmy's Greek Kitchen
24-52 28th Street, Astoria, NY 11102
Phone: (555) 274-5672   Fax: (555) 274-5671
Email: Jimmysgreek@comcast.net
Web site: <www.jimmysgreekkitchen.com>

July 16, 20XX

Adriana Nikolaidis
26-22 30th Street #5
Astoria, NY 11102

Dear Ms. Nikolaidis:

Are you in the mood to sample the best Greek food in the neighborhood absolutely free of charge? We at the newly opened Jimmy's Greek Kitchen would like to say "Thank you for having us in your neighborhood" by inviting you to sample a variety of our authentic Greek specialties. ← • Opens with an attention-grabbing question

If you've heard of or visited the famous Jimmy's in Chicago, you know that our fare has been pleasing Chicago diners for over 40 years. At long last, we have opened a companion restaurant in Astoria, and we are proud to offer you the same high-quality appetizers, entrees, and desserts, prepared to perfection. In fact, I trained our Astoria chef myself. ← • Describes the long history and appeal of the restaurant

Ranging from charbroiled meats and grilled seafoods to vegetarian specialties and Greek favorites like tzatziki, pastitsio, and moussaka, Jimmy's is truly the best in town. Please have a look at the enclosed menu to see the full range of tasty foods we offer. ← • Further maintains appeal by describing the menu

Please take advantage of this special offer while it lasts. From now until August 31, just bring this letter to Jimmy's and lunch or dinner is on the house. You may choose any appetizer, entree, side order, beverage, and dessert on the menu—all free of charge. We hope that you will not only enjoy the dining experience but will tell others and come back to see us frequently. ← • Ends by asking the reader to take action

Thank you,

Jimmy Lekkas

Jimmy Lekkas

FIGURE 10.11 A sales letter

STRATEGIES
for Sales Letters

▸ **Begin with a question or other attention-grabbing statement.**

▸ **Get to the point.** People resist reading long opening passages, especially if the message is unsolicited.

▸ **Spell out the benefits for the recipients.** Answer this implied question: "What do I stand to gain from this?"

▸ **Persuade with facts and with appeals to the senses.** Facts (such as the history of your company) appeal to logic. Graphic descriptions (such as the colors of your new cars or the types of food you offer) appeal to a different part of the brain—the emotions. Use both.

▸ **Tell the truth.** Despite your desire to sell something, it is unethical to lie, distort, exaggerate, or underestimate to make the sale.

▸ **Close by asking readers to take action.** Either ask for some reasonable action (such as "go to our Web site") or offer an incentive (such as a free sample) to encourage follow-up.

Adjustment Letters

Positive and negative adjustment letters

Adjustment letters are written in response to a claim letter from a customer. Even though most people never make formal complaints or follow up on warranties or product guarantees, companies generally will make a requested adjustment that seems reasonable.

Rather than quibbling over questionable claims, companies usually honor the request and show how much they appreciate the customer, as in Figure 10.12. In this example, writer Jane Duval apologizes graciously for a mistake. She omits an explanation because the error is obvious: Someone sent the wrong software. Once the reader has the information and apology, Duval shifts attention to a positive feature: the gift certificate. Note the "you" perspective and friendly tone.

Of course, if a claim is unreasonable or unjustified, the recipient usually will refuse the request. In refusing to grant a refund for a 10-speed bicycle, company representative Anna Jenkins faces a delicate balance (Figure 10.13). On the one hand, she must explain why she cannot grant the customer's request; on the other hand, she must be diplomatic in how she asserts that the customer is mistaken. Although Mrs. Gower may not be pleased by the explanation, it is thorough and reasonable.

FIGURE 10.12
A positive adjustment letter

Software Unlimited
421 Fairview Road
Tulsa, Oklahoma 74321

May 2, 20XX

Mr. James Morris
P.O. Box 176
Little Rock AR 54701

Dear Mr. Morris:

Your software should arrive by May 15. Sorry for the mixup. We don't make a practice of sending Apple software to PC owners, but we do slip up once in a while. ◄──● Apologizes immediately

In appreciation for your patience and understanding, I've enclosed a $50 gift certificate. You can give it to a friend or apply it toward your next order. If you order by phone, just give the certificate number, and the operator will credit your account. ◄──● Offers compensation

Keep your certificate handy because you will be getting our new catalog soon. It features 15 new business and utility programs that you might find useful. ◄──● Looks toward the future

Sincerely,

Jane Duval

Jane Duval
Sales Manager

Encl. Gift Certificate

STRATEGIES
for Adjustment Letters

▸ **If you need to apologize, do so immediately and in active voice.** Don't say "An error was made…"; instead, say "We are sorry we made an error…"

▸ **Be polite and professional.** Even if you must say no to a request, you can do so respectfully.

▸ **Use passive voice if you want to avoid sounding accusatory.** If your customer made a mistake in assembling the device, you could say "The wrong bolts were used" rather than "You used the wrong bolts."

▸ **If appropriate, offer an incentive.** You can create a lot of goodwill if you reach out with even a small gift certificate or in-store credit.

▸ **Close on a positive note.** Thank the person for writing and for being a customer.

People Power, Inc.

101 Salem Street, Springfield, Illinois 32456

March 8, 20XX

Mrs. Alma Gower
32 Wood Street
Lewiston, IL 32432

Dear Mrs. Gower:

Introduction starts off with the facts →

When we advertise the Windspirit as the toughest, most durable ten-speed, we stress it's a racing or cruising bike built to withstand the long, grueling miles of intense competition. The bike is built of the strongest, yet lightest, alloys available, and each part is calibrated to within 1/1000 of an inch. That's why we guarantee the Windspirit against defects resulting from the strain of competitive racing.

Writer doesn't accuse; she explains in a friendly tone →

The Windspirit, though, is not built to withstand the impact of ramp jumps such as those attempted by your son. The rims and front fork would have to be made from a much thicker gauge alloy, thereby increasing weight and decreasing speed. Since we build racing bikes, such a compromise is unacceptable.

Refusal is professional, direct, and reasonable →

To ensure that buyers are familiar with the Windspirit's limits, in the owner's manual we stress that the bike should be carried over curbings and similar drops because even an eight-inch drop could damage the front rim. Damage from such drops is not considered normal wear and so is not covered by our guarantee.

Closing is helpful →

Since your son appears to be more interested in a bike capable of withstanding the impact of high jumps, you could recoup a large part of the Windspirit's price by advertising it in your local newspaper. Many novice racers would welcome the chance to buy one at a reduced price. Or, if you prefer having it repaired, you could take it to Jamie's Bike Shop, the dealer closest to you.

Yours truly,

Anna Jenkins

Anna Jenkins
Manager, Customer Services

FIGURE 10.13 A negative adjustment letter

CHECKLIST
for Memos and Letters

MyWritingLab™

MEMO

☐ Does my memo contain all the necessary parts (To, From, Date, Subject, body copy)?

☐ Is the text of my memo clear and direct?

☐ Does my memo follow a standard format, beginning with an introductory paragraph, explaining my points in the body of the memo, then ending with a short conclusion?

☐ Is the tone of my memo professional and polite?

☐ Have I considered whether to take a direct or an indirect approach?

☐ Does my memo focus on one topic?

☐ Is my memo directed at the right people?

LETTER

☐ Does my letter contain all the necessary parts (sender's address, date, inside address, salutation/attention line, body text, closing signature)?

☐ Is the tone of my letter professional, polite, and appropriately formal?

☐ Have I considered whether to take a direct or an indirect approach?

☐ Have I put my reader's interests first (the "you" perspective)?

☐ If making a difficult request, am I being tactful yet clear about what I want?

☐ Am I writing in clear language?

APPLICATIONS

GENERAL APPLICATION   MyWritingLab™

Write a memo as the sales director of a company to in-house sales department employees and to sales representatives. Announce and outline a new dress code policy and diplomatically explain why the policy is more strict for the sales reps. Remember to keep an informal but professional tone, format the memo properly, and keep it brief but complete.

TEAM APPLICATIONS

1. In groups of two to three, assume that you are co-owners of a condominium complex that has been invaded by carpenter ants. Have a meeting to discuss your plans to find a way that the ants can be eliminated, using an insecticide that is proven to be nontoxic to humans. Ask each team member to write a follow-up memo that summarizes the meeting and recommends next steps for each team member to take. Compare memos and discuss the decisions each person made for how to organize and structure the memo.

2. Working in groups, respond to the following scenario. Appoint one group member to present the letter in class.

> Luke Harrington wants a $1200 refund for four Douglas fir trees that have died since your workers planted them in his yard two years ago. Because you guarantee your transplants for three years, he wants his money returned. After checking Harrington's contract, you recall his problem: You wouldn't guarantee the five Douglas firs he ordered because he wanted them planted in a wet, marshy area, and Douglas firs need well-drained soil. A check of Harrington's lot confirms that four trees planted in the wet area have died of root rot. Write to him, reminding him of the contract and refusing the adjustment. As you did two years ago, suggest that he plant balsam firs in the wet area. Although balsam needles are slightly darker than the Douglas firs', both trees have the shape he wants. The balsams would retain the symmetry of his tree line. Harrington's address: 921 Daisy Lane, Churchill, MO 61516.

GLOBAL APPLICATION   MyWritingLab™

Interview a person whose work takes him or her to one or more countries outside the United States. Ask that person to describe the way letters are used for international communication and whether any special issues involving grammar, forms of address, direct or indirect organizational patterns, or other features make letter writing different when addressing international audiences.

DIGITAL AND SOCIAL MEDIA APPLICATION   MyWritingLab™

Word processing programs such as Microsoft Word or Apple Pages offer a variety of templates for writing letters. Templates can help you get started with the writing; templates can also be a problem, however, because instead of thinking for yourself about the audience, purpose, and appropriate organizational pattern and language usage, you may end up letting the template do the thinking. Look at the various templates available in your word processing program, and make a list of ways in which the template may or may not work for your purposes.

MyWritingLab™   Visit Chapter 10, *Memos and Letters*, in MyWritingLab to complete this chapter's applications, to explore this chapter's overview, checklist, and flashcards, and to test your understanding of the chapter objectives.

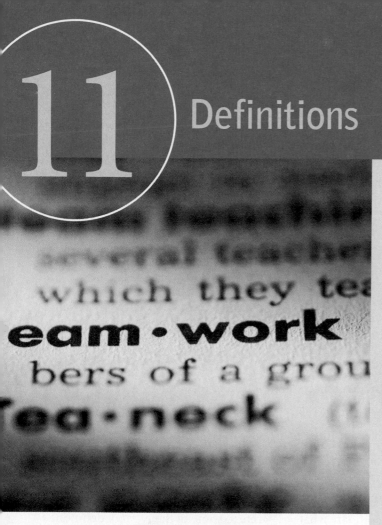

11

Definitions

CHAPTER OUTLINE

LET'S GET STARTED:
Definitions *206*

Audience and Purpose
of Definitions *207*

Legal, Ethical, and Societal
Implications of Definitions *208*

Types of Definitions *209*

Methods for Expanding
Definitions *210*

Using Multiple Expansion
Methods *214*

Placement of Definitions *216*

STRATEGIES for Definitions *217*

CHECKLIST for Definitions *218*

Applications *218*

LEARNING OBJECTIVES FOR THIS CHAPTER

▸ Research and write clear definitions

▸ Understand the legal, ethical, and societal
implications of definitions

▸ Use the three types of definitions

▸ Use various methods to expand a definition,
as the situation requires

▸ Place definitions in your document

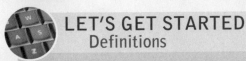

In your college major, you become familiar with technical or specialized terms that don't mean much to people outside the field. Think about a group of readers who don't know much about what you are studying. Without reading this chapter, make a list of five specialized terms or phrases used in your major, and write definitions of these terms or phrases that would be understandable to the readers you have selected. (Do not consult dictionaries or other sources in preparing these definitions.)

Questions to ask about the definitions you wrote as you review the material in this chapter:

▶ Do the definitions all answer the question "What is it?" or "What does it entail?" in a way that will make sense for these readers?

▶ Do the definitions use metaphors, references to history, or other devices that will make it easy for these readers to understand?

▶ Would the definitions benefit from the use of visuals?

At the end of this chapter, read through the definitions you wrote for this Let's Get Started exercise. Compare what you wrote to some of the types of definitions described in this chapter. Share your definitions with a student in class who is not in your major field of study. Revise your definitions based on what your student reader tells you and what you learned in this chapter.

Meaning and
importance of
definitions

Definitions explain terms or concepts that are specialized and may be unfamiliar to people who don't have expertise in a particular field. In many cases, a term may have more than one meaning or different meanings in different fields. Consider a word such as *atmosphere*: To a meteorologist, it would refer to the envelope of gases that surrounds a planet ("the Earth's atmosphere"); to a politician or office manager it would typically mean the mood of the country or the workplace ("an atmosphere of high hopes"); to a geologist it would have to do with the weather conditions in a particular area ("the atmosphere of the Hawaiian forests is lush and volcanic"); to a physicist it would stand for a unit of pressure ("a standard atmosphere is 101,325 pascal"); and to a novelist it would be associated with the mood of a novel ("a gothic atmosphere").

As you can see, precision is important, especially in specialized fields, in which field-specific terminology is common and undefined terms may prevent the overall meaning of a technical document from making sense. Engineers talk about *elasticity* or *ductility*; bankers discuss *amortization* or *fiduciary relationships*. In a technical document, these terms must be defined if people both inside and outside of those fields are to understand the meaning of the document as a whole. Imagine if a doctor continually used the words *myocardial infarction* in a patient brochure without ever defining the term. The fact that a myocardial infarction is the medical name for one form of *heart attack* would be lost on patients who might benefit from a clear understanding of the brochure.

AUDIENCE AND PURPOSE OF DEFINITIONS

Definitions make a document usable for an audience by answering one of two questions: "What, exactly, does it entail?" or "What, exactly, is it?" The first question spells out for audience members how they are affected by the item defined. For example, a person buying a new computer needs to understand exactly what "manufacturer's guarantee" or "expandable memory" means in the context of that purchase. The second question spells out for your audience what makes an item, concept, or process unique. For example, an engineering student needs to understand the distinction between *elasticity* and *ductility*. Inside or outside any field, people have to grasp precisely what "makes a thing what it is and distinguishes that thing from all other things" (Corbett 38).

Audience considerations

Consider the purpose of using particular terms in your document by answering the question "Why does my audience need to know it?" The level of technicality you use must match the audience's background and experience. For a group of mechanical engineering students, your definition of a *solenoid*, for example, can be brief and to the point, and you can use highly technical language:

Purpose considerations

> A solenoid is an inductance coil that serves as a tractive electromagnet.

A highly technical version

For general audiences, your definition will require language they can understand:

> A solenoid is a metal coil that converts electrical energy to magnetic energy capable of performing mechanical functions.

A nontechnical version

Unless you are certain that your audience can grasp the exact meaning, always define a term the first time you use it.

LEGAL, ETHICAL, AND SOCIETAL IMPLICATIONS OF DEFINITIONS

Definitions have legal implications

Precise definition is essential because you (or the organization, if you write a technical document on its behalf) are legally responsible for that document. The more clear and precise your definitions, the more confident both you and your readers can be that they share a mutual understanding of the document's meaning. For example, contracts are detailed (and legally binding) definitions of the specific terms of an agreement. If you lease an apartment or a car, the printed contract will define both the *lessee's* and *lessor's* specific responsibilities. Likewise, an employment contract or employee handbook will spell out responsibilities for both employer and employee. In preparing an employee handbook for your company, you would need to define such terms as *acceptable job performance*, *confidentiality*, *sexual harassment*, and *equal opportunity*.

Definitions have ethical implications

Definitions have ethical requirements, too. For example, the term *acceptable risk* had an ethical impact on January 28, 1986, when the space shuttle *Challenger* exploded 73 seconds after launch, killing all seven crew members aboard. (Two rubber O-ring seals in a booster rocket had failed, allowing hot exhaust gases to escape and igniting the adjacent fuel tank.) Hours earlier—despite vehement objections from the engineers—management had decided that going ahead with the launch was a risk worth taking, under the understood meaning of *acceptable risk*. This definition of *acceptable risk* was based not on the engineering facts but rather on bureaucratic pressure to launch on schedule. In this case, a faulty definition not only was ethically questionable but also cost lives. Agreeing on meaning in such cases rarely is easy, but you are ethically bound to convey an accurate interpretation of the facts as you understand them.

Definitions have societal implications

Clear and accurate definitions help the public understand and evaluate complex technical and social issues. For example, as a first step in understanding the debate over the term *genetic engineering*, we need at least the following basic definition:

> Genetic engineering refers to [an experimental] technique through which genes can be isolated in a laboratory, manipulated, and then inserted stably into another organism. Gene insertion can be accomplished mechanically, chemically, or by using biological vectors such as viruses. (Office of Technology Assessment 20)

Of course, to follow the debate, we would need increasingly detailed information (about specific procedures, risks, benefits, and so on). But the above definition gets us started on the course to a healthy debate by enabling us to visualize the basic concept and mutually agree on the basic meaning of the term.

TYPES OF DEFINITIONS

Definitions fall into three distinct categories: *parenthetical*, *sentence*, and *expanded* definitions. When you define terms within a document, decide how much detail your audience actually requires in order to grasp your exact meaning: Do you need to quickly define a word in parentheses or in a sentence, or do you need to go into significant detail explaining a complex concept?

Three categories of definitions

Parenthetical Definitions

Often, you can clarify the meaning of a word by using a more familiar synonym or a clarifying phrase in parentheses immediately after the word. This is known as a parenthetical definition and is used when a definition is relatively simple and doesn't need detailed elaboration, as in these two examples:

When to use parenthetical definitions

> The *leaching field* (sievelike drainage area) requires crushed stone.
>
> The trees on the site are mostly *deciduous* (shedding foliage at season's end).

Parenthetical definitions

On a Web page or online help system, parenthetical definitions can be linked to the main word or phrase rather than placed in parentheses after the word. Readers who click on *leaching field*, say, would be taken to a window containing a brief definition.

Sentence Definitions

A slightly longer way to define a phrase is to use the "term-class-features" method to form a sentence definition. Begin by stating the term. Then indicate the broader class to which this item belongs, followed by the features that distinguish it from other items in that general grouping. Use a sentence definition when a concept requires further elaboration than a parenthetical definition could offer. Here are some examples:

When to use sentence definitions

Term	Class	Features
A carburetor	is a mixing device	in gasoline engines that blends air and fuel into a vapor for combustion within the cylinders.
Diabetes	is a metabolic disease	caused by a disorder of the pituitary gland or pancreas and characterized by excessive urination, persistent thirst, and inability to metabolize sugar.
Stress	is an applied force	that strains or deforms a body.

Sentence definitions (term-class-features)

The previous elements may be combined into one or more complete sentences:

A complete sentence definition

> Diabetes is a metabolic disease caused by a disorder of the pituitary gland or pancreas. This disease is characterized by excessive urination, persistent thirst, and inability to metabolize sugar.

Sentence definitions are especially useful if you plan to use a term frequently and need to establish a working definition that you will not need to repeat throughout the document:

A working definition

> Throughout this report, the term *disadvantaged student* will refer to all students who lack adequate funds to pay for on-campus housing, food services, and medical care, but who are able to pay for their coursework and books through scholarships and part-time work.

Expanded Definitions

When to use expanded definitions

Brief definitions such as parenthetical and sentence definitions are fine when your audience requires only a general understanding of a term or when a term is not particularly complex to define. For example, the parenthetical definition of *leaching field* on page 209 might be enough to prevent reader confusion without providing excessive detail, or the above sentence definition of *disadvantaged student* might be enough to get a simple concept across. However, a document that requires more detail (such as a public health report on groundwater contamination from leaching fields) or a highly complex term would call for an expanded definition.

Depending on audience and purpose, an expanded definition may be a short paragraph or may extend to several pages. For example, if a device, such as a digital dosimeter (used for measuring radiation exposure), is being introduced for the first time to an audience that needs to understand how this instrument works, your definition would require at least several paragraphs, if not pages.

METHODS FOR EXPANDING DEFINITIONS

An expanded definition can be created in any number of ways as described below. The method or methods you decide to use will depend on the questions you expect the audience will want answered, as illustrated in Figure 11.1.

As you read through the following sections, refer to the following sentence definition of the word *laser*, and consider how each expansion method provides further detail in a different way:

Sentence definition

> A laser is an electronic device that emits a highly concentrated beam of light.

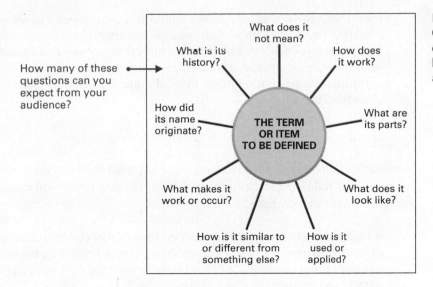

FIGURE 11.1
Questions to determine the best expansion approach

Etymology

Sometimes, a word's origin (its development and changing meanings), also known as the word's etymology, can help clarify its meaning. For example, *biometrics* (the statistical analysis of biological data) is a word derived from the Greek *bio*, meaning life, and *metron*, meaning measure. You can use a dictionary to learn the origins of most words. Not all words develop from Greek, Latin, or other roots, however. For example, some terms are acronyms, derived from the first letters or parts of several words. Such is the case with the word *laser* (derived from *light amplification by stimulated emission of radiation*); therefore, to expand the sentence definition of *laser* on page 210, you might phrase your definition as follows:

"How did its name originate?"

> The word *laser* is an acronym for *light amplification by stimulated emission of radiation* and is the name for an electronic device that emits a highly concentrated beam of light.

History

In some cases, the history of a term, concept, or procedure can be useful in expanding a definition. Specialized dictionaries and encyclopedias are good background sources. You might expand the definition of a laser by describing how the laser was invented:

"What is its history?"

> The early researchers in fiber optic communications were hampered by two principal difficulties—the lack of a sufficiently intense source of light and the absence of a medium which could transmit this light

free from interference and with a minimum signal loss. Lasers emit a narrow beam of intense light, so their invention in 1960 solved the first problem. The development of a means to convey this signal was longer in coming, but scientists succeeded in developing the first communications-grade optical fiber of almost pure silica glass in 1970. (Stanton 28)

Negation

"What does it not mean?"

Some definitions can be clarified by explaining what the term *does not* mean. For example, the following definition of a laser eliminates any misconceptions an audience might already have about lasers:

A laser is an electronic device that emits a highly concentrated beam of light. It is used for many beneficial purposes (including corrective eye and other surgeries), not—as science fiction might tell you—as a transport medium to other dimensions.

Operating Principle

"How does it work?"

The following example not only defines what a laser is but also shows the operating principle behind it:

Basically, a laser [uses electrical energy to produce] coherent light: light in which all the waves are in phase with each other, making the light hotter and more intense. (Gartaganis 23)

Analysis of Parts

"What are its parts?"

Be sure to list all of the parts to create a complete picture, and, if necessary, define the individual parts as well, as in the following expanded definition of a laser:

A laser is an electronic device that emits a highly concentrated beam of light. To get a better idea of how a laser works, consider its three main parts:

1. [Lasers require] a source of energy, [such as] electric currents or even other lasers.

2. A resonant circuit...contains the lasing medium and has one fully reflecting end and one partially reflecting end. The medium—which can be a solid, liquid, or gas—absorbs the energy and releases it as a stream of photons [electromagnetic particles that emit light]. The photons...vibrate between the fully and partially reflecting ends of the resonant circuit, constantly accumulating energy—that is, they are amplified. After attaining a prescribed level of energy, the photons can

pass through the partially reflecting surface as a beam of coherent light and encounter the optical elements.

3. Optical elements—lenses, prisms, and mirrors—modify size, shape, and other characteristics of the laser beam and direct it to its target. (Gartaganis 23)

Visuals

Make sure any visual you use is well-labeled. Always introduce and explain your visual and place the visual near your discussion. If the visual is borrowed, credit the source. The following visual accompanies the previous analysis of parts:

"What does it look like?"

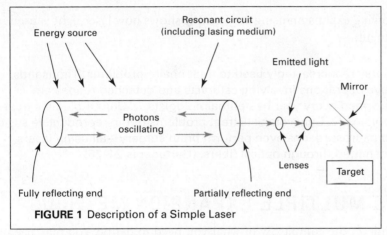

FIGURE 1 Description of a Simple Laser

Source: Gartaganis, Arthur. "Lasers." *Occupational Outlook Quarterly.*

Comparison and Contrast

By comparing (showing similarities) or contrasting (showing differences) between new information and information your audience already understands, you help build a bridge between what people already know and what they don't. The following example uses both comparison and contrast to expand upon a more basic definition of a laser:

"How is it similar to or different from something else?"

> Fiber optics technology results from the superior capacity of light waves to carry a communications signal. Sounds waves, radio waves, and light waves can all carry signals; their capacity increases with their frequency. Voice frequencies carried by telephone operate at 1000 cycles per second, or hertz. Television signals transmit at about 50 million hertz. Light waves, however, operate at frequencies in the hundreds of trillions of hertz. (Stanton 28)

Required Conditions

In the following example, additional information on optics adds to the definition of a laser:

> In order to emit a highly concentrated beam of light, the laser must absorb energy through the reflecting end of a resonant circuit, amplify the photons produced between the reflecting and partially reflecting end of the resonant circuit, and release the photons as a beam of light via a set of lenses, prisms, and mirrors.

Examples

The following expansion using an example shows how laser light is used in medical treatment:

> Lasers are increasingly used to treat health problems. Thousands of eye operations involving cataracts and detached retinas are performed every year by ophthalmologists.... Dermatologists treat skin problems.... Gynecologists treat problems of the reproductive system, and neurosurgeons even perform brain surgery—all using lasers transmitted through optical fibers. (Gartaganis 24–25)

USING MULTIPLE EXPANSION METHODS

Depending on the complexity of what you need to define, you may need to combine multiple expansion methods, as in Figure 11.2.

Like a good essay, this multiparagraph definition is unified and coherent: Each paragraph is developed around one main idea and logically connected to other paragraphs. Transitions emphasize the connection between ideas. The level of technicality connects with the intended audience.

Because this definition deals with a vital community issue, the author uses multiple methods to ensure that readers have a solid basis for understanding the situation: A water reservoir is threatened by chemical seepage and depleted by drought. This definition forms part of the introduction to a report that analyzes the severity of the problems and explores possible solutions.

To understand the problems, readers first need to know what a water table is, how it is formed, what conditions affect its level and quality, and how it figures into town planning decisions. The concepts of *recharge* and *permeability* are vital to understanding the problem, so these terms are defined parenthetically. This audience has no interest in geological or hydrological (study of water resources) theory. Audience members simply need the broadest possible picture.

FIGURE 11.2
An expanded
definition

EXPANDED DEFINITION: WATER TABLE

The water table is the level below the earth's surface at which the ground is saturated with water. Figure 1 shows a typical water table that might be found in the East. Wells driven into such a formation will have a water level identical to that of the water table.

◄ ● Sentence definition

◄ ● Example

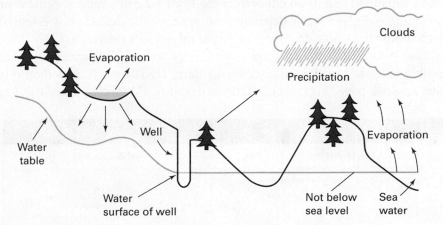

FIGURE 1 A Typical Water Table (Eastern United States)

The world's freshwater supply comes almost entirely as precipitation that originates with the evaporation of sea and lake water. This precipitation falls to earth and follows one of three courses: It may fall directly onto bodies of water, such as rivers or lakes, where it is directly used by humans; it may fall onto land, and either evaporate or run over the ground to the rivers or other bodies of water; or it may fall onto land, be contained, and seep into the earth. The latter precipitation makes up the water table.

◄ ● Operating principle

Similar in contour to the earth's surface above it, the water table generally has a level that reflects such features as hills and valleys. Where the water table intersects the ground surface, a stream or pond results.

◄ ● Comparison

A water table's level, however, will vary, depending on the rate of recharge (replacement of water). The recharge rate is affected by rainfall or soil permeability (the ease with which water flows through the soil). A water table therefore is never static; rather, it is the surface of a body of water striving to maintain a balance between the forces that deplete it and those that replenish it. In areas of Florida and some Western states where the water table is depleted, the earth caves in, leaving sinkholes.

◄ ● Operating principle

◄ ● Example

The water table's depth below ground is vital in water resources engineering and planning. It determines an area's suitability for wastewater disposal or a building lot's ability to handle sewage. A high water table could become contaminated by a septic system. Also, bacteria and chemicals seeping into a water table can pollute an entire town's water supply. Another consideration in water table depth is the cost of drilling wells. These conditions obviously affect an industry's or homeowner's decision on where to locate.

◄ ● Special conditions
and examples

The rising and falling of the water table give an indication of the pumping rate's effect on a water supply (drawn from wells) and of the sufficiency of the recharge rate in meeting demand. This kind of information helps water resources planners decide when new sources of water must be made available.

◄ ● Special conditions

PLACEMENT OF DEFINITIONS

Placing printed
definitions

Each time readers encounter an unfamiliar term or concept, that item should be defined in the same area on the page or screen. In a printed text, you can place brief definitions in parentheses or in the document's margin, aligned with the terms being defined. Sentence definitions should be part of the running text. Place an expanded definition either near the beginning of a long document or in an appendix (see page 312)—depending on whether the definition is essential to understanding the whole document or serves merely as a reference.

Using hyperlinked
definitions

On a Web site, hyperlinks are a great way to make expanded definitions accessible because readers can click on an item, read about it, and then return to the original page. Figure 11.3 defines usability ("What is Usability?") and

**FIGURE 11.3
A hyperlinked
expanded
definition**

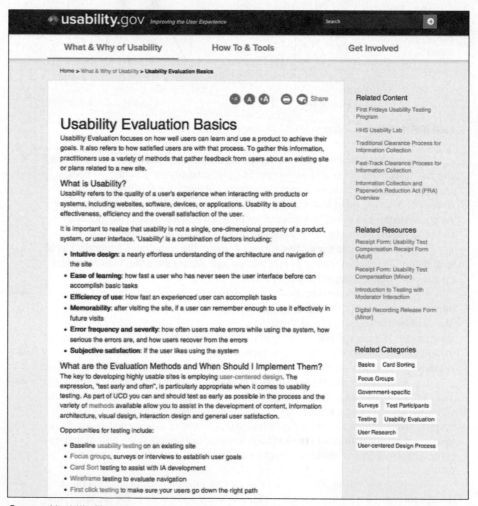

Source: UsabilityNet

then provides expanded definitions via links at the bottom of the page (usability testing; focus groups; Card Sort; and so on). The previous Web page provides a thorough definition of "usability," but the "user-centered designed" material is at a deeper level of detail; rather than disrupting the discussion of "usability," the hyperlink allows readers to jump to it if they wish.

STRATEGIES
for Definitions

▸ **Decide on the level of detail you need.** Definitions vary greatly in length and detail, from a few words in parentheses to a multipage document. How much does this audience need in order to follow your explanation or grasp your point?

▸ **Classify the item precisely.** The narrower your class, the clearer your meaning. *Stress* is classified as an applied force; to say that stress "is what…" or "takes place when…" fails to denote a specific classification. Diabetes is precisely classified as a *metabolic disease*, not as a *medical term*.

▸ **Differentiate the item accurately.** If the distinguishing features are too broad, they will apply to more than this one item. A definition of *brief* as a "legal document used in court" fails to differentiate briefs from all other legal documents (wills, affidavits, and the like).

▸ **Avoid circular definitions.** Do not repeat, as part of the distinguishing feature, the word you are defining. "Stress is an applied force that places stress on a body" is a circular definition.

▸ **Expand your definition selectively.** Begin with a sentence definition and select the best expansion strategy or combination of expansion strategies for your audience and purpose.

▸ **Use visuals to clarify your meaning.** No matter how clearly you explain, as the saying goes, a picture can be worth a thousand words—even more so when used with readable, accurate writing.

▸ **Know "how much is enough."** Don't insult people's intelligence by giving needless details or spelling out the obvious.

▸ **Consider the legal implications of your definition.** What does an *unsatisfactory job performance* mean in an evaluation of a company employee: that the employee could be fired, required to attend a training program, or given one or more chances to improve (Performance Appraisal 3–4)? Failure to spell out your meaning invites a lawsuit.

▸ **Consider the ethical implications of your definition.** Be sure your definition of a fuzzy or ambiguous term such as *safe levels of exposure, conservative investment*, or *acceptable risk* is based on fair and accurate interpretation of the facts.

STRATEGIES *continued*

Consider, for example, a U.S. cigarette company's claim that cigarette smoking in the Czech Republic promoted *fiscal benefits*, defined, in this case, by the fact that smokers die young, thus eliminating pension and health care costs for the elderly!

▶ **Place your definition in an appropriate location.** Allow readers to access the definition and then return to the main text with as little disruption as possible.

▶ **Cite your sources, as needed.** See Appendix A.

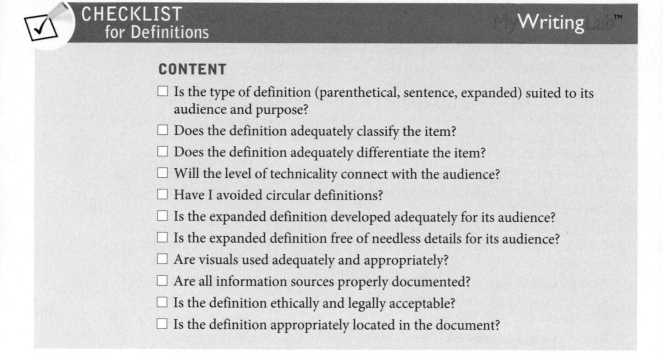

CHECKLIST
for Definitions

MyWritingLab™

CONTENT

☐ Is the type of definition (parenthetical, sentence, expanded) suited to its audience and purpose?

☐ Does the definition adequately classify the item?

☐ Does the definition adequately differentiate the item?

☐ Will the level of technicality connect with the audience?

☐ Have I avoided circular definitions?

☐ Is the expanded definition developed adequately for its audience?

☐ Is the expanded definition free of needless details for its audience?

☐ Are visuals used adequately and appropriately?

☐ Are all information sources properly documented?

☐ Is the definition ethically and legally acceptable?

☐ Is the definition appropriately located in the document?

APPLICATIONS

GENERAL APPLICATION   MyWritingLab™

Choose a situation and an audience, and prepare an expanded definition specifically designed for this audience's level of technical understanding. Use at least four expansion strategies, including at least one visual. In preparing your expanded definition, consult no fewer than four outside references. Cite and document each source as shown in Appendix A.

TEAM APPLICATION

Divide into groups by majors or interests. Appoint one person as group manager. Decide on an item, concept, or process that would require an expanded definition for laypersons; some examples follow:

From computer science: an algorithm, binary coding, or systems analysis

From nursing: a pacemaker, coronary bypass surgery, or natural childbirth

Complete an Audience and Purpose Profile (page 46). Once your group has decided on the appropriate expansion strategies, the group manager will assign each member to work on one or two specific strategies as part of the definition. As a group, edit and incorporate the collected material into an expanded definition, revising as often as needed. The group manager will assign one member to present the definition in class.

GLOBAL APPLICATION   MyWritingLab™

Any definition you write may be read by someone who may not speak English as a first language. Locate an expanded definition on Wikipedia that may be difficult for a non-American or non-native English speaker to understand for one reason or another (use of idioms, use of abbreviations, use of American metaphors such as sports metaphors not used in other countries). Explain how the definition could be reworded so that most readers would be able to understand it.

DIGITAL AND SOCIAL MEDIA APPLICATION   MyWritingLab™

If you could convert your expanded definition from the General Application into a Web page or other digital document, which items would be best suited for hyperlinks?

MyWritingLab™   Visit Chapter 11, *Definitions*, in MyWritingLab to complete this chapter's applications, to explore this chapter's overview, checklist, and flashcards, and to test your understanding of the chapter objectives.

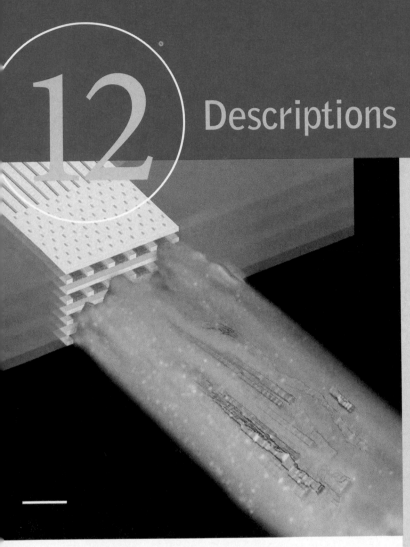

12 Descriptions

CHAPTER OUTLINE

LET'S GET STARTED:
Descriptions *221*

Audience and Purpose
of Descriptions *222*

Objectivity in Descriptions *222*

Elements of Descriptions *223*

Product and Process
Descriptions *225*

A Complex Product
Description *228*

A Complex Process
Description *232*

STRATEGIES for Descriptions *235*

Specifications *236*

STRATEGIES for
Specifications *238*

CHECKLIST for Descriptions
and Specifications *239*

Applications *240*

LEARNING OBJECTIVES FOR THIS CHAPTER

▸ Understand the importance of descriptions
in workplace communication

▸ Maintain objectivity in descriptions

▸ Differentiate between product descriptions
and process descriptions

▸ Write a long product or process description

▸ Differentiate product or process descriptions
from specifications

▸ Compose a set of specifications

Suppose your company has invented a useful gadget—such as a staple remover or paper punch (or some other ordinary but somewhat complex item with multiple parts). Choose such an item—one that you can get your hands on and study, weigh, measure, and possibly take apart. Begin describing this object by assigning descriptive details to it, recording every detail on a piece of paper or in a word-processed document. Weed out the subjective details (such as "pretty" or "ugly") from the objective details (such as—for a staple remover—"prongs," "finger grips," and "spring mechanism"). Then decide on the most logical sequence for describing this item: bottom to top, exterior to interior, and so on (such as—for the staple remover—"plastic finger grips" to "hollow metal prongs with pointed tips" to "coil-spring extensor mechanism," and so on). Finally, compose a full description of the product, using visuals as needed.

Questions to ask about the description you wrote as you review the material in this chapter:

▸ Were you able to maintain objectivity when writing your description?

▸ Does your description contain all of the typical elements?

▸ Did you include appropriate visuals?

▸ Did you follow the appropriate descriptive sequence(s) for your purpose and audience?

At the end of this chapter, review your initial Let's Get Started description with your instructor or with a group of students to see how much you might change or modify the description based on what you have learned from the chapter.

D escriptions are essential in workplace writing because, like definitions, they help ensure that readers understand the full meaning of any technical document. Descriptions and definitions often go hand in hand. For example, to return to the *myocardial infarction* example in the previous chapter (page 207), a medical student reading a document about myocardial infarctions would need to know not only that

Meaning and
importance of
descriptions

a myocardial infarction is a form of heart attack (definition) but also what causes such a heart attack (description).

This chapter will explore how to write technical descriptions from a variety of angles and for a variety of purposes.

AUDIENCE AND PURPOSE OF DESCRIPTIONS

As with any technical document, consider your audience and your document's purpose carefully before writing a description.

Audience considerations

While definitions answer the questions "What is it?" or "What does it entail?" descriptions often include definitions first and then must answer the additional questions "What does it look like?" "What are its parts?" "What does it do?" "How does it work?" or "How does it happen?"

Assume that most readers won't be familiar with the product or process you are describing and write your description at the appropriate level of technicality. An audience of medical technicians will easily understand jargon related to that field, but nonexperts will need language with which they are familiar. For example, the sentence "A tumor is a neoplasm" would make sense to most medical professionals; however, for an audience outside that field, you would need to use more accessible language, such as "A tumor is a growth of cells that occurs independently of surrounding tissue and serves no useful function."

Purpose considerations

Consider exactly what you want readers to know and why they need to know it. You may want to write out a purpose statement before you start writing your description, such as: "The purpose of this description is to help plumbing apprentices understand the parts of the Heatwave home water heater and how those parts work together to produce hot water."

OBJECTIVITY IN DESCRIPTIONS

Subjective versus objective descriptions

A description can be mainly *subjective* (based on feeling) or *objective* (based on fact). Subjective descriptions do more than simply convey factual information; subjective descriptions use sensory and judgmental ideas such as "The weather was miserable" or "The room was terribly messy." In contrast, objective descriptions present an impartial view, filtering out personal impressions and focusing on details any viewer could observe ("All day, we had freezing rain and gale-force winds").

Why descriptions should be objective

Except in cases of promotional writing, descriptions should be objective. Pure objectivity is, of course, humanly impossible. Each writer filters the facts and their meaning through his or her own perspective and therefore chooses what to include and what to omit. Nonetheless, when writing descriptions, you should communicate the facts as we know and understand them. Even positive claims made in promotional writing (for example, "reliable," "rugged") should be based on objective and verifiable evidence.

Being objective does not, however, mean forsaking personal evaluation in cases in which a product or process may be unsafe or unsound. An ethical communicator, in the words of one expert, "is obligated to express her or his opinions of products, as long as these opinions are based on objective and responsible research and observation" (MacKenzie 3).

Descriptions have ethical implications

One way to maintain objectivity when writing descriptions is to always provide details that are visual, not emotional. Ask yourself what any observer would recognize or what a camera would record. For example, instead of saying, "His office has a depressing atmosphere" (not everyone would agree), say "His office has broken windows looking out on a brick wall, missing floorboards, broken chairs, and a ceiling with chunks of plaster missing."

How to be objective

A second way to maintain objectivity is to use precise and informative language. For instance, specify location and position, exact measurements, weights, and dimensions instead of using inexact and subjective words like *large*, *long*, and *near*. Be careful, though, not to confuse precise language with overly complicated technical terms or needless jargon. For example, don't say *phlebotomy specimen* instead of *blood*, *thermal attenuation* instead of *insulation*, or *proactive neutralization* instead of *damage control*. General readers prefer nontechnical language—as long as the simpler words do the job.

ELEMENTS OF DESCRIPTIONS

All descriptions should include a forecasting title, an orienting introduction, a logical sequence of topics, clarifying visuals, and a summarizing conclusion.

Title

Promise exactly what the document will deliver—no more nor less. For example, assume you are describing the braking mechanism of a particular brand and type of bicycle: Be clear in your title by referring to the exact brand and type of bicycle, and be limited in your title by indicating that you will only describe the braking mechanism. The title "A Description of a Bicycle" is neither clear nor limited. A better title would be "A Description of the Velo Racing Bicycle's Center-Pull Caliper Braking Mechanism."

Provide a clear and limiting title

Introduction

Descriptions rarely call for a standard topic or thesis statement because the goal of these documents is to catalog details to help readers visualize the product or process. Any description, however, should begin by telling readers what to look for. If you have written a purpose statement to help you orient yourself prior to writing the description, simply reuse it here. For example, you might say in your

Provide an introduction that orients readers

introduction, "The goal of this description is to introduce apprentice road construction workers to the parts and function of a standard jackhammer." You may also simply want to start with a brief definition of what you will describe.

Sequence of Topics

For longer descriptions, choose the sequence, or organizational pattern that is most logically consistent with your purpose.

To describe how something looks, including its parts, use a *spatial* sequence. Follow the same spatial patterns readers would follow when viewing the item. Do you want to move from top to bottom, inside to outside, or right to left or follow some other pattern? For example, when describing a laptop keyboard, you might follow an outside to inside spatial sequence, first describing the "on/off" and mouse keys, then moving inward to the "page up," "page down," "shift," "tab," "caps lock," and function keys, and finally moving to the interior number, letter, and punctuation keys.

To describe how something works, use a *functional* sequence. Describe the workings (functions) of the device in the order in which the parts function. For example, if you want to describe how a solar home heating system works, proceed from source to outlet: from the heat collectors on the roof through intermediate components to the heating vents.

To describe how something is assembled, use a *chronological* sequence. Parallel the order in which parts are assembled or stages occur. For example, if you want to describe how to put together a small desk, describe how to put together the main parts first and the smaller, more decorative parts last.

Spatial, functional, and chronological sequencing are not mutually exclusive; you can combine these sequences as needed. For example, in describing the appearance, use, and assembly of an atomic alarm clock, you would employ a spatial sequence to help readers recognize this item, a functional sequence to show how it works, and a chronological sequence to help readers assemble it correctly.

Visuals

You can explain a product or process as clearly as you like in words, but a clear diagram or other visual can show your readers the actual look and feel of the product or process. The diagram (top view) in Figure 12.1 adds much-needed visual impact to what would be a complicated prose description. In addition to the picture, labels help readers interpret what they are seeing.

Conclusion

A conclusion should be short and to the point and not introduce any new material. It should provide readers with a brief summary of what the description

---

Marginal notes:

Provide a logical and appropriate sequence of topics

Spatial sequence: How something looks

Functional sequence: How something works

Chronological sequence: How something is assembled or occurs

Combine sequencing when appropriate

Provide visuals to enhance and clarify prose descriptions

Provide a concise conclusion to give readers a sense of finality

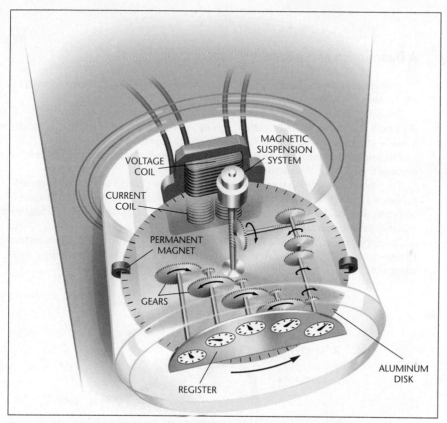

FIGURE 12.1
A descriptive
visual

Source: "Description of an Electricity Meter" illustration by George Retseck, from "Electricity Meters" by Les Rosenau, from *Scientific American*, March 2000, Volume 108. Reprinted with permission.

has attempted to accomplish. It also should give readers a sense that they now understand everything they need to know about the product or process.

PRODUCT AND PROCESS DESCRIPTIONS

Descriptions generally divide into two broad categories: *product descriptions* and *process descriptions*. Anyone learning the parts of a particular device (say, a standard microscope) relies on a product description. Anyone wanting to understand the steps or stages in a complex event (say, how lightning is produced) relies on a process description.

Product and process descriptions

For example, the product description in Figure 12.2 gives beginning paramedical or nursing students a clear image of the overall device (a stethoscope) and its parts. The process description in Figure 12.3, on the other hand, helps surveyors or environmentalists understand the steps or stages by which contaminants may be removed from the soil using the "lasagna process."

FIGURE 12.2
A product description

A Description of the Standard Stethoscope

The stethoscope is a listening device that amplifies and transmits body sounds to aid in detecting physical abnormalities.

This instrument has evolved from the original wooden, funnel-shaped instrument invented by French physician R. T. Lennaec in 1819. Because of his female patients' modesty, he found it necessary to develop a device, other than his ear, for auscultation (listening to body sounds).

This description explains to the beginning paramedical or nursing student the structure, assembly, and operating principle of the stethoscope.

The standard stethoscope is roughly 24 inches long and weighs about 5 ounces. The instrument consists of a sensitive sound-detecting and amplifying device whose flat surface is pressed against a bodily area. This amplifying device is attached to rubber and metal tubing that transmits the body sound to a listening device inserted in the ear.

The stethoscope's Y-shaped structure contains seven interlocking pieces: (1) diaphragm contact piece, (2) lower tubing, (3) Y-shaped metal piece, (4) upper tubing, (5) U-shaped metal strip, (6) curved metal tubing, and (7) hollow ear plugs. These parts form a continuous unit (Figure 1).

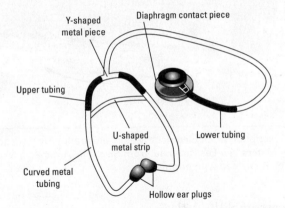

FIGURE 1 Stethoscope with Diaphragm Contact Piece (Front View)

The seven major parts of the stethoscope provide support for the instrument, flexibility of movement for the operator, and ease in use.

In an operating cycle, the diaphragm contact piece, placed against the skin, picks up sound impulses from the body's surface. These impulses cause the plastic diaphragm to vibrate. The amplified vibrations, in turn, are carried through a tube to a dividing point. From here, the amplified sound is carried through two separate but identical series of tubes to hollow ear plugs.

FIGURE 12.3
A process
description

The Lasagna Process

Dubbed the "lasagna" process because of its layers, this technology cleans up liquid-borne organic and inorganic contaminants in dense, claylike soils. Initial work is focused on removing chlorinated solvents.

Because clay is not very permeable, it holds groundwater and other liquids well. Traditional remediation for this type of site requires that the liquid in the soil (usually groundwater) be pumped out. The water brings many of the contaminants with it, then is chemically treated and replaced—a time-consuming and expensive solution.

The lasagna process, on the other hand, allows the soil to be remediated *in situ* (on site) by using low-voltage electric current to move contaminated groundwater through treatment zones in the soil. Depending on the characteristics of the individual site, the process can be done in either a vertical or horizontal configuration. (See figure below.)

The first step in the lasagna process is to "fracture" the soil, creating a series of zones. In a vertical configuration, a vertical borehole is drilled and a nozzle inserted; a highly pressurized mixture of water and sand (or another water/solid mix) is injected into the ground at various depths. The result: a stack of pancake-shaped, permeable zones in the denser, contaminated soil. The top and bottom zones are filled with carbon or graphite so they can conduct electricity. The zones between them are filled with treatment chemicals or microorganisms that will remediate the contaminants.

When electricity is applied to the carbon and graphite zones, they act as electrodes, creating an electric field. Within the field, the materials in the soil migrate toward either the positive or negative electrode. Along with the migrating materials, pollutants are carried into the treatment zones, where they are neutralized or destroyed.

The horizontal configuration works in much the same way, differing only in installation. Because the electrodes and treatment zones extend down from the surface, this configuration does not require the sophisticated hydraulic fracturing techniques that are used in the vertical configuration.

Schematic Diagram of the Lasagna Process

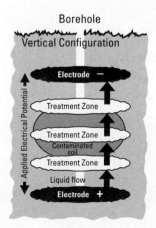

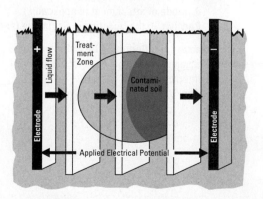

Source: Adapted from Japikse, Catharina. "Lasagna in the making." *EPA Journal,* 20.3.

A COMPLEX PRODUCT DESCRIPTION

Figure 12.4 is a complex product description. The audience for the standard bumper jack description would be car and truck owners and other general readers. This audience needs to know only the basics—what it is, what it looks like, what its parts are, and how, generally, it works—before actually using the jack safely and effectively.

To plan this description, the writer has created an outline for what details to include and how to organize the material. Also, the writer has determined what *not* to include: for example, basic dimensions and measurements are included, but they are not the precise and detailed dimensions and measurements an engineering audience might require. Finally, the writer has kept the language simple and free of jargon that this audience might not understand.

Writer's outline for planning the complex description →

I. Introduction: General Description
   A. Definition, Function, and Background of the Item
   B. Purpose (and Audience—for classroom only)
   C. Overall Description (with general visuals, if applicable)
   D. Principle of Operation (if applicable)
   E. List of Major Parts

II. Description and Function of Parts
   A. Part One in the Descriptive Sequence
      1. Definition
      2. Shape, dimensions, material (with specific visuals)
      3. Subparts (if applicable)
      4. Function
      5. Relation to adjoining parts
      6. Mode of attachment (if applicable)
   B. Part Two in the Descriptive Sequence (and so on)

III. Summary and Operating Description
   A. Summary (used only in a long, complex description)
   B. Interrelation of Parts
   C. One Complete Operating Cycle

FIGURE 12.4 A complex product description

1

Description of a Standard Bumper Jack

Introduction—General Description

The standard bumper jack is a portable mechanism for raising the front or rear of a car through force applied with a lever. This jack enables even a frail person to lift one corner of a 2-ton automobile.

The jack consists of a molded steel base supporting a free-standing, perpendicular, notched shaft (Figure 1). Attached to the shaft are a leverage mechanism, a bumper catch, and a cylinder for insertion of the jack handle. Except for the main shaft and leverage mechanism, the jack is made to be dismantled. All its parts fit neatly in the car's trunk.

The jack operates on a leverage principle, with the operator's hand traveling 18 inches and the car only $\frac{3}{8}$ of an inch during a normal jacking stroke. Such a device requires many strokes to raise the car off the ground but may prove a lifesaver to a motorist on some deserted road.

Five main parts make up the jack: base, notched shaft, leverage mechanism, bumper catch, and handle.

Description of Parts and Their Function

Base. The rectangular base is a molded steel plate that provides support and a point of insertion for the shaft (Figure 2). The base slopes upward to form a platform containing a 1-inch depression that provides a stabilizing well for the shaft. Stability is increased by a 1-inch cuff around the well. As the base rests on its flat surface, the bottom end of the shaft is inserted into its stabilizing well.

Shaft. The notched shaft is a steel bar (32 inches long) that provides a vertical track for the leverage mechanism. The notches, which hold the mechanism in position on the shaft, face the operator.

The shaft vertically supports the raised automobile, and attached to it is the leverage mechanism, which rests on individual notches.

Leverage Mechanism. The leverage mechanism provides the mechanical advantage needed for the operator to raise the car. It is made to slide up and down the notched shaft. The main body of this pressed-steel mechanism contains two units: one for transferring the leverage and one for holding the bumper catch.

The leverage unit has four major parts: the cylinder, connecting the handle and a pivot point; a lower pawl (a device that fits into the notches to allow forward and prevent backward motion), connected directly to the cylinder; an upper pawl, connected at the pivot point; and an "up-down" lever,

Clear and limiting title tells readers exactly what to expect

Introduction orients readers via a definition

Overall description of the product uses spatial sequencing ("What does it look like?")

Description of parts uses chronological sequencing ("How is it assembled?")

FIGURE 12.4 *(Continued)*

2

Clearly labeled visual enhances prose descriptions of parts

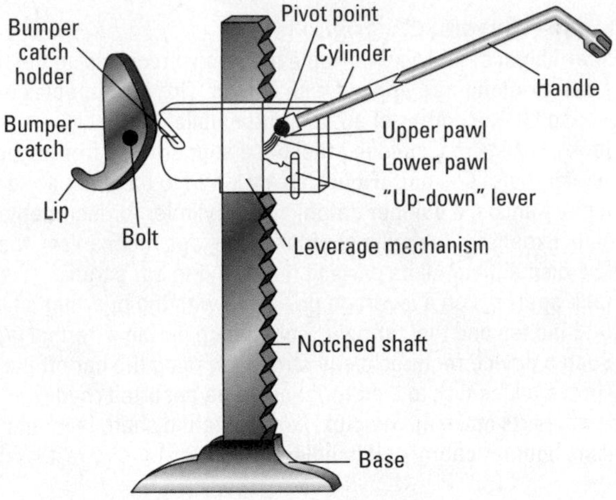

FIGURE 1 A Side View of the Standard Bumper Jack

which applies or releases pressure on the upper pawl by means of a spring (Figure 1). Moving the cylinder up and down with the handle causes the alternate release of the pawls and, thus, movement up or down the shaft—depending on the setting of the "up-down" lever. The movement is transferred by the metal body of the unit to the bumper catch holder.

The holder consists of a downsloping groove, partially blocked by a wire spring (Figure 1). The spring is mounted in such a way as to keep the bumper catch in place during operation.

Bumper Catch. The bumper catch is a 9-inch molded plate that attaches the leverage mechanism to the bumper and is bent to fit the shape of the bumper. Its outer $\frac{1}{2}$ inch is bent up to form a lip (Figure 1), which hooks behind the bumper to hold the catch in place. The two sides of the plate are bent back 90 degrees to leave a 2-inch bumper contact surface, and a bolt is riveted between them. This bolt slips into the groove in the leverage mechanism and provides the attachment between the leverage unit and the car.

Jack Handle. The jack handle is a steel bar that serves both as lever and lug bolt (or lugnut) remover. This round bar is 22 inches long, $\frac{5}{8}$ inch in diameter, and bent 135 degrees roughly 5 inches from its outer end. Its outer

FIGURE 12.4 *(Continued)*

3

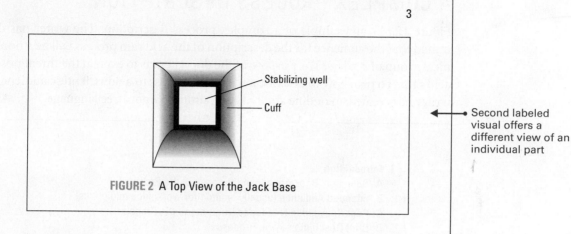

FIGURE 2 A Top View of the Jack Base

Second labeled visual offers a different view of an individual part

end is a socket wrench made to fit the wheel's lug bolts. Its inner end is beveled to form a bladelike point for prying the wheel covers and for insertion into the cylinder on the leverage mechanism.

Conclusion and Operating Description

One quickly assembles the jack by inserting the bottom of the notched shaft into the stabilizing well in the base, the bumper catch into the groove on the leverage mechanism, and the beveled end of the jack handle into the cylinder. The bumper catch is then attached to the bumper, with the lever set in the "up" position.

As the operator exerts an up-down pumping motion on the jack handle, the leverage mechanism gradually climbs the vertical notched shaft until the car's wheel is raised above the ground. When the lever is in the "down" position, the same pumping motion causes the leverage mechanism to descend the shaft.

Conclusion uses functional sequencing ("How does it work?")

FIGURE 12.4 *(Continued)*

A COMPLEX PROCESS DESCRIPTION

Figure 12.5 is an example of a complex process description. The writer has determined that the audience for the description of the acid rain process will be a nontechnical group of readers. The purpose of the document is to explain the threat posed by acid rain. To plan how to describe a scientific process to a nonscientific audience, the writer has created an outline and has used simple, jargon-free language.

Writer's outline for planning the complex description →

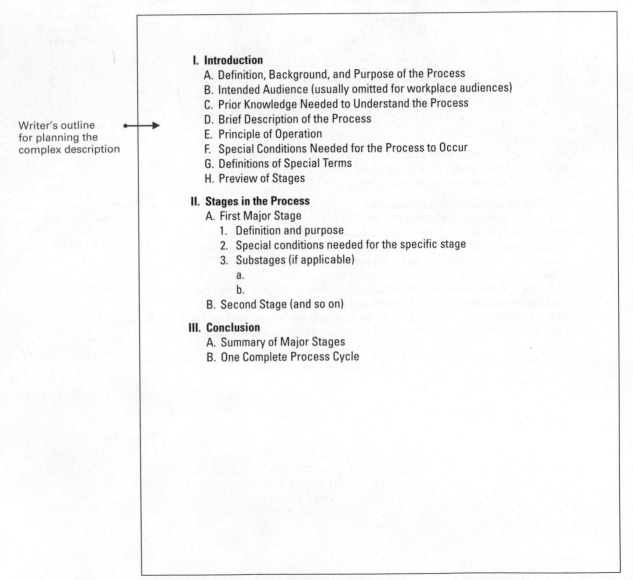

I. **Introduction**
   A. Definition, Background, and Purpose of the Process
   B. Intended Audience (usually omitted for workplace audiences)
   C. Prior Knowledge Needed to Understand the Process
   D. Brief Description of the Process
   E. Principle of Operation
   F. Special Conditions Needed for the Process to Occur
   G. Definitions of Special Terms
   H. Preview of Stages

II. **Stages in the Process**
   A. First Major Stage
      1. Definition and purpose
      2. Special conditions needed for the specific stage
      3. Substages (if applicable)
         a.
         b.
   B. Second Stage (and so on)

III. **Conclusion**
   A. Summary of Major Stages
   B. One Complete Process Cycle

FIGURE 12.5 A complex process description

1

HOW ACID RAIN DEVELOPS, SPREADS, AND DESTROYS

Introduction

Acid rain is environmentally damaging rainfall that occurs after fossil fuels burn, releasing nitrogen and sulfur oxides into the atmosphere. Acid rain increases the acidity level of waterways because these nitrogen and sulfur oxides combine with the air's normal moisture. The resulting rainfall is far more acidic than normal rainfall. Acid rain is a silent threat because its effects, although slow, are cumulative.

Power plants burning oil or coal are primary causes of acid rain. The burnt fuel is not completely expended, and residue enters the atmosphere. Although this residue contains several potentially toxic elements, sulfur oxide and, to a lesser extent, nitrogen oxide are the major problems: These chemical culprits combine with moisture to form sulfur dioxide and nitric acid, which then rain down to earth.

The Process

HOW ACID RAIN DEVELOPS. Once fossil fuels have been burned, their usefulness ends. It is here that the acid rain problem begins (Figure 1).

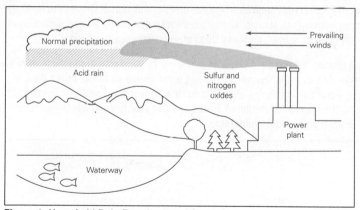

Figure 1 How Acid Rain Develops and Spreads

Acid level is measured by pH readings. The pH scale runs from 0 through 14—a pH of 7 is neutral. (Distilled water has a pH of 7.) Numbers above 7 indicate increasing alkalinity. (Household ammonia has a pH of 11.) Numbers below 7 indicate increasing acidity. Movement in either direction on the scale means multiplying by 10. Lemon juice, with a pH value of 2, is 10 times more acidic than apples, with a pH of 3, and 1,000 times more acidic than carrots, with a pH of 5.

Right margin annotations:

Clear title tells readers what to expect and also promotes awareness of the issue

Introduction orients readers via a definition

Initial description of the process uses functional sequencing ("How does it work?"), as does the remainder of the description

Headers in "The Process" section mirror and follow through on the description's title

Clearly labeled visual enhances prose description of process

Additional definition introduces a new concept ("pH")

FIGURE 12.5 *(Continued)*

FIGURE 12.5
(Continued)

2

Because of carbon dioxide (an acid substance) normally present in air, unaffected rainfall has a pH of 5.6. At this time, the pH of precipitation in the northeastern United States and Canada is between 4.5 and 4. In Massachusetts, rain and snowfall have an average pH reading of 4.1. A pH reading below 5 is considered abnormally acidic and therefore a threat to aquatic populations.

HOW ACID RAIN SPREADS. Although we might expect areas containing power plants to be most severely affected, acid rain can in fact travel thousands of miles from its source. Stack gases escape and drift with the wind currents, traveling great distances before they return to earth as acid rain (Figure 1).

For roughly two to five days after emission, the gases follow the prevailing winds far from the point of origin. About 50 percent of the acid rain that affects Canada originates in the United States; conversely, 15 to 25 percent of U.S. acid rain originates in Canada.

The tendency of stack gases to drift makes acid rain a widespread menace. More than 200 lakes in the Adirondacks, hundreds of miles from any industrial center, cannot support life because their water has become so acidic.

HOW ACID RAIN DESTROYS. Acid rain causes damage wherever it falls. It erodes various types of building rock such as limestone, marble, and mortar. Damage to buildings, houses, monuments, statues, and cars is widespread. Many priceless monuments have already been destroyed, and even trees of some varieties are dying.

More crucial is damage to waterways (Figure 2). Acid rain gradually lowers the pH in lakes and streams, eventually making a waterway so acidic that it dies. In areas with natural acid-buffering elements such as limestone, the dilute acid has less effect. The northeastern United States and Canada, however, lack this natural protection and so are most vulnerable.

Second labeled visual provides graphic illustration of the process ●——→

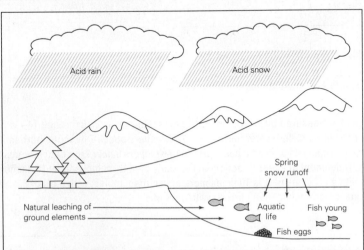

Figure 2 How Acid Rain Infiltrates Waterways

FIGURE 12.5
(Continued)

3

The pH level in an affected waterway drops so low that some species cease to reproduce. A pH of 5.1 to 5.4 means that entire fisheries are threatened: Once a waterway reaches a pH of 4.5, fish reproduction ceases.

In the northeastern United States and Canada, the acidity problem is compounded by the runoff from acid snow. During winter, acid snow sits with little melting, so that by spring thaw, the acid released is greatly concentrated. Aluminum and other heavy metals normally present in soil are also released by acid rain and runoff. These concentrated toxins leach into waterways, affecting fish in all stages of development.

Summary

Acid rain develops from nitrogen and sulfur oxides emitted by the burning of fossil fuels. In the atmosphere, these oxides combine with ozone and water to form precipitation with a low pH. This acid precipitation returns to earth miles from its source, damaging waterways that lack natural buffering agents. The northeastern United States and Canada are the most severely affected areas in North America.

Conclusion summarizes the process and implicitly solicits audience support

STRATEGIES
for Descriptions

▸ **Take a look at the product or process.** Study your subject. For a product description, get your hands on the item if you can; weigh it, measure it, take it apart. For a process description, observe the process yourself, if possible.

▸ **Analyze your audience.** Determine your primary and secondary audiences. Then ask yourself exactly what your audience needs to know: "What does it look like?" "What are its parts?" "What does it do?" "How does it work?" or "How does it happen?" Decide upon the appropriate level of technicality for your audience.

▸ **Analyze your purpose.** Ask yourself why your audience needs your description.

▸ **Maintain objectivity.** Think in terms of visual (not emotional) details and specific language when describing location, measurements, weights, and dimensions.

▸ **Be concise.** Provide only what your audience needs.

▸ **Include all necessary parts.** Include a clear and limiting title, an orienting introduction, the appropriate sequence of topics (spatial, functional, chronological—or a combination), and a conclusion that brings readers full circle.

▸ **Incorporate visuals.** Enhance your verbal description using visuals, particularly if the product or process is too complicated to describe only in words.

SPECIFICATIONS

Specifications (or "specs") are a type of description used by professionals. Specifications build on definitions and descriptions by asking the question "How is this process or procedure performed according to regulations?" Airplanes, bridges, computer software, medical procedures, and nearly all modern products and processes are produced according to specifications. The minimum standards are identified; then the specific methods or materials for meeting those standards are proposed, reviewed, and revised until they are approved. Specifications are vital because they prescribe standards for consistency, quality, and safety.

Specifications are important when everyone in your audience needs to understand and agree on what is to be done and how it is to be done. In other words, specifications ensure consistency, helping prevent misunderstandings that may lead to errors, slowdowns, or even lawsuits. For example, Figure 12.6 shows partial specifications drawn up by an architect designing a medical clinic (these specs are for the exterior of the building only; additional specs would be written for the interior). These specifications help ensure that contractors, architects, landscapers, and others have a consistent master plan regarding parts, materials, and designs that everyone can interpret identically.

Specifications describe features such as methods for manufacturing, building, or installing a product; materials and equipment used; and size, shape, and weight. Professionals must therefore carefully consider the quality of the product they produce. They must ask themselves "Does this product exceed or at the very least meet governmental standards?" "How do the standards compare with those of others in the field?" and "How will our standards be perceived by our customers?" In the medical clinic specifications (Figure 12.6), for example, the quality of materials must meet not only government regulations but also the medical profession's requirements for quality. As a result, those specifications call for a reinforced foundation, exterior, and roof; high-quality insulated windows; and a relaxing landscape that will appeal to both highly stressed medical staff and patients.

Perhaps most important, specifications are always written with public safety in mind. For example, the U.S. Department of Energy (DOE) issues specifications that prescribe minimum design requirements for the shipping containers (or casks) used to transport (via rail or road) spent nuclear fuel to permanent storage facilities. In the private sector, any product that fails to meet federal or industry specifications may provide grounds for a lawsuit.

When injury or death results (as in a bridge collapse or an airline accident), a product will be inspected to be sure it was designed and maintained according to the appropriate specifications. If not, the contractor, manufacturer, or supplier may be liable. The architectural specifications in Figure 12.6, for instance, must meet government standards for building safety as well as the medical profession's standards for a building in which patient safety is paramount.

FIGURE 12.6
**Specifications
to ensure
consistency,
quality, and
safety**

Ruger, Filstone, and Grant
Architects

SPECIFICATIONS FOR THE POWNAL CLINIC BUILDING

Foundation

    footings: 8" x 16" concrete (load-bearing capacity: 3,000 lbs. per sq. in.)

    frost walls: 8" x 4' @ 3,000 psi

    slab: 4" @ 3,000 psi, reinforced with wire mesh over vapor barrier

Exterior Walls

    frame: eastern pine #2 timber frame with exterior partitions set inside posts

    exterior partitions: 2" x 4" kiln-dried spruce set at 16" on center

    sheathing: 1/4" exterior-grade plywood

    siding: #1 red cedar with a 1/2" x 6' bevel

    trim: finished pine boards ranging from 1" x 4" to 1" x 10"

    painting: 2 coats of Clear Wood Finish on siding; trim primed and finished
            with one coat of bone white, oil base paint

Roof System

    framing: 2" x 12" kiln-dried spruce set at 24" on center

    sheathing: 5/8" exterior-grade plywood

    finish: 240 Celotex 20-year fiberglass shingles over #15 impregnated felt
            roofing paper

    flashing: copper

Windows

    Anderson casement and fixed-over-awning models, with white exterior
        cladding, insulating glass and screens, and wood interior frames

Landscape

    driveway: gravel base, with 3" traprock surface

    walks: timber defined, with traprock surface

    cleared areas: to be rough graded and covered with wood chips

    plantings: 10 assorted lawn plants along the road side of the building

Audience for
specifications

Specifications may be written for a wide range of readers, including customers, designers, contractors, suppliers, engineers, programmers, and inspectors. If your audience consists primarily of technical experts (such as architects) you can use specialized language and brief explanations. But if your audience is mixed, you may need to include more detail or refer readers to other sources of information, such as a glossary, appendix (see page 316), or Web site.

STRATEGIES
for Specifications

- ▶ **Analyze your audience.** Determine who will be reading the specs.
- ▶ **Know the minimum governmental and industry standards.** If your product is for specific customers, also consider the standards they will expect you to meet.
- ▶ **Keep consistency, quality, and safety at the forefront.** Specifications fulfill all three purposes. Everyone who reads the document needs to be "on the same page" (consistency); the product you describe must meet minimal quality requirements; and it must also meet safety requirements.
- ▶ **Use a standard format when applicable.** If your organization uses a standard format for specifications, follow that format.
- ▶ **Include a brief introduction or descriptive title.** Include some kind of overview, be it a one- or two-sentence introduction, a brief summary, or an abstract (see Chapter 14 for more on summaries and abstracts). For an audience completely familiar with the material, a clear and descriptive title will suffice.
- ▶ **List component parts or materials.** List all the parts or materials your readers will need to know about. Group items into categories if needed.
- ▶ **Refer to other documents or specs, as needed.** Often one set of specifications will refer to another set or to government or industry standards. If your specifications are online, link to other specifications you refer to.
- ▶ **Use a consistent terminology.** Use the same terms for the same parts or materials throughout your specifications. If you refer to an "ergonomic adapter" in one section, do not substitute "iMac mouse adapter" in a later section.
- ▶ **Include retrieval aids.** Especially in longer specifications, some readers may be interested in only one portion. For example, someone working on a subset of a larger project may want to look up technical details for his or her part of the project only. Use clear headings and a table of contents.
- ▶ **Keep it simple.** People look at specifications because they want quick access to items, parts, technical protocols, and so on. If you can, limit your specs to short lists, using longer prose passages only as necessary.
- ▶ **Check your use of technical terms.** Use terms that are standard for the field.

CHECKLIST
for Descriptions and Specifications

PRODUCT OR PROCESS DESCRIPTIONS

☐ Have I studied the product or process to get a clear view of how it looks or what it does?

☐ Have I recorded the details of the product or process objectively?

☐ Have I written a clear purpose statement upon which to base my description?

☐ Does the title promise exactly what the description delivers?

☐ Have I provided an introduction based on my purpose statement (and a definition, if necessary)?

☐ Have I written the description using a spatial, functional, or chronological sequence or a combination of sequences?

☐ Are relationships among parts or stages clearly explained?

☐ Do visuals appear whenever they can provide clarification?

☐ Have I provided a conclusion to bring readers full circle?

☐ Is the use of technical terminology appropriate for this audience?

SPECIFICATIONS

☐ Are the specifications appropriately detailed for the audience?

☐ Do the specifications meet the requirements for consistency, quality, and safety?

☐ Do the specifications adhere to prescribed standards?

☐ Do the specifications follow a standard format, if applicable?

☐ Have I included a brief introduction or descriptive title?

☐ Have I listed the component parts or materials?

☐ Are other specifications or documents referred to, if needed?

☐ Is my terminology consistent?

☐ Are the specifications easy to navigate, with clear headings and other retrieval aids?

☐ Do I provide short lists instead of long prose passages wherever possible?

☐ Are technical terms standard for the field?

APPLICATIONS

GENERAL APPLICATIONS

MyWritingLab™

1. Choose a product requiring a description. Identify the audience and purpose, and prepare a description for this audience's level of technical understanding. As you prepare your description, refer to the Strategies on page 235. Be sure to include a clear and limiting title; an orienting introduction; a spatial, functional, or chronological sequence of topics; at least one visual; and a conclusion. Also remain as objective as possible.

2. Select a specialized process that you understand well and that has several distinct steps. Begin by analyzing your audience and purpose. Using the process description on page 233 as a model, explain this process to classmates who are unfamiliar with it.

3. The bumper jack description in this chapter is aimed toward a general audience. Evaluate its effectiveness for this audience. In one or two paragraphs, discuss your evaluation and suggest revisions.

4. How do specifications function in your workplace or home? Find one example of specifications used in your home or workplace and analyze it in terms of its usability. Are the specifications written for consistency, quality, and safety? How? What could the writers have done to improve the usability of this document?

TEAM APPLICATIONS

1. Divide into groups. Assume your group works in the product development division of a diversified manufacturing company. Your division has just thought of an idea for an inexpensive consumer item with a potentially vast market (choose a simple mechanism, such as nail clippers or a stapler). Your group's assignment is to prepare three descriptions of this invention:

   a. one for company executives who will decide whether to produce and market the item

   b. one for the engineers, machinists, and so on, who will design and manufacture the item

   c. one for the customers who might purchase and use the item

   Before writing for each audience, complete an Audience and Purpose Profile (page 46). Appoint a group manager, who will assign tasks to members (visuals, typing, etc.). When the descriptions are prepared, the group manager will appoint one member to present the documents and explain their differences in class.

2. Select a specialized process you understand well or that you can learn about quickly by searching the Web (e.g., how gum disease develops, how an earthquake occurs, how steel is made, how a computer compiles and executes a program). Write a brief description of the process, incorporating at least one visual. Exchange your description with a classmate. Study your classmate's description for 15 minutes and then write the description in your own words. Now, evaluate your classmate's version of your original description. Does it show that your description was understood? If not, why not? Discuss your conclusions in a memo to your instructor, submitted with all samples. Be sure to document your information sources.

3. Assume your group is an architectural firm designing buildings at your college. Develop a set of specifications for duplicating the interior of the classroom in which this course is held. Focus only on materials, dimensions, and equipment (whiteboard, desk, etc.), and use visuals as appropriate. Your audience includes the firm that will construct the classroom, teachers, and school administrators. Use the same format as in Figure 12.6, or design a better one. Appoint one member to present the completed specifications in class. Compare versions from each group for accuracy and clarity.

GLOBAL APPLICATION   MyWritingLab™

Descriptions, especially those for nonspecialized or nontechnical audiences, are often written by comparing the item being described to an item that is already familiar to readers. For instance, the human heart is often described as a pump and compared to a pump people already know about (the pump on a swimming pool or a car's water pump). While descriptions based on these types of comparisons can be useful, they can also be problematic if your readers are from different countries and cultures. For instance, if you describe the human heart in relation to the pump on a swimming pool, people from countries or parts of the United States that don't have pools would not be able to understand the comparison. Working with two to three other students, pick an item for which you'd like to write a description that will be distributed both within the United States and to at least one other country. Discuss whether to use a comparison and how you would decide which comparisons to use.

DIGITAL AND SOCIAL MEDIA APPLICATION   MyWritingLab™

Go online and search for a description of a product or process that is related to your field of study. Look for places where the description might be confusing for general readers, and rewrite the description for their understanding.

MyWritingLab™   Visit Chapter 12, *Descriptions,* in MyWritingLab to complete this chapter's applications, to explore this chapter's overview, checklist, and flashcards, and to test your understanding of the chapter objectives.

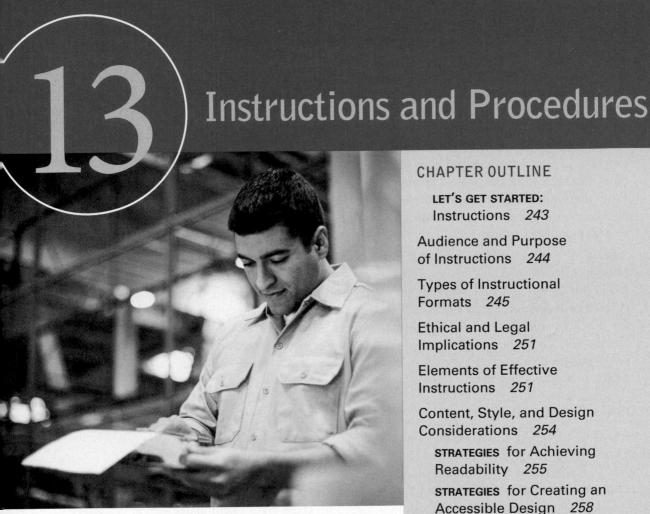

13 Instructions and Procedures

CHAPTER OUTLINE

LET'S GET STARTED:
Instructions *243*

Audience and Purpose
of Instructions *244*

Types of Instructional
Formats *245*

Ethical and Legal
Implications *251*

Elements of Effective
Instructions *251*

Content, Style, and Design
Considerations *254*

  STRATEGIES for Achieving
  Readability *255*

  STRATEGIES for Creating an
  Accessible Design *258*

Procedures *261*

Usability Testing *263*

  STRATEGIES for Instructions
  and Procedures *263*

  CHECKLIST for Instructions
  and Procedures *265*

Applications *265*

LEARNING OBJECTIVES FOR THIS CHAPTER

▸ Identify various types of instructions and their uses

▸ Understand the ethical and legal implications of instructions

▸ Understand the components of instructions

▸ Determine the level of detail and technicality necessary for a given set of instructions

▸ Write instructions with a readable style and accessible design

▸ Understand the components of procedures

▸ Write a set of procedures

▸ Test instructions and procedures for usability

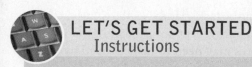

LET'S GET STARTED
Instructions

Almost everyone writes instructions. Think about the last time someone asked you how to get to your apartment or house. You may have told them to look it up on Google Maps, but you probably also gave some simple step-by-step instructions ("Get off at Exit 12. Turn left. Go about 1/2 mile…."). Before reading the material in this chapter, write instructions that tell a new student how to get from your classroom to the student union (or to a good pizza place or somewhere similar).

Questions to ask about the instructions you wrote as you review the material in this chapter:

- ► Did I provide enough of an introduction?
- ► Are steps listed in order?
- ► Are the steps visually easy to follow?
- ► Am I using imperative verb forms?
- ► Am I providing enough detail? Too much?

At the end of this chapter, review your initial Let's Get Started instructions with your instructor or with a group of students to see how much you might change or modify the instructions based on what you have learned from the chapter.

I*nstructions* spell out the steps required for completing a task or series of tasks (for example, installing a video card in your computer or operating an electron microscope). The audience for a set of instructions might be someone who doesn't know how to perform the task or someone who has performed the task but can't remember how or wants to perform it more effectively. In any case, well-written and carefully designed instructions enable readers to get the job done safely and efficiently.

Definition of instructions

Procedures, a special type of instructions, serve as official guidelines for people who typically are already familiar with a given task (say, firefighters who are evacuating a high-rise building). Procedures ensure that all members of a group

Definition of procedures

coordinate their activities when performing a task. More so than instructions, procedures may need to be reviewed and approved by an official body of some sort. For example, official surgical procedures may need to be approved by a hospital's safety and ethics board.

Formats of
instructions
and procedures

Instructions and procedures can be written and designed in a wide variety of formats, from brochures to user manuals to Web pages. Increasingly, instructions and procedures are available in both print and digital formats; for instance, PDF versions of consumer user manuals are often available for download from a company's Web site. The format should be chosen based on the people who will be using the material and the environment where the material will be used. For example, instructions for connecting a battery charger to your car's battery should not be provided on a CD because most people will not have a laptop computer handy while performing this task. Instead, these instructions should be printed directly on the charger itself, with a longer brochure (containing safety information) included in the box.

This chapter will first explore various aspects of instructions, followed by procedures.

AUDIENCE AND PURPOSE OF INSTRUCTIONS

Audience
considerations

Before writing instructions, find out how much your readers already know about the task. For instance, if you are writing for technicians who have done a similar task with a different piece of equipment, you may not need as much detail or context. If, on the other hand, you are writing for a general audience, such as consumers who are trying to assemble a new stereo cabinet or use a new Bluetooth headset, you will need more details but in a less technical presentation. If you have a mixed audience (some experienced with the task, others less experienced), you will need a layered approach, offering a "quick start up" document for those in the know and a more comprehensive user guide for the novices.

Readers across the globe, some who may not speak English as a first language, might use your instructions. Therefore, write in a straightforward style with plenty of visuals, and remain sensitive to cultural differences.

Purpose
considerations

The purpose of instructions is simply to help people perform a task or series of tasks. As you write, keep the following questions in mind: "How is the task done?" "What materials are needed in order to complete the task?" "In which order should the steps in the task be completed?" "What could go wrong?" and "Are any safety issues involved?" Ask yourself if the primary purpose is to allow people to complete the task quickly (as when people are trying to assemble a new stereo cabinet and don't want to take all day) or to complete the task incrementally and over a longer period (as when people are using a kit to test for radon in their homes).

TYPES OF INSTRUCTIONAL FORMATS

As discussed above, instructions and procedures alike come in many formats. The most common formats for instructions are instructional brochures, user manuals, quick reference cards, Web-based instructions, and online instructions.

Instructional Brochures

Instructional brochures can be posted, handed out, mailed, put on a Web site, or otherwise distributed to a broad audience. Typically, brochures contain both text and visuals, which helps increase the audience appeal. Figure 13.1 shows an

Features of effective instructional brochures

BAC (foodborne bacteria) could make you and those you care about sick. In fact, even though you can't see BAC—or smell him, or feel him—he and millions more like him may have already invaded the food you eat. But you have the power to *Fight BAC!®*.

Foodborne illness can strike anyone. Some people are at a higher risk for developing foodborne illness, including pregnant women, young children, older adults and people with weakened immune systems. For these people the following four simple steps are critically important:

CLEAN: *Wash hands and surfaces often*

Bacteria can be spread throughout the kitchen and get onto hands, cutting boards, utensils, counter tops and food. To *Fight BAC!®*, always:

- Wash your hands with warm water and soap for at least 20 seconds before and after handling food and after using the bathroom, changing diapers and handling pets.
- Wash your cutting boards, dishes, utensils and counter tops with hot soapy water after preparing each food item and before you go on to the next food.
- Consider using paper towels to clean up kitchen surfaces. If you use cloth towels wash them often in the hot cycle of your washing machine.
- Rinse fresh fruits and vegetables under running tap water, including those with skins and rinds that are not eaten.
- Rub firm-skin fruits and vegetables under running tap water or scrub with a clean vegetable brush while rinsing with running tap water.

SEPARATE: *Don't cross-contaminate*

Cross-contamination is how bacteria can be spread. When handling raw meat, poultry, seafood and eggs, keep these foods and their juices away from ready-to-eat foods. Always start with a clean scene—wash hands with warm water and soap, and wash cutting boards, dishes, countertops and utensils with hot water and soap.

- Separate raw meat, poultry, seafood and eggs from other foods in your grocery shopping cart, grocery bags and in your refrigerator.
- Use one cutting board for fresh produce and a separate one for raw meat, poultry and seafood.
- Never place cooked food on a plate that previously held raw meat, poultry, seafood or eggs.

COOK: *Cook to safe temperatures*

Food is safely cooked when it reaches a high enough internal temperature to kill the harmful bacteria that cause illness. Refer to the chart on the back of this brochure for the proper internal temperatures.

- Use a food thermometer to measure the internal temperature of cooked foods. Make sure that meat, poultry, egg dishes, casseroles and other foods are cooked to the internal temperature shown in the chart on the back of this brochure.
- Cook ground meat or ground poultry until it reaches a safe internal temperature. Color is not a reliable indicator of doneness.
- Cook eggs until the yolk and white are firm. Only use recipes in which eggs are cooked or heated thoroughly.
- When cooking in a microwave oven, cover food, stir and rotate for even cooking. Food is done when it reaches

the safe internal temperature as measured with a food thermometer.

- Bring sauces, soups and gravy to a boil when reheating.

CHILL: *Refrigerate promptly*

Refrigerate foods quickly because cold temperatures slow the growth of harmful bacteria. Do not over-stuff the refrigerator. Cold air must circulate to help keep food safe. Keeping a constant refrigerator temperature of 40ºF or below is one of the most effective ways to reduce the risk of foodborne illness. Use an appliance thermometer to be sure the temperature is consistently 40ºF or below. The freezer temperature should be 0ºF or below.

- Refrigerate or freeze meat, poultry, eggs and other perishables as soon as you get them home from the store.
- Never let raw meat, poultry, eggs, cooked food or cut fresh fruits or vegetables sit at room temperature more than two hours before putting them in the refrigerator or freezer (one hour when the temperature is above 90ºF).
- Never defrost food at room temperature. Food must be kept at a safe temperature during thawing. There are three safe ways to defrost food: in the refrigerator, in cold water, and in the microwave. Food thawed in cold water or in the microwave should be cooked immediately.
- Always marinate food in the refrigerator.
- Divide large amounts of leftovers into shallow containers for quicker cooling in the refrigerator.
- Use or discard refrigerated food on a regular basis. Check USDA cold storage information at **www.fightbac.org** for optimum storage times.

FIGURE 13.1 An instructional brochure

Source: "Four Simple Steps to Food Safety" from *Fight BAC!* Copyright © 2011 by the Partnership for Food Safety Education. Reprinted with permission.

instructional brochure. Notice its user-friendly design: In addition to the cartoon illustration at the top, which immediately catches a reader's attention, clear visuals reinforce each main section ("Clean," "Separate," "Cook," and "Chill"). Each main section also begins with an action verb, includes a brief introduction, and uses bulleted lists (which also use action verbs) to break up the text into easy-to-digest chunks. Finally, a Web address at the end points readers to further information.

User Manuals

Features of effective user manuals

User manuals tend to be the most comprehensive form of instructions: Manuals often contain instructions for using a product, along with descriptions and specifications, warnings, maintenance and troubleshooting advice, and any other information the reader is likely to need. For complex products (for example, a spreadsheet program), the user manual can be a sizable book. Given the cost of printing and distributing such a large book and keeping print material current, companies are increasingly providing smaller ("Getting Started") manuals that contain the basic operating tips and then placing the more lengthy information on a Web site. In some cases (for legal or other reasons), full-scale user manuals are still being produced, but the trend is toward smaller documents and digital information.

Figure 13.2 is a table of contents from a photocopier user manual. Although most people will go directly to sections 2 and 3 on loading paper and making copies, other sections are available for learning about the copier, using its peripheral devices, performing maintenance, and entering text.

Quick Reference Materials

Features of effective quick reference materials

Quick reference materials are a form of instructions typically written and designed to fit on a single sheet of paper, a small or wallet-sized card, or a Web page. The instructions focus on the basic steps for people who only want enough information to perform a specific task rapidly and continue on with their work.

Figure 13.3 shows Web-based quick reference material (keyboard shortcuts) for Internet Explorer. The first screen organizes the content into high level categories so that people can find what they need quickly. After clicking on a category, readers would see detailed information (shown on the second screen) about particular tasks in the left column, with the corresponding keyboard shortcuts listed in the right column. The two-column approach and clean design make the page easy to navigate.

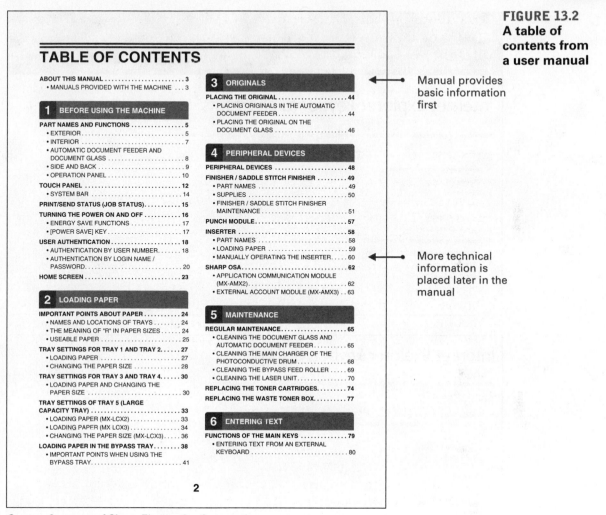

TABLE OF CONTENTS

ABOUT THIS MANUAL 3
• MANUALS PROVIDED WITH THE MACHINE . . . 3

1 BEFORE USING THE MACHINE

PART NAMES AND FUNCTIONS 5
• EXTERIOR 5
• INTERIOR 7
• AUTOMATIC DOCUMENT FEEDER AND
  DOCUMENT GLASS 8
• SIDE AND BACK 9
• OPERATION PANEL 10
TOUCH PANEL 12
• SYSTEM BAR 14
PRINT/SEND STATUS (JOB STATUS) 15
TURNING THE POWER ON AND OFF 16
• ENERGY SAVE FUNCTIONS 17
• [POWER SAVE] KEY 17
USER AUTHENTICATION 18
• AUTHENTICATION BY USER NUMBER 18
• AUTHENTICATION BY LOGIN NAME /
  PASSWORD 20
HOME SCREEN 23

2 LOADING PAPER

IMPORTANT POINTS ABOUT PAPER 24
• NAMES AND LOCATIONS OF TRAYS 24
• THE MEANING OF "R" IN PAPER SIZES 24
• USEABLE PAPER 25
TRAY SETTINGS FOR TRAY 1 AND TRAY 2 27
• LOADING PAPER 27
• CHANGING THE PAPER SIZE 28
TRAY SETTINGS FOR TRAY 3 AND TRAY 4 30
• LOADING PAPER AND CHANGING THE
  PAPER SIZE 30
TRAY SETTINGS OF TRAY 5 (LARGE
CAPACITY TRAY) 33
• LOADING PAPER (MX-LCX2) 33
• LOADING PAPER (MX LCX3) 34
• CHANGING THE PAPER SIZE (MX-LCX3) 36
LOADING PAPER IN THE BYPASS TRAY 38
• IMPORTANT POINTS WHEN USING THE
  BYPASS TRAY 41

3 ORIGINALS

PLACING THE ORIGINAL 44
• PLACING ORIGINALS IN THE AUTOMATIC
  DOCUMENT FEEDER 44
• PLACING THE ORIGINAL ON THE
  DOCUMENT GLASS 46

4 PERIPHERAL DEVICES

PERIPHERAL DEVICES 48
FINISHER / SADDLE STITCH FINISHER 49
• PART NAMES 49
• SUPPLIES 50
• FINISHER / SADDLE STITCH FINISHER
  MAINTENANCE 51
PUNCH MODULE 57
INSERTER 58
• PART NAMES 58
• LOADING PAPER 59
• MANUALLY OPERATING THE INSERTER 60
SHARP OSA 62
• APPLICATION COMMUNICATION MODULE
  (MX-AMX2) 62
• EXTERNAL ACCOUNT MODULE (MX-AMX3) . . 63

5 MAINTENANCE

REGULAR MAINTENANCE 65
• CLEANING THE DOCUMENT GLASS AND
  AUTOMATIC DOCUMENT FEEDER 65
• CLEANING THE MAIN CHARGER OF THE
  PHOTOCONDUCTIVE DRUM 68
• CLEANING THE BYPASS FEED ROLLER 69
• CLEANING THE LASER UNIT 70
REPLACING THE TONER CARTRIDGES 74
REPLACING THE WASTE TONER BOX 77

6 ENTERING TEXT

FUNCTIONS OF THE MAIN KEYS 79
• ENTERING TEXT FROM AN EXTERNAL
  KEYBOARD 80

2

Manual provides basic information first

More technical information is placed later in the manual

FIGURE 13.2
A table of contents from a user manual

Source: Courtesy of Sharp Electronics Corporation.

Web-based Instructions

Instructions that are set up as a Web page allow readers to click on hyperlinks to explore more information, access definitions of technical words and phrases, and learn more about topics they may not fully understand. Web-based instructions are useful in situations where your audience may be a mix

Features of effective Web-based instructions

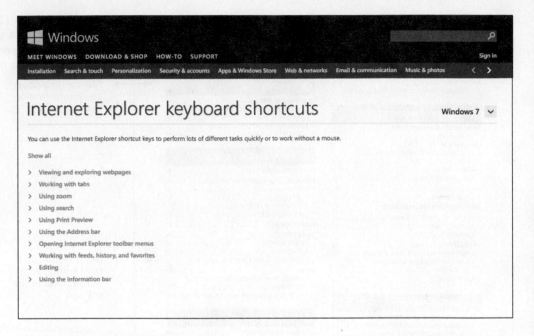

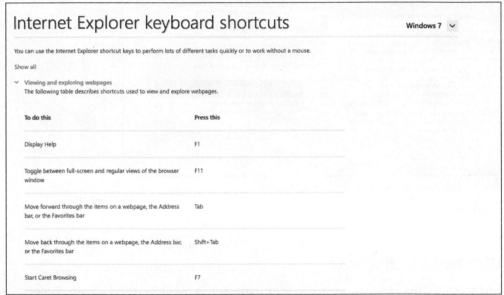

FIGURE 13.3 A quick-reference Web page (partial view)
Source: Microsoft product screen shot reprinted with permission from Microsoft Corporation.

of people who know something about the topic and people who don't know as much. For instance, Figure 13.4 shows Web-based instructions for how to apply for Energy Star status for a building. Some readers may already be familiar with the eligibility requirements, but people who need more information can click on the link.

Web-based instructions are also useful because it's easy for organizations to keep the information updated by simply revising the Web site (rather than, say, printing thousands of new brochures).

FIGURE 13.4 Web-based instructions
Source: U.S. Environmental Protection Agency.

Online Instructions

Features of effective
online instructions

Many products, especially software, have done away with large user manuals and instead provide instructions that can be accessed directly through the software. Word processing programs (Microsoft Word or Apple Pages or other) are good examples of online instructions. If you are working on a document and forget how to create a table or set up footnotes, you simply type your question or topic into the help box to access the instructions. This content is always up to date because it is linked to the company's database of help information or is updated when your computer or software does an automatic update.

Online instructions are typically "context sensitive"—that is, the help system recognizes what you are trying to accomplish and not only provides instructions but also guides you to the menu function you are looking for. Figure 13.5 is a typical online help screen.

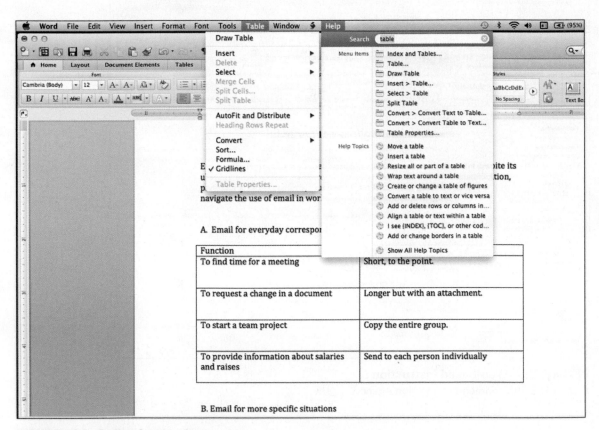

FIGURE 13.5 Online instructions

Source: Microsoft product screen shot reprinted with permission from Microsoft Corporation.

ETHICAL AND LEGAL IMPLICATIONS

Instructional documents carry profound ethical and legal obligations on the part of those who prepare them. Among all technical documents, therefore, instructions involve the strictest requirements for accurate information in an accessible format.

Countless injuries result from misuse of products such as power tools, car jacks, or household cleaners. This type of misuse is often caused by defective instructions. Clear, easy-to-follow instructions that contain just the right amount of detail can prove to be the difference between the unsafe and safe use of a product.

Ethical implications of instructions

Any person injured because of unclear, inaccurate, or incomplete instructions can sue the writer as well as the manufacturer. Courts have ruled that a writing defect in product support literature carries the same type of liability as a design or manufacturing defect in the product itself (Girill 37). Some of the legal liabilities resulting from faulty instructions include

Legal implications of instructions

- Failure to provide instructions and cautions for the proper use of a product: for example, a household cleaning product that should not be mixed with other products

- Failure to warn against hazards from proper use of a product: for example, the risk of cutting one's fingers on a vegetable slicer

- Failure to warn against the possible misuses of a product: for example, the danger of improperly installing a child safety seat

ELEMENTS OF EFFECTIVE INSTRUCTIONS

All instructions must include a title, a brief overview or introduction, a body section (including the required steps involved in following the instructions), and a conclusion. In addition, most instructions should also include visuals as well as notes, cautions, warnings, and/or danger notices.

Title

Be sure your title provides a clear and exact preview of the required task. For example, the title "Instructions for Cleaning the DVD Drive of a Laptop Computer" tells people what to expect: instructions for a specific procedure involving one selected part. But the title "The Laptop Computer" gives no such forecast; a document with a general title like this might contain a history of the laptop, a description of each part, or a wide range of related information.

Include a clear and exact title

Overview or Introduction

Provide a brief
overview or
introduction to orient
readers before they
begin the task

Explain the purpose of the instructions and describe what they cover. You don't want to bury readers in an overly long overview/introduction, nor do you want to set them loose without adequate preparation. Know your audience—what it needs and doesn't need. For example, you might begin with a short paragraph:

> These instructions provide complete information for the use of the lab's electron microscope. The first section explains the setup steps, and the second section describes how to create a slide and view it with the microscope.

Body

Include a body
section with task
steps in correct order

Explain each step and substep in the correct order. Insert notes, cautions, warnings, dangers, and visuals as needed (see below for more on these elements). Begin each step with a definition or a purpose statement, as appropriate. People who understand the reasons for a step will do a better job. Segment the steps with a numbered list. Begin each substep of a complex process on a new line.

Conclusion

Wrap up with
a conclusion, if
appropriate

The conclusion of a set of instructions might summarize the main steps of the task, describe the results readers should experience, offer follow-up advice, or provide troubleshooting tips. You might do all of these things in the conclusion—or none of them. If the body section has provided all the necessary information, omit the conclusion altogether.

Visuals

Provide visuals to
enhance usability

Visuals in instructions play a vital role: They show what to do, attract the reader's attention, and help keep words to a minimum. (For more on visuals, see Chapter 8.) Visuals can illustrate any step that might be hard for people to picture. For instance, describing in words how to locate something is a lot less effective than simply showing the location with a drawing or photograph. Visuals can also help tell the whole story, offering the big picture in one glance, something that would be far less effective using words only. Figure 13.6 enables readers to visualize a task. Figure 13.7 shows readers the complete process at a glance.

Notes, Cautions, Warnings, and Danger Notices

Always include
notes, cautions, and
warnings for user
safety

Notes provide additional information, while cautions, warnings, and danger notices prevent damage, injury, or even death. Use these items only when needed. Overuse will dull their effect, and readers may overlook their importance.

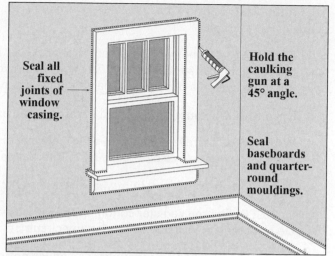

FIGURE 13.6
A visual that illustrates a task (how to apply weatherstrip caulking)

Seal all fixed joints of window casing.

Hold the caulking gun at a 45° angle.

Seal baseboards and quarter-round mouldings.

Source: From U.S. Department of Energy <www.nrel.gov/docs/fy01osti/28039.pdf>.

A note clarifies a point, emphasizes vital information, or describes options or alternatives. For example:

> NOTE: If you don't name a newly initialized disk, the computer automatically names it "Untitled."

Notes are designed to enhance performance and prevent errors; cautions, warnings, and danger notices are used for safety reasons.

When to use notes

When to use cautions

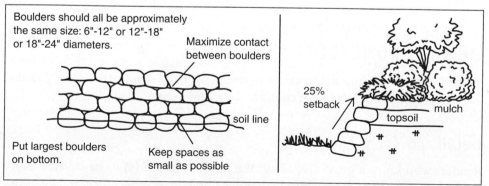

FIGURE 13.7
A visual that shows the full picture (how to build a boulder wall) in one glance

Boulders should all be approximately the same size: 6"-12" or 12"-18" or 18"-24" diameters.

Maximize contact between boulders

soil line

Put largest boulders on bottom.

Keep spaces as small as possible

25% setback

topsoil

mulch

Source: From University of Michigan Sustainable Urban Landscape Information Series Web site, <www.sustland.umn.edu>. Copyright © 2006 by University of Minnesota Extension. Reprinted with permission.

Cautions prevent possible mistakes that could result in injury or equipment damage. For example:

> CAUTION: A momentary electrical surge or power failure will erase the contents of internal memory. To avoid losing your work, every few minutes save on a backup file what you have just typed into the computer.

When to use warnings

Warnings alert readers to potential hazards to life or limb. For instance:

> WARNING: To prevent electrical shock, always disconnect your printer from its power source before cleaning internal parts.

When to use a danger notice

Danger notices identify an immediate hazard to life or limb. For example:

> DANGER: The red canister contains DEADLY radioactive material. Do not break the safety seal under any circumstances.

When you include cautions, warnings, or danger notices, be sure to provide the appropriate visual symbol or icon to indicate these conditions, as in Figure 13.8.

**FIGURE 13.8
Caution, warning, and danger symbols**

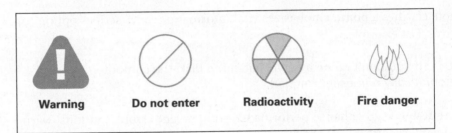

CONTENT, STYLE, AND DESIGN CONSIDERATIONS

In addition to including all the necessary elements in a set of instructions, you also need to decide about matters of content, style, and design.

Detail and Technicality

Provide an adequate level of detail and technicality

Readers who know a great deal about the product or task(s) to be covered don't need a lot of detail and can typically handle a high level of technical information. But readers who are new to the situation need more detail and fewer technical terms. Use the techniques described in Chapter 3 to determine how much your readers already know.

Unless you learn that your audience has the relevant background and skills, write for more general readers. For example, if you are writing instructions for providing first aid to a victim of electrical shock, you might write the following for an audience with extensive medical background:

FIRST AID FOR ELECTRICAL SHOCK

1. Check vital signs.

2. Establish an airway.

3. Administer CPR as needed.

4. Treat for medical shock.

Instructions for a technical audience

But for an inexperienced audience, not only will the above details be inadequate, but also terms such as "vital signs" and "CPR" will be too technical. Such instructions posted for workers in a high-voltage area who are not medically trained would be useless. Illustrations and explanations would be needed, as demonstrated in Figure 13.9.

Style

Instructions must always be clear and easy to follow upon first reading because people usually take immediate action. Follow the Strategies below.

Write with a readable style

STRATEGIES
for Achieving Readability

▶ **Use direct address, active voice, and imperative mood.** To emphasize the reader's role, write in the second person, as direct address. Begin all steps and substeps with action verbs, using the active voice and imperative mood. In certain cases, you may want to provide a clarifying word or phrase that precedes the verb:

Say this	Not this
Insert the disk. *or* [To run the program,] insert the disk.	You should insert the disk.
Key in your access code. *or* [To log on,] key in your access code.	The user keys in her access code.
Plug in the power cord. *or* [When you are ready to power up,] plug in the power cord.	The power cord is plugged in.

→

▶ **Use short and logically shaped sentences.** Use short sentences—one sentence for each step—so that readers can perform one step at a time. If a single step covers two related actions, describe these actions in their required sequence:

| Before switching on the computer, insert the CD in the drive.
OR
| Insert the CD in the drive. Then switch on the computer.

▶ **Use parallel phrasing.** Parallelism is especially important in instructions because the repeating grammatical forms emphasize the step-by-step organization. Notice how all the sentences below are structured identically:

| To log on to the VAX 380, follow these steps:
| 1. Switch the terminal to "on."
| 2. Press the CONTROL key and the C key simultaneously.
| 3. Type "logon," and then press the ESCAPE key.
| 4. Type your user name, and then press the ESCAPE key.

▶ **Use affirmative phrasing.** Negative phrasing is harder to understand.

Say this	Not this
Examine your disk for dust contamination.	Verify that your disk is not contaminated with dust.

▶ **Use transitions to mark time and sequence.** Transitional expressions provide a bridge between related ideas. Some transitions ("first," "next," "meanwhile," "finally," "after," "then") mark time and sequence and are therefore especially useful in instructions, emphasizing their step-by-step nature:

| First, plug in the power cord, and then turn on the printer.
| After the printer warms up, insert the paper in the paper slot.
| Finally, hit the "print" button.

Design

Create an accessible design

Instructions rarely receive undivided attention. The reader, in fact, is doing two activities more or less at once: interpreting the instructions and performing the required task.

THE ABC'S OF CARDIOPULMONARY RESUSCITATION (CPR)

Cardiopulmonary resuscitation (CPR) is an emergency medical procedure for restoring breathing and heartbeat to persons who have suffered an electrical shock, heart attack, or other instance of cardiac arrest. CPR keeps oxygenated blood flowing to the brain until medical professionals arrive. Following are three simple "ABC" steps for CPR.

Step 1: A for Airway: Make sure the airway is not constricted.
- First, call 911 immediately or have someone else call.
- Check if the victim is breathing. If not, carefully roll the victim onto his or her back in one movement.
- Gently push back the forehead with one hand and lift the chin with your other hand to unblock tongue from airway.
- Listen for breathing and watch for chest movement. Move quickly to Step 2 if the victim is still not breathing.

Step 2: B for Breathing: Administer rescue breathing to keep the blood oxygenated.
- Continue to hold down the forehead and lift the neck to keep the airway open.
- Pinch the nose with the thumb and forefinger of the hand holding back the forehead.
- Take a deep breath and seal your lips around the victim's mouth.
- Blow one breath steadily into the mouth for one second; then administer a second breath.
- Do not wait to see if the victim resumes independent breathing. Move quickly to Step 3.

Step 3: C for Circulation: Perform chest compressions to keep the blood circulating.
- Kneel at the side of the victim's head and shoulders. Do not spend time checking for a pulse.
- Place the heel of one hand over the notch at the center of the victim's chest.
- Place the palm of your other hand over the first hand and, using your body weight, press down firmly and quickly, compressing the chest about two inches.
- Allow the chest to return to its original position before the next compression.
- Administer chest compressions at about two compressions per second for 20 seconds.
- Return to Step 2, first ensuring that the airway is open.
- Cycle between Steps 2 and 3 thereafter until help arrives.

Step 1   Step 2   Step 3

FIGURE 13.9 **Adequate detail and technicality for a general audience**

An effective instructional design conveys the sense that the task is within a qualified person's range of abilities. Therefore, design your instructions so that people can leave and return to the document as needed and easily find their place.

STRATEGIES
for Creating an Accessible Design

▸ **Use informative headings.** Clear headings tell readers what to expect, emphasize what is most important, and provide cues for navigation. A heading such as "How to Format Your Portable USB Drive" is more informative than "Portable USB Drive Formatting."

▸ **Arrange all steps in a numbered list.** Unless the procedure consists of simple steps, list and number each step. Numbered steps not only announce the sequence of required actions, but also help readers remember where they left off.

▸ **Separate each step visually.** Single space within steps and double space between.

▸ **Make cautions, warnings, and danger notices highly visible.** Use ruled boxes or highlighting and plenty of white space to make these items stand out. Also, include symbols if possible; if not, use bold text and capital letters for emphasis.

▸ **Make visual and verbal information redundant.** Let the visual repeat, restate, or reinforce the prose rather than provide entirely new information.

▸ **Place visuals and prose steps that are connected close together.** If room allows, place a visual that goes with a step right beside the step; if not, right after the step. Set off the visual with plenty of white space.

▸ **Keep the design simple and easy to navigate.** Readers may be overwhelmed by an excessively complex or inconsistent design.

▸ **For lengthy instructions, consider a layered approach.** In a complex manual, for instance, you might add a "Quick-Use Guide" for getting started or a table of contents with page references to more detailed and technical information.

Figure 13.10 shows instructions that have been prepared for general readers who need to make a common home repair.

HOW TO REPLACE A WORN FAUCET WASHER

Introduction

A leaking faucet, caused by a worn washer, can lose up to fifteen gallons of water per day. This loss can result in a higher water bill, overuse of the septic system and well pump, an increase in your hot-water bill, and rust or chlorine deposits in your sink basin. These instructions detail how to replace the washer. No special knowledge or skills are necessary.

Overview

The typical faucet consists of a round knob or a handle (Figure 1) that, when turned, causes the stem to screw down until the washer sits snugly over the seat. With the washer in place, the flow of water is stopped. A worn washer loses the ability to form a tight seal, causing a leak or drip to develop. Replacing the worn washer eliminates the leak.

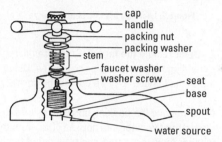

Figure 1. Typical faucet in exploded view

Equipment and Material Needed

• pliers
• regular or Phillips (crossed head) screwdriver
• new washer of same size and shape as worn washer
• valve for shutting off water supply

Note and Caution These instructions apply only to faucets that have washers. Avoid using any excessive force on the threaded parts because they are made of soft metal and could easily strip.

INSTRUCTIONS

1. Shut off the water supply. Look under the sink or fixture for the shutoff valve. If you are unable to find a valve in this location, use the main shutoff valve located in the basement or beneath the house. The water pipe (one-half to one inch in diameter) usually originates from an inside cellar wall. Locate the shutoff valve by following the pipe from the wall to an attached valve, usually within a few feet of the wall (Figure 2). Turn this valve fully clockwise. With your water supply shut off, you can take the faucet apart.

FIGURE 13.10
A complete set of instructions

• Clear title announces the document's exact purpose

• Introduction provides appropriate detail for people with no experience with this task

• Brief overall description and principle of operation

• Visual reinforces the prose

• Required items are listed

• Note and caution alert readers before they take action

• The body section provides step-by-step guidance

FIGURE 13.10
(Continued)

2

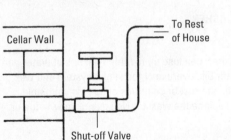

Figure 2. Location of main shut-off valve

2. Disassemble the faucet. Before removing the handle, open the faucet to allow remaining water in the pipe to escape. Using your screwdriver, remove the screw on top of the handle. If a cap covers the screw, pry it off (Figure 1). Remove the handle.

Next, remove the packing nut, using pliers to turn the nut counter-clockwise. The flat circular nut washer can now be lifted from the faucet base. With packing nut and washer removed, screw the stem out of the base by turning the faucet in the "open" direction. Lift the stem out of the base and proceed to step 3.

3. Replace the worn washer. Using your screwdriver, remove the screw holding the washer at the base of the stem (Figure 1). Remove the worn washer and replace it with a new one of the same size, using the washer screw to hold it in place. (Washers of various sizes can be purchased at any hardware store.) If the washer screw is worn, replace it. When the new washer is fixed in place, proceed to step 4.

4. Reassemble the faucet. To reassemble your faucet, reverse the sequence described in step 2.

Caution: Do not overtighten the packing nut!

Using pliers, screw the stem into the base until it ceases to turn. Next, place the packing washer and nut over the threads in the collar. Tighten the packing nut using the strength of one hand. Finally, secure the handle with your screwdriver. When the faucet is fully assembled, turn the handle to the "off" position and proceed to step 5.

5. Turn on the water supply. First, check to see that your faucet is fully closed. Next, turn the water on slowly (about one-half turn each time) until the shutoff valve is fully open. These slow turns prevent a sudden buildup of pressure, which could damage the pipes. Your faucet should now be as good as new.

Caution
precedes step

Because the body section has given readers all they need, no conclusion is required

PROCEDURES

Procedures provide rules and guidance for people who are required to follow accepted practice. For example, different people in your organization might perform the same task (say, monitoring groundwater pollution) at different times, with different equipment, or under different circumstances. This task may need to be standardized to ensure that all work is done with the same accuracy and precision.

Function of procedures

Audience and Purpose Considerations

Unlike instructions, which will be read mostly by people unfamiliar with the given task, procedures may be used by people already familiar with the task but who need to follow a standard. For example, if apprentice chefs in a famous restaurant who normally prepare salads and appetizers are asked to take over on the preparation of special sauces, those workers probably already know the basics but would need more information on the specific sauces required, amounts of ingredients, reduction techniques, and so on.

Consider your audience

Determine how your readers will use these procedures. Will they be following the procedures in a hurry while evacuating a building? Would the procedures be better distributed on paper, on a Web site, or as an email attachment? Once you know exactly how the procedures will be used, you can make decisions about the document's length, format, level of detail, and medium.

Consider your purpose

Types of Procedures

The most common types of procedures are standard operating procedures (SOPs), general safety procedures, and medical or health procedures.

Standard operating procedures are formal procedures designed to give an organization an official record of the procedure and how it should be performed. SOPs, kept up to date and in a location or format available to employees, are required by law in many workplace environments, including those that deal with chemicals or industrial waste. SOPs are also written to inform the public about how a particular procedure is performed.

Standard operating procedures

Safety procedures, as in Figure 13.11, are required in many settings. Hotel rooms typically list fire exit procedures on the back of the entry door. Most organizations have official procedures for dealing with emergencies.

Safety procedures

Medical procedures can be written for medical professionals or for consumers. Procedures for medical professionals might include SOPs on hand washing, surgical techniques, and other steps involved in patient care in the hospital. Today, with the vast amount of medical information available online, many medical procedures are written for nonexperts.

Medical procedures

FIGURE 13.11
A set of procedures (safety procedures)

Title ("Evacuating High-Rise Buildings") is clear and easy to spot

Overview/ introduction section defines the issue and provides background

Headings in the form of reader questions help people find the information they need

Bullets, instead of numbered lists of steps, are appropriate for this document

Evacuating High-Rise Buildings

OSHA**FACT***Sheet*

The National Fire Protection Association defines "high-rise building" as a building greater than 75 feet (25 m) in height where the building height is measured from the lowest level of fire department vehicle access to the floor of the highest occupiable story. Appropriate exits, alarms, emergency lighting, communication systems, and sprinkler systems are critical for employee safety. When designing and maintaining exits, it is essential to ensure that routes leading to the exits, as well as the areas beyond the exits, are accessible and free from materials or items that would impede individuals from easily and effectively evacuating. State and local building code officials can help employers ensure that the design and safety systems are adequate.

When there is an emergency, getting workers out of high-rise buildings poses special challenges. Preparing in advance to safely evacuate the building is critical to the safety of employees who work there.

What actions should employers take to help ensure safe evacuations of high-rise buildings?

- Don't lock fire exits or block doorways, halls, or stairways.
- Test regularly all back-up systems and safety systems, such as emergency lighting and communication systems, and repair them as needed.
- Develop a workplace evacuation plan, post it prominently on each floor, and review it periodically to ensure its effectiveness.
- Identify and train floor wardens, including back-up personnel, who will be responsible for sounding alarms and helping to evacuate employees.
- Conduct emergency evacuation drills periodically.
- Establish designated meeting locations outside the building for workers to gather following an evacuation. The locations should be a safe distance from the building and in an area where people can assemble safely without interfering with emergency response teams.
- Identify personnel with special needs or disabilities who may need help evacuating

and assign one or more people, including back-up personnel, to help them.
- Ensure that during off-hour periods, systems are in place to notify, evacuate, and account for off-hour building occupants.
- Post emergency numbers near telephones.

What should workers know before an emergency occurs?

- Be familiar with the worksite's emergency evacuation plan;
- Know the pathway to at least two alternative exits from every room/area at the workplace;
- Recognize the sound/signaling method of the fire/evacuation alarms;
- Know who to contact in an emergency and how to contact them;
- Know how many desks or cubicles are between your workstation and two of the nearest exits so you can escape in the dark if necessary;
- Know where the fire/evacuation alarms are located and how to use them; and
- Report damaged or malfunctioning safety systems and back-up systems

What should employers do when an emergency occurs?

- Sound appropriate alarms and instruct employees to leave building.
- Notify police, firefighters, or other appropriate emergency personnel.
- Take a head count of employees at designated meeting locations, and notify emergency personnel of any missing workers.

What should employees do when an emergency occurs?

- Leave the area quickly but in an orderly manner, following the worksite's emergency evacuation plan. Go directly to the nearest fire-free and smoke-free stairwell recognizing that in some circumstances the only available exit route may contain limited amounts of smoke or fire.

Source: U.S. Occupational Safety and Health Administration.

USABILITY TESTING

Any technical document must be written and designed for the right audience. With instructions and procedures, however, accuracy and ease of use are especially important. Otherwise, readers could make costly and dangerous errors.

To identify which parts of the document work or don't work, conduct a usability analysis, using the Basic Usability Survey in Figure 13.12. The survey is designed for both the writers and the readers. Essentially it asks one main question (broken into more specific questions): "Do these instructions or procedures enable you to carry out the task safely, efficiently, and accurately?" Notice how the phrasing encourages responses containing examples instead of merely yes or no answers.

The importance of usability testing of instructions and procedures

What a basic usability survey asks

STRATEGIES
for Instructions and Procedures

▸ **Analyze your audience.** For instructions, assume a general audience that does not know how to perform a task. For procedures, assume that your audience does know something about the procedure but needs a set of standard guidelines.

▸ **Analyze your purpose.** Consider where the document will be used and how to present the information for maximum usability.

▸ **Always remember the ethical and legal implications.** Instructions and procedures must always be written with reader safety at the forefront.

▸ **Use standard organization and include all needed elements.** Always include a clear and exact title; include an overview or introduction for instructions (but only if appropriate for procedures); include a body section (in numbered list format for instructions, but not necessarily for procedures); and include visuals, notes, cautions, warnings, danger notices, and a conclusion as appropriate.

▸ **Provide an appropriate level of detail and technicality.** Do not give readers too much or too little detail, and use only as much technical language as your audience will understand.

▸ **Write with a readable style.** Refer to the Strategies for Achieving Readability (pages 255–256).

▸ **Design for maximum accessibility.** Refer to the Strategies for Creating an Accessible Design (page 258).

▸ **Always test for usability.** Instructions and procedures must be easy to grasp in one reading, lead to successful completion of a task or procedure, and ensure reader safety. Make sure each word and image is just right.

Basic Usability Survey

1. Briefly describe why this document is used. _____
   _____

2. Evaluate the *content:*
   - Identify any irrelevant information. _____
     _____

   - Indicate any gaps in the information. _____
     _____

   - Identify any information that seems inaccurate. _____
     _____

   - List other problems with the content. _____
     _____

3. Evaluate the *organization:*
   - Identify anything that is out of order or hard to locate or follow. ____
     _____

   - List other problems with the organization. _____
     _____

4. Evaluate the *style:*
   - Identify anything you misunderstood on first reading. _____
     _____

   - Identify anything you couldn't understand at all. _____
     _____

   - Identify expressions that seem wordy, inexact, or too complex. _____
     _____

   - List other problems with the style. _____
     _____

5. Evaluate the *design:*
   - Indicate any headings that are missing, confusing, or excessive. _____
     _____

   - Indicate any material that should be designed as a list. _____
     _____

   - Give examples of material that might be clarified by a visual. _____
     _____

   - Give examples of misleading or overly complex visuals. _____
     _____

   - List other problems with the design. _____
     _____

6. Identify anything that seems misleading or that could create legal problems or
   cross-cultural misunderstanding. _____
   _____

7. Please suggest other ways of making this document easier to use. _____
   _____

FIGURE 13.12 A basic usability survey

Source: Adapted from Carliner 258; Daugherty 17–18; Hart 53–57.

CHECKLIST
for Instructions and Procedures

MyWritingLab

INSTRUCTIONS

- ☐ Have I determined what type of instructional format I should use?
- ☐ Have I assessed the ethical and legal implications of my instructions?
- ☐ Have I provided a clear and exact title?
- ☐ Have I included an orienting overview or introduction?
- ☐ Have I provided step-by-step instructions in the body?
- ☐ Have I used visuals to enhance usability?
- ☐ Have I included notes, cautions, warnings, and dangers whenever necessary?
- ☐ Have I provided the appropriate level of detail and technicality for my audience?
- ☐ Have I followed the strategies for writing with a readable style?
- ☐ Have I followed the strategies for creating an accessible design?
- ☐ Have I performed a Basic Usability Survey?

PROCEDURES

- ☐ Have I considered my audience and purpose?
- ☐ Have I provided a clear and exact title?
- ☐ Have I provided a clear introduction and numbered steps or visuals if appropriate?
- ☐ Have I included notes, cautions, warnings, and dangers whenever necessary?
- ☐ Have I provided a conclusion?
- ☐ Have I provided an appropriate level of detail, a readable style, and an accessible design?
- ☐ Have I performed a Basic Usability Survey?

APPLICATIONS

GENERAL APPLICATION

MyWritingLab™

Select part of a technical manual in your field—or instructions or procedures for a general audience—and make a copy of the material. Using the Checklist above, evaluate the sample. In a memo to your instructor, discuss the document's strong and weak points, or be prepared to explain them in class.

TEAM APPLICATION

Divide into small groups and go online to look for a quick reference guide for something you own (your cell phone or laptop; a coffee pot or other appliance; the office copier). Look specifically for fairly brief instructions that could use revision for improved content, organization, style, or format. Make sure the instructions cover a task that you will be able to carry out. Make a copy of the instructions. Test these instructions for usability and revise as needed. Submit all materials to your instructor, along with a memo explaining the improvements, or be prepared to discuss your revision in class.

GLOBAL APPLICATION   MyWritingLab™

In many cultures, the use of imperative mood is considered impolite or too direct. For instance, instructions that state "Place the disk into the disk drive" may sound bossy and inconsiderate. Find a set of instructions that use imperative mood (for example, Figure 13.10 in this chapter) and rewrite these for a cross-cultural audience where the imperative mood would be offensive. For instance, you might use an indirect imperative ("Be sure to insert the disk into the drive").

DIGITAL AND SOCIAL MEDIA APPLICATION   MyWritingLab™

Think of a real situation in which you are trying to fix a product you own but can't find the original user manual. For instance, you might need to access the password settings for your Wi-Fi router but not remember how to do so. Go online and find the user manual (Hint: You will need the device name, brand, and model number). How easy or difficult was it to find the manual and then find the information you needed? Based on ideas from this chapter, are there other ways the information could have been written or made available to make your task easier?

MyWritingLab™   Visit Chapter 13, *Instructions and Procedures*, in MyWritingLab to complete this chapter's applications, to explore this chapter's overview, checklist, and flashcards, and to test your understanding of the chapter objectives.

14

Summaries

CHAPTER OUTLINE

LET'S GET STARTED:
Summaries *268*

Audience and Purpose
of Summaries *268*

Elements of Effective
Summaries *269*

Writing Summaries
Step by Step *270*

Special Types of Summaries *273*

Ethical Considerations
in Summarizing Information *276*

STRATEGIES for Summaries *278*

CHECKLIST for Summaries *279*

Applications *279*

LEARNING OBJECTIVES FOR THIS CHAPTER

▸ Summarize a long document using
step-by-step strategies

▸ Identify the purpose and placement of the
four types of summaries: closing summaries,
informative abstracts, descriptive abstracts,
and executive summaries

▸ Recognize ethical issues when
writing summaries

LET'S GET STARTED
Summaries

MyWritingLab™

Locate a technical article related to your undergraduate major that begins with a summary (the summary may use the name "summary," "abstract," or "executive summary"). For instance, if you are majoring in electrical engineering, use the library to find an article from a journal in that field. Most peer-reviewed articles begin with a brief summary of the article. Read this summary and make notes about the use of language, the order in which information is presented, and the level of technicality. See if you can understand the entire article simply by reading the summary. Then read the entire article.

Questions to ask about the summary you've located as you review the material in this chapter may include the following:

- ▸ What role does the summary play for the readers of this journal?
- ▸ How well does the summary characterize the full report or article?
- ▸ What decisions did the writer make about word choice, and why?

As you read this chapter, come back to your notes and the answers to the above questions and modify them based on what you learn from the chapter and in-class discussion.

Definition of summary

A *summary* is a restatement of the main ideas in a longer document. Summaries are used to convey the general meaning of the ideas in the original source without all the specific details or examples that may appear in the original. When you write a summary, take care to provide the essential information clearly and concisely in your own words, leaving out anything that isn't absolutely central to an understanding of the original.

AUDIENCE AND PURPOSE OF SUMMARIES

Audience considerations

Formal reports and proposals (discussed in Chapters 16 and 17) and other long documents are typically submitted to busy people: researchers, developers, managers, vice presidents, customers, and so on. For readers who must act quickly or only need to know the "big picture," reading an entire long report may not only be too time-consuming but also irrelevant. As a result, most long reports, proposals, and other long documents are commonly preceded by a summary.

The purpose of summaries, then, is to provide only an overview and the essential facts. Whether you summarize your own writing or someone else's, your summary should do three things for readers: (1) describe, in short form, what the original document is all about; (2) help readers decide whether to read all of the long document, parts of it, or none of it; and (3) give readers a framework for understanding the full document that will follow if they do plan to read it.

Purpose of summaries

To get a basic idea of how summaries fulfill audience needs, consider the examples in Figures 14.1 and 14.2.

Scientists know with virtual certainty that human activities are changing the composition of Earth's atmosphere. Increasing levels of greenhouse gases like carbon dioxide (CO_2) since pre-industrial times are well-documented and understood. The atmospheric buildup of CO_2 and other greenhouse gases is largely the result of human activities such as the burning of fossil fuels. Increasing greenhouse gas concentrations tend to warm the planet. A warming trend of about 0.7 to 1.5°F occurred during the 20th century in both the Northern and Southern Hemispheres and over the oceans. The major greenhouse gases remain in the atmosphere for periods ranging from decades to centuries. It is therefore virtually certain that atmospheric concentrations of greenhouse gases will continue to rise over the next few decades.

Source: Adapted from *State of Knowledge*, by the U.S. Environmental Protection Agency.

FIGURE 14.1
A passage to be summarized

Figure 14.2 shows a summary of the complex passage in Figure 14.1. Note how it captures the original's main ideas but in a compressed and less technical form that busy readers and general audiences would appreciate. The summary does not, however, change the essential meaning of the original—it merely boils the original down to its basic message.

Scientists are virtually certain that greenhouse gases largely produced by human activities are warming the planet. Temperatures have risen worldwide during the 20th century and undoubtedly will continue.

Source: From *State of Knowledge*, by the U.S. Environmental Protection Agency.

FIGURE 14.2
A summarized version of Figure 14.1

ELEMENTS OF EFFECTIVE SUMMARIES

Whether you summarize your own document or someone else's, always keep in mind that all summaries have four key characteristics: accuracy, completeness, conciseness, and nontechnical style.

Four characteristics of summaries

Accuracy

Readers expect a precise sketch of the content, emphasis, and line of reasoning used in the original document. Be careful not to alter the essential meaning of the original. For example, in Figure 14.2 on page 269, the summary uses different wording but remains true to the original document's central point (scientists feel that global warming is "virtually certain," not "somewhat certain"), retains the emphasis made in the original (the fact that human activity is responsible), and follows the same logical sequence (global warming has occurred and will continue to occur).

Completeness

Readers will also expect your summary to include everything essential in the original document—everything they need at a glance to grasp its full meaning. For example, in Figure 14.2, nothing has been left out to prevent readers from getting a complete overview of the original. Readers will know exactly what to expect from the longer document, only in fuller detail.

Conciseness

Readers expect a summary to exclude superfluous details—as well as any new details, examples, or opinions—not found in the original. Although the summary in Figure 14.2 doesn't omit anything essential, it does omit lesser details such as statistics ("0.7 to 1.5°F"), examples (set off by "like," "such as," "and other"), and overly long passages ("in both the Northern and Southern Hemispheres and over the oceans" is replaced with "the planet"). Also the summary in no way embellishes upon the original content.

Nontechnical Style

Unless your readers are all experts (and most of the time they will not be), always summarize a document using plain English rather than carrying the original's technical jargon or scientific and mathematical data into the summary. The summary in Figure 14.2, for example, omits expressions such as "atmospheric buildup" and "greenhouse gas concentrations," while also leaving out the specific temperatures mentioned.

WRITING SUMMARIES STEP BY STEP

Step-by-step nature of summaries

More so than for other types of documents, writing summaries involves a straightforward process: reading and rereading the original document, marking the key information, and writing and revising your summary while checking it against the original. The Strategies for Summaries on pages 278–279 provide an overview of these steps, along with audience and purpose considerations.

Step 1: Read the Original Document

Before you can effectively summarize a document, you need a solid understanding of what it says. Read the original from start to finish, without highlighting or taking notes. An initial read will give you a general understanding of the document's main point and key subpoints.

Do an initial read to get the big picture

Step 2: Reread and Mark Essential Material

Read the document again, this time using a highlighter or pen (if working on hard copy) or your computer's highlighting feature (after copying and pasting the document into a word processing file). Pay close attention to key words or phrases to help you identify the essential points. In Figure 14.3, key sentences are underlined, while the less important information is not.

Reread and highlight for a sharper understanding

Step 3: Cut and Paste the Key Information

If you are working from a hard copy of the original, rekey the material you highlighted into a new document. If you are working from an electronic version of the original, copy and paste only the highlighted portions into a new file. Don't worry about the overall organization or sentence construction at this point; just gather everything you need.

Create a new document from the highlighted information

Step 4: Redraft the Information into Your Own Organizational Pattern and Words

At this point, reorganize the material from the original source into patterns that work well in a smaller space. Use your own wording to express the original concepts. Don't worry about length just yet. You just want to get your own wording down on paper.

Turn the cut-and-paste version into your own version

Step 5: Edit Your Draft

In the previous step, the goal was to get your own wording down on paper. Now, edit your version. Keeping sentences clear and grammatical, cross out needless words; get rid of any asides; combine related concepts; and look for any repetitions. Note how Figure 14.4 is as pared down as it can be.

Focus on shortening your version

Step 6: Compare Your Version with the Original Document

As a final step, double-check that you have not altered the meaning, intent, or emphasis of the original document. Reread the original and then immediately reread your own version. As you can see, Figure 14.4 remains true to the original source but is only about 25% of the original's length.

Make sure you preserve the intent of the original

FIGURE 14.3
An article to be summarized

Open with basic claim

Omit background details

Include key comparison

Omit inessential detail

Include essential definition

Compress list of examples

Omit repetition and inessential statistic

Include key fact

Compress list of benefits

Include key comparison

Include key point

Dietary Fats and Your Health

Scientific evidence shows that consumption of <u>saturated fat, trans fat, and dietary cholesterol raises low-density lipoprotein (LDL), or "bad" cholesterol levels, which increases the risk of coronary heart disease (CHD).</u> According to the National Heart, Lung, and Blood Institute of the National Institutes of Health, more than 12.5 million Americans have CHD, and more than 500,000 die each year. That makes CHD one of the leading causes of death in the United States.

The <u>Food and Drug Administration has required that saturated fat and dietary cholesterol be listed on food labels since 1993. With trans fat added to the Nutrition Facts panel, you will know for the first time how much of all three—saturated fat, trans fat, and dietary cholesterol—are in the foods you choose.</u> Identifying saturated fat, trans fat, and dietary cholesterol on the food label gives you information you need to make food choices that help reduce the risk of CHD. This revised label will be of particular interest to people concerned about high blood cholesterol and heart disease. However, everyone should be aware of the risk posed by consuming too much saturated fat, trans fat, and dietary cholesterol.

But what is trans fat, and how can you limit the amount of this fat in your diet?

What Is Trans Fat?
Basically, <u>trans fat is made when manufacturers add hydrogen to vegetable oil—a process called hydrogenation.</u> Hydrogenation increases the shelf life and flavor stability of foods containing these fats. <u>Trans fat can be found in vegetable shortenings, some margarines, crackers, cookies, snack foods, and other foods made with or fried in partially hydrogenated oils.</u> Unlike other fats, the majority of trans fat is formed when food manufacturers turn liquid oils into solid fats like shortening and hard margarine. <u>A small amount of trans fat is found naturally, primarily in dairy products, some meat, and other animal-based foods.</u>

Trans fat, like saturated fat and dietary cholesterol, raises the LDL cholesterol that increases your risk for CHD. Americans consume on average 4 to 5 times as much saturated fat as trans fat in their diets. Although saturated fat is the main dietary culprit that raises LDL, trans fat and dietary cholesterol also contribute significantly.

Are All Fats Bad?
Simply put: <u>No. Unsaturated fat is a major source of energy for the body and aids in the absorption of vitamins A, D, E, and K, and carotenoids.</u> Both animal- and plant-derived food products contain fat, and when eaten in moderation, <u>unsaturated fat is important for proper growth, development, and maintenance of good health.</u> As a food ingredient, <u>unsaturated fat provides taste, consistency, and stability</u> and helps you feel full. In addition, parents should be aware that unsaturated <u>fats are an especially important source of calories and nutrients for infants and toddlers</u> (up to 2 years of age), who have the highest energy needs per unit of body weight of any age group.

<u>While unsaturated fats</u> (monounsaturated and polyunsaturated) <u>are beneficial when consumed in moderation, saturated and trans fats are not.</u> Saturated fat and trans fat raise LDL cholesterol levels in the blood. Dietary cholesterol also raises LDL cholesterol and may contribute to heart disease even without raising LDL. Therefore, it is advisable to <u>choose foods low in saturated fat, trans fat, and dietary cholesterol as part of a healthful diet.</u>

< continued >

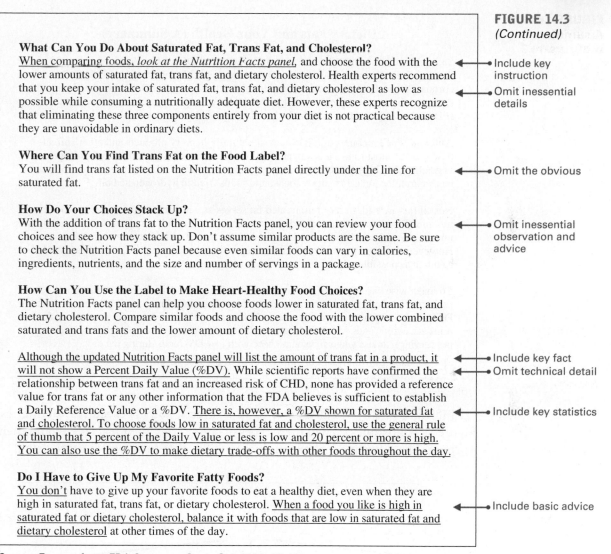

FIGURE 14.3
(Continued)

What Can You Do About Saturated Fat, Trans Fat, and Cholesterol?
When comparing foods, *look at the Nutrition Facts panel,* and choose the food with the
lower amounts of saturated fat, trans fat, and dietary cholesterol. Health experts recommend
that you keep your intake of saturated fat, trans fat, and dietary cholesterol as low as
possible while consuming a nutritionally adequate diet. However, these experts recognize
that eliminating these three components entirely from your diet is not practical because
they are unavoidable in ordinary diets.

→ Include key instruction
→ Omit inessential details

Where Can You Find Trans Fat on the Food Label?
You will find trans fat listed on the Nutrition Facts panel directly under the line for
saturated fat.

→ Omit the obvious

How Do Your Choices Stack Up?
With the addition of trans fat to the Nutrition Facts panel, you can review your food
choices and see how they stack up. Don't assume similar products are the same. Be sure
to check the Nutrition Facts panel because even similar foods can vary in calories,
ingredients, nutrients, and the size and number of servings in a package.

→ Omit inessential observation and advice

How Can You Use the Label to Make Heart-Healthy Food Choices?
The Nutrition Facts panel can help you choose foods lower in saturated fat, trans fat, and
dietary cholesterol. Compare similar foods and choose the food with the lower combined
saturated and trans fats and the lower amount of dietary cholesterol.

Although the updated Nutrition Facts panel will list the amount of trans fat in a product, it
will not show a Percent Daily Value (%DV). While scientific reports have confirmed the
relationship between trans fat and an increased risk of CHD, none has provided a reference
value for trans fat or any other information that the FDA believes is sufficient to establish
a Daily Reference Value or a %DV. There is, however, a %DV shown for saturated fat
and cholesterol. To choose foods low in saturated fat and cholesterol, use the general rule
of thumb that 5 percent of the Daily Value or less is low and 20 percent or more is high.
You can also use the %DV to make dietary trade-offs with other foods throughout the day.

→ Include key fact
→ Omit technical detail
→ Include key statistics

Do I Have to Give Up My Favorite Fatty Foods?
You don't have to give up your favorite foods to eat a healthy diet, even when they are
high in saturated fat, trans fat, or dietary cholesterol. When a food you like is high in
saturated fat or dietary cholesterol, balance it with foods that are low in saturated fat and
dietary cholesterol at other times of the day.

→ Include basic advice

Source: Excerpt from *FDA Consumer* Sept.–Oct. 2003: 12–18.

SPECIAL TYPES OF SUMMARIES

In preparing a report, proposal, or other document, you might summarize
the work of other people as part of your presentation. The previous sections
have described how to summarize documents written by others. But in other
situations, you will often need to summarize your own material. Various types
of reports, proposals, and other long documents require internal summaries.
Depending on the length, purpose, and audience, your document might include
one or more of four special types of summaries, in different locations, with different levels of detail. These four types of summaries are (1) closing summaries,

**FIGURE 14.4
A summary
of Figure 14.3**

Dietary Fats and Your Health (A Summary)

Saturated fat is a principal cause of bad cholesterol (LDL, or low density lipoprotein), but dietary cholesterol and trans fat also play a role. High LDL is a major risk factor for coronary heart disease, a leading killer in the United States. In addition to the listing of saturated fat and dietary cholesterol on food labels, the Food and Drug Administration (FDA) now requires that trans fat be listed.

Although small amounts of trans fat exist naturally in dairy products and other animal-based foods, most trans fat is a byproduct of hydrogenation, the addition of hydrogen to vegetable oil. This process increases shelf life and stabilizes the flavor of foods such as hard margarine, crackers, snack foods, and foods fried in hydrogenated oil.

Not all fats are bad. In fact, unsaturated fat serves as a major energy source, promotes vitamin absorption, enhances food taste, and helps us feel full. Consumed in moderation, unsaturated fat is essential to health and provides a vital calorie source for infants. However, saturated fats and trans fats, along with dietary cholesterol, should be avoided as much as possible.

To make wise choices about fats and cholesterol, read the Nutrition Facts label on packaged foods. Note the serving size, number of servings in the package, and the Percent Daily Value (%DV) of each ingredient. Although no Daily Value is yet established for trans fat, avoid foods with a high saturated fat or cholesterol DV (greater than 20 percent per serving), unless you can balance these with low DV foods during the day.

Source: Excerpt from *FDA Consumer* Sept.–Oct. 2003: 12–18.

(2) informative abstracts, (3) descriptive abstracts, and (4) executive summaries. Figure 14.5 illustrates each of these types of summaries, their placement, and their purpose. The following sections discuss and illustrate each type in more detail.

**FIGURE 14.5
Special types
of summaries**

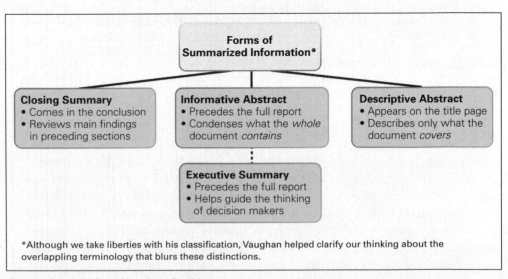

*Although we take liberties with his classification, Vaughan helped clarify our thinking about the overlappling terminology that blurs these distinctions.

Source: Adapted from Vaughan, David.

Closing Summaries

A *closing summary* appears in the concluding section of a formal report or proposal. The closing summary helps readers review and remember the major findings that have preceded it. This look back at "the big picture" also helps readers appreciate the conclusions and recommendations that typically follow the closing summary. Figure 14.6 shows a closing summary at the end of a report that analyzes the feasibility of a career in technical marketing. This summary appears just before the "Recommendations" portion that ends the report.

Purpose and placement of closing summaries

Summary of Findings
Technical marketing and sales requires solid technical background, motivation, communication skills, and interpersonal skills. This career offers job diversity and excellent income potential, balanced against hard work and relentless pressure to perform.

College graduates interested in this field confront four entry options: (1) direct entry with on-the-job training, (2) a formal training program, (3) prior experience in a technical specialty, and (4) graduate programs. Each option has benefits and drawbacks based on immediacy of income, rate of advancement, and long-term potential.

**FIGURE 14.6
A closing
summary**

Informative Abstracts

An *informative abstract* is a capsule version of a formal report or proposal that appears on a separate page, just after the document's title page. Informative abstracts provide readers with a snapshot of a long document—a clear picture of what is to come. Some readers, such as busy executives, may want just the "bottom line" without having to read the entire report or proposal. The informative abstract summarizes what the full document says: it identifies the need or issue that prompted the document; it describes the research methods used; it reviews the main facts and findings; and it condenses the conclusions and recommendations. (See page 317 of the formal report in Chapter 16 or page 340 of the formal proposal in Chapter 17 for an example.) An informative abstract may simply be labeled as an "abstract."

Purpose and placement of informative abstracts

Descriptive Abstracts

More compressed than an informative abstract, a *descriptive abstract* is usually only one to three sentences long and appears on the title page of a report or proposal. A descriptive abstract merely states what a document *covers*; it doesn't get into detail about what the document contains. Such an abstract helps people decide whether to read the report. Compare, for example, the descriptive abstract

Purpose and placement of descriptive abstracts

FIGURE 14.7
A descriptive abstract

> The origin of trans fat, its relation to saturated fat and dietary cholesterol, and its causative role in heart disease is explained, and advice for consumers is provided.

in Figure 14.7 with the article summary in Figure 14.4 The descriptive abstract conveys only the basic nature and extent of the longer document.

Executive Summaries

Purpose and placement of executive summaries

An *executive summary* is similar to an informative abstract; however, it not only summarizes the long document but also tells readers what they should think about it. Placed on a separate page just after a long document's title page (just like an informative abstract), an executive summary is aimed at decision makers rather than technical audiences. Unlike informative abstracts, executive summaries are written to persuade readers to act on the information. Executive summaries are crucial in cases when readers have no time to read the entire original document and when they expect the writer to help guide their thinking ("Tell me how to think about this," instead of, "Help me understand this"). Unless the readers (the organization or company) stipulate a specific format, organize your executive abstract to answer the following questions:

Questions to answer in an executive summary

- What is the issue?
- What was found?
- What does it mean?
- What should be done?

The executive summary in Figure 14.8 falls at the beginning of a much longer 40-page report. This one page summarizes the more detailed report. Notice how the executive summary answers all the above questions.

ETHICAL CONSIDERATIONS IN SUMMARIZING INFORMATION

Summaries in the information age

Information in summary format is increasingly attractive to today's readers, who often feel bombarded by more information than they can handle. Consider, for example, the popularity of the *USA Today* newspaper, with its countless news items offered in brief snippets for overtaxed readers. In contrast, the *New York Times* offers lengthy text that is information rich but more time-consuming to digest. Summaries are especially adaptable to the hypertext-linked design of online documents. Instead of long blocks of text, Web pages are often designed with concise modules, or "chunks," of information that stand alone, are easy to scan, and require little or no scrolling. Moreover, magazine Web sites such as *Forbes* or *The Economist* offer email summaries of their hard copy articles.

Status Report: Market Share for Goldilocks Breakfast Cereals (GBC)

In response to a request from GBC's Board of Directors, the accounting division analyzed recent trends in the company's sales volume and profitability. ← • What is the issue?

Findings

- Even though GBC is the cereal industry leader, its sales for the past four years increased at a mere average of 2.5 percent annually, to $5.2 billion, and net income decreased 12 percent overall, to $459 million.

- This weak sales growth apparently results from consumer resistance to retail ← • What was found? price increases for cereal, totaling 91 percent in slightly more than a decade.

- GBC introduces an average of two new cereal products annually (most recently, "Coconut Whammos" and "Spinach Crunchies"), but such innovations do little to increase consumer interest.

- A growing array of generic cereal brands have been underselling GBC's products by more than $1 per box, especially in giant retail outlets.

- This past June, GBC dropped its cereal prices by roughly 20 percent, but by this time the brand had lost substantial market share to generic cereal brands.

Conclusions

- Slow but progressive loss of market share threatens GBC's dominance as industry leader.

- GBC must regain consumer loyalty to reinvigorate its market base. ← • What does it mean?

- Our new cereal products have done more to erode than to enhance GBC's brand image.

Recommendations

To regain lost market share and ensure continued dominance, GBC should implement the following recommendations:

1. Curtail development of new cereal products, and invest in improving the taste ← • What should and nutritional value of GBC's traditional products. be done?

2. Capitalize on GBC's brand recognition with an advertising campaign to promote GBC's "best-sellers" as an "all-day" food (a healthful snack or inexpensive alternative to microwave dinners).

3. Examine the possibility of high-volume sales at discounted prices through giant retail chains.

FIGURE 14.8 A one-page executive summary from a much longer (40-page) report

While such capsules or "digests" of information are an efficient way to stay informed, summaries carry with them potential pitfalls, as media critic Ilan Greenberg points out (65):

Ethical pitfalls of summaries

- A condensed version of a complicated document may provide a useful overview, but this superficial treatment often fails to communicate the document's full complexity—that is, the complete story. Whoever summarizes a lengthy document makes decisions about what to leave out and what to leave in, what to emphasize, and what to ignore. During the selection process, the original message could very well be distorted. Therefore, be careful that any summary (except a descriptive abstract) conveys the full picture of what the original document says.

- In a summary of someone else's writing, the tone or "voice" of the original author often disappears—along with that writer's way of seeing. Be careful that you not only carry the essential facts of an original document into your summary, but that in the process of condensing you don't distort the original writer's intent. If a writer says, as in Figure 14.1, "Scientists know with virtual certainty" that human activities are leading to global warming, make sure that this critical point carries into your summary. Downplaying ("some scientists suspect") or overplaying ("scientists are 100% certain") the original writer's intent is a distortion.

Although summaries do have their place in our busy world, the more complex the topic, the more readers need the whole story.

STRATEGIES
for Summaries

> **Start the summary process by reading the original document.** Read the document all the way through without highlighting or taking notes to get a clear sense of its main point and most important subpoints.

> **Reread the original while highlighting essential information.** A second read, combined with highlighting or underlining, will give you a sharper picture of important points.

> **Save only the key information.** Delete the inessential information from the original document to create a rough draft of the original document's wording.

> **Rewrite the key information in your own words.** Initially don't worry about length. Avoid using any of the original document's words unless a key term or phrase is indispensable. If you must quote a passage directly, use quotation marks around the quoted words.

> **Edit your version.** When you have included everything readers need, edit your work for conciseness, getting rid of wordiness, combining related ideas, and eliminating repetition.

STRATEGIES *continued*

- ▸ **Finally, check your version against the original.** Verify that you have added no personal observations (unless you are writing an executive abstract) and have not altered the meaning, intent, or emphasis of the original.

- ▸ **Indicate the exact source of the summarized material.** When you are summarizing someone else's work, immediately follow your summary with a reference to the original source.

- ▸ **Use the appropriate types of summaries in your own formal documents.** Formal reports and proposals always include informative abstracts (when the intent is simply to provide a snapshot) or executive summaries (when the intent is to persuade readers how to think about the longer document). Closing summaries are always helpful in such reports. Descriptive abstracts can be helpful when included on the title page of a formal report or proposal.

- ▸ **Remain aware of ethical considerations.** A summary that adds material not found in the original document or omits critical information from the original is misleading and unethical. Likewise, misrepresenting the original document's point of view is unethical.

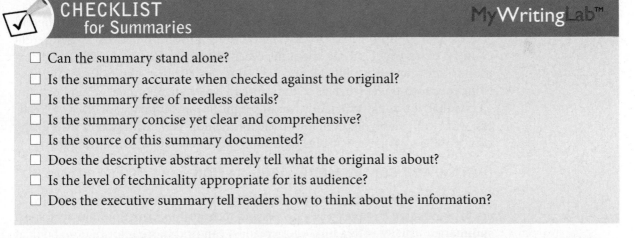

CHECKLIST
for Summaries

MyWritingLab™

- ☐ Can the summary stand alone?
- ☐ Is the summary accurate when checked against the original?
- ☐ Is the summary free of needless details?
- ☐ Is the summary concise yet clear and comprehensive?
- ☐ Is the source of this summary documented?
- ☐ Does the descriptive abstract merely tell what the original is about?
- ☐ Is the level of technicality appropriate for its audience?
- ☐ Does the executive summary tell readers how to think about the information?

APPLICATIONS

GENERAL APPLICATIONS
MyWritingLab™

1. Find an article about your major field or area of interest and write both an informative abstract and a descriptive abstract for the article.

2. Find a long article (at least five pages) and summarize it, following the step-by-step process described in this chapter and keeping accuracy, completeness,

conciseness, and nontechnical language always in mind. Capture the essence and main points of the original article in no more than one-fourth the length. Use your own words, and do not distort the original. Submit a copy of the original along with your summary.

TEAM APPLICATION

Organize into small groups and choose a topic for discussion: an employment problem, a campus problem, plans for an event, suggestions for energy conservation, or the like. (A possible topic: Should employers have the right to require lie detector tests or drug tests for their employees?) Discuss the topic for one class period, taking notes on significant points and conclusions. Afterward, organize and edit your notes in line with the directions for writing summaries. Write a summary of the group discussion in no more than 200 words. As a group, compare your individual summaries for accuracy, emphasis, conciseness, and clarity.

GLOBAL APPLICATION   MyWritingLab™

Find a long article (longer than five pages) from a technical, scientific, financial, or similar publication. Pick an article that deals with an issue that is global in scope (for instance, an article about the use of pesticides in different countries or an article about the ways in which financial decisions have worldwide impacts). Summarize this article for an audience of nonspecialists, but for two different groups: one group of U.S. citizens and another group of citizens in a different country. Learn what you can about the other country by looking online and determining key scientific, political, or financial issues. Or bring knowledge you have from your own travel (such as a study abroad experience) or background or from a class that you took. What will you highlight in the summary for the U.S. readers, what will you highlight in the article for the non-U.S. readers, and why? Bring copies of the original article plus each summary to class to discuss with others.

DIGITAL AND SOCIAL MEDIA APPLICATION   MyWritingLab™

When used for workplace communication, Twitter and Facebook require writers to summarize complex news stories and technical information into very short summaries, usually with a link where readers can find more information. Look at the Twitter feed or Facebook page for your campus or for a technical or scientific government agency (such as the National Weather Service). How effective are these short summaries? What techniques do the writers use to keep these summaries accurate yet interesting? Summarize your findings in two to three sentences for your instructor.

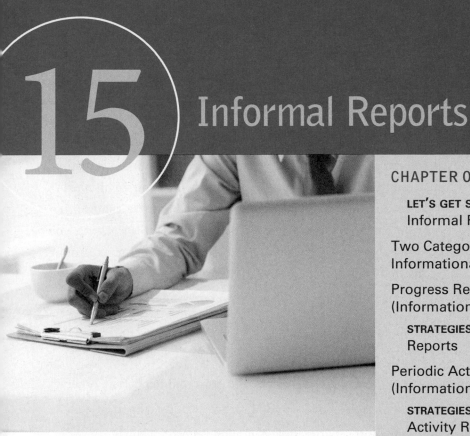

15 Informal Reports

CHAPTER OUTLINE

LET'S GET STARTED:
Informal Reports   *282*

Two Categories of Reports:
Informational and Analytical   *283*

Progress Reports
(Informational)   *283*
   STRATEGIES for Progress
   Reports   *284*

Periodic Activity Reports
(Informational)   *287*
   STRATEGIES for Periodic
   Activity Reports   *287*

Trip Reports (Informational)   *287*
   STRATEGIES for Trip Reports   *289*

Meeting Minutes (Informational)   *292*
   STRATEGIES for Meeting
   Minutes   *292*

Feasibility Reports (Analytical)   *293*
   STRATEGIES for Feasibility
   Reports   *294*

Recommendation Reports
(Analytical)   *296*
   STRATEGIES for
   Recommendation Reports   *296*

Peer Review Reports (Analytical)   *298*
   STRATEGIES for Peer Review
   Reports   *298*
   CHECKLIST for Informal
   Reports   *300*

Applications   *300*

LEARNING OBJECTIVES FOR THIS CHAPTER

▸ Define and understand the role
   of informal reports

▸ Identify the difference between informational
   and analytical reports

▸ Plan and write effective informational reports

▸ Plan and write effective analytical reports

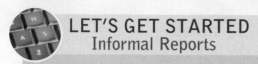

LET'S GET STARTED
Informal Reports

MyWritingLab™

You have probably written a short informal report at one time or another (at school, for an internship, or on the job). Make some notes about that situation, and then think about a different real-life situation for which you might need to write a short informal report. For instance, you may need to write a short progress report for your employer about what you accomplished this week. Or you may want to write a feasibility report addressed to your instructor, explaining and justifying the final project you propose to do for class. Use a memo format to write your short report.

Questions to ask about the short report you wrote as you review the material in this chapter:

- ▶ Is the purpose of the report clear (status update, recommendation, other)?
- ▶ Have I used headings and bullets, and, if so, are these used appropriately?
- ▶ Is the tone of my short report personal enough yet professional?
- ▶ Is the report's length appropriate?
- ▶ Is the subject line clear?

At the end of this chapter, review your initial Let's Get Started report with your instructor or with a group of students to see how much you might change or modify the report based on what you have learned from the chapter.

Definition of informal reports

When you think of reports, you probably picture long, formal documents that contain many pages of research, information, charts and graphs, footnotes, and other details. Yet in the workplace, for every long, formal report dozens of shorter reports are written, reports focused on only one or two very specific issues. These *informal reports* help people make informed decisions on matters such as the most comfortable office chairs to buy or the best recruit to hire for management training. Unlike long formal reports (discussed in Chapter 16), most informal reports require no extended planning, are prepared quickly, contain little or no background information, and have no *front* or *end matter* (title page, table of contents, glossary, works cited, index).

Despite being so focused and concise, informal reports do provide the information and analysis that readers need every day on the job. Although various formats can be used, informal reports, especially those intended for internal audiences, most often take the form of a memo. (Depending on the company or organization, the words "memo" or "memorandum" may or may not be used, but a general memo format is followed.) Because informal reports are typically longer than what would be suitable for the body of an email message, these reports are usually sent as attachments. Informal reports are typically written using a word processing program (like Microsoft Word, Apple Pages, or Google Docs), but the final version should be saved as a PDF file to retain formatting and page breaks. PDF files can be read on a computer or mobile device or printed and read on paper.

Format of informal reports

TWO CATEGORIES OF REPORTS: INFORMATIONAL AND ANALYTICAL

In the professional world, decision makers rely on two types of informal reports: Some reports focus primarily on information ("what we're doing now," "what we did last month," "what our customer survey found," "what went on at the department meeting"), while others may also include analysis ("what this information means for us," "what courses of action should be considered," "what we recommend, and why").

Informational versus analytical reports

The purpose of an *informational report* is to inform; that is, to provide data and other information to answer basic questions, such as how much progress has been made on a project (progress reports), what activity has taken place over the course of a certain period of time (activity reports), what activity occurred during a business trip (trip reports), or what discussions took place in a meeting (meeting minutes). These reports help keep an organization running from day to day by providing short, timely updates on important activities.

Purpose of informational reports

Unlike informational reports, *analytical reports* offer both information and conclusions based on the information. Analysis is the heart of technical communication. Analysis involves evaluating information, interpreting it accurately, drawing valid conclusions, and making persuasive recommendations. Although gathering and reporting information are essential workplace skills, analysis is ultimately what professionals do to earn their pay. Analytical reports analyze and evaluate whether a project or situation is feasible (feasibility reports), make recommendations on how to proceed (recommendation reports), or constructively critique the work of others (peer review reports).

Purpose of analytical reports

PROGRESS REPORTS (INFORMATIONAL)

Organizations depend on *progress reports* (also called status reports) to monitor progress and problems on various projects. Progress reports may be written either for internal personnel or outside clients. In the case of internal audiences,

Purpose, audience, and frequency of progress reports

managers use progress reports to evaluate projects, monitor employees, decide how to allocate funds, and keep track of delays or expense overages that could dramatically affect outcomes and project costs. In the case of external audiences, progress reports explain to clients how time and money are being spent and how difficulties have been overcome. The reports can therefore be used to assure the client that the project will be completed on schedule and on budget.

Many contracts stipulate the dates and stages when progress will be reported. Failing to report on time may invoke contractual penalties. Some organizations require regular progress reports (daily, weekly, monthly), while others use such reports only as needed, such as when a project milestone has been reached.

Elements of progress reports

Figure 15.1 shows a progress report from a training manager to a company vice president. Because the audience is internal, the writer has chosen memo format. A report like this to an external client might be written in letter format and on company letterhead as a legal record. Notice also how the report provides only those details essential to the reader. In addition, it follows a timeline structure, beginning with a summary of progress on the project (or since the last progress report) and concluding with the next steps to be completed. The text of this report (without the heading guide, company logo, and copy notation) also appears on pages 88–89.

STRATEGIES
for Progress Reports

▶ **Choose an appropriate format.** Routine, regular reports may be delivered in email format, whereas more infrequent reports might be better delivered via a signed memo (or a letter, when the report is for an external client).

▶ **Provide a clear subject line.** All progress reports should clearly identify their purpose in the subject line of a memo or email or in the introduction to a letter.

▶ **Present information efficiently.** Because readers of progress reports are managers or clients who want the bottom-line information as quickly as possible, chunk the information into logically headed sections and use bulleted or numbered lists. Leave out information readers will already know, but do not omit new information.

▶ **Make sure your report answers the anticipated questions.** First identify what has been accomplished since the last report; then discuss any important details such as outcomes of meetings, problems encountered and solutions implemented or proposed, deadlines met or missed, resources/materials needed, and so on. Conclude with steps to be completed in time for the next report, with specific dates, if available.

FIGURE 15.1
A progress report

BETA National

To: P. J. Stone, Senior Vice President
From: B. Poret, Group Training Manager *B.P.*
Date: June 6, 20XX
Subject: *Progress Report: Equipment for New Operations Building*   ◄────● Subject line identifies
                                                                                exact purpose of the
                                                                                report

Work Completed

Our training group has met twice since our May 12 report. In our first meeting,   ◄────● Summarizes first
we identified the types of training we anticipate.   achievement

Types of Training Anticipated

- Loan Officer Work Experience
- Divisional Systems Training
- Divisional Clerical Training (Continuing)
- Divisional Clerical Training (New Employees)
- Divisional Management Training (Seminars)
- Special/New Equipment Training

In our second meeting, we considered various areas for the training room.

Training Room Assignment and Equipment   ◄────● Summarizes
                                                       second achievement

The frequency of training necessitates having a training room available daily. The
large training room in the Corporate Education area (10th floor) would be ideal.
Please confirm that this room can be assigned to us on a full-time basis.

To support the training programs, we purchased this equipment:

- Audioviewer
- Large flat screen monitor
- Digital video camera and tripod
- Software for computer-assisted instruction

This equipment will allow us to administer training in varied modes, ranging from
programmed and learner-controlled instruction to seminars and workshops.

Work Remaining

To support the training, we need to furnish the room appropriately. Because the types   ◄────● Describes work
of training will vary, the furniture should provide a flexible environment. Outlined here   remaining
are our anticipated furnishing needs.

- Tables and chairs that can be set up in many configurations. These would allow   ◄────● Bulleted list
  for individual or group training and large seminars.   breaks up dense
- Portable room dividers. These would provide study space for training with   information
  programmed instruction, and allow for simultaneous training.
- Built-in storage space for audiovisual equipment as well as training supplies.
  This storage space should be multipurpose, providing work or
  display surfaces.
- A flexible lighting system, for audiovisual presentations and individualized study.

The project is on schedule. As soon as we receive your approval of these specifications,   ◄────● Concludes with
we will send out bids for room dividers and have plans drawn for built-in storage.   request for approval
                                                                                                   of next phase

The next example (Figure 15.2) is a progress report written by a student. As you work on a longer report or term project, your instructor might require a progress report. In this example, the student writer documents the progress she has made on her term project: a causal analysis examining the impact of a recently formed town committee.

PROGRESS REPORT

TO: Dr. J. Lannon

FROM: T. Fitzgerald, Student *T.F.*

DATE: April 27, 20XX

SUBJECT: Analytical Report

                 A STUDY OF THE IMPACT OF THE SANDWICH HISTORIC DISTRICT
                 COMMITTEE ON THE TOWN'S ARCHITECTURAL CHARACTER

WORK COMPLETED TO DATE

March 22:   Completed report on Sandwich Historic District Committee.

April 11:   Obtained maps of Sandwich, legislation, certificates of appropriateness, exemption, and appeals from Town Hall.

April 12, 14, 15:   Investigated district area by car, noted differences in historic and nonhistoric areas.

April 18:   Photographed sampling of areas in district. Twenty photos taken, fifteen returned by developer.

April 19:   Divided master map into sections, redefining district.

April 20:   Completed tentative outline.

April 22:   Interviewed chairman of Committee, Donald Bourne. Received new set of rules and regulations for district.

WORK IN PROGRESS: Drawing maps of present district and redefined area.

WORK TO BE COMPLETED

April 28:   Interview Edward Cain, committee member.

May 2:   Interview Gary Sosa committee member.

DATE FOR COMPLETION: May 11, 20XX

FIGURE 15.2 Progress report on a term project

PERIODIC ACTIVITY REPORTS (INFORMATIONAL)

Periodic activity reports resemble progress reports in that they summarize activities over a specified period. But unlike progress reports, which summarize specific accomplishments on a particular project, periodic activity reports summarize general activities during a particular period. Periodic activity reports are almost always internal, written by employees to keep their supervisors up to date on their activities as a whole in order to help managers monitor workload. In many companies, these reports, usually written weekly or monthly, are called "status reports."

Figure 15.3 shows a periodic activity report, in the form of a weekly status report. Notice how Laura Hardin presents the most vital information first (the ongoing user manuals project) and ends with necessary but less pressing details (vacation time and "other"). The report contains only the information and level of detail her supervisor needs.

Purpose, audience, and frequency of periodic activity reports

Elements of periodic activity reports

STRATEGIES
for Periodic Activity Reports

▸ **Choose an appropriate format.** Periodic activity reports are usually written in email or memo format to a supervisor. However, some organizations may require a predesigned form.

▸ **Provide a clear subject line.** As with any report, identify the exact purpose of a periodic activity report by providing a subject line, such as "Monthly activity report for August."

▸ **Present information efficiently.** All report readers want the bottom line. Omit minor details but include all the essentials. Use headers to chunk information and bulleted and numbered lists to break up dense prose for easier reading.

▸ **Make sure your report answers the expected questions.** Begin by describing your most important accomplishments during the period (such as progress on an ongoing project). Then describe any other relevant activity since the last report (such as completion of one-time projects, attendance at meetings, supplies needed, conflicts or problems encountered, schedule changes, vacation time taken or upcoming, and so forth).

TRIP REPORTS (INFORMATIONAL)

Trip reports resemble periodic activity reports in that they detail activities during a given period, but they focus specifically on business-related travel rather than a variety of workplace activities. These reports, like periodic activity reports,

Purpose and audience of trip reports

Email format
indicates routine
nature of report

Subject line clearly
indicates purpose
of report

Progress on most
important ongoing
projects presented
first

Bold introductions
and double spaces
between items
highlight and
separate categories
of information

Less vital
information
presented at
the end

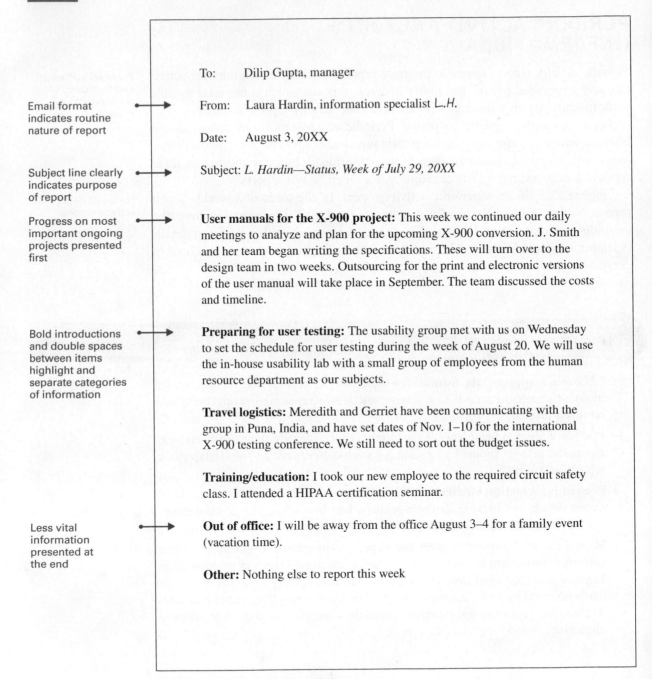

To: Dilip Gupta, manager

From: Laura Hardin, information specialist *L.H.*

Date: August 3, 20XX

Subject: *L. Hardin—Status, Week of July 29, 20XX*

User manuals for the X-900 project: This week we continued our daily meetings to analyze and plan for the upcoming X-900 conversion. J. Smith and her team began writing the specifications. These will turn over to the design team in two weeks. Outsourcing for the print and electronic versions of the user manual will take place in September. The team discussed the costs and timeline.

Preparing for user testing: The usability group met with us on Wednesday to set the schedule for user testing during the week of August 20. We will use the in-house usability lab with a small group of employees from the human resource department as our subjects.

Travel logistics: Meredith and Gerriet have been communicating with the group in Puna, India, and have set dates of Nov. 1–10 for the international X-900 testing conference. We still need to sort out the budget issues.

Training/education: I took our new employee to the required circuit safety class. I attended a HIPAA certification seminar.

Out of office: I will be away from the office August 3–4 for a family event (vacation time).

Other: Nothing else to report this week

FIGURE 15.3 A periodic activity report

are written to help a supervisor monitor employee activities. In the case of trip reports, when employers pay for employee travel, managers need to know that the company is getting its money's worth. Managers also need to know what employees learn through their travels.

Figure 15.4 shows a trip report written by an employee who has traveled to a branch office to inspect the site and interview those employees about absenteeism and hiring problems at that branch. Because the report is informational, not analytical, it sticks only to the facts. Note also that Bill Moskowicz begins the report with a purpose statement, accounts for how he spent his time, identifies the people with whom he met, offers a summary of what he learned, and provides a conclusion.

Elements of trip reports

For more on trip reports, see the Strategies below.

STRATEGIES
for Trip Reports

▸ **Take good notes and make accurate transcriptions of interviews.** If you must interview people, either ask their permission to record the conversation or take careful notes. Transcribe interviews immediately, while the discussion is still fresh in your mind. If you investigate a location or site, take careful notes of what you observe.

▸ **Write down the names of people and places.** Make sure you are able to indicate whom you spoke with (spelling their names correctly and getting their job titles right) and the names of places visited.

▸ **Account for times and locations.** Demonstrate a good use of your time by accounting for it (but not exhaustively). If you visit more than one location, be clear about what occurred at each.

▸ **Provide a clear title and purpose statement.** A clear title indicates exactly which trip you are referring to, including date(s), while a purpose statement at the beginning of the report prevents any possible confusion as to your reasons for taking the trip.

▸ **Use a format that is easy to navigate.** As you would in any report, provide clear headings to break up chunks of information and use bulleted/numbered lists, double spacing, and so on, for ease of readability.

▸ **Describe findings completely and objectively.** Don't omit vital information or include irrelevant information, and don't insert personal impressions—stick to the facts.

▸ **Offer to follow up.** Because trip reports may lead to further questions from a supervisor, indicate that you are available to help answer those questions. Unless you have been asked to do so, do not make recommendations.

FIGURE 15.4
A trip report

Subject line
identifies trip
and date   ●━━▶

Starts with a
purpose statement   ●━━▶

Provides an
accounting of how
time was spent   ●━━▶

Includes discussion
of what was learned   ●━━▶

Uses bulleted list
(and headings) to
break up text and
identify key points   ●━━▶

To: Monica Herrera, Director of Human Resources, Boston office
From: Bill Moskowicz, Human Resources Specialist *B. M.*
Date: March 30, 20XX
Subject: *Visit to the Eastfield Office*

PURPOSE
On March 20, I visited the Eastfield office to explore these two issues:
• Higher-than-average rate of employee absenteeism at that office
• Difficulties hiring qualified employees to work and live in or near the
  Eastfield Fort Channel area

To pinpoint the causes of these problems, I decided to interview three individuals
face to face in hopes of getting more candid and detailed responses than I would
via phone or email, particularly regarding the sensitive absenteeism problem.

SCHEDULE
I spoke with the following people individually: Susan Sheehan, Director of
HR (9:00 a.m.–10:00 a.m.); Sammy Lee, Marketing Manager for the gourmet
desserts division (10:00 a.m.–11:00 a.m.); and Megan Fields, an Administrative
Assistant in the distribution division (11:00 a.m.–12:00 p.m.). Then we all had
lunch and continued the discussion between noon and 2:00 p.m., at which time
I transcribed my recordings and headed back to Boston.

INTERVIEWS
The interviews were illuminating. Essentially all three pointed out how the
absenteeism and hiring problems are not entirely separate issues; in fact, they
are closely linked. While once a thriving, safe, and low-crime city (including
the branch's Fort Channel area), Eastfield has now fallen upon difficult
economic times, particularly in the last year. All three employees identified
the following problems:
• Increased gang activity and vagrancy in the Fort Channel area
• Lack of safe public transportation to and from the office or a secure, on-site
  parking facility

FIGURE 15.4
(Continued)

- An increasing decline in amenities, especially lunch venues or safe public areas nearby
- Decreased security resulting from a busy police force and high security guard turnover

While Susan and Sammy can both afford to occasionally take cabs and leave the Fort Channel area for lunch, Megan pointed out her limitations due to salary and an insufficient reimbursement program.

The Fort Channel area's problems have all had a direct impact on employee hiring in recent months. Both Susan and Sammy reported losing promising potential employees following interviews. According to Susan, while United Foods manufactures and distributes gourmet products, attracting those who wish to work in an upscale environment, potential employees are often frightened away, preferring employment at either the Boston office or with competitors located elsewhere in the state. At the same time, very few have opted to relocate from the Boston to Eastfield offices to help account for imbalances.

CONCLUSION

While the goal of this trip was not for me to make recommendations, I have some specific ideas. I would be glad to speak with you further to answer any questions and to share those ideas with you.

Provides an offer to follow up

MEETING MINUTES (INFORMATIONAL)

Purpose, audience, and distribution of meeting minutes

Many team or project meetings require someone to record the proceedings. *Meeting minutes* are the records of such meetings. Copies of minutes usually are distributed (often via email) to all members and interested parties to track the proceedings and to remind members about their responsibilities. Usually one person is appointed to record the minutes. Often, the person assigned will type minutes on a laptop computer and email them out as soon as the meeting is completed. Be sure to proofread the minutes, check the spelling of the attendees' names, and consider how you have described any politically sensitive or confidential issues before sending. Remember, email can travel widely.

Figure 15.5 shows minutes from a personnel manager's meeting.

STRATEGIES
for Meeting Minutes

▸ **Take good notes during the meeting.** Don't rely on your memory, even if you write up the minutes immediately after the meeting. Write down who said what, especially if a particularly important point was raised.

▸ **Complete the minutes immediately after the meeting.** Even if you take good notes, you may forget the context of a particular point if you wait too long. Write up the minutes immediately.

▸ **Include a clear title with the meeting date.** A clear title should indicate the meeting's exact purpose ("sales conference planning meeting"), and always include the meeting date to prevent confusion with similar meetings.

▸ **List attendees.** List everyone who attended. If the meeting was chaired or moderated, indicate by whom.

▸ **Describe all agenda items.** Make sure all topics discussed are recorded. Your own memory of meeting topics and those of other meeting attendees are usually fleeting.

▸ **Record all decisions or conclusions.** If everyone agreed on a point or if a vote was taken, be sure to include those results in your minutes.

▸ **Make sure the minutes are easy to navigate.** Use headings, lists, and other helpful design features.

▸ **Make sure the minutes are precise and clear.** Describe each topic fully yet concisely. Don't leave out important nuances, but stick to the facts.

▸ **Keep personal commentary, humor, and "sidebar" comments out of meeting minutes.** Comments ("As usual, Ms. Jones disagreed with the committee") or judgmental words ("good," "poor," "irrelevant") are not appropriate.

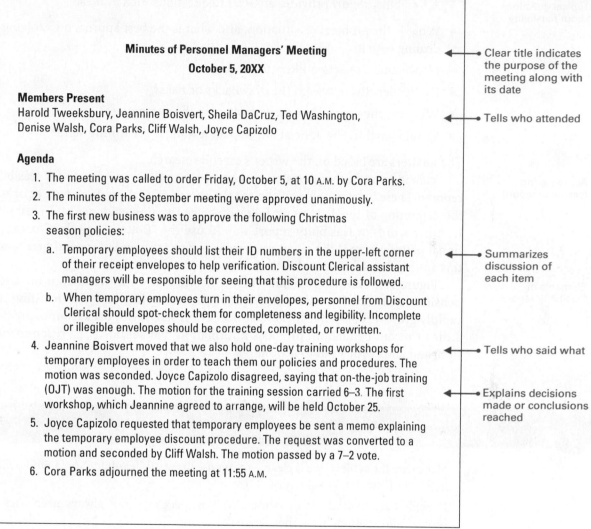

Minutes of Personnel Managers' Meeting
October 5, 20XX

Members Present

Harold Tweeksbury, Jeannine Boisvert, Sheila DaCruz, Ted Washington, Denise Walsh, Cora Parks, Cliff Walsh, Joyce Capizolo

Agenda

1. The meeting was called to order Friday, October 5, at 10 A.M. by Cora Parks.

2. The minutes of the September meeting were approved unanimously.

3. The first new business was to approve the following Christmas season policies:

   a. Temporary employees should list their ID numbers in the upper-left corner of their receipt envelopes to help verification. Discount Clerical assistant managers will be responsible for seeing that this procedure is followed.

   b. When temporary employees turn in their envelopes, personnel from Discount Clerical should spot-check them for completeness and legibility. Incomplete or illegible envelopes should be corrected, completed, or rewritten.

4. Jeannine Boisvert moved that we also hold one-day training workshops for temporary employees in order to teach them our policies and procedures. The motion was seconded. Joyce Capizolo disagreed, saying that on-the-job training (OJT) was enough. The motion for the training session carried 6–3. The first workshop, which Jeannine agreed to arrange, will be held October 25.

5. Joyce Capizolo requested that temporary employees be sent a memo explaining the temporary employee discount procedure. The request was converted to a motion and seconded by Cliff Walsh. The motion passed by a 7–2 vote.

6. Cora Parks adjourned the meeting at 11:55 A.M.

Annotations (right margin):
- Clear title indicates the purpose of the meeting along with its date
- Tells who attended
- Summarizes discussion of each item
- Tells who said what
- Explains decisions made or conclusions reached

FIGURE 15.5 Meeting minutes

FEASIBILITY REPORTS (ANALYTICAL)

Feasibility reports are used when decision makers need to assess whether an idea, plan, or course of action is realistic and practical. Sometimes an idea may make perfect sense from one perspective, but may not be feasible at the moment for one reason or another, usually because of timing. For example, a manufacturing company may want to switch to a more automated process, which would greatly reduce costs over the long term. But in the short term, the resulting layoffs would have a negative impact on morale.

Purpose of feasibility reports

Typical questions about feasibility

A feasibility report provides answers to questions such as these:

- What is the problem or situation, and what is the best approach to solving or dealing with it?
- Is this course of action likely to succeed?
- Do the benefits outweigh the drawbacks or risks?
- What are the pros and cons, and what are the alternatives?
- Should anything be done at all? Should it wait? Is the timing right?

The answers are based on the writer's careful research.

Audience for feasibility reports

Managers and other decision makers are the primary audience for feasibility reports. These busy people want to see the recommendation or answer at or near the beginning of the document, followed by supporting evidence and reasoning. In other words, a feasibility report should use the "bottom line first" organizational pattern: here is the situation; here is our recommendation; and here is why this approach is feasible at this time.

Elements of feasibility reports

Figure 15.6 shows a feasibility report in which a securities analyst for a state pension fund reports to the fund's manager on the feasibility of investing in a rapidly growing computer maker. Notice how it starts with background, provides a direct recommendation, provides information that supports the recommendation, and ends with a call to action.

STRATEGIES
for Feasibility Reports

- ▶ **Make sure the subject line is clear.** Always use the word "feasibility" (or a synonym) in the title ("Subject: Feasibility of …").
- ▶ **Provide background information.** Your readers may not always need background information, but if they do, make it short.
- ▶ **Offer the recommendation near the beginning of the report.** Because readers of feasibility reports are interested primarily in the "bottom line," state it explicitly at the very beginning of the report or just after the background information.
- ▶ **Provide the details, data, and criteria after the recommendation section.** Include supporting data, such as costs, equipment needed, results expected, and so on. Don't overdo the supporting data, but include everything directly relevant that will persuade readers to support your recommendation.
- ▶ **Explain why your recommendation is the most feasible of all the possible choices.** Your readers may prefer other choices. Persuade them that yours is the best choice.
- ▶ **End with a call to action.**

State Pension Fund

MEMORANDUM

To: Mary K. White, Fund Manager

From: Martha Mooney ᴍᴍ

Date: April 1, 20XX

Subject: **The Feasibility of Investing in WBM Computers, Inc.**

Our Treasury bonds, composing 3.5 percent of the Fund's investment portfolio, mature on April 15. Current inflationary pressures make fixed-income investments less attractive than equities. As you requested, I have researched and compared investment alternatives based on these criteria: market share, earnings, and dividends.

Recommendation

Given its established market share, solid earnings, and generous dividends, WBM Computers, Inc., is a sound and promising company. I recommend that we invest our maturing bond proceeds in WBM's Class A stock.

Market Share

Though only ten years old, WBM competes strongly with established computer makers. Its market share has grown steadily for the past five years. This past year, services and sales ranked 367th in the industrial United States, with orders increasing from $750 million to $1.25 billion. Net income places WBM 237th nationally and 13th on return to investors.

Earnings

WBM's net profit on sales is 9 percent, a roughly steady figure for the past three years. Whereas 2006 earnings were only $.09 per share, this year's are $1.36 per share. Included in these ten-year earnings is a two-for-one stock split issued November 2, 2010. Barring a global sales downturn WBM's outlook for continued strong earnings is promising.

Dividends

Investors are offered two types of common stock. The assigned par value of both classes is $.50 per share. Class A stock pays an additional $.25 per share dividend but restricts voting privileges to one vote for every ten shares held by the investor. Class B stock does not pay the extra dividend but carries full voting rights. The additional dividend from Class A shares would enhance income flow into our portfolio.

WBM shares now trade at 14 times earnings and current share price of $56.00, a bargain in my estimation. An immediate investment would add strength and diversity to our portfolio.

Clear subject line leaves no doubt as to purpose of report

Gives brief background

Makes a direct recommendation

Explains the criteria supporting the recommendation

Encourages reader action

FIGURE 15.6 A feasibility report

RECOMMENDATION REPORTS (ANALYTICAL)

Purpose and audience of recommendation reports

While a feasibility report sets out to prove that a particular course of action is the right one to take, a *recommendation report* shortens or even skips the feasibility analysis (since it has already taken place or been discussed) and gets right to the point of making a recommendation. Recommendation reports, like feasibility reports, may include supporting data, but they also state an affirmative position ("Here's what we should do and why") rather than examining whether the approach will work ("Should we do it?"). Like feasibility reports, recommendation reports are for the eyes of decision makers, and these documents take a direct stance.

Elements of recommendation reports

Figure 15.7 shows a recommendation report from a health and safety officer at an airline company to a vice president regarding the workstation comfort of the company's reservation and booking agents. Notice that it is organized similarly to a feasibility report but takes a more authoritative stance based on previous analysis, emphasizing expected rather than possible benefits. Also, a description of the problem and its causes precedes the recommendations.

This is just one example of countless short reports used to examine a workplace problem and recommend a solution.

STRATEGIES
for Recommendation Reports

▸ **Provide a clear subject line.** As always, make sure the subject of the report is brief and directly to the point.

▸ **Keep background information short.** Keep the background history brief, but do discuss how feasibility has already been determined.

▸ **Discuss the problem or situation prior to making recommendations.** In addition to the brief background information, outline the problem or situation that the recommended actions will resolve. Then discuss the recommendations in as much detail as necessary.

▸ **Use an authoritative tone.** Take a strong stance and write with confidence, knowing that the recommendation has already been determined to be feasible.

▸ **Use headings and make them as informative as possible.** Instead of using the vague heading "Problem," be specific ("Causes of Agents' Discomfort"). Don't forget that you are writing to a "bottom line" audience.

▸ **End with a list of benefits for taking action.** Rather than appealing for action, assume that it will be taken by reemphasizing the benefits.

FIGURE 15.7
**A recommen-
dation report**

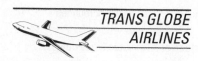
**TRANS GLOBE
AIRLINES**

MEMORANDUM

To: R. Ames, Vice President, Personnel

From: B. Doakes, Health and Safety *B.D.*

Date: August 15, 20XX

Subject: **Recommendations for Reducing Agents' Discomfort**
◄── • Subject line directly states exact purpose of report

In our July 20 staff meeting, we discussed physical discomfort among reservation and booking agents, who spend eight hours daily at workstations. They complain of headaches, eyestrain, blurred or double vision, backaches, and stiff joints. This report outlines the apparent causes and recommends ways of reducing discomfort.
◄── • Provides immediate orientation by giving brief background and main point

Causes of Agents' Discomfort
Last year, we replaced all older CRT monitors with LCD screens. Ergonomics consultants have adjusted the brightness and contrast settings for each user and have advised us that the monitors themselves are not causing headaches and eyestrain. Instead, these problems seem to be caused by excessive glare from background lighting. Other concerns, such as backaches and stiffness, result from agents who are sitting in one position for up to two hours between breaks.
◄── • Statement of problem or situation precedes recommendations

Recommended Changes
We can eliminate much discomfort by improving background lighting, workstation conditions, and work routines and habits.
◄── • Makes general recommendations

Background Lighting. To reduce the glare on display screens, I recommend these changes in background lighting:

1. Decrease all overhead lighting by installing lower-wattage LED bulbs.
◄── • Expands on each recommendation

2. Keep all curtains and adjustable blinds on the south and west windows at least half-drawn to block direct sunlight.

3. Install shades to direct the overhead lighting straight downward, so that it is not reflected on the screens.

Workstation Conditions. I recommend the following changes in the workstations:

1. Reposition all screens so light sources are neither at front nor back.

2. Clean the surface of each screen weekly.

3. Adjust each screen so the top is slightly below the operator's eye level.

4. Adjust all keyboards so they are 27 inches from the floor.

5. Replace all fixed chairs with pneumatic, multi-task chairs.

<continued>

FIGURE 15.7
(Continued)

Work Routines and Habits. These are recommended changes in agents' work routines and habits:

1. Allow frequent rest periods (10 minutes hourly instead of 30 minutes twice daily).

2. Provide yearly eye exams for agents as part of our routine healthcare program.

3. Train agents to adjust screen contrast and brightness whenever the background lighting changes.

4. Offer workshops on improving posture.

Discusses benefits of following the recommendations → These changes will give us time to consider more complex options such as installing hoods and antiglare filters on display screens, replacing fluorescent lighting with LED or other options, covering surfaces with nonglare paint, or other disruptive procedures.

cc: J. Bush, Medical Director
     M. White, Manager of Physical Plant

PEER REVIEW REPORTS (ANALYTICAL)

Purpose and audience of peer review reports

Peer review reports are written between employees, providing a way for people (peers) to give each other constructive criticism and feedback. Because peer review reports are shared by colleagues wishing to preserve good workplace relationships, they must be written with tact.

Figure 15.8 illustrates the use of constructive criticism in peer review and can serve as a model for reviewing the work of other students in the classroom.

STRATEGIES
for Peer Review Reports

▶ **Start with the positives.** Briefly state the good points of the reviewed document as a way of leading into and balancing against the criticisms.

▶ **Organize by topic area.** Provide separate sections for suggestions about the reviewed document's writing style, design, use of visuals, and other areas.

▶ **Always provide constructive criticism.** Remember that you are reviewing the work of a colleague or colleagues. Review their work tactfully, as you would want them to review your work. However, don't ignore problem areas.

▶ **Support your criticisms with examples and advice.** Point to particular examples in the reviewed document as you discuss them. Suggest alternatives, if possible. Point to helpful resources, if applicable.

▶ **Close positively.** End with a friendly, encouraging tone. If the reviewed document is particularly problematic, state as much—but diplomatically.

FIGURE 15.8
A peer review report

TO: Catie Noll, Advertising Associate
FROM: David Summer, Advertising Supervisor D.S.
DATE: May 1, 20XX
SUBJECT: Review of Your Feasibility Report for the Garvey Account

I have reviewed the first draft of your report for the Garvey account. Thank you for your good work! You have done a great job organizing the material and getting started. I would like to offer the following suggestions:

Voice: You use passive voice in a number of places where active voice would be more appropriate. For instance, at the bottom of page 7, you might want to change "A mistake was made" to "We made a mistake." I would recommend that you review the entire draft for this usage.

Organization: As a reader, I did not know what you were recommending in this report until I reached the very end. I would suggest that you move your recommendation up to the beginning of the report, then follow it with the supporting data. Our supervisors will want to know the bottom line right away.

Research: I noticed that most of your research was based on commercial Web sites. You should probably look at more reliable peer-reviewed sources, such as well-respected business newspapers, journal articles, and online publications of professional organizations.

Visuals/font: Great use of images, especially the maps on page 9. You might want to increase the font size of the base text.

I hope my recommendations are helpful as you complete this project. Your report is well on the way, offering solid reasons that should persuade the managers to try winning the Garvey account from our competitors. Please let me know if you have any questions.

Report starts with a friendly tone and says something positive before offering suggested changes

Suggested changes are clear and organized by area

Writer provides rationale behind suggestions

Writer provides specific advice to help the writer improve the reviewed document

Report uses a polite closing

CHECKLIST
for Informal Reports

MyWritingLab™

☐ Have I determined the right report type (status report, recommendation report, etc.) for this situation?

☐ When preparing a progress or status report, have I determined how much detail is necessary to include?

☐ When taking minutes for a meeting, have I included all the key decisions and discussion items and left out unnecessary detail?

☐ If I have decided to write a recommendation report, has the feasibility of the project or idea already been determined, or is a feasibility study and report more appropriate at this time?

☐ For all forms of informal reports, have I used a memo format?

☐ Is the subject line clear?

☐ Is the tone professional and polite but direct?

☐ For any report, have I done enough research so that my position is credible?

☐ Have I reviewed the Strategies box for my specific report type?

APPLICATIONS

GENERAL APPLICATIONS

MyWritingLab™

1. For this or another class, write a progress report to your instructor, describing the progress you've made on a project you are working on (your final project, for instance). Use the strategies suggested in this chapter. Or write a peer review report of a classmate's draft of an upcoming assignment.

2. For a current or past job or internship, write a periodic activity report in which you report on the past week's activities (actual or typical). Be sure to follow the strategies for periodic activity reports in this chapter.

3. Take notes at the next group event or meeting that you attend. Write up minutes for the meeting, thinking about how much detail to include and what kinds of information will be useful to the other members of the team.

TEAM APPLICATIONS

1. With two or three other classmates, identify a dangerous or inconvenient area or situation on campus or in your community (endless cafeteria lines,

an unsafe walkway, slippery stairs, a bad campus intersection). Observe the problem for several hours during a peak use period. Write a recommendation report to a specifically identified decision maker (the head of campus security, for example) describing the problem, listing your observations, and making a recommendation.

2. Convert the same report into a feasibility report by discussing several different approaches that might be taken and then recommending the feasibility of the approach you prefer.

GLOBAL APPLICATION   MyWritingLab™

Assume that you are a team leader of a company that is based in the United States but has offices worldwide. You have been assigned a new manager who is a citizen of another country. This week you need to write a report recommending that all the staff on your team receive bonuses. You know the tone you would take if your manager were from the United States, but you are uncertain about what tone or level of politeness is appropriate for this new manager. Pick a country and do some research on the Internet about tone, style, and politeness in different cultures, remembering that not everyone in a country or culture is exactly alike. Write a short memo to your instructor explaining what you have learned and how you would shape your recommendation report in this situation.

DIGITAL AND SOCIAL MEDIA APPLICATION   MyWritingLab™

As the examples in this chapter illustrate, most informal reports are written for internal audiences. Yet with the rise of social media, organizations are making some informal reports available to the public. Look at the Twitter feed for agencies like the Environmental Protection Agency (EPA) or the U.S. Department of Agriculture (USDA) and find links to one to two short, informal reports. Compare these reports to the examples in this chapter. What are the differences in formatting, tone, and style when these reports are written for external audiences?

MyWritingLab™   Visit Chapter 15, *Informal Reports*, in MyWritingLab to complete this chapter's applications, to explore this chapter's overview, checklist, and flashcards, and to test your understanding of the chapter objectives.

16 Formal Reports

CHAPTER OUTLINE

LET'S GET STARTED:
Formal Reports   *303*

Audience and Purpose of Formal Reports   *304*

Elements of Effective Formal Reports   *306*

Parts of Formal Reports   *309*

STRATEGIES for Formal Reports   *312*

A Sample Formal Report   *313*

CHECKLIST for Formal Reports   *324*

Applications   *325*

LEARNING OBJECTIVES FOR THIS CHAPTER

▸ Differentiate between informal and formal reports

▸ Determine the audience and purpose of a formal report

▸ Identify the characteristics of the three analytical approaches: comparative, causal, and feasibility

▸ Write a formal report that incorporates all the vital elements

▸ Include all the essential parts in a formal report (front matter, text elements, end matter)

LET'S GET STARTED
Formal Reports

MyWritingLab™

Formal reports are more complex and longer than informal reports (discussed in Chapter 15). Whether written for the workplace or for a class, formal reports are usually the culmination of many weeks or months of research, planning, drafting, and revising.

Think about a situation where you will need to write a formal report (for work, for this class, or for another class). Draft an initial plan by writing a one- to two-page memo to your instructor. In your plan, consider the intended audience, purpose of the report, intended use of the report, main question(s) the report is intended to answer, research and sources of information you will need to look at, and so on. Also create a rough outline for your report.

Questions to ask about the formal report as you review the material in this chapter may include the following:

► Who is my audience?

► Are there any secondary audiences (other readers)?

► What is the purpose of the report? To inform? To persuade?

► What would be the right length for this report?

► Should I use visuals? What kind?

► What types of research will I need to undertake?

At the end of this chapter, review your Let's Get Started report planning memo with your instructor or with a group of students and determine how much you might change or modify your plan based on what you have learned in this chapter.

M uch like the shorter analytical reports (feasibility and recommendation reports) discussed in Chapter 15, long, formal reports are analytical reports that often lead to recommendations. The formal report format replaces the informal memo format when the topic requires lengthy discussion. Formal reports generally include a title page, a table of contents, a system of headings, a list of references or works cited, and other front-matter and end-matter supplements. An

Formal versus informal reports

essential component of workplace problem solving, formal reports are designed to answer these questions:

- Based on the information gathered about this issue, what do we know?
- What conclusions can we draw?
- What should we do or not do?

Scenario for a formal report

For instance, imagine you work on a team of alternative energy experts (engineers, policy analysts, technical writers, lawyers), and the state department of energy has asked your organization for a report on the feasibility of producing biodiesel fuel in your state. First you will have to learn everything you can about the nature of the energy situation in your state at this time. Then you will need to compare the advantages and disadvantages of various options based on the *criteria* you are using to assess feasibility, such as cost-effectiveness, time required versus time available to begin biodiesel production, potential risk to the public and the environment, and so on. As you consider all the factors, you might find that the cheapest biodiesel option might also pose the greatest environmental risk; on the other hand, the most environmentally friendly option might be too expensive.

The importance of research in formal reports

This type of situation requires critical thinking and research. Aside from the technical knowledge about biodiesel production that your team already has, you may need additional research about the state or about the relationship of biodiesel to other sectors of the agricultural economy. Sources for this research may be available using secondary research (online or through the library), or you may need to answer these questions through primary research (surveys and interviews). For more information on how to conduct research, review Chapter 2.

AUDIENCE AND PURPOSE OF FORMAL REPORTS

Audience considerations

Because of their major impact on the decision-making process, formal reports are almost always written for an audience of decision makers: for example, government officials, corporate managers. You need to know whether the report will be read primarily by an individual, a team, or a series of individuals with differing roles in the company.

Purpose considerations

To determine the purpose of the report, consider what question or questions it will ultimately answer. Also, consider why this particular topic is timely and useful to the intended audience. Use the Audience and Purpose Profile Sheet on page 46 to begin mapping out your audience and purpose for the report.

Next, determine which of the following three analytical categories best fits your purpose: the comparative analysis ("Which is better, X or Y?"), the causal analysis ("Why does X occur?"), or the feasibility analysis ("Is X a good idea?"). Note that not all formal reports fall neatly into one of these categories. Some reports blend two or all three. For instance, some reports will present a feasibility analysis but will also offer a great deal of comparative information.

Comparative Analysis

Comparative analysis rates similar items on the basis of specific criteria. For example, you may need to answer a question such as "Which type of security procedure—firewall or encryption—should we install in our company's computer system?"

Features of a comparative analysis

For a comparative analysis, base the comparison on clear and definite criteria: costs, uses, benefits/drawbacks, appearance, results. Identify your specific criteria and then rank these in order of importance. Give each item balanced treatment. Support and clarify the comparison or contrast through credible examples. Use research, if necessary, for examples that readers can visualize.

In a report titled "A Comparison of Different Methods for Uploading Digital Photographs," the abstract of which is shown in Figure 16.1, Christina Romano compares three different upload methods. Romano, a freelance photographer, was asked to write this report for a local photography club. Notice how the abstract makes clear the comparative approach of the report.

FIGURE 16.1
Abstract for a formal report that takes a primarily comparative approach

Abstract

This report compares three different methods for uploading digital photographs from camera to computer. Each method has strengths and weaknesses, depending on the needs and skill level of the photographer.

The first method involves connecting the camera to the computer with a USB cable, then uploading the photographs through whatever software is used (Picasa, iPhoto, other). This method is the easiest but does not give users very much control on where the photo files are stored.

The second method requires users to remove the storage card from the camera, insert it into a device called a card reader, and then connect the card reader to the computer's USB or firewire port. This method is quicker than the first one described, but it is also more complicated for users not experienced with the directories on their computer.

The final method uses the camera and computer's Bluetooth wireless communication feature. This method does not require any cables or card readers, but it can be slow.

For beginning photographers, this report recommends the first method. For more advanced photographers, the second method is often preferred.

Causal Analysis

Causal analysis explains the causes or the effects of an event, a problem, or a decision. For example, medical researchers may need to explain why so many apparently healthy people have sudden heart attacks. Or you might need to anticipate the possible effects of a proposed corporate merger on employee morale.

Features of a causal analysis

For a causal analysis, be sure the cause fits the effect. Faulty causal reasoning is extremely common, especially when people ignore other possible causes or when they confuse mere coincidence with causation. Make the links between effect and cause clear. Identify the immediate cause (the one most closely related to the effect) as well as the distant cause(s) (the ones that precede the immediate cause). For example, the immediate cause of an airplane crash might be a fuel-tank explosion, caused by a short circuit in frayed wiring. This wiring defect, it turns out, was caused by faulty design or poor quality control by the manufacturer. Discussing only the immediate cause merely scratches the surface of the problem.

The sample formal report by Crystal Cunningham, "Effects of Periodontal Disease on Preterm Low Birth Weight Babies," provided later in this chapter (see pages 314–323), takes a primarily causal approach. The writer examines the research literature on the question of whether periodontal disease in mothers might cause low birth weight in babies.

Feasibility Analysis

Features of a feasibility analysis

Feasibility analysis assesses the practicality of an idea or plan. For example, if your company needs to know whether increased business will justify the cost of maintaining a corporate blog for customers, you would do some research and describe your findings in a formal feasibility report. In some cases, you (the writer) can't actually determine the feasibility; all you can do is provide enough information so that the readers of your report can make the final decision.

For a feasibility analysis, consider the strength of supporting reasons. Choose the best reasons for supporting the action or decision being considered—based on your collected evidence. Also consider the strength of opposing reasons. Remember that people usually see only what they want to see. Avoid the temptation to overlook or downplay opposing reasons, especially for an action or decision you have been advocating. Consider alternate points of view and examine and evaluate all the evidence. After weighing the pros and cons, recommend a realistic and well-reasoned course of action.

In their report "A Study on the Feasibility of Biodiesel Production in Georgia" (the conclusion section is shown in Figure 16.2), Professor George A. Shumaker and his coauthors provide decision makers with the information needed to decide on a vital component of one state's energy policy. Their conclusion is a good example of how a feasibility study can take into account criteria that would have to be met (in this case cost-effectiveness) for a proposed plan to be feasible.

ELEMENTS OF EFFECTIVE FORMAL REPORTS

Readers expect a report that is based on thorough research, critical analysis of the evidence, and clear presentation of the material.

FIGURE 16.2
Conclusion of a formal report that takes a feasibility approach

---

Conclusion

There exist a variety of potential feedstocks both in Georgia and nearby states that could be utilized to produce biodiesel. These feedstocks vary significantly in price depending on supply and demand conditions, as well as market structural conditions. Feedstock costs represent between 50 and 75 percent of the cost of producing biodiesel, and thus a reliable source of low priced feedstocks is critical to success. A 15 million gallon biodiesel plant would require about 27% of the vegetable and animal fats currently available within the State of Georgia. This facility would produce 750 million gallons of 2% blend for approximately twice the state demand. A 20% blend will create 75 million gallons of B20 or roughly 20% of the Georgia diesel market.

The processing technology for producing biodiesel is well established and presents little technological risk. The production of biodiesel is a very efficient process, returning about 3.2 units of energy for each unit used in production. Biodiesel is thus an excellent renewable fuel source. Biodiesel can be very easily integrated into the existing petroleum distribution system from the handling, chemical, physical, and performance perspectives.

Lacking government mandates or subsidies, a feedstock cost of about 10 cents per pound or less, given current diesel fuel prices, is needed for biodiesel to be cost effective.

Source: From "A Study on the Feasibility of Biodiesel Production in Georgia" by Professor George A. Shumaker et al. Copyright © 2003 by The University of Georgia's Center on Agribusiness & Economic Development. Reprinted with permission.

Accurate, Appropriate, and Clearly Interpreted Data

Make sure your information is accurate and, to the best of your ability, unbiased. Use reputable information sources (particularly for statistical data), such as government documents, peer-reviewed sources, and sound reporting from nationally respected newspapers and similar sources. Make sure you interpret information fairly and provide valid conclusions based on your best research. Assume, for example, that you are writing a report to recommend the best brand of chain saw for a logging company. If, in reviewing test reports on various chain saw brands, you learn that one brand, Bomarc, is the easiest to operate but also has the fewest safety features, include both pieces of information in your report—even if you personally prefer this brand.

Choose and interpret the source material critically

Clearly Identified Purpose Statement

Begin by defining the primary question the report will need to answer, and then identify any secondary questions. The biodiesel report discussed earlier may have begun with a question from a state legislator: "Will producing biodiesel benefit the state of Georgia?" Answering this question is the report's primary purpose (feasibility analysis); however, this question leads to others, such as "What are the advantages and drawbacks of biodiesel use versus other types of fuels?" (comparative analysis) or "How does biodiesel fuel affect the environment?" (causal analysis). Create a purpose statement that addresses both primary and secondary purpose,

Address both primary and secondary purposes in the purpose statement

such as "The purpose of this report is to examine the feasibility of biodiesel production in the state of Georgia by comparing biodiesel fuels to other alternatives and assessing their environmental effects."

Understandable Structure

Use outlining, chunking, sequencing, paragraphing, and heading strategies

Structure your report for ease of navigation. Begin by outlining your report and adjusting that outline as you go. Then chunk the text so that large passages of dense information don't overwhelm your readers. Next, sequence all your data in a logical order (spatial, chronological, problem-solution, cause and effect). After that, order information within your paragraphs for maximum readability. Finally, use clarifying headings and subheadings to announce what each section contains. For example, the heading "Data Analysis" does not really say much, whereas the heading "Physiological Effects and Health Risks" offers a clear, informative preview.

Readable Style

Write clearly, concisely, fluently, and personably

Readers don't want to be bogged down with cumbersome prose. Make your writing clear by avoiding ambiguous pronoun references and modifiers, using active voice, avoiding nominalizations, unstacking modifying nouns, and avoiding unnecessary jargon. Make your writing concise by avoiding wordiness and eliminating repetition and redundancy. Make your writing fluent by combining related ideas, varying sentence construction and length, and using parallel structure. Write personally by choosing the appropriate tone and avoiding sexist and biased language. Ask a colleague or editor to copyedit your report before it is printed. Proofread the final version carefully.

Audience-centered Visuals

Use graphs, tables, charts, illustrations, diagrams, and photographs as appropriate

Provide as much visual information as appropriate to make complex statistics and numeric data easy to understand. Graphs are especially useful for analyzing rising or falling trends, levels, and long-term forecasts. Tables and charts are helpful for comparing data. Illustrations, diagrams, and photographs are an excellent way to show a component or special feature. Place each visual near the accompanying text and be careful not to overuse visuals. The biodiesel feasibility study mentioned earlier uses visuals effectively. For instance, on page 18 of the report (see Figure 16.3), the writers quantify the reduction in emissions when biodiesel fuel is used. In that example, a table provides an excellent way to compare information without the requirement of reading a lot of dense prose.

User-friendly Design

Design for consistency, cohesiveness, navigation, and emphasis

Remember that a well-designed document demonstrates consistency and cohesiveness via grid patterns, margins, paragraphs, justification, line spacing, font style, and font size. A good design also aids navigation and adds emphasis via headings, color, shading, bold, italic, underlining, color, bulleted and numbered lists, and running heads and feet (see Chapter 8).

FIGURE 16.3
Effective use of a visual in a formal report

18

Gelling of biodiesel varies depending upon the chemical composition of the feedstock used in its production. The higher the saturated fat of the feedstock, such as in animal fats, the higher the temperature at which gelling occurs. The converse is also true. Canola oil, with low levels of saturated fats, derived biodiesel provides the lowest gelling temperature biodiesel. Pure biodiesel should be stored and transported at temperatures above 50 F and blending temperatures should be above 40 F.

Environmental Impacts of Biodiesel Use

Studies completed by the Environmental Protection Agency (NREL/TP 2001) state that a 20% blend is "basically a trade off between cost, emissions, cold weather, material compatibility and solvency issues." Researchers believe the 20% blend to be the best blend for general use without encountering major issues. Higher blends often cause problems in winter and with nitrogen oxide emissions.

Table 10. Emission Changes with Biodiesel Fuels.

Emission	100% Biodiesel*	20% Biodiesel Blend*
Carbon Monoxide	-43.2%	-12.6%
Hydrocarbons	-56.3%	-11%
Particulates	-55.4%	-18%
Nitrogen Oxides	+5.8%	+1.2%
Air Toxics	-60% to -90%	-20%
Mutagenicity	-80% to -90%	-20%
Carbon Dioxide**	-78.3%	-15.7%

* Average of data from 14 EPA FTP Heavy duty test cycle tests, variety of stock engines
** Life Cycle Emission

◄── ● The table enables readers to compare data easily

It would appear that the use of biodiesel can be an effective means for reducing exhaust emissions. The relevant question becomes, how does the cost of reducing emission using biodiesel compare to other means of obtaining the same level of emission reduction? The answer to that question is beyond the scope of this inquiry.

Impact Analysis

Impact analysis is a key component of any feasibility study. An impact analysis indicates the effect of a new venture on the economy. Building a new biodiesel facility in Georgia will impact the economy on two levels. The new plant will generate output as it begins selling biodiesel and its by-products. These sales will, in turn, generate additional sales as the plant purchases inputs. The suppliers to the plant will increase the purchase of their inputs, thus

Source: From "A Study on the Feasibility of Biodiesel Production in Georgia" by Professor George A. Shumaker et al. Copyright © 2003 by The University of Georgia's Center on Agribusiness & Economic Development. Reprinted with permission.

PARTS OF FORMAL REPORTS

Most formal reports consist of the front matter, the text of the report, and the end matter. (Some parts of the front and end matter may be optional.) The following sections describe these various parts.

Letter of Transmittal

Many formal reports include a letter of transmittal, addressed to a specific reader or readers, which precedes the report. This letter might acknowledge individuals or organizations that helped with the report, refer readers to sections of special interest, discuss any limitations of the study or any problems in gathering data, offer personal (or off-the-record) observations, or urge readers to take immediate action. See page 314 (Figure 16.4) for a sample letter of transmittal.

Front Matter

Preceding the text of the report is the front matter: the title page, table of contents, list of tables and figures if appropriate, and abstract or executive summary.

Title Page. The title page provides the report title, the names of all authors and their affiliations (and/or the name of the organization that commissioned the report), and the date the report was distributed to readers. The title announces the report's purpose and subject by using descriptive words such as *analysis*, *proposal*, *feasibility*, or *recommendation*. Be sure the title fully describes your report, but avoid an overly long and involved title. Design the page so that the title is the most prominent item, highest on the page, followed by the name of the recipient(s), the author(s), and the date of submission. See page 315 (Figure 16.4) for a sample title page.

Table of Contents. A table of contents is essential for any long report, helping readers find what they seek by providing the page number for each major section, including any front matter that falls after the table of contents. (Do not include the letter of transmittal, title page, or table of contents itself, but do include the list of tables and figures, along with the abstract or executive summary.)

Indicate page numbers for front matter in lowercase Roman numerals (i, ii, iii). Note that the title page, though not numbered itself or listed on the table of contents, is counted as page i. Number the report text pages using Arabic numerals (1, 2, 3), starting with the first page of the report. Number end matter using Arabic numerals continuing from the end of the report's text.

Make sure headings and subheadings in the table of contents match exactly the headings and subheadings in the report. Indicate headings of different levels (a-level, b-level, c-level) using different type styles or indentations. Use *leader lines* (........) to connect headings with their page numbers. For a sample table of contents, see page 316 (Figure 16.4).

List of Tables and Figures. On a separate page following the table of contents (or at the end of the table of contents, if it fits), list the tables and figures in the report. If the report contains only one or two tables and figures, you may skip this list. Because Figure 16.4 contains no illustrations, it includes no such list in the front matter.

Abstract or Executive Summary. Instead of reading an entire formal report, readers interested only in the big picture may consult the abstract or executive summary that commonly precedes the report proper (see Chapter 14). The purpose of this summary is to explain the issue, describe how you researched it, and state your conclusions (and, in the case of an executive summary, indicate what action the conclusions suggest). Busy readers can then flip through the document to locate sections important to them.

Make the abstract or executive summary as brief as you can. Summarize the report without adding new information or leaving out critical information.

Write for a general audience and follow a sequence that moves from the reason the report was written, to the report's major findings, to conclusions and recommendations. For an example of an abstract, see page 317 (Figure 16.4).

Text of the Report

The text of the report consists of the introduction, the body, and the conclusion.

Introduction. The introduction engages and orients the audience and provides background as briefly as possible. Readers don't generally need a long history lesson. In your introduction, identify the topic's origin and significance, define or describe the problem or issue, and explain the report's purpose. Briefly identify your research methods (interviews, literature searches, and so on). List working definitions, but if you have more than five, place definitions in a glossary. Finally, if you have not done so in the abstract or executive summary, state your conclusion. Don't make readers wade through the entire report to find out what you are recommending or advising. For a sample introduction to a formal report, see page 318 (Figure 16.4).

Body. The body describes and explains your findings. Present a clear and detailed picture of the evidence, interpretations, and reasoning on which you will base your conclusion. Divide topics into subtopics, and use informative headings as aids to navigation, as described earlier in this chapter. The body of your report will vary greatly, depending on the audience, topic, purpose, and situation. The body of Figure 16.4 begins after the introduction on page 1 of the report and ends with the recommendation on page 4 of the report (pages 318–321 in this book).

Conclusion. The conclusion is vital because it answers the questions that originally sparked the analysis. In the conclusion, you summarize, interpret, and recommend. Although you have interpreted evidence at each stage of your analysis, your conclusion presents a broad interpretation and suggests a course of action (where appropriate). Your conclusion should provide a clear and consistent perspective on the whole document. Don't introduce new ideas, facts, or statistics. See page 321 (Figure 16.4) for a sample conclusion.

End Matter

Following the text of the report (as needed) is the end matter, which may include a list of references cited in your report, a glossary, and/or appendices. Readers can refer to any of these supplements or skip them altogether, according to their needs.

References or Works Cited List. If you have used outside sources in your report (and typically you should), you must provide a list of References (per APA style) or of Works Cited (per MLA style) just after the text of the report or on a separate page. For detailed advice on documenting sources using APA or MLA style, see Appendix A of this book. The long report in Figure 16.4 uses APA style and includes a References list (page 322).

Glossary. Use a glossary if your report contains more than five technical terms that may not be understood by all intended readers. If five or fewer terms need defining, place them in the report's introduction as working definitions or use footnote definitions. If you do include a separate glossary, announce its location when you introduce technical terms defined there ("see the glossary at the end of this report"). Figure 16.4 includes working definitions in the appendix (page 323).

Appendices. If you have large blocks of material or other documents that are relevant but will bog readers down, place these in an appendix. For example, if your report on the cost of electricity at your company refers to another report issued by the local utility company, you may wish to include this second report as an appendix. Other items that belong in an appendix might include complex formulas, interview questions and responses, maps, photographs, questionnaires and tabulated responses, texts of laws and regulations, and the like.

Do not stuff appendices with needless information or use them to bury bad or embarrassing news that belongs in the report itself. Title each appendix clearly: "Appendix A: Projected Costs." Mention the appendices early in the introduction, and refer readers to them at appropriate points in the report: "(see Appendix A)". The sample report in Figure 16.4 includes an appendix on page 323.

STRATEGIES
for Formal Reports

▸ **Determine your audience.** Be sure that you understand what your audience needs to know or do as a result of reading your report.

▸ **Determine your analytical approach.** Decide whether the primary purpose of the report is to compare items, look for a cause, or determine feasibility. Because formal reports are complex, also consider if the report will have a secondary purpose or purposes.

▸ **Do your research and document your sources.** For a long, formal report, research is paramount. Strive for accurate, appropriate, and clearly interpreted data. Always think critically about the sources you consult during the research process. Document all your sources within the report (using parenthetical citation—see pages 413, 425) and at the end of the report (in a References or Works Cited list—see pages 322, 414, 426).

➔

▸ **Work from a clear purpose statement.** You may need to revise your purpose statement during the research process as you uncover new information, but make sure the statement is finalized before you start writing your final draft of the report.

▸ **Use an understandable structure.** Follow the strategies in Chapter 5 for outlining, chunking, sequencing, paragraphing, and using headings.

▸ **Write with a readable style.** Follow the strategies in Chapter 6 to write with a clear, concise, fluent, and personable style.

▸ **Include audience-centered visuals.** Follow the strategies in Chapter 7 for using graphs, tables, charts, illustrations, diagrams, and photographs as appropriate to enhance, not decorate, the report.

▸ **Create a user-friendly design.** Follow the strategies in Chapter 8 for consistency, cohesiveness, navigation, and emphasis.

▸ **Include all appropriate front matter.** If appropriate, include a letter of transmittal. Always include a title page as well as a table of contents and an abstract or executive summary. If your report contains plentiful visuals, include a list of tables and figures.

▸ **Provide an introduction, body, and conclusion.** In the text of the report, include an introduction to orient readers and provide background; a body with a clear and detailed presentation of findings; and a conclusion that answers the question or questions posed by the report, possibly with recommendations.

▸ **Include the appropriate end matter.** Always include a list of References (APA style) or of Works Cited (MLA style) on a separate page at the report's end. If your report includes more than five technical terms to be defined, place them in a glossary after the Works Cited or References page; otherwise, define the terms in your introduction or via footnotes in the report. Relevant secondary information that will not fit within the report (surveys, complex formulas, interviews, maps, and so on) belongs in an appendix at the very end.

▸ **Proofread.** If possible, get someone else to read and edit your report.

A SAMPLE FORMAL REPORT

Figure 16.4 is a formal report. Its author, Crystal Cunningham, was a student in the B.S. program in dental hygiene at the University of Minnesota. For a final project in her technical writing class, she chose a real-life research situation that fit nicely with her major. Crystal chose to examine the relationship between periodontal disease in mothers and low birth weights in their babies. Her research is

FIGURE 16.4
A sample formal report

Letter of transmittal targets and thanks specific reader and provides additional context

15 Timber Drive
St. Paul, MN 55666

28 August, 20XX

Professor Janet Belding
University of Minnesota
School of Dentistry
Minneapolis, MN 55444

Dear Dr. Belding:

Thank you for providing me with this opportunity to research the potential impacts of periodontal disease on birth weights. Enclosed in this envelope is my final report, "Effects of Periodontal Disease on Preterm Low Birth Weight Babies." In the Appendix to this report, I recommend that we develop a proposal to explore this potential causal connection.

If I can provide any other information as you review this report, please don't hesitate to contact me. I look forward to meeting with you at a later date to hear your thoughts. I hope this report is useful in your research program.

Yours truly,

Crystal Cunningham

Crystal Cunningham, B.S., Dental Hygiene

FIGURE 16.4
(Continued)

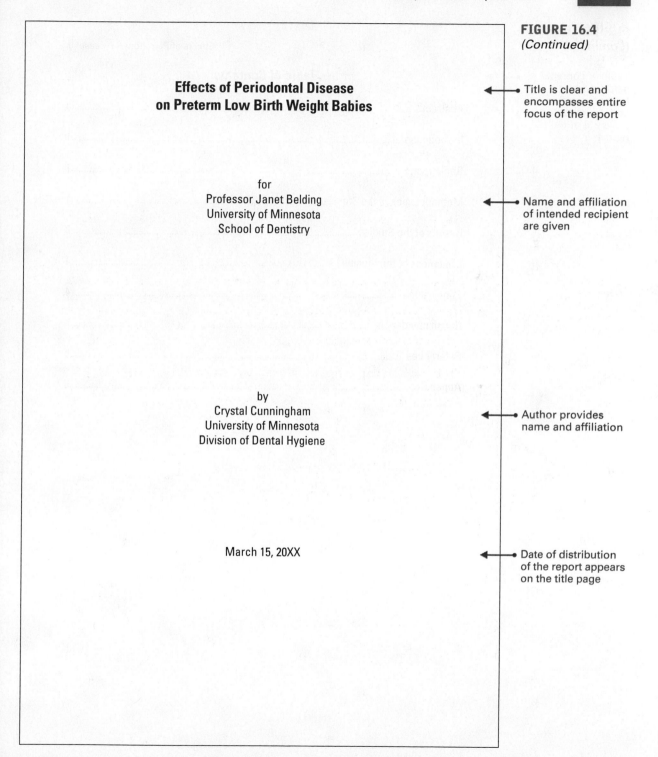

**Effects of Periodontal Disease
on Preterm Low Birth Weight Babies**

Title is clear and
encompasses entire
focus of the report

for
Professor Janet Belding
University of Minnesota
School of Dentistry

Name and affiliation
of intended recipient
are given

by
Crystal Cunningham
University of Minnesota
Division of Dental Hygiene

Author provides
name and affiliation

March 15, 20XX

Date of distribution
of the report appears
on the title page

FIGURE 16.4
(Continued)

Table of contents helps readers find information and visualize the structure of the report

Table of Contents

Abstract iii

Introduction 1

Background 1

Methodologies of the Studies 1

Results of the Studies 3

Limitations of the Studies 4

Conclusion 4

Recommendation..4

References 5

Appendix 6

FIGURE 16.4
(Continued)

Effects of Periodontal Disease iii

Abstract

The purpose of this report is to assess ten recent studies concerning periodontal disease and its association with preterm and low birth weight infants and to recommend, based on the inconclusiveness of these studies, that a new study be undertaken at the University. A number of these studies have found a correlation between periodontal disease and premature birth/low birth weight. However, a number of them have been limited in their scope and the results have been contradictory, indicating the need for further research.

Abstract fully summarizes the content of the report

FIGURE 16.4
(Continued)

Introduction sets up the problem and clearly indicates the report's causal analytical approach

Introduction

In the last ten to fifteen years, interesting findings in dental and obstetric research have linked periodontal disease in mothers to preterm low birth weight conditions in their babies. Many studies have found a correlation, while adequately controlling for confounding variables; the variables include age, smoking, diabetes, and other factors already contributing to preterm low birth weight babies. However a definitive link has yet to be found. This report examines the existing studies, charting their methodologies and results, and concludes with a recommendation for future research.

Background section provides helpful but not overly detailed context

Background

The world has seen a rise in preterm low birth weight births in the last few decades. This fact has alarmed many physicians and obstetricians because there have been so many advancements in the medical field aiming to promote the health and longevity of life. Many reasons have been proposed to explain the reasons for preterm low birth weight births, but no conclusive answers have yet emerged. In the last ten years, some researchers have suggested that gingivitis and periodontal disease may be to blame for this occurrence. One possible cause could be the increase in harmful bacteria entering the bloodstream.

Preterm birth is considered to be any birth that occurs before 37 weeks of gestation; low birth weight is recognized as a weight of fewer than 2,500 grams. Many studies since the mid-1990s have attempted to find a correlation between periodontal disease and preterm low birth weight babies. However, research related to the possibility that periodontal disease increases the risk for preterm low birth weight babies has varied immensely over the years.

Clear purpose statement leads into the body of the report

This report is an assessment of ten peer–reviewed journal articles that seek to examine whether periodontal disease has any correlation with preterm low birth weight babies. The goal of this report is to find a correlation between gingivitis/periodontal disease and preterm low birth weight infants in previous studies and offer a brief recommendation to conduct a new study (see Appendix).

Methodologies of the Studies

Following is a summary of the methodologies used in the various studies:

Subheads within the Methodologies section make the section easy to follow

Time

Studies by Farrell, Ide, and Wilson (2006) and Dortbudak, Eberhardt, Ulm, and Persson (2005) examined women during pregnancy. In the Farrell et al. study, pregnant women were recruited at 12 weeks of gestation (p. 116). Subjects were excluded if gestational age was below 10 weeks or above 15 weeks. The Dortbudak et al. study maintained that it was crucial to examine patients during weeks 15–20 of gestational age because a sample of amniotic fluid is needed to assess for particular bacteria (p. 46). However, most studies waited to collect fluid samples until immediately after the birth.

FIGURE 16.4
(Continued)

Effects of Periodontal Disease 2

Setting

Most of these studies were conducted in hospital settings. The remaining studies were conducted after the subjects returned home from the hospital and were either instructed to return to their dental office or wait for an examiner to visit their home within 48 hours after birth. Some studies had a lengthier time frame to collect data following the birth, such as 72 hours, or five days as in a UK study (Buduneli et al., 2005, p. 176; Moore, Randhawa, & Ide, 2005, p. 3).

Sentence variety and clear prose give the report a readable style

Examiners

Examiners in these studies were calibrated and blind, and often a single examiner was used (Alves & Ribeiro, 2006, p. 322; Bassani, Olinto, & Kreiger, 2007, p. 37; Gazolla et al., 2007, p. 844; Jarjoura et al., 2005, p. 516; Moliterno, Monteiro, Figueredo, & Fischer, 2005, p. 887; Moore et al., 2005, p. 2). The study by Farrell et al. (2006) involved three examiners, which allowed more subjects to be evaluated (p. 117).

Exclusion Criteria

A questionnaire/interview was given to patients (Bassani et al., 2007, p. 32; Bosnjak, Relja, Vucicevic-Boras, Plasaj, & Plancak, 2006, p. 712; Farrell et al., 2006, p. 117; Jarjoura et al., 2005, p. 516; Moliterno et al., 2005, p. 888; Moore et al., 2005, p. 3). These questions pertained to socioeconomic status, race, education, occupation, marital status, smoking, drinking, medications, pregnancies, preterm deliveries, and prenatal care (Gazolla et al., 2007, p. 843).

Writer uses accurate and clearly interpreted data

The information gathered from questions and patients' medical records excluded many subjects from the study. Exclusion criteria included diabetes, anemia, cardiovascular disorders, hepatic deficiency, high blood pressure, TB, cancer, seizure disorders, psychopathology, asthma, STD, HIV, fetal or uterine anomalies, cervical incompetence, labor induction, and multiple birth pregnancies (Buduneli et al., 2005, p. 177; Gazolla et al., 2007, p. 844; Jarjoura et al., p. 516; Moliterno et al., p. 887; Moore et al., p. 4). Another common exclusion involved subjects who required prophylactic antibiotics prior to dental treatment (Farrell et al., p. 117; Jarjoura et al., p. 513; Moore et al., p. 3).

No year needed for work that follows closely after the initial reference

Data Collection

The most common measurements in each trial were pocket depths, clinical attachment levels, and bleeding on probing. A periodontal probe of varying markings was used to assess the extent of periodontal involvement. A few studies included a plaque index along with the previously mentioned tests (Farrell et al., 2006, p. 117; Jarjoura et al., 2005, p. 515; Moore et al., 2005, p. 3). One study, by Alves and Ribeiro, also included calculus detection (2006, p. 319). DMFT scores were taken into account in two other studies (Bosnjak et al., 2006, p. 712; Buduneli et al., 2005, p. 176).

All information from outside sources is documented in text

Most of the studies gathered periodontal measurements from six different sites on one tooth throughout the entire dentition (Alves & Ribeiro, 2006, p. 319; Bassani et al., 2007, p. 36; Buduneli et al., 2005, p. 176; Gazolla et al., 2007, p. 845;

Writer not only describes but critiques the previous studies examined

FIGURE 16.4
(Continued)

Effects of Periodontal Disease 3

Moliterno et al., 2005, p. 887). However other studies assessed fewer sites, for example mesial, distal, buccal, and lingual surfaces (Bosnjak et al., 2006, p. 711; Dortbudak et al., 2005, p. 47). Columbia University collected data from three sites: mesiobuccal, midbuccal, and distobuccal in two randomly selected quadrants (Jarjoura et al., 2005, p. 514). The fewest measurements were taken from one tooth at only two sites, in a UK study. These sites were midbuccal and mesiobuccal in the maxillary and midlingual and mesiolingual in the mandibular (Moore et al., 2005, p. 3).

Three studies included a subgingival plaque sample from the mesial and distal aspect of certain teeth. The sample was obtained by placing a paperpoint into the sulcus and analyzing the type of bacteria collected (Buduneli et al., 2005, p. 177; Dortbudak et al., 46; Jarjoura et al., 518).

An interesting study was conducted by Dortbudak et al. A periodontal exam was completed as in other studies; however, this study included collection of amniotic fluid at 15–20 weeks. These women were already scheduled to have amniocentesis tests for medical purposes. Two milliliters of additional fluid were collected and analyzed for particular bacteria. The results concluded that an increased number of certain bacteria from the fluid placed these women at a higher risk for premature birth. An obvious limitation to this study, however, was that women undergoing an amniocentesis are already at an increased risk for problems during their pregnancy, or they would not be having the test in the first place (p. 51).

Results of the Studies

The research analyzed for this report demonstrates varying degrees of correlation between periodontal disease and birth weight of preterm low weight babies (PTLWB). See Table 1 for summary.

Writer provides bottom-line results of previous studies ➤

Table 1. Results of major studies

Correlation	Correlation percentages	Comments
High correlation:		
Alves and Ribeiro 2006, p. 323	84.21%	High correlation found.
Bosnjak et al. 2006, p. 716	73.26%	Similar correlation found between PTLWB and tobacco use (p. 716).
Dortbudak et al. 2005, p. 52	83%	No bacteria found in amniotic fluid: authors still believe maternal periodontitis could be causal.
Jarjoura et al. 2005, p. 522; Moliterno et al. 2005, p. 890	No percentages given.	Both found statistically significant casual connections.
Low correlations:		
Bassani et al. 2007, p. 39	No significant correlation.	While 59% of subjects had periodontal disease, causality was not established.
Buduneli et al. 2005, p. 181; Farrell et al. 2006, p. 120	No significant correlation.	No differences established.
Gazolla et al. 2007, p. 879	No significant correlation.	Note that the group not treated with scaling/root planing had 79% PTLWB.

FIGURE 16.4
(Continued)

Effects of Periodontal Disease 4

As summarized in Table 1 (previous page), recent studies offer conflicting results about the relationship between periodontal disease and the birth of preterm low weight babies. The two studies to establish high, statistically significant correlations are Alves and Ribeiro (2006) and Dortbudak et al. (2005), but as noted, Dortbudak et al. did not actually find bacteria in the amniotic fluid, thus requiring the authors to make something of casual leap. As noted in the next section, there were also other limitations to all these studies.

Limitations of the Studies

All these studies involved limitations, the most obvious being the sample size. Two studies had a sample of less than 100 subjects (Alves & Ribeiro, 2006, p. 318; Dortbudak et al., 2005, p. 45). Another limitation was the location of the studies. Many well-known studies were conducted outside the United States, in countries such as Croatia, United Kingdom, Turkey, and two in Brazil.

Almost all of these studies were conducted in lower socioeconomic areas, in developing countries, with more uniform ethnic and racial groups. Pregnant Croatian women were studied because they tend to develop more pronounced periodontal disease (Bosnjak et al., 2006, p. 710).

Limitations in only a couple cases were the ages of the subjects. It is well known that having a child above or beneath a certain age poses potential problems for the mother and child, not to mention the strong correlation between age and increased periodontal disease. Only two studies imposed a restriction on age. One study only allowed an age range of 18 to 35 years (Buduneli et al., 2005, p. 174); another only allowed an age range of 18 to 30 years (Gazolla et al., 2007, p. 842).

● The writer is careful to list the limitations of previous studies

Conclusion

In conclusion, several studies found a correlation between periodontal disease and preterm low birth weight babies, even when accounting for possible confounding variables. On the other hand, many found no correlation between periodontal disease and preterm low birth weight babies. These researchers make the argument that their counterparts who did find a correlation did not account for all confounding variables.

The research conducted pertaining to the correlation between preterm low birth weight babies and periodontal disease, then, continues to result in conflicting conclusions. More research is needed in order to arrive at definitive conclusions.

● Conclusion provides a summary of the report

● Because the report takes the causal approach, writer is careful to show that correlation does not always equal causation

Recommendation

See Appendix for a brief discussion about a proposed new study.

FIGURE 16.4
(Continued)

Reference page
immediately follows
the report and
lists all sources
consulted in APA
style

References

Alves, R. T., & Ribeiro, R. A. (2006). Relationship between maternal periodontal disease and birth of preterm low weight babies. *Pesquisa Odontologica Brasileira, 20*(4), 319–323.

Bassani, D. G., Olinto, M. T., & Kreiger, N. (2007). Periodontal disease and perinatal outcomes: A case-control study. *Journal of Clinical Periodontology, 34*(1), 32–39.

Bosnjak, A., Relja, T., Vucicevic-Boras, V., Plasaj, H., & Plancak, D. (2006). Pre-term delivery and periodontal disease: A case-control study from Croatia. *Journal of Clinical Periodontology, 33*(10), 710–716.

Buduneli, N., Baylas, H., Buduneli, E., Turkoglu, O., Kose, T., & Dahlen, G. (2005). Periodontal infections and pre-term low birth weight: A case-control study. *Journal of Clinical Periodontology, 32*(2), 174–181.

Dortbudak, O., Eberhardt, R., Ulm, M., & Persson, G. R. (2005). Periodontitis, a marker of risk in pregnancy for preterm birth. *Journal of Clinical Periodontology, 32*(1), 46–52.

Farrell, S., Ide, M., & Wilson, R. F. (2006). The relationship between maternal periodontitis, adverse pregnancy outcome and miscarriage in never smokers. *Journal of Clinical Periodontology, 33*(2), 116–120.

Gazolla, C. M., Ribeiro, A., Moyses, M. R., Oliveira, L. A., Pereira, L. J., & Sallum, A. W. (2007). Evaluation of the incidence of preterm low birth weight in patients undergoing periodontal therapy. *Journal of Periodontology, 78*(5), 842–849.

Jarjoura, K., Devine, P. C., Perez-Delboy, A., Herrera-Abreu, M., D'Alton, M., & Papapanou, P. N. (2005). Markers of periodontal infection and preterm birth. *American Journal of Obstetrics and Gynecology, 192*(2), 513–522.

Moliterno, L. F., Monteiro, B., Figueredo, C. M., & Fischer, R. G. (2005). Association between periodontitis and low birth weight: A case-control study. *Journal of Clinical Periodontology, 32*(8), 887–890.

Moore, S., Randhawa, M., & Ide, M. (2005). A case-control study to investigate an association between adverse pregnancy outcome and periodontal disease. *Journal of Clinical Periodontology, 32*(1), 2–4.

FIGURE 16.4
(Continued)

Appendix

Recommendation for Future Research

← Content that is not central to the report goes into an appendix

Overview

Based on the existing studies described in this report, I recommend we propose a new study to explore a possible correlation between periodontal disease and preterm low birth weight babies. This study would measure six surfaces on every tooth; most importantly, it would gather a baseline periodontal reading within eight weeks after conception. Using this approach, we can measure to see if there has been any significant difference in periodontal disease during pregnancy or if the subject has always had the same level of disease. This more exacting approach should increase the accuracy and reliability of the findings.

In a forthcoming proposal, I will describe this study in detail. For the purposes of this Appendix, I have outlined several key areas.

Research Design

The research design of this study involves no manipulation of subjects; patients are only observed for changes in their periodontal status. Therefore, the design of this study is quantitative, nonexperimental, and correlational.

Sample

The sample will include 500 women from the Twin Cities Area. Women cannot be more than eight weeks pregnant to be included in the study. Exclusion criteria include women with diabetes and other systemic illnesses, previous birth complications, and previous abuse of alcohol or other illegal substances.

Credentials of Project Personnel

Crystal Cunningham is a recent graduate from the school of dentistry at the University of Minnesota, Division of Dental Hygiene. She is well prepared to perform a study in this particular area due to the extensive background research she has completed in this area. As the project director, who will also be working in collaboration with highly educated professionals from the University of Minnesota, the author anticipates that this research will be successfully carried out.

aimed at other dental hygiene experts; in particular, she wants to send her report to a professor in her department who might wish to continue this research.

With this audience in mind, Crystal makes appropriate choices about technical language, statistical analysis, and reference to scientific articles. While these approaches would not be suitable for a nonexpert audience, they are just right for an audience of other scientists. She understands that her primary purpose is to see if the literature can show a causal relationship. Another purpose is to convince her readers to take her work seriously so that her work might be continued and possibly published in a scientific journal.

CHECKLIST
for Formal Reports

My WritingLab™

- ☐ Have I determined the audience for this report?
- ☐ Have I decided on the purpose, and have I chosen the right analytical approach (comparative, causal, feasibility) to fit this purpose?
- ☐ Did I evaluate all sources consulted while researching?
- ☐ Are my data accurate, appropriate, and clearly interpreted?
- ☐ Does my report have a clearly defined purpose statement early in the report?
- ☐ Is the structure of the report logical and appropriate for this setting?
- ☐ Is the writing style clear and professional?
- ☐ If there are visuals in my report, are the visuals supportive of what is in the text?
- ☐ Are the pages well designed and easy to follow?
- ☐ Is there a distinct introduction, body, and conclusion?
- ☐ Does the introduction provide enough of an orientation to the issue or problem without being too long?
- ☐ Does the body of the report offer a clear picture of the issue or problem?
- ☐ Does the conclusion answer the question that originally sparked the analysis?
- ☐ Have I included all the required and appropriate front and end matter?
- ☐ Have I documented all my sources both in the text and in a References or Works Cited list?

APPLICATIONS

GENERAL APPLICATIONS   MyWritingLab™

1. Choose a specific audience and purpose, based on a real-life situation at school or at work, and write out some ideas for how you would determine whether this situation is an appropriate one for a formal report. List all possible readers (audience members) and all possible purposes. List the kinds of questions your report will need to answer, and then list the kinds of research you will need to do in order to write the report. Bring this document to class for a discussion.

2. Prepare a formal report using causal, comparative, or feasibility analysis (or some combination). As you prepare your report, refer to the Strategies for Formal Reports on pages 312–313, the Checklist, and other materials in this chapter.

TEAM APPLICATION

In the workplace, it is common for reports to be written not by one individual but in teams. Thinking of an idea you might have for a report for this class, ask yourself whether this report might be a team project. How would you divide the tasks and ensure that the work was being done fairly? What are the advantages and disadvantages of a team approach to a report? In groups of two to three, discuss these issues. If your instructor indicates that your report is to be team-based, write a memo (as a team) to your instructor indicating the role of each team member and the timeline.

GLOBAL APPLICATION   MyWritingLab™

Go online and look for reports written in English by government agencies of different countries. See if you can use the material from this chapter to determine if the reports fall into causal, comparative, or feasibility categories. Look for similarities to the reports you are familiar with within the United States (or the one you are preparing for class), as well as differences in features such as structure and organization, word choice, formatting, use of visuals, levels of politeness, and so on.

DIGITAL AND SOCIAL MEDIA APPLICATION   MyWritingLab™

Many reports, particularly government reports, are turned into PDF documents and are available on the Web (often via a link on a Twitter or Facebook posting). When you have a draft of your report, experiment with turning it into a PDF document. Check to be sure the PDF conversion maintained your original formatting. Then write a brief tweet or Facebook posting about the report that would entice readers to click on the link to learn more.

MyWritingLab™   Visit Chapter 16, *Formal Reports*, in MyWritingLab to complete this chapter's applications, to explore this chapter's overview, checklist, and flashcards, and to test your understanding of the chapter objectives.

17 Proposals

CHAPTER OUTLINE

LET'S GET STARTED: Proposals *327*

Audience and Purpose of Proposals *328*

Types of Proposals *328*

Organization of Informal and Formal Proposals *332*

STRATEGIES for Proposals *335*

A Sample Formal Proposal *336*

CHECKLIST for Proposals *347*

Applications *347*

TECHNICAL PROPOSAL
CONTENTS

ription Item............. Page 2
tion 1.0 .... Page 4
.... Page 6
.... Page 7
.... Page 9
.... Page 16
.... Page 18
.... Page 25
.... Page 55
.... Page 56
.... Page 66
.... Page 87
.... Page 104

LEARNING OBJECTIVES FOR THIS CHAPTER

▸ Differentiate between solicited and unsolicited proposals

▸ Differentiate between informal and formal proposals

▸ Understand the different functions of planning, research, and sales proposals

▸ Write an informal proposal

▸ Write a formal proposal

LET'S GET STARTED
Proposals

MyWritingLab™

Most people have had experience making verbal proposals. For instance, a student may want a new computer but will need to propose that his or her parents share the cost. ("If I contribute XX dollars from my summer job, will you help me with the rest of the payment?") Workplace proposals require a more detailed, research-oriented approach, but the concept is the same: You are proposing a particular plan of action, and you need to make your best case. Before reading this chapter, think of a proposal you may wish to make to your manager, the supervisor of your internship, or your instructor. What, exactly, would you like to see happen and why and how? After specifying your goal, make a list of the supporting reasons that you think will be most persuasive in this case.

Questions to ask about your proposal ideas as you review the material in this chapter may include the following:

▸ Do I have a strong enough case?

▸ How will my audience react?

▸ What other ideas might my audience counterpropose, and am I ready for these arguments?

▸ Did someone ask for my proposal, or does it originate from me?

▸ What sort of format (number of pages, uses of visuals, organizational structure) is best suited to my plan?

At the end of this chapter, review your initial Let's Get Started list with your instructor or with a group of students to see how much you might change or modify it based on what you have learned from the chapter.

Proposals encourage an audience to take some form of direct action: to authorize a project, purchase a service or product, or support a specific plan for solving a problem. Although proposals often contain the same basic elements as reports (see Chapters 15 and 16), they have *one* specific purpose: to persuade the audience to say "Yes, let's move ahead with this plan." This purpose may sound similar to the purpose of a recommendation report. However, while a recommendation

How proposals and reports differ

report answers the question "What should we do, and why?" a proposal maps out the steps for getting it done: "Here's what we should do and here's how we can do it." (Note the difference, for example, between the discussion of existing studies in the long report on birth weight in Chapter 16 and the idea for a proposed study and a longer proposal outlined in that report's appendix.)

Proposals are called for in a variety of situations: a request to fund a training program for new employees, a suggestion to change the curriculum of your English or biology department, a bid to the U.S. Defense Department on a missile contract, and so on. Depending on the situation, proposals may be short (informal) or long (formal) and may be written in the form of a report, a letter, or a memo. As a student or as an intern at a nonprofit agency, you might submit a formal grant proposal requesting financial support for a research or community project. If your job depends on funding from outside sources, proposals might be the most important documents you produce.

AUDIENCE AND PURPOSE OF PROPOSALS

Audience considerations

In science, business, industry, government, and education, proposals are written for any number of audiences: managers, executives, directors, clients, board members, or community leaders. Inside or outside the organization, these people review various proposals and then decide whether the plans are worthwhile, the projects will materialize, and the services or products are useful.

Purpose considerations

The singular purpose of proposals is to persuade your audience to say yes to your plan.

TYPES OF PROPOSALS

Solicited and unsolicited proposals

Proposals may be either *solicited* or *unsolicited*. Solicited proposals are those that have been requested by a manager, client, or customer. For example, if you represent an engineering firm specializing in highway construction, you may receive a request for proposal (RFP) from a local township asking you to bid on a road project. Typically, an RFP is issued to numerous companies, and your proposal will need to stack up against all the others. Unsolicited proposals are those that have not been requested. If you are a new advertising agency in town, you may send out short unsolicited proposals to local radio stations suggesting that they use your agency for their advertising needs.

Because the audience for a solicited proposal has made a specific request, you will not need to spend time introducing yourself or providing background on the product or service. For an unsolicited proposal (sometimes termed a "cold call" in sales), you will need to catch readers' attention quickly and provide incentives for them to continue reading: perhaps by printing a price comparison of your fees on the first page, for example.

Proposals may also be *informal* or *formal*. Informal proposals, like informal reports, can take the form of an email or memo (if distributed within an organization) or a letter (when sent outside an organization). Formal proposals, meanwhile, take on the same format as formal reports (see Chapter 16), including front matter, the text of the report, and end matter, if applicable. Formal proposals will be discussed later in this chapter.

Informal and formal proposals

Both solicited and unsolicited proposals, whether informal or formal, fall into three categories: planning proposals, research proposals, and sales proposals.

Planning Proposals

Planning proposals offer solutions to a problem or suggestions for improvement. A planning proposal might be a request for funding to expand the campus newspaper (as in the formal proposal at the end of this chapter), an architectural plan for new facilities at a ski area, or a plan to develop energy alternatives to fossil fuels.

Characteristics of planning proposals

Figure 17.1 is a solicited, informal planning proposal that will be used by bank loan officers when deciding whether to grant a construction loan. Because this document is addressed to external readers, it is cast as a letter. For specific advice on how to approach planning proposals, read the annotations accompanying Figure 17.1 and see the Strategies for Proposals on pages 335–336.

Research Proposals

Research (or grant) proposals request approval and funding for research projects. For example, a chemist at a university might address a research proposal to the Environmental Protection Agency for funds to identify toxic contaminants in local groundwater. Research proposals are solicited by many agencies, including the National Science Foundation and the National Institutes of Health. Each agency has its own requirements and guidelines for proposal format and content. Successful research proposals follow these guidelines and carefully articulate the goals of the project. In these cases, proposal readers will generally be other scientists, so writers can use language that is appropriate for other experts (as in the Appendix in Figure 16.4, page 323).

Characteristics of research proposals

Figure 17.2 is a solicited, informal research proposal from an employee in the marketing and research department to her supervisor, proposing to conduct research into management–employee relations at a single location of the company that has experienced problems in this area. Because this document is addressed to an internal reader (the supervisor), it has been cast as a memo. It could also have taken the form of an email. For specific advice on how to approach research proposals, read the annotations accompanying Figure 17.2 and see the Strategies for Proposals on pages 335–336.

FIGURE 17.1
A planning
proposal

P.O. Box 185
Amherst, MA 01002

March 15, 20XX

Ambrose Savings Bank
South Haley Street
Weaton, MA 09758

SUBJECT: *Proposal to erect a new dwelling*

Dear Mr. Smith:

As we discussed in our meeting on March 6, this letter is in application for a construction loan in the amount of $300,000, on an interest-only basis, for the construction of the described residence (plans and specifications are enclosed) on Lot #6 of my Leverett property. Anticipated sales price of the completed home is $398,000, including the standard realtor's commission. I have already completed clearing work and some excavation, and I expect weather conditions to permit the commencement of foundation work within the next three weeks. Construction time is projected at approximately five months, with completion targeted for September 1, 20XX.

The quality of construction materials and workmanship will be comparable to the adjacent three homes, which you have inspected. Exterior woodwork will be executed in Western Red Cedar, while interior finishes will comprise masonry, dry-wall, and Philippine mahogany. All sashes, doors, flooring, cabinets, and special millwork will be designed and custom fabricated. Water supply and waste disposal will be handled on-site; the appropriate permits have already been obtained. The heating system will be oil-fired hot air, ducted for the later addition of air conditioning. All windows and skylights will be double-glazed and insulation will be maximized.

Thank you for giving this proposal your immediate attention. I will be pleased to provide any additional information you may require.

Very truly yours,

Gerald A. Jackson

Gerald A. Jackson

GAJ/ch

Enclosures: architect's drawings
                      specifications

Provides a clear subject line →

Introduction states purpose, identifies plan, gives background, and provides a timetable →

Body paragraph spells out details (what will be done, qualifications, obtaining permits) →

Concluding paragraph thanks the reader and encourages acceptance of the proposal →

FIGURE 17.2
A research proposal (memo format)

MEMORANDUM

To: James Granger, Vice President, Marketing and Research Division
From: Anne Hickett, Analyst, Marketing and Research Division *A.H.*
Date: March 4, 20XX
Subject: *Report proposal regarding the South Dennis location*

Proposed Study

In answer to your March 2 request for a research report due May 10, I propose to study the ongoing problem of low employee morale at our Foodstuff Supermarket in South Dennis. Following are the specifications:

→ Opens with general description of the problem and a proposed study

Statement of Problem

During my two years as a part-time employee at Foodstuff, I worked at a location with similar problems. I have witnessed firsthand the high turnover and general employee dissatisfaction over the work situation and store management policies. Because we have heard continuing complaints about management–employee relations at the South Dennis location, including from top management, I propose to research the situation and offer potential solutions.

→ Describes the problem in detail, as well as the writer's qualifications

Scope of Proposed Study

My study will explore the following issues:

1. An assessment of the efficiency of Foodstuff's South Dennis management by drawing parallels and contrasts between the actual management operation and principles of effective management that I will identify and collect from my secondary sources.
2. A consideration of the direct or indirect effects that any management problem might have on employee morale.
3. An assessment of the management's effectiveness in employee motivation.
4. An assessment of the role of effective communication in all management–employee relations.

→ Details overall scope of study

Methods and Data Sources

My secondary research will include library resources on the topic of management, as well as reliable Web resources. Primary research will include personal observation at the South Dennis site, which I will visit next Thursday; a survey (see attached) to be distributed to all of the South Dennis management and employees; and interviews with both employee and management representatives at the South Dennis location. All conclusions and any recommendations for positive change will be based on the collected evidence in my report.

→ Details specific approaches to the research

If you have any further questions, I will be happy to discuss this proposal with you at your convenience.

→ Encourages reader acceptance

Sales Proposals

Sales proposals offer services or products and may be solicited or unsolicited. If solicited, several firms may be competing for the same contract, so submitted proposals may be ranked by a committee. Sales proposals can be cast as letters if the situation calls for them to be brief. If the situation requires a longer proposal, include the various parts and elements of formal proposals. A successful sales proposal persuades customers that your product or service surpasses those of any competitors. What you include in a sales proposal is determined by the guidelines from the client or by a thorough analysis of the kinds of information your audience needs.

Figure 17.3 is an example of a solicited, informal sales proposal, in which the writer explains why her machinery is best for the job, what qualifications her company can offer, and what costs are involved. As with Figure 17.1, because this document is addressed to external readers, it is cast as a letter. For specific advice on how to approach sales proposals, read the annotations accompanying Figure 17.3 and see the Strategies for Proposals on pages 335–336.

ORGANIZATION OF INFORMAL AND FORMAL PROPOSALS

No matter the type, all proposals must move in a logical direction from problem/situation to solution/resolution. All effective proposals typically include a clear title or subject line; background information; a statement of the problem or situation; a description of how to solve the problem or resolve the situation; a breakdown of costs, timing, or qualifications (if applicable); and a conclusion that induces readers to act.

Include front matter
and end matter as
needed

Formal proposals typically require *front matter* including a title page, a table of contents, an abstract or executive summary, and possibly a letter of transmittal. *End matter* would include appendices and a list of sources cited (if the formal proposal has entailed research, which it usually will). For more information on these components, see Chapter 16 (pages 309–312); front matter and end matter are presented in the same way in a formal proposal as in a formal report.

Clear Title or Subject Line

State the proposal's purpose with a clear and complete title, such as "Recommended Wastewater Treatment System for the MudPie Resort and Spa," (for a formal proposal) or a subject line (in an informal proposal). Avoid being vague or overly general. An overworked decision maker facing a stack of proposals might very well decide that one that lacks a clear, focused title or subject line probably will be unclear and unfocused in its content.

FIGURE 17.3
A sales proposal

Modern Landscaping
23–44 18th Street
Sunnyside, NY 11104

October 4, 20XX

Martin Haver
35–66 114th Avenue
Jamaica, NY 11107

Subject: *Proposal to dig a trench and move boulders at Bliss site*

Dear Mr. Haver:

I've inspected your property and would be happy to undertake the landscaping project necessary for the development of your farm. ← • Describes the subject and purpose

The backhoe I use cuts a span 3 feet wide and can dig as deep as 18 feet—more than an adequate depth for the mainline pipe you wish to lay. Because this backhoe is on tracks rather than tires and is hydraulically operated, it is particularly efficient in moving rocks. I have more than twelve years of experience with backhoe work and have completed many jobs similar to this one. ← • Gives the writer's qualifications

After examining the huge boulders that block access to your property, I am convinced they can be moved only if I dig out underneath and exert upward pressure with the hydraulic ram while you push forward on the boulders with your D-9 Caterpillar. With this method, we can move enough rock to enable you to farm that now inaccessible tract. Because of its power, my larger backhoe will save you both time and money in the long run. ← • Explains how the job will be done
← • Maintains a confident tone throughout

This job should take 12 to 15 hours, unless we encounter subsurface ledge formations. My fee is $200 per hour. The fact that I provide my own dynamiting crew at no extra charge should be an advantage to you because you have so much rock to be moved. ← • Gives a qualified cost estimate

Please phone me any time for more information. I'm sure we can do the job economically and efficiently. ← • Encourages reader acceptance by emphasizing economy and efficiency

Sincerely yours,
Sharon Ingram
Sharon Ingram

Background Information

Provide your readers with background context

A background section can be brief or long. In Figure 17.1, the writer's opening sentence ("As we discussed in our meeting on March 6...") provides a quick reminder of the context for the project. This sentence is brief because the reader is already familiar with the project. For a new audience or in an unsolicited proposal, you may need to provide a longer paragraph (or, in the case of a formal proposal, a full introduction) with background information on the project. If the topic warrants, the background section may take up several pages.

Statement of Problem or Situation

Clearly describe the problem or situation

The problem or situation and its resolution form the backbone of any proposal. Describe the problem or situation statement in either the background portion of your proposal or in its own headed section. For example, a good statement of the problem or situation might be: "Complaints about noise in our college library call for a plan that will make areas of the library quiet enough for serious study."

Description of Solution or Resolution

Fully explain how you plan to solve the problem or resolve the situation

The bulk of the proposal should map out your plan to solve the problem or resolve the situation. Include in this section as much detail as needed for your audience to evaluate the soundness of your plan. If the plan is vague or unrealistic, the proposal will be rejected.

Costs, Timing, and Qualifications

Spell out any particulars involving money, time, and expertise

If your proposal involves financial outlay, timing sensitivity, or proof of your qualifications, provide separate sections dealing with these factors. Make sure that your breakdown of costs and timing is accurate, easy to understand, and realistic. If you work with an accountant or other financial specialist, ask that person to check your cost figures. If the proposal is solicited, make sure you follow the client's guidelines for establishing a budget and/or schedule.

Conclusion

End with a call to action

The conclusion reaffirms the need for your plan and induces the audience to act. A conclusion does not need to be more than a sentence or two in an informal proposal (longer, of course, in a formal proposal), but no matter the length, always end on a strong note, with a conclusion that is assertive, confident, and encouraging.

STRATEGIES
for Proposals

▸ **Consider your audience and purpose.** Remember that your audience consists of decision makers; therefore, the purpose of any proposal must be to convince the decision makers to say yes to what you propose.

▸ **Understand the audience's needs.** The proposal audience members want specific suggestions to meet their specific needs. Their biggest question will be "What will this plan do for me?" Make your proposal demonstrate a clear understanding of the audience's problem or situation, and then offer an appropriate solution or resolution.

▸ **Perform research as needed.** To make your plan convincing, do your research. For example, you might research the very latest technology for solving a problem or resolving a situation; compare the costs, benefits, and drawbacks of various approaches; contact others in your field for their suggestions; find out what competitors are up to; and so on.

▸ **Be sure to credit information sources and contributors.** Complex proposals rarely emerge from thin air, and proposals are often a result of a team effort. If anything in your proposal represents the work or input of others, document the sources or acknowledge fellow contributors.

▸ **Use an appropriate format.** For an informal proposal distributed internally, use email or memo format. For an informal proposal distributed externally, use letter format. For a formal proposal, include all the required components, including a title page, table of contents, abstract or executive summary, introduction, body, and conclusion. If applicable, include a letter of transmittal and appendices.

▸ **Provide a clear title or subject line and background information.** Draw readers into your proposal with a title or subject line that describes the content of the proposal exactly, and orient your readers with the appropriate background information.

▸ **Follow a problem-to-solution or situation-to-resolution organizational pattern.** All proposals should move in this sequence from beginning to end.

▸ **Spell out the problem (and its causes) or situation clearly and convincingly.** Provide enough detail for your audience to appreciate the importance of the problem or situation. Answer the implied question, "Why is this such a big deal?"

▸ **Point out the benefits of solving the problem.** Answer the implied question, "Why should we spend time, money, and effort to do this?"

▸ **Offer a realistic solution or resolution.** Stick to claims or assertions you can support. Answer the implied question, "How do we know this will work?" If the solution or resolution involves accounting for costs, budgeting time, or proving your qualifications, include this information.

▸ **Address anticipated objections to your solution.** Decision makers typically approach a proposal with skepticism, especially if the project will cost them money and time. Answer the implied question, "Why should we accept the things that seem wrong with your plan?"

▸ **Include all necessary details, but don't overload.** Include as much supporting detail as you need to induce readers to say yes to your proposal. Leave nothing to guesswork. At the same time, don't overload your readers with information that is not directly relevant.

▸ **Write clearly and concisely.** Make sure your document is easy to read, uses action verbs, and avoids puffed-up language or terms that are too technical for your audience. If necessary for a mixed audience with differing technical levels, include a glossary.

▸ **Express confidence.** You are trying to sell yourself, your ideas, or your services to a skeptical audience. Be upfront about the supporting facts ("For the third year in a row, our firm has been ranked as the number 1 architecture firm in the Midwest") and state your case directly ("We know you will be satisfied with the results").

▸ **Make honest and supportable claims.** Because they often involve large sums of money, investments of time, and contractual obligations, proposals require a solid ethical and legal foundation. False promises not only damage the writer's or company's reputation but also invite lawsuits. If the solutions you offer have limitations, make sure you say so.

▸ **Induce readers to act.** Decide exactly what you want readers to do, and give reasons why they should be the ones to act. In your conclusion, answer the implied question, "What action am I supposed to take?"

A SAMPLE FORMAL PROPOSAL

Figure 17.4 has been written because a state university's newspaper is struggling to meet rising costs. The paper's yearly budget is funded by the Student Fee Allocation Committee, which disburses money to various campus organizations. Because of drastic budget cuts for all state schools, the newspaper has received no funding increase for three years. Bill Trippe, the *Torch*'s business manager, must justify a requested increase of 20.6 percent for the coming year's budget.

Before drafting his proposal, Bill constructed a detailed profile of his audience and purpose: He determined that the primary audience (the Allocation Committee) would use the document as perhaps the sole basis for deciding whether to grant the additional funds and that his primary purpose must be to provide a convincing rationale. To achieve his goal, he has included a detailed plan for reducing existing operating costs, a section outlining next year's projected costs, and an appendix comparing the *Torch*'s performance with that of other nearby college newspapers. All these materials demonstrate how Bill has anticipated his audience's possible objections.

FIGURE 17.4
A formal proposal

SMU *Torch*

Old Westport Road
North Dartmouth, Massachusetts 02747

May 1, 20XX

Charles Marcus, Chair
Student Fee Allocation Committee
Southeastern Massachusetts University
North Dartmouth, MA 02747

Dear Dean Marcus:

No one needs to be reminded about the effects of increased costs on our campus community. We are all faced with having to make do with less.

Accordingly, we at the *Torch* have spent long hours devising a plan to cope with increased production costs—without compromising the newspaper's tradition of quality service. I think you and your colleagues will agree that our plan is realistic and feasible. Even the "bare-bones" operation that will result from our proposed spending cuts, however, will call for a $6,478.57 increase in next year's budget.

We have received no funding increase in three years. Our present need is absolute. Without additional funds, the *Torch* simply cannot continue to function as a professional newspaper. I therefore submit the following budget proposal for your consideration.

Respectfully,

William Trippe

William Trippe
Business Manager, SMU *Torch*

Letter of transmittal provides additional context and persuasion

FIGURE 17.4
(Continued)

Provides a clear
title

**A Funding Proposal
for
The SMU *Torch***
(20XX–XX)

Prepared for
The Student Fee Allocation Committee
Southeastern Massachusetts University
North Dartmouth, Massachusetts

Writer, affiliation,
and date always
appear on the
title page

by
William Trippe
Torch Business Manager

May 1, 20XX

FIGURE 17.4
(Continued)

ii

TABLE OF CONTENTS

PAGE

INFORMATIVE ABSTRACT iii

INTRODUCTION 1
    Overview 1
    Background 1
    Statement of Problem 1
    Need 2
    Scope 2

PROPOSED PLAN 2
    Methods 2
    Costs 3
    Feasibility 5
    Personnel 5

CONCLUSION 5

APPENDIX (Comparative Performance) 6

Table of contents orients readers and demonstrates proposal's structure

FIGURE 17.4
(Continued)

Abstract
accurately
encapsulates
entrie document

INFORMATIVE ABSTRACT

The SMU *Torch*, the student newspaper at Southeastern Massachusetts University, is crippled by inadequate funding, having received no budget increase in three years. Increased costs and inadequate funding are the major problems facing the *Torch*. Increases in costs of technology upgrades and in printing have called for cutbacks in production. Moreover, our low staff salaries are inadequate to attract and retain qualified personnel. A nominal pay increase would make salaries more competitive.

Our staff plans to cut costs by reducing page count and by hiring a new press for the *Torch*'s printing work. The only proposed cost increase (for staff salaries) is essential.

A detailed breakdown of projected costs establishes the need for a $6,478.57 budget increase to keep the paper a weekly publication with adequate page count to serve our campus.

Compared with similar newspapers at other colleges, the *Torch* makes much better use of its money. The comparison figures in the Appendix illustrate the cost-effectiveness of our proposal.

FIGURE 17.4
(Continued)

Funding Proposal   1

INTRODUCTION

Overview

Our campus newspaper faces the contradictory challenge of surviving ever-growing production costs while maintaining its reputation for quality. The following proposal addresses that crisis. This plan's ultimate success, however, depends on the Allocation Committee's willingness to approve a long-overdue increase in the *Torch*'s upcoming yearly budget.

Opens with an overview of the situation

Background

In ten years, the *Torch* has grown in size, scope, and quality. Roughly 6,000 copies (24 pages/issue) are printed weekly for each fourteen-week semester. Each week, the *Torch* prints national and local press releases, features, editorials, sports articles, announcements, notices, classified ads, a calendar column, and letters to the editor. A vital part of university life, our newspaper provides a forum for information, ideas, and opinions—all with the highest professionalism. This year we published an online version as well.

Provides relevant background

Statement of Problem

With much of its staff about to graduate, the *Torch* faces next year with rising costs in every phase of production and the need to replace outdated and worn equipment.

Describes the problem concisely

Our newspaper also suffers from a lack of student involvement: Despite gaining valuable experience and potential career credentials, few students can be expected to work without some kind of remuneration. Most staff members do receive nominal weekly salaries: from $20 for the distributor to $90 for the Editor-in-Chief. But salaries averaging barely $5 per hour cannot possibly compete with the minimum wage. Since more and more SMU students must work part-time, the *Torch* will have to make its salaries more competitive.

The newspaper's operating expenses can be divided into four categories: hardware and software upgrades, salaries, printing costs, and miscellaneous (office supplies, mail, and so on). The first three categories account for nearly 90 percent of the budget. Over the past year, costs in all categories have increased: from as little as 2 percent for miscellaneous expenses to as much as 19 percent for technology upgrades. Printing costs (roughly one-third of our total budget) rose 9 percent in the past year, and another price hike of 10 percent has just been announced.

FIGURE 17.4
(Continued)

Proposes a
logical solution to
the problem, based
on evidence

Previews the plan
before getting into
details

Itemizes realistic
ways to save money
and retain staff

Need

Despite growing production costs, the *Torch* has received no increase in its yearly budget allocation ($37,400) in three years. Inadequate funding is virtually crippling our newspaper.

Scope

The following plan includes
1. Methods for reducing production costs while maintaining the quality of our staff
2. Projected costs for technology upgrades, salaries, and services during the upcoming year
3. A demonstration of feasibility, showing our cost-effectiveness
4. A summary of attitudes shared by our personnel

PROPOSED PLAN

This plan is designed to trim operating costs without compromising quality.

Methods

We can overcome our budget and staffing crisis by taking these steps:

Reducing Page Count. By condensing free notices for campus organizations, abolishing "personal" notices, and limiting press releases to one page, we can reduce page count per issue from 24 to 20, saving nearly 17 percent in production costs. (Items deleted from hard copy could be linked as add-ons in the *Torch*'s online version.)

Reducing Hard-Copy Circulation. Reducing circulation from 6,000 to 5,000 copies barely will cover the number of full-time students, but will save 17 percent in printing costs. The steadily increasing hits on our Web site suggest that more and more readers are using the electronic medium. (We are designing a fall survey to help determine how many readers rely on the online version.)

Hiring a New Press. We can save money by hiring Arrow Press for printing. Other presses (including our present printer) bid at least 25 percent higher than Arrow. With its state-of-the art production equipment, Arrow will import our "camera-ready" digital files to produce the hard-copy version. Moreover, no other company offers the rapid turnover time (from submission to finished product) that Arrow promises.

FIGURE 17.4
(Continued)

Funding Proposal   3

Upgrading Our Desktop Publishing Technology. To meet Arrow's specifications for submitting digital files, we must upgrade our equipment. Upgrade costs will be largely offset the first year by reduced printing costs. Also, this technology will increase efficiency and reduce labor costs, resulting in substantial payback on investment.

Increasing Staff Salaries. Although we seek talented students who expect little money and much experience, salaries for all positions must increase by an average of 25 percent. Otherwise, any of our staff could earn as much money elsewhere by working only a little more than half the time. In fact, many students could exceed the minimum wage by working for local newspapers. To illustrate: The *Standard Beacon* pays $60 to $90 per news article and $30 per photo; the *Torch* pays nothing for articles and $6 per photo.

A striking example of low salaries is the $4.75 per hour we pay our desktop publishing staff. Our present desktop publishing cost of $3,038 could be as much as $7,000 or even higher if we had this service done by an outside firm, as many colleges do. Without this nominal salary increase, we cannot possibly attract qualified personnel.

Costs

Our proposed budget is itemized in Table 1, but the main point is clear: If the *Torch* is to remain viable, increased funding is essential for meeting our projected costs.

Table 1 Projected Costs and Requested Funding for Next Year's *Torch* Budget

PROJECTED COSTS

Hardware/Software Upgrades	
Apple iMac w/8 GB memory, 1TB HD (Intel Core i7)	$1,162.00
HP Pavilion 2709m 27" (second monitor)	355.00
Seagate 8 TB external hard drive (for backups)	128.99
Olympus Stylus 9000 digital camera	299.98
HP Scanjet 5000 sheet-feed scanner	799.00
Microsoft Office 2013 Professional Upgrade	499.00
Adobe Creative Suite 5 Master Collection	2,450.00
Subtotal	**$5,693.97**

Provides detailed breakdown of costs—the central issue in the situation

FIGURE 17.4
(Continued)

Funding Proposal   4

PROJECTED COSTS (*continued*)

Wages and Salaries

Desktop-publishing staff (35 hr/wk at $6.00/hr x 28 wk)	$5,880.00
Editor-in-Chief	3,150.00
News Editor	1,890.00
Features Editor	1,890.00
Advertising Manager	2,350.00
Advertising Designer	1,575.00
Webmaster	2,520.00
Layout Editor	1,890.00
Art Director	1,260.00
Photo Editor	1,890.00
Business Manager	1,890.00
Distributor	560.00
Subtotal	**$26,745.00**

Miscellaneous Costs

Graphics by SMU art students (3/wk @ $10 each)	$ 840.00
Mailing	1,100.00
Telephone	1,000.00
Campus print shop services	400.00
Copier fees	100.00
Subtotal	**$3,440.00**

Fixed Printing Costs (5,000 copies/wk x 28/wk)	**$24,799.60**

TOTAL YEARLY COSTS	**$60,678.57**
Expected Advertising Revenue ($600/wk x 28 wks)	**($16,800.00)**
Total Costs Minus Advertising Revenue	**$45,109.39**

TOTAL FUNDING REQUEST	**$43,878.57**

FIGURE 17.4
(Continued)

Funding Proposal   5

Feasibility

Beyond exhibiting our need, we feel that the feasibility of this proposal can be measured through an objective evaluation of our cost-effectiveness: Compared with newspapers at similar schools, how well does the *Torch* use its funding?

In a survey of the four area college newspapers, we found that the *Torch*—by a sometimes huge margin—makes the best use of its money per page. Table 1A in the Appendix shows that, of the five newspapers, the *Torch* costs students the least, runs the most pages weekly, and spends the least money per page, *despite a circulation two to three times the size of the other papers.*

The *Torch* has the lowest yearly cost of all five newspapers, despite having the largest circulation. With the requested budget increase, the cost would rise by only $0.88, for a yearly cost of $9.00 to each student. Although Alden College's newspaper costs each student $8.58, it is published only every third week, averages 12 pages per issue, and costs more than $71.00 yearly per page to print—in contrast to our yearly printing cost of $55.65 per page. As the figures in the Appendix demonstrate, our cost management is responsible and effective.

Assesses probability of success

Personnel

The *Torch* staff is determined to maintain the highest professionalism. Many are planning careers in journalism, writing, editing, advertising, photography, Web design, or public relations. In any *Torch* issue, the balanced, enlightened coverage is evidence of our judicious selection and treatment of articles and our shared concern for quality.

Addresses important issue of personnel

CONCLUSION

As a broad forum for ideas and opinions, the *Torch* continues to reflect a seriousness of purpose and a commitment to free and responsible expression. Its role in campus life is more vital than ever during these troubled times.

Every year, allocations to student organizations increase or decrease based on need. Last year, for example, eight allocations increased by an average of $4,332. The *Torch* has received no increase in three years.

Presumably, increases are prompted by special circumstances. For the *Torch*, these circumstances derive from increasing production costs and the need to update vital equipment. We respectfully urge the Committee to respond to the *Torch*'s legitimate needs by increasing next year's allocation to $43,878.57.

Reemphasizes need and encourages action

FIGURE 17.4
(Continued)

APPENDIX (Comparative Performance)

Table 1A Allocations and Performance of Five Local College Newspapers

Appendix provides detailed breakdown of cost comparsions →

	Stonehorse College	Alden College	Simms University	Fallow State	SMU
Enrollment	1,600	1,400	3,000	3,000	5,000
Fee paid (per year)	$65.00	$85.00	$35.00	$50.00	$65.00
Total fee budget	$104,000	$119,000	$105,000	$150,000	$325,000
Newspaper budget	$18,300	$8,580	$36,179	$52,910	$37,392
					$45,109[a]
Yearly cost per student	$12.50	$8.58	$16.86	$24.66	$8.12
					$9.00[a]
Publication rate	Weekly	Every third week	Weekly	Weekly	Weekly
Average no. of pages	8	12	18	12	24
Average total pages	224	120	504	336	672
					560[a]
Yearly cost per page	$81.60	$71.50	$71.78	$157.47	$55.65
					$67.12[a]

[a]These figures are next year's costs for the SMU *Torch.*

Source: Figures were quoted by newspaper business managers in April 20XX.

CHECKLIST
for Proposals

- ☐ Have I identified whether my proposal is solicited or unsolicited, and have I planned accordingly?
- ☐ Have I determined whether my proposal should be informal or formal?
- ☐ Have I identified whether my proposal is a planning, research, or sales proposal?
- ☐ Does my proposal follow a problem-solution or situation-resolution pattern?
- ☐ Have I done adequate research?
- ☐ Have I provided a clear title or subject line?
- ☐ Is the problem or situation clearly identified in the introduction?
- ☐ Is the background section appropriate for this audience's needs?
- ☐ Does the proposal maintain a clear focus on benefits?
- ☐ Is the proposed solution or resolution appropriate and realistic?
- ☐ Is the cost, budget, and/or qualifications section accurate and easy to understand?
- ☐ Are my claims honest and supportable?
- ☐ Are all foreseeable limitations identified?
- ☐ Are visuals, if needed, used effectively?
- ☐ Is my writing style clear, concise, and confident?
- ☐ Does the proposal end with a call to action?

APPLICATIONS

GENERAL APPLICATIONS

1. After identifying your primary and secondary audience, write a short planning proposal for improving an unsatisfactory situation in the classroom, on the job, or in your dorm or apartment (e.g., poor lighting, drab atmosphere, health hazards, poor seating arrangements). Choose a problem or situation whose solution or resolution is more a matter of common sense and lucid observation than of intensive research. Be sure to (a) identify the problem clearly, give a brief background, and stimulate interest; (b) clearly state the methods proposed to solve the problem; and (c) conclude with a statement designed to gain audience support.

2. Write a research proposal to your instructor (or an interested third party) requesting approval for your final term project (a formal analytical report or formal proposal).

Verify that adequate primary and secondary sources are available. Convince your audience of the soundness and usefulness of the project.

3. As an alternate term project to the formal analytical report (Chapter 16), develop a long proposal for solving a problem, improving a situation, or satisfying a need in your school, community, or job. Choose a subject sufficiently complex to justify a formal proposal, a topic requiring research (mostly primary). Identify an audience (other than your instructor) who will use your proposal for a specific purpose. Complete an Audience and Purpose Profile.

TEAM APPLICATION

Working in groups of four, develop an unsolicited planning proposal for solving a problem, improving a situation, or satisfying a need in your school, community, or workplace. Begin by brainstorming as a group to come up with a list of possible issues or problems to address in your proposal. Narrow your list, and work as a group to focus on a specific issue or idea. Your proposal should address a clearly identified audience of decision makers and stakeholders in the given issue. Complete an Audience and Purpose Profile.

GLOBAL APPLICATION   MyWritingLab™

Compare the sorts of proposals regularly done in the United States with those created in other countries. For example, is the format the same? Are there more proposals for certain purposes in the United States than in another country? You can learn about this topic by interviewing an expert in international business (someone you meet on the job, during an internship, or through your adviser). You can also search the Web for information on international technical communication. Describe your findings in a short memo that you will share with your classmates.

DIGITAL AND SOCIAL MEDIA APPLICATION   MyWritingLab™

Solicited proposals are usually written in response to a formal "request for proposal" (RFP). The National Science Foundation's Web site and Facebook page have links for research funding opportunities for undergraduate and graduate students, K-12 educators, and many program areas such as engineering, geosciences, and so on. Find an area of interest to you and locate an RFP. Write a memo to your instructor explaining why you are interested in this research and what focus your proposal would take.

MyWritingLab™   Visit Chapter 17, *Proposals*, in MyWritingLab to complete this chapter's applications, to explore this chapter's overview, checklist, and flashcards, and to test your understanding of the chapter objectives.

PART 4

Digital Media and Presentations

18 Email and Text Messages

19 Blogs, Wikis, and Web Pages

20 Social Media

21 Oral Presentations and Video Conferencing

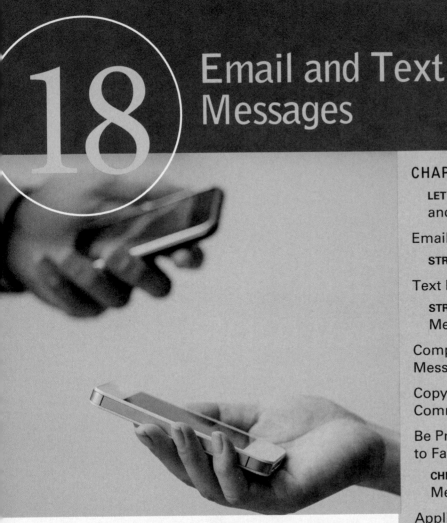

18 Email and Text Messages

CHAPTER OUTLINE

LET'S GET STARTED: Email and Text Messages *351*

Email *351*

STRATEGIES for Email *356*

Text Messages *357*

STRATEGIES for Text Messages *358*

Comparing Email and Text Messaging *358*

Copyright and Privacy in Digital Communication *358*

Be Prepared for Technology to Fail *360*

CHECKLIST for Email and Text Messages *360*

Applications *361*

LEARNING OBJECTIVES FOR THIS CHAPTER

- ▸ Identify advantages of using email in the workplace
- ▸ Determine if email is the correct form of communication in a given situation
- ▸ Write a well-organized, stylistically appropriate workplace email
- ▸ Identify advantages and disadvantages of using text messages in the workplace
- ▸ Conduct a successful workplace communication using text messages
- ▸ Recognize basic issues about copyright and privacy in digital communication

LET'S GET STARTED
Email and Text Messages

MyWritingLab™

Think about how quickly most email messages are written and sent. Before reading this chapter, compose an email message to a professor whom you have never met, asking for more information about a course that she or he is teaching next semester. Consider that the professor probably receives a lot of email, doesn't know you, and is busy with current students.

Questions to ask about the email you wrote as you review the material in this chapter:

- ▸ What did I write in the subject line?

- ▸ Is my tone informal, formal, or in between?

- ▸ Is my request clear?

- ▸ Did I use any emoticons (such as smiley faces)?

- ▸ What differences should be considered between an email sent to a friend and an email sent to a professor, potential employer, or current employer?

At the end of this chapter, review your initial Let's Get Started email with your instructor or with a group of students to see how much you might change or modify the document based on what you have learned from the chapter.

As described in previous chapters, workplace communication typically involves a combination of both print and digital media. Email is the most common form of digital communication on the job; email can be used on its own or as a way to send an attachment. Text messaging is also popular at work, especially for short messages that need to be seen quickly. This chapter explores both email and text messages as forms of workplace communication.

EMAIL

Email is the primary way people communicate in today's workplace and professional settings, largely replacing the paper memo and letter. Unlike paper, email offers both rapid speed and wide reach: With one keystroke, an email message can quickly reach the inboxes of thousands of people. These readers can easily forward the email to others.

Advantages of workplace email

Email is useful when people are in different time zones or have different working schedules: You can send an email at 2:00 A.M. if you are a night owl, and your early-bird colleague can read it in the morning. Or, if you are based in the eastern United States and your colleagues are in China, the 12-hour time difference means that email is essential to your work. Email also provides written documentation—an electronic trail, so to speak—that helps track a project or conversation or that may become important for legal reasons down the road.

Email is often the primary means of communication, but it might also be used as a vehicle for sending attachments (long reports, formal memos, letters on letterhead, or working documents such as word processing files). Either way, email messages tend to be conversational in tone and are therefore best suited for simple, straightforward messages that are not too long and that do not leave a lot of room for misunderstanding. Even writers who are extremely careful with traditional paper correspondence sometimes ignore spelling and grammar as they dash off various emails. However, as the uses for email broaden and as the software evolves, workplace emails are starting to look more polished. Writers are paying greater attention to style and correctness and making their emails look more professional.

The changing character of email

Audience and Purpose of Email

Unlike paper documents, with email you have little control over the final audience. You might send your message to only a small group, but because of easy forwarding, your audience could turn out to be much larger. People also tend to be more casual and off-the-cuff on email, sometimes more than in person; therefore, audience considerations become crucial.

Audience considerations

Suppose, for example, that after a long week of work on a particularly tough engineering design project, you send a quick email to another manager. In your message, you complain about one of the engineers not holding up his end. You quickly press "Send" and head out for the weekend. At a Monday status meeting, you are surprised to find that your message was forwarded to several other engineers. Clearly, your original message was not intended for them, but—inadvertently or deliberately—someone forwarded it along.

Remember this cardinal rule about email: Always assume that your message will travel far beyond its intended recipient, and never send anything private or confidential via email.

Email accomplishes various purposes: to schedule meetings, update team members on a project, send simple memos in electronic form, and send attached documents to colleagues both within and outside of an organization.

Purpose considerations

Think carefully about whether email is the best medium for the given message. If you want your message to be private or confidential or if your message is too complex for email, set up a personal meeting or phone call. You can always follow up with a brief email that summarizes the main points. Also keep in mind how much email people get on a daily basis: Important items, even if marked as such, often get ignored or accidentally deleted. Finally, be sure to check before you send large attachments, such as long reports, proposals, or legal correspondence.

Components and Organization of Email

A typical email message combines features from both memos and letters. Emails usually begin with a heading, containing "To," "From," "Date," and "Subject" fields. Most email programs also feature the courtesy copy ("cc") and blind courtesy copy ("bcc") fields. Use "cc" for people who need to know but are not central to the conversation. Use "bcc" for a very long list of recipients or for individuals who need to be in the loop but may not want their email address visible. Attachments (such as PDF files or other documents too large or too formal for the email itself) take the place of the "enclosure" notation on a paper memo or letter. Depending on the level of formality, email may sometimes be written with openings and closings ("Dear John," "Sincerely, Linda").

Email components

Regardless of length, an effective email should contain a brief introduction (even a single sentence) that gets right to the point, a clear body section with transitions, and a brief conclusion that usually ask readers to take action (such as "Please get back to me by 5:00 P.M. on Monday"). Visually, longer emails are easier for readers to process if information is broken into chunks, such as short paragraphs and bulleted lists. However, because email can be viewed on a range of screen sizes (computer, tablet, smart phone), be careful about using too much formatting. Keep email messages to about the size of one computer screen or less.

Email organization

Figure 18.1 illustrates the components and organization of a standard workplace email.

Appropriate Style for Workplace Email

Personal email often contains deliberately misspelled or abbreviated words, a disregard for grammatical rules, a lax attitude toward proper punctuation, a highly informal tone, and an emphasis on brevity over completeness. Workplace email, however, should use proper spelling, grammar, and punctuation and should avoid words or phrases in all capital letters, as well as text-message style abbreviations ("LOL," "imho," and the like) and emoticons (facial expressions, such as smiley faces, created using type). In addition, adopt a professional, respectful tone and express complete thoughts. An email that is too casual (e.g., using such words as "uh huh," "whatever," and "cool") or is incomplete will undermine the writer's professionalism.

Workplace email style

Be sure to avoid *flaming* (angry, sarcastic, insulting messages that will only lead to repercussions), using sexist or otherwise biased language that demeans or excludes some potential readers, and blaming others. Also, do not forward a particularly sensitive email without permission, edit a forwarded email, or send enormous attachments.

Workplace email etiquette

Figure 18.2 shows an email that is lacking in professional style. Although the writer and recipient are close personal friends in addition to their employee–supervisor relationship, an email like this should never be written in the workplace.

(*Text continues on p. 356.*)

**FIGURE 18.1
A workplace
email**

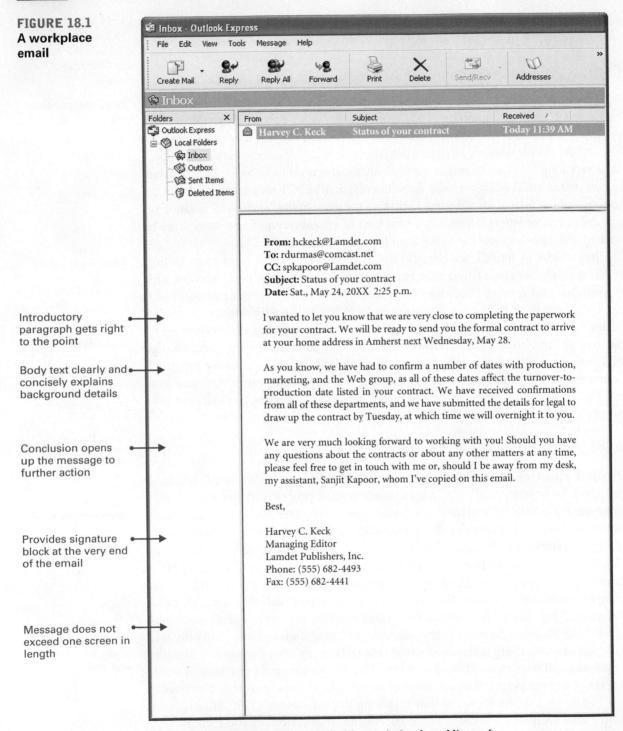

Introductory
paragraph gets right
to the point

Body text clearly and
concisely explains
background details

Conclusion opens
up the message to
further action

Provides signature
block at the very end
of the email

Message does not
exceed one screen in
length

From: hckeck@Lamdet.com
To: rdurmas@comcast.net
CC: spkapoor@Lamdet.com
Subject: Status of your contract
Date: Sat., May 24, 20XX 2:25 p.m.

I wanted to let you know that we are very close to completing the paperwork for your contract. We will be ready to send you the formal contract to arrive at your home address in Amherst next Wednesday, May 28.

As you know, we have had to confirm a number of dates with production, marketing, and the Web group, as all of these dates affect the turnover-to-production date listed in your contract. We have received confirmations from all of these departments, and we have submitted the details for legal to draw up the contract by Tuesday, at which time we will overnight it to you.

We are very much looking forward to working with you! Should you have any questions about the contracts or about any other matters at any time, please feel free to get in touch with me or, should I be away from my desk, my assistant, Sanjit Kapoor, whom I've copied on this email.

Best,

Harvey C. Keck
Managing Editor
Lamdet Publishers, Inc.
Phone: (555) 682-4493
Fax: (555) 682-4441

Source: Outlook Express frame used with permission from Microsoft.

FIGURE 18.2
A workplace email lacking professional style

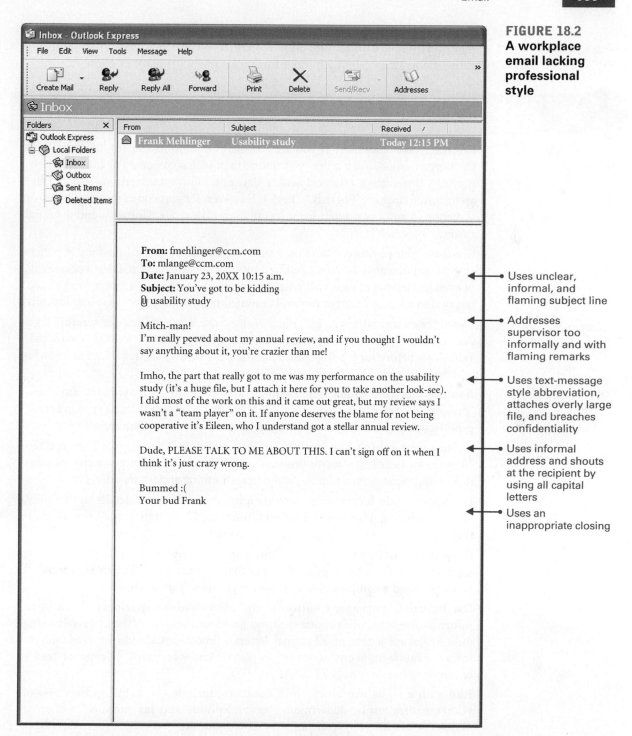

Source: Outlook Express frame used with permission from Microsoft.

Not only does the message in Figure 18.2 have legal implications in terms of the writer's job performance and future employment, but it also violates another employee's confidentiality. It is also much too informal for any workplace document.

STRATEGIES
for Email

▸ **Consider your audience.** If you are writing to a customer, client, or superior in your organization, use a more formal tone than with a coworker or immediate supervisor. If you know your recipient well, use an informal salutation ("Hello") and an informal closing ("Regards," "Best"). However, for someone you don't know or someone in authority, use a formal salutation ("Dear Dr. Gomez") and a formal closing ("Sincerely").

▸ **Consider your purpose.** Don't use email when a more personal medium is preferable. Sometimes an issue is best resolved by talking face to face, making a phone call, or even just leaving a voice mail. Don't use email to resign from a job, request a raise, respond to a formal letter, or respond to something that may have legal implications.

▸ **Consider confidentiality.** Email may not be the best medium for sending legal documents, confidential company files, or anything else that should remain private. Also, before forwarding a message, obtain permission from the sender, who may have intended the message for you only.

▸ **Assume that your email is permanent and readable by anyone at any time.** "Forensic software" can find virtually any file that has been deleted, so don't make promises you cannot keep or expect anything else you say to disappear forever.

▸ **Write a clear subject line.** Instead of "Test Data" or "Data Request," be specific: "Request for Beta Test Data for Project 18." This line helps recipients decide whether to read the message immediately, and it helps for filing and future reference.

▸ **Use appropriate formatting.** Provide a brief introduction, details in the body, and a conclusion. Use bullets, headings, numbered lists, italics, and other formatting features to make your message easy to read.

▸ **Keep it short.** Readers are impatient and don't want to scroll through long screens of information. Messages longer than one screen will often go unread. If you must send a complex message, put longer details in an attachment.

▸ **Use informal language, emoticons, and abbreviations sparingly.** Even in an informal message, use proper spelling, grammar, and mechanics (avoid using only lowercase letters or all capital letters). Emoticons should be used only in informal messages to coworkers or people you know very well. The same goes for common abbreviations (FYI, ASAP, OMG).

▸ **End with a signature block.** In most cases, include the name and address of your organization or department, your telephone and fax number, and other contact information by using an automatic signature block.

→

> STRATEGIES *continued*

> ► **Proofread thoroughly before hitting "send."** Every message reflects your image, so double-check any email with your name on it. Also be careful that the email goes only to your intended recipients.

> ► **Be professional.** Take time to read email carefully; respond in a timely manner; avoid flaming (angry or personal attacks) and sexist or biased language; do not edit forwarded emails without the sender's permission; and do not send large attachments.

TEXT MESSAGES

A faster medium than email, text messages (often called "texts" for short) allow you to communicate quickly using a cell phone or smart phone. When you send a text, it is received almost immediately. Texts can be sent to one person or to several. Long popular for personal communication, texting has recently become common in the workplace for short, quick exchanges (e.g., to let someone know you'll be late for a meeting or tell a colleague your plane has landed). Although few rules govern the use of texting on the job, many companies recognize the value of short, instantaneous messages and are increasingly accepting the text message as legitimate communication.

Advantages of workplace text messages

Similar to text messages, instant messages (IMs, also called "chats" or "chatting") allow for text-based conversations in real time using a computer or tablet (iPad, for example) instead of a cell phone. The writer types a message into a pop-up box or other interface, and the recipient can respond instantly. Instant messaging can be used one to one or with groups, allowing people to converse and collaborate from various locations. One advantage of IMs over text messaging is that typically, IM conversations can be captured on the screen, whereas text messages on cell phones disappear after a short time.

Audience and Purpose of Workplace Text Messages

Consider your audience carefully before deciding to use text messaging for workplace communication. Texting can be useful in place of a phone call for short questions or notifications. But keep in mind that most people receive text messages on their personal cell phone number and may be charged a fee per message, so only send text messages if the recipient has agreed to communicate this way.

Audience considerations

In most cases, defer to using email, which requires timely, but not instant and rapid-fire, responses. Texting is not a good medium for the kind of written communication that requires careful planning, composing, and editing. For such messages, consider using email or print instead of texting. Importantly, text messages are typically not archived, so if you should need to review a message weeks or months later, you may not be able to find the information.

Purpose considerations

► **Consider your audience and purpose.** Use texts to communicate with people who are comfortable with this medium or who don't mind texts interrupting their work. Use texts for quick conversations on single topics that don't require a paper trail.

► **Keep each text conversation separate.** Stick to the topic at hand.

► **Keep text messages short.** Texting is more informal than email, so feel free to use abbreviations, as long as everyone understands them.

► **Stay connected if you are in the middle of a communication.** Texting requires you to stay connected until you complete your text conversation. If you need to end a conversation, alert the other people involved.

► **Know when to end the conversation.** Don't digress. When you've exhausted the topic, say goodbye.

► **Be professional.** Avoid flaming and sexist or biased language, maintain confidentiality, and respond to messages in a timely manner.

► **Avoid emoticons and icons.** These features can be easily misunderstood and are not suitable for workplace communication.

COMPARING EMAIL AND TEXT MESSAGING

Email and text messaging are common forms of communication, both personally and on the job. Yet when deciding which one to use for a workplace situation, you may want to take a moment to consider a more detailed comparison about audience, purpose, and style. Table 18.1 will help you compare email and text messaging so you can choose the most appropriate tool for the situation.

COPYRIGHT AND PRIVACY IN DIGITAL COMMUNICATION

Because the various forms of digital communication discussed in this and the next two chapters are often written quickly and distributed widely, you need to keep in mind the importance of copyright and privacy issues.

Copyright protects many forms of work including digital communication

Copyright is a system of legal protection for original works of authorship (books, photographs, user manuals, music) that are "fixed in a tangible medium." In other words, copyright applies when an idea becomes recorded or written down or otherwise fixed, as in a printed book, an email message, a Web site, or a recorded piece of music.

TABLE 18.1 When to choose a text message or an email

Audience	Purpose	Writing style and content	Email or text?
Student	Let someone know you'll be late for a meeting	Brief, timely, to the point	Text message (short, no need for permanent record)
Instructor/professor	Ask about your grade on a quiz	Brief but polite	Email (provides a record, is more accessible because most instructors don't give out cell numbers)
Your manager	Indicate that you'd like to take a vacation day	Businesslike, to the point	Email unless your manager has specifically requested the use of texting
Coworkers	Start a discussion about a new project	Professional style and content	Email, in most instances
Customers or clients	Send a thank you note	Polite, with some detail	Email (or even paper letter)

In technical writing and communication, especially with digital communication, there are a few key aspects of copyright to be aware of. In the workplace, if you are a full-time employee, most of what you write and create is typically owned by the company. So be careful about posting material to a blog or Web site without first obtaining permission from the company. Also, you may find a photograph or piece of music or image on a Web site and think it's the perfect visual for the report you are writing. But unless your use is for educational purposes or the piece is clearly marked as "copyright free" or "in the public domain," you probably need to seek permission to use the item. (See pages 383 and 436–438 for more on fair use.)

If you are unsure about the copyright status of a work, it's best to consult with a librarian or with the author of the material, keeping in mind that sometimes the author is a corporate, not individual, author.

Digital communication also raises privacy issues. For example, avoid forwarding an email without checking with the sender first. Likewise, don't forward proprietary information (information that originates in your company) to unauthorized recipients outside the company. Texts are not always archived, but they can still be used to violate a sender's privacy or a company's confidential information.

Digital communication and workplace privacy

BE PREPARED FOR TECHNOLOGY TO FAIL

Have a backup plan when communicating digitally

Digital communication is "virtual" and can therefore disappear temporarily or permanently when technology fails. Before the advent of the Internet, paper copies and written notes allowed for a permanent record. Barring some disaster, once something was recorded, a physical document would be retrievable from the file cabinet.

Today we can rely on technology to preserve everything for us. However, computer crashes, server failures, faulty flash drives, and viruses compromise the permanence of virtual communications. So, have a backup plan. Use email rather than texts to record important ongoing conversations, and print out or back up digital work to an external hard drive or server routinely. Don't rely on continuous online access. Along with regular electronic backups, make regular print copies, too.

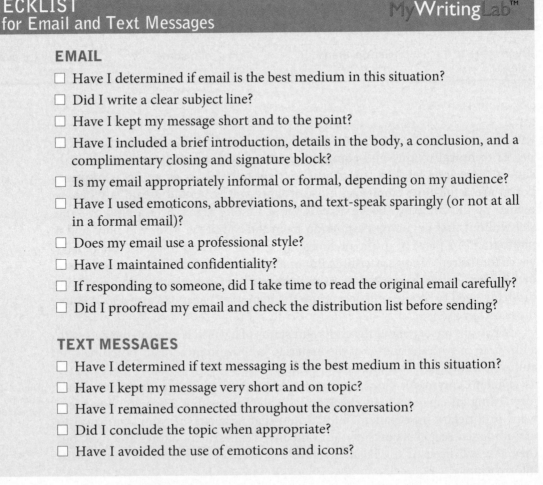

CHECKLIST
for Email and Text Messages

MyWritingLab™

EMAIL

☐ Have I determined if email is the best medium in this situation?

☐ Did I write a clear subject line?

☐ Have I kept my message short and to the point?

☐ Have I included a brief introduction, details in the body, a conclusion, and a complimentary closing and signature block?

☐ Is my email appropriately informal or formal, depending on my audience?

☐ Have I used emoticons, abbreviations, and text-speak sparingly (or not at all in a formal email)?

☐ Does my email use a professional style?

☐ Have I maintained confidentiality?

☐ If responding to someone, did I take time to read the original email carefully?

☐ Did I proofread my email and check the distribution list before sending?

TEXT MESSAGES

☐ Have I determined if text messaging is the best medium in this situation?

☐ Have I kept my message very short and on topic?

☐ Have I remained connected throughout the conversation?

☐ Did I conclude the topic when appropriate?

☐ Have I avoided the use of emoticons and icons?

 **APPLICATIONS**

GENERAL APPLICATIONS MyWritingLab™

1. Choose a topic and an audience, and write an email complaining about something that bothers you, written in a way that follows proper email format, includes all the required components, and avoids flaming.

2. Do some online research to learn how corporations are using text messaging for workplace communication. Write a brief recommendation report, arguing that your company or organization or department (you can invent a company or organization if you are not currently on the job) should or should not allow work-related text messaging.

TEAM APPLICATION

Work with a team to write a collaborative version of the complaint email (Application 1 in General Applications).

GLOBAL APPLICATION MyWritingLab™

Copyright and privacy are subject to the laws of a country or region. The Internet and other technologies complicate matters because data can easily travel around the world without regard for borders. The World Intellectual Property Organization (WIPO) is an international group that oversees the global implications of intellectual property issues. If you can, talk to a communication professional who deals with international audiences. Ask about any difficulties the person has encountered with copyright or privacy. Review the WIPO Web site with this professional, and ask how the information on this site might affect the way she or he would write, design, and distribute various digital communications.

DIGITAL AND SOCIAL MEDIA APPLICATION MyWritingLab™

Take Table 18.1 from this chapter, and expand on it to include other audiences/purposes where you might need to choose between sending a text or sending an email. Compare your additions to others in class.

MyWritingLab™ Visit Chapter 18, *Email and Text Messages*, in MyWritingLab to complete this chapter's applications, to explore this chapter's overview, checklist, and flashcards, and to test your understanding of the chapter objectives.

19 Blogs, Wikis, and Web Pages

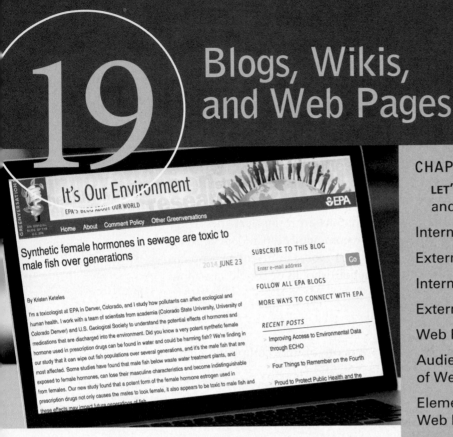

CHAPTER OUTLINE

LET'S GET STARTED: Blogs, Wikis, and Web Pages *363*

Internal Blogs *363*

External Blogs *364*

Internal Wikis *365*

External Wikis *365*

Web Pages *365*

Audience and Purpose of Web Pages *366*

Elements of Effective Web Pages *367*

Ethical Considerations *371*

STRATEGIES for Blogs, Wikis, and Web Pages *371*

CHECKLIST for Blogs Wikis, and Web Pages *373*

Applications *374*

LEARNING OBJECTIVES FOR THIS CHAPTER

▸ Differentiate between internal and external blogs and wikis

▸ Understand how to write for blogs and wikis

▸ Consider audience and purpose before designing and writing a Web page

▸ Design and write an effective Web page

LET'S GET STARTED
Blogs, Wikis, and Web Pages

Blogs, wikis, and Web pages can be useful tools to help companies and other organizations stay in touch with customers and reach potential new employees. Think of a group you are involved with—a club, a volunteer organization, a study group, a part-time or full-time job—and, in teams of three people, compile a list of ideas about how you might use a blog, wiki, or Web page to increase visibility for your organization.

Questions to ask may include the following:

► Why would we use a blog? A wiki? A Web page?

► What tone and style should we use when writing for these sites?

► Should we include visuals?

At the end of this chapter, review your initial Let's Get Started list with your instructor to see how much you might change or adapt your initial strategy based on what you have learned here.

B logs, wikis, and Web pages are important forms of workplace communication for companies and organizations. Blogs began as forums for people to write about and discuss political topics, hobbies, and personal interests. Today, blogs are also used to help employees network with each other (internal blogs) and stay in touch with customers and clients (external blogs). Wikis, both internal and external, allow organizations to keep technical and scientific content updated and current, based on input from individual contributors. Web pages are essential for almost all organizations, large or small, as ways to advertise, maintain a visible presence, and provide information to customers.

Advantages of blogs, wikis, and Web pages

INTERNAL BLOGS

Internal blogs enhance workflow and morale. In large organizations, blogs can provide an alternative to email for routine in-house communication. Anyone in the network can post a message or comment on other messages. In the blogging environment, meetings can be conducted without the time and location constraints of face-to-face meetings. Employee training can be delivered, and updates

How a blog can enhance a company's internal conversation

about company developments can be circulated. Blogs are especially useful for collaborating. For example, someone in a company's engineering department can create a forum to discuss various solutions to a technical problem.

EXTERNAL BLOGS

How a blog can enhance a company's public conversation

External blogs facilitate customer feedback on products and services, enhance marketing and public relations, and help personalize a large corporation in the eyes of customers and consumers. Blogs give businesses a chance to show a personal, informal side, to respond amiably and quickly to customer concerns, and to allow customers to provide ideas and feedback. Tone, of course, is critical in a corporate blog; it needs to sound friendly, welcoming, and sincere.

Marriott International, for example, has created a "Marriott on the Move" blog (Figure 19.1), which provides customers with updates about travel and hotel specials. The most prominent feature, as on any blog, is the daily post. Customers can make comments, providing the company with immediate feedback. In addition, this blog (like most) includes a search option, a sign-in feature for receiving email alerts, and an RSS feed option (RSS stands for "really simple syndication"

FIGURE 19.1 An external blog

Source: Reproduced with permission of Marriott International, Inc.

and is also known as a Web feed or a news feed.) Nonprofits and government organizations, such as the Centers for Disease Control and Prevention (CDC) and the National Wildlife Federation, also use blogs aimed primarily at external audiences and designed to keep the public updated on timely topics.

INTERNAL WIKIS

A wiki (from the Hawaiian phrase *wiki wiki*, meaning "quick") is used primarily to collect information and keep it updated. Most people are familiar with Wikipedia, an online encyclopedia for which anyone can write or revise the content. In the workplace, wikis also allow for the sharing and updating of content, but they serve a different function: to allow employees within a company (or outside the company, if given password access) to update information. Each person with access may log on to the wiki and make changes to content, overwriting previous versions. Despite the potential for abuse created by such alterations, a well-managed wiki can be a valuable resource among trustworthy contributors. To ensure that serial edits do not end up distorting the original posting, copies of the original along with each subsequent edit are saved for later reference.

How internal wikis enhance team communication

EXTERNAL WIKIS

While some wikis are used only internally by a company or organization, others are used by external audiences in specific scientific or technical areas. Because these wikis are open to countless people with knowledge in the fields, these sites can be excellent external sources of information. But as with Wikipedia, the lack of gatekeeping by a central editor also creates the potential for inaccuracy. A well-managed wiki, one that balances open access with editorial control, can be a valuable resource. If you search for a wiki related to your undergraduate major (nursing, chemistry, engineering, technical writing), you may find some useful resources. Or you may find that a Wikipedia entry on this topic contains a link to a more specific external wiki.

Advantages and disadvantages of using external wikis

WEB PAGES

Most organizations, whether private or public, large or small, have a Web site. When compared with print, online information can be updated quickly and easily. Also, Web sites are interactive: People can provide input, download files, place orders, and follow hyperlinks to new or related information. Figure 19.2 shows a Web page from the U.S. Food and Drug Administration on bug bites and bee stings. Interactive features include a list of consumer updates and questions that readers can click on for more information, a search box, and a resources section.

Advantages of Web pages

FIGURE 19.2
An interactive Web page

Links to more information →

Questions that readers might ask →

Downloadable newsletter →

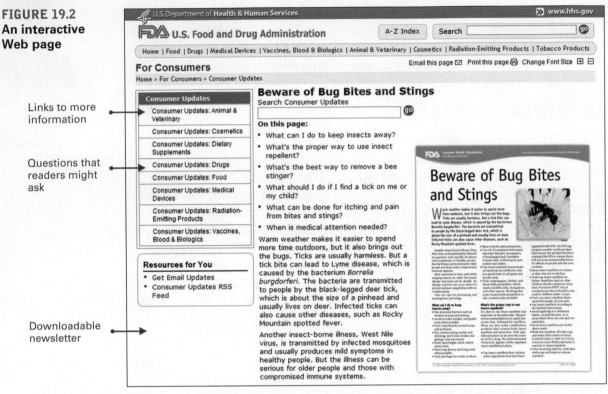

Source: U.S. Food and Drug Administration from <http://www.fda.gov/ForConsumers/ConsumerUpdates/ucm048022.htm>.

Note that *Web site* refers to an entire site with all related pages; *Web page* refers to one single page. The rest of this section discusses elements of effective Web page writing and design.

Web site development in the workplace

Web site development is a complex process that changes as related technologies change. Professional Web site development requires training in visual communication, information design, and programming. Moreover, Web development is primarily a collaborative process, often involving content providers, information architects, graphic designers, computer programmers, and marketers. Nevertheless, especially in small businesses and nonprofit organizations, writing and designing for the Web often become the responsibility of everyday employees. This section introduces the basics of writing and designing Web pages. The Strategies on pages 371–372 provide a basic overview of the process.

AUDIENCE AND PURPOSE OF WEB PAGES

As with any technical documents you must first think carefully about your intended audience and purpose before designing and writing a Web page.

Consider the audience for a Web page by filling out an Audience and Purpose Profile Sheet (see Chapter 3). Does the primary audience consist of potential customers or others who are seeking information, of people buying a product or service, of customers needing product support, or of some combination? Who is the secondary audience?

Will your audience members be proficient at navigating a complex Web page, or will they need a help menu and a feedback mechanism (email address, phone number) if they have questions? Will the page be read by audiences fluent in English or nonnative speakers of English or nonspeakers of English? Unless your page is aimed at a highly technical audience, use plain, noncolloquial English that is easily understood by anyone with basic English proficiency and easily translatable into other languages.

Is the Web page's purpose to publish information, explain a task, sell a product or promote an idea, solicit customer feedback, or some combination? If you want to sell something to technologically savvy young audiences, the page will need to convey a cutting-edge image, employing the latest Web technologies (animation, interaction, complex design). Begin by writing a purpose statement, such as "The purpose of this Web page is both to sell our new mp3 and video players to a young, hip audience and to provide instructions, contact information, downloads, and feedback options for those who already own one."

Audience considerations

Purpose considerations

ELEMENTS OF EFFECTIVE WEB PAGES

Both print documents and Web pages must follow the same basic principles of understandable structure (Chapter 5), readable style (Chapter 6), audience-centered visuals (Chapter 7), and a user-friendly design (Chapter 8). However, because Web pages and print pages are read differently, some of these elements play out differently in the online environment. As you read though this section, refer to Figure 19.3, a user-friendly Web page, and note how structure, style, visual, and design elements both resemble and differ from print pages.

Print documents versus Web pages

Structure

As discussed in Chapter 5, the three approaches in planning a print document's structure are outlining, chunking, and sequencing. This section discusses how these approaches apply to Web pages.

Outlining (Storyboarding). For a simple print document you would create a basic introduction–body–conclusion outline. A longer print document would require a more detailed formal outline using alphanumeric notation, as in Figure 5.3 in Chapter 5. But instead of outlining a Web page, create a storyboard (a handwritten sketch of the page, as in Figure 19.3). This type of storyboard for a Web site is often called a site map.

Create a storyboard rather than an outline

FIGURE 19.3
A storyboard sketch for a home page

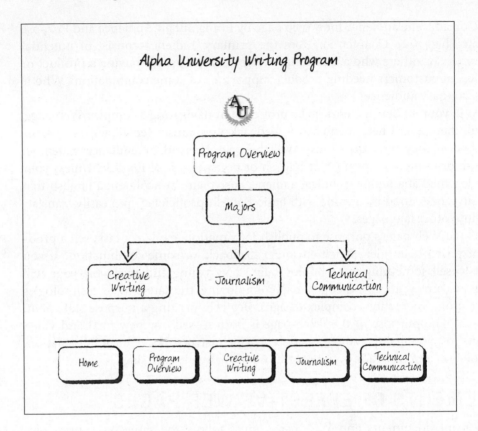

Why storyboards are important

Most of us have visited Web pages that have no apparent logical organization. A well-designed Web page is storyboarded in advance so that readers can follow the information flow and locate what they seek. The page should be organized so that its main purpose stands out.

In Figure 19.4, the home page of the National Park Service Web site, the name of the organization stands out prominently on the page in white text over a black background. This header and the pull-down menus directly beneath grab readers' attention and encourage them to explore the site further. Other information on the page has been storyboarded into subcategories for further exploration.

Always chunk informsation into small segments

Chunking. Readers expect information to be in small and easy-to-digest chunks. Computers are associated with speed, and users are impatient with long blocks of online information. Also, the flickering light patterns of computer screens tire the eyes.

How you chunk the information depends on how your audience will interact with the site. Imagine that you are writing text for a Web site intended to explain a medical procedure to patients. You decide to organize this information by questions users might ask: "How long will the surgery last?" or "When will I be able to return to work?" You would chunk your information into those categories, possibly making each an individual link.

Figure 19.4 chunks its content by News, Events, and Photos and Multimedia.

Sequencing. A print document follows a logical, linear sequence: spatial, chronological, problem-solution, or cause-and-effect. A Web page should also follow a logical sequence even though people tend not to read Web pages in linear fashion. A typical site displays information in a hypertext format, allowing readers to move from link to link, often randomly. Each chunk of text on a Web page must therefore make sense by itself, regardless of its order in the original sequence.

Use logical sequencing, but don't expect users to follow it

In Figure 19.4, the information is sequenced from general (Find a park) to specific (News; Events).

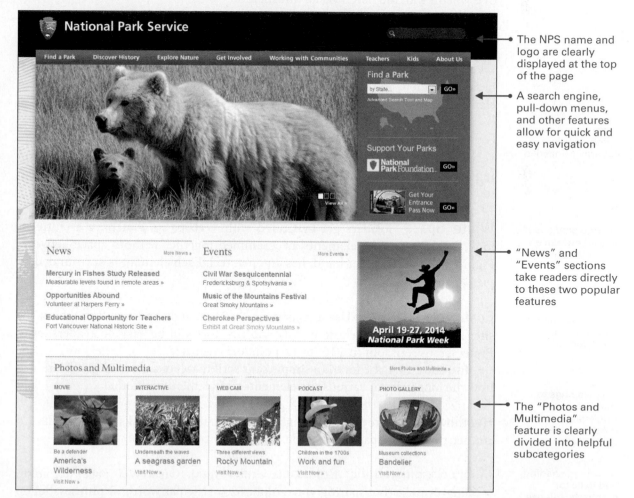

The NPS name and logo are clearly displayed at the top of the page

A search engine, pull-down menus, and other features allow for quick and easy navigation

"News" and "Events" sections take readers directly to these two popular features

The "Photos and Multimedia" feature is clearly divided into helpful subcategories

FIGURE 19.4 A user-friendly Web page

Source: From the National Park Service <www.nps.gov/index.htm>

Style

As explained previously, information on the Web must be presented in small, easy-to-digest chunks. Be especially attentive to conciseness by avoiding wordiness and eliminating repetition and redundancy. Figure 19.4 uses short headings and phrases to help readers find the section they are looking for.

Visuals

As discussed in Chapter 8, use visuals to perform a function rather than merely dress up the page. Figure 19.4 uses photos nicely, at the top of the page and then for each section. The photos help draw the reader to the page, but they do not overwhelm with too much visual information.

Design

Like printed documents, Web pages must be designed for consistency, cohesiveness, navigation, and emphasis (see Chapter 8); however, some individual design elements serve a different function online than in print documents.

Grid Patterns. Web pages typically use a combination of horizontal and vertical grid patterns, as in Figure 19.4. The key information on the page is presented horizontally and takes visual precedence; other information is presented in columns.

Combine grid patterns as needed

White Space. Readers get frustrated with Web pages that have a cluttered look, where too many elements are crammed together without space between. Figure 19.4, on the other hand, has an open feel. Each element is surrounded by plenty of white space.

Provide ample white space between all page elements

Font Style and Size. Use a consistent base font style and size throughout the site. In addition, choose a font style and size that will be easy on readers' eyes. Prefer a sans serif font in a 10- to 12-point or larger size.

In Figure 19.4, the font is a simple sans serif that looks professional. Note also how the font styles of various site elements complement each other.

Use a readable font style and size, and use it consistently

Headings. In Figure 19.4, headings set off each item, and links enable readers to connect to separate pages they want to view.

Use headings to chunk text on a single page, and links to connect to other pages

Color, Shading, Italic, Bold, and Underlining. On a Web page, use color, shading, or italic (but sparingly) to emphasize particular words or phrases, but do not use bold or underlining, which signifies a hyperlink.

Use color, shading, and italic for emphasis, but use bold or underlining for hyperlinks only

Bulleted and Numbered Lists. Bulleted and numbered lists enhance readability by extracting from a dense paragraph interrelated items or items that fall into a sequence or process. Because the Web environment calls for small chunks of texts and ease of reading on a screen, use lists generously.

Use bulleted and numbered lists to further chunk text

ETHICAL CONSIDERATIONS

The power of a Web page to convey information instantaneously and worldwide increases the writer's or designer's need for sound ethical judgment.

Consider the speed of the Internet, its global reach, and a Web page's ability to combine sound, color, images, text, and interactivity. These features create the potential for manipulation and distortion. Imagine a Web site for an herbal remedy that some people feel is helpful for anxiety. This herbal remedy may not have Food and Drug Administration approval and may have harmful side effects. But a Web site promoting this product could easily, and at very little cost, be set up to look extremely scientific and factual. Fancy logos from quasi-scientific organizations might give the page a sense of professional credibility. Statistics, charts, and links to other Web sites might create the appearance of a valid medical site. As a communicator setting up such a site, you need to question the possible risks for users.

How a Web page can be unethical

Web pages raise important privacy concerns as well, especially in regard to gathering the personal information of visitors to the site. Many organizations create privacy statements that can be accessed on their Web sites. Such statements let readers know how information will be used and what rights readers have. Privacy statements should be readily available on a site, and they should be written in language that anyone can understand. As a technical communicator, you may be asked to help write such a privacy statement.

Invasion of privacy

STRATEGIES
for Blogs, Wikis, and Web Pages

BLOGS AND WIKIS

▶ **When writing for blogs and wikis, keep content brief, to the point, and concise.** Avoid wordiness and repetition.

▶ **Write differently for internal versus external audiences.** Internal audiences do not require as much background. External audiences may need more explanation.

- **For an external blog, focus on the customer's priorities and needs.** A friendly, encouraging tone goes a long way in good customer relations.
- **Check blog and wiki entries for credibility.** Check the content to see when the blog or wiki was last updated (usually under the "history" tab on a wiki).

WEB PAGES

- **Identify the intended audience.** Who is the primary audience? Who is the secondary audience? Will your audience be Web savvy? Will the audience include worldwide readers?
- **Decide on the page's purpose.** Is the purpose to inform, instruct, persuade, or some combination?
- **Decide what the page will contain.** Will it display print only or a combination of print and graphics? Will it include audio and video? Will links be provided and, if so, how many and to where? Will user feedback be solicited and, if so, in what form: surveys, email comments, or other?
- **Create an understandable structure.** Map out your Web page with a storyboard that illustrates which parts of the page will go where and that provides ways to navigate. Chunk information into short passages that are easy to access and quick to read. Provide a logical sequence (even if readers won't necessarily follow the given sequence).
- **Write with a readable style.** Write clearly, concisely, fluently, and personably, with special emphasis on conciseness.
- **Use visuals.** Include visuals that serve a useful purpose, not merely a decorative one. Select simple and complementary colors.
- **Design a Web-friendly page.** Combine grid patterns as needed; provide ample margins, consistent justification, plenty of white space, consistent line spacing, and a simple and readable font. Use headings to chunk text on a single page, color/shading/italic for emphasis, and lists whenever appropriate.
- **Proofread your page.** Verify the accuracy of numbers, dates, and data; check for spelling or grammar errors.
- **Attend to ethical considerations.** Consider whether your page in any way exploits users. If you use copyrighted information, be aware of fair use guidelines. See pages 383 and 436–438 for more on copyright and fair use. When in doubt, request permission. If your page asks individuals for private information, create a privacy statement.
- **Maintain your page.** Review and update the page often and redesign as needed.

CHECKLIST
for Blogs, Wikis, and Web Pages

My WritingLab™

BLOGS AND WIKIS

☐ Have I determined if a blog or wiki should be internal (for employees only) or external (for outside audiences)?

☐ Are blog or wiki entries written clearly, avoiding wordiness and repetition?

☐ Have I checked blog or wiki entries for credibility and truthfulness?

☐ For external blogs or wikis, have I provided enough background and context for this audience?

☐ For external blogs or wikis, is the tone friendly, welcoming, and sincere?

☐ Have I determined if the blog or wiki should include an RSS feed?

WEB PAGES

☐ Have I assessed my audience and purpose before planning the Web page?

☐ Did I create a storyboard to plan the overall structure?

☐ Have I chunked information into small pieces for ease of reading on the Web?

☐ Did I sequence the information logically (even if it may not be read in its original order on the Web)?

☐ Have I followed the same style guidelines that apply to print documents, with special attention to conciseness?

☐ Did I use (but not overuse) visuals, including color?

☐ Have I used consistent grid patterns when creating multiple Web pages for the same site?

☐ Have I provided ample white space?

☐ Have I used a consistent and readable font style and size?

☐ Did I use headings to chunk text on a single Web page and links to navigate to other pages?

☐ Does the page include any color, shading, and italics to highlight key information?

☐ Have I avoided the use of bold and underlining, except to indicate hyperlinks?

☐ Have I provided a search option and links to other pages within or outside of my site?

☐ Have I attended to ethical considerations?

☐ Have I proofread the page before going "live"?

APPLICATIONS

GENERAL APPLICATIONS   MyWritingLab™

1. Locate one or more blogs related to technical communication or to your major. Follow the discussion for a few days, and write a brief analysis of the chosen blog, its intended audience, its content areas, and its value to members in the field.

2. With a classmate, locate one or two Web sites you might use as research sources for a project. Using the guidelines in this chapter, assess these Web sites for the quality of their structure, style, use of visuals, and design. Write up your findings in an email message to your instructor. Include the Web address for each of the sites you used.

TEAM APPLICATION

In teams of two, find a blog written for an external audience, similar to the blog shown in Figure 19.1. Analyze the writing style and tone of the blog. In what ways does the blog maintain a professional tone but still sound personal and friendly? Is the blog used mainly to provide updates, or is there also some commenting or other interaction on the site? How are visuals used on the blog? Write a short summary of your thoughts to share with class.

GLOBAL APPLICATION   MyWritingLab™

Blogs, wikis, and Web pages have global reach—you can use these tools to collaborate with team members from other countries. Locate a wiki related to your major. See if the wiki is available in languages other than English. Write a memo to your instructor explaining what you found.

DIGITAL AND SOCIAL MEDIA APPLICATION   MyWritingLab™

Do some research to develop your own "top 10" list of effective Web writing principles. Hint: Look online for Web writing guidelines by experts such as the Nielsen Norman Group, college and university sites, and others. Based on what you find, assemble your list. Using your list as a guide, find three Web sites that exemplify the principles of effective Web design and style. Prepare a short presentation on your exemplary sites, and explain why you selected them as examples.

MyWritingLab™   Visit Chapter 19, *Blogs, Wikis, and Web Pages,* in MyWritingLab to complete this chapter's applications, to explore this chapter's overview, checklist, and flashcards, and to test your understanding of the chapter objectives.

20 Social Media

CHAPTER OUTLINE

LET'S GET STARTED: Social
Media   *376*

Considering Audience
and Purpose   *377*

Social Media in Technical
and Workplace
Communication   *379*

Ethical and Legal Issues   *382*

STRATEGIES for Social Media   *383*

CHECKLIST for Social Media   *384*

Applications   *384*

LEARNING OBJECTIVES FOR THIS CHAPTER

▸ Understand audience and purpose considerations
when using social media

▸ Recognize the difference between social media for
personal use and for workplace use

▸ Understand how to use social media for workplace
communication

▸ Write for social media with professional style and
tone

▸ Identify social media that are most used for job
search and career advancement

▸ Understand appropriate ways of presenting
yourself and your company or organization on
social media

Social media offer an effective way to communicate with thousands of people, especially in situations where time is critical. Select a government agency (such as the Food and Drug Administration) that uses social media regularly to keep the public informed. Visit its Facebook page, read its Twitter feed, and look at any other social media it may be using. Make a list of items you notice about the writing style, use of visuals, and frequency of communication.

Questions to ask before reading this chapter may include the following:

- ▸ Does the writing style sound as if the posts were written by one person or several different people?
- ▸ How are visuals used on these sites?
- ▸ Do readers post comments? If so, how frequently?
- ▸ Can you tell whom the presumed audience is for most of these postings?

At the end of this chapter, review your initial Let's Get Started list with your instructor to see if you can add any items based on what you have learned here.

The phrase "social media" refers to Web sites and applications ("apps") that allow people to network and share information, updates, photos, videos, and more. The most popular social media sites for workplace communication include the following:

- Customer review sites, such as Yelp and TripAdvisor, which allow individuals to post reviews of restaurants, hotels, businesses, doctors, and more
- Facebook, originally developed for college students but now used by friends, family, professional associates, businesses, nonprofits, and other organizations
- Google+, a network that includes email, friends and workplace associates, document and photo sharing, and more
- *LinkedIn* and other job sites, used for professional networking, job postings, job searches, and resume and job application materials
- Twitter, used for sending short messages ("tweets") to people who subscribe to a particular Twitter feed
- YouTube, where videos about how to perform a task or how to understand a technical concept or idea are posted for viewing and public comment

Blogs and wikis, and even some Web pages, might also be considered social media, depending on how they are used. This chapter focuses on the more obvious forms of social media, listed above. See Chapter 19 for information about workplace blogs, wikis, and Web pages.

As you read this chapter, keep in mind that your interactions with social media in the workplace can take two forms: as a consumer and user of such sites (using *LinkedIn* for the job search, for instance) and as a creator and writer of such media (writing and maintaining your organization's Facebook site or Twitter feed).

Social media are playing an increasingly important role in the workplace. In technical communication, social media can serve as a resource for staying in touch with colleagues, acquiring information from technical experts, learning more about customer preferences, sharing updated information with customers, and keeping professionals connected. On the job, you might use social media to research a report or proposal, to post a job announcement, or to learn more about the professional background of a job candidate. You might also be asked to help create, maintain, update, and post to these sites.

Social media in the workplace

Social media can help organizations disseminate cutting-edge technical and scientific research—and get feedback from people who may not be experts but who have firsthand experience. In one case, the Mayo Clinic used Twitter to announce a new research study about celiac disease (an autoimmune disease that prevents the digestion of wheat gluten). Mayo was able to track how the Twitter messages spread and to send a prepublication copy of the article to select readers from the Twitter stream. Mayo gave these readers permission to blog about the study (adapted from Ruiz).

Increasingly, organizations are hiring social media directors to help determine the most strategic uses of social media to reach customers and others. These jobs will continue to be on the rise as social media use increases in the workplace. Social media directors require strong writing abilities, an ability to understand the complex nature of audience and purpose in online settings, and skills with digital technology. Technical communicators, engineers, medical professionals, and others with specialized expertise may at one time or another find themselves called to contribute to an organization's social media sites and strategies.

Jobs in social media

CONSIDERING AUDIENCE AND PURPOSE

Most organizations maintain a social media site to highlight or promote a particular product or service or to provide updates and keep in touch with customers. Initially, a social media site such as Facebook may be designed with one particular audience in mind. But when set up as open to the public, Facebook and other social media sites can be viewed by thousands (if not more) people. So, your audience and

Audience and purpose for social media

purpose may soon be far more expansive than originally envisioned. For example, the Centers for Disease Control and Prevention (CDC) reports that its initial Facebook page was set up for an audience interested in health and safety updates. But as interest grew, the organization had to expand its Facebook presence, eventually supporting "multiple Facebook profiles connecting users with information on a range of CDC health and safety topics" ("CDC Social Media Guidelines," 1).

For most large organizations, it has become imperative not only to have a social media presence but also to have a social media *policy*. From government agencies to colleges and universities to businesses, social media policies describe everything from appropriate use of visuals to the tone, style, and word count best suited when writing for that organization's social media site. Simon Fraser University (see Figure 20.1), for example, suggests limiting a Facebook

FIGURE 20.1
A sample social media policy

Source: Simon Fraser University

post to 35 words or less and keeping voice and tone professional and consistent, no matter how many people are maintaining and writing for the site (Simon Fraser University).

Audience as Contributor

External audience members can be important contributors to social media sites. For instance, many companies encourage customers to provide feedback via a customer review site, such as Yelp or TripAdvisor. Increasingly, product instructions and user documentation (see Chapter 13) are posted online, with a comment section available so readers can report on or update the documentation if they notice problems or errors. When audience members become contributors, there are more chances to collect important information. But there is also a greater need for fact-checking.

As one technical communication expert noted:

> "The challenge for the professional communicator is to contribute at a higher level, welcoming community involvement and building on it. For the technical writer, that may mean doing less writing and more curating of content—for example, identifying and promoting the best wiki contributions, correcting errors, clarifying unclear language, adding illustrations, and improving organization." (Carr)

See "Ethical and Legal Issues," page 382 in this chapter.

Impact of audience participation

SOCIAL MEDIA IN TECHNICAL AND WORKPLACE COMMUNICATION

The most common social media sites for workplace communication are discussed below.

Customer Review Sites

For companies such as restaurants, hotels, and entertainment venues, word of mouth can be the most important—or the most damaging—form of advertising. Customer review sites (Yelp and TripAdvisor are two of the most popular) allow registered members to post feedback in the form of short reviews. People can also rate the business using a number of stars. In some cases, companies are able to write a follow-up response, which can be especially important if the customer review is not favorable.

Business uses of Yelp and other customer review sites

Facebook

As previously mentioned, Facebook is used by government agencies, nonprofit organizations, and companies both large and small, across the United States and, increasingly, around the globe. Facebook provides a way to keep readers informed about news, updates, products and services, and so forth. Like customer review sites, Facebook also allows readers to participate on the site, posting questions and comments. Social media directors and others who manage the site often need to sift through these comments to ensure accuracy and keep "flame wars" and negative information to a minimum.

Another equally important feature of Facebook, however, involves your personal use. As a student, you may envision your audience as only those people you have chosen to see your posts (your friends or a custom list). But keep in mind that as with all social media, Facebook postings can travel far beyond your initial audience, and they can last for years. Many people have come to regret a Facebook posting when it comes time for a job interview.

Google+

Google+ is a suite of applications that includes email, document collaboration and sharing, and a network of friends and workplace associates that you can use to stay in touch and share information. Google+ allows you to create special lists of people you want to communicate with: for example, business associates, friends, acquaintances, and so on. In this way, you can customize the audience for your message. Google+ also offers real-time ways to interact with your audience, such as Google Hangouts and Google Chat.

LinkedIn and Other Job Sites

Social networking sites can help you stay connected, discover job openings, and advertise yourself. One popular professional networking site is *LinkedIn* (see Figure 20.2). On this and similar sites, you can keep your profile (work experience, references, and so forth) updated and make this profile available to professional contacts, potential employers, and job recruiters. Importantly, you can connect with former colleagues and classmates. These people are often your best bet for learning about job openings. Don't be shy about contacting people you don't know firsthand but with whom you have some mutual connection through a third party (a former coworker, for example).

Twitter is also becoming a popular tool for employment-related communication. Many companies use Twitter to announce job openings. By using Twitter, companies can reach hundreds of potential employees quickly and inexpensively.

FIGURE 20.2 *LinkedIn,* **a Professional Networking Site** *LinkedIn* and similar sites let you connect with potential employers as well as with other people in your field.

Twitter

As mentioned, Twitter can be used for employment information. Twitter also provides real-time postings and updates in a concise format. Individuals as well as companies, government agencies, and other organizations maintain Twitter feeds to keep friends, business associates, customers, and citizens informed and updated. Called "tweets," the form of writing on Twitter is concise, with a limit of 140 characters. A tweet may contain a Web address directing readers to a Web site for more information.

Twitter can be especially effective in situations that require a rapid response. For example, when a major weather event (such as a hurricane or blizzard) interrupts air travel, airlines become inundated with calls from customers. A Twitter feed can be a very effective method for providing customers with up-to-date information, by the minute, on flight cancellations, contingency plans, and resources for more information. See Figure 20.3—note the short, compact, informational tweets that are written with a professional, friendly tone.

Other uses of Twitter

FIGURE 20.3
Twitter feed during a weather emergency
Posts are written with a friendly yet professional style and tone.

PineTree Airways	**PT Airways** @PTAirways @ LauraG Sorry you can't get through by phone. Blizzard has slowed things down. Please rebook online if you can bit.ly/LGjEcl/11 ^CF
PineTree Airways	**PT Airways** @PTAirways @ NitaR International connections are still being rebooked. Check with a gate agent when you get in. ^CF
PineTree Airways	**PT Airways** @PTAirways @ AnetaD Please call us again at the new 800 no. we just posted on the website. Have your confirmation no. handy. ^MC
PineTree Airways	**PT Airways** @PTAirways @ greg_s Greg, did you check your flight status on our website? Here's the link bit.ly/XYZGEx ^MC
PineTree Airways	**PT Airways** @PTAirways @ joan_kc MSP is providing meals and blankets if you are stranded. Please see a gate agent. Thank you for your patience. ^CF
PineTree Airways	**PT Airways** @PTAirways @ Geoff_travels Geoff, that flight is delayed two hours. Keep checking our website if you can bit.ly/LGjEcl/11 thank you. ^CF
PineTree Airways	**PT Airways** @PTAirways Dear customers, as storm conditions improve, we will be updating all flight statuses so please stay tuned to Twitter and our website.

YouTube

Using YouTube to post instructions

For workplace communication, YouTube offers an easy-to-access site where customers can watch videos that help explain a concept or demonstrate how to perform a task. Many organizations create video instructions in addition to print or online user guides. Viewers can post comments and ideas to the video's Web page; these comments provide valuable feedback on the product or idea being featured and give audience members a chance to offer their input directly to the company or organization.

ETHICAL AND LEGAL ISSUES

Potential for information abuse

Social media can be an effective way to reach customers, stay connected, and do research. But it also harbors potential for information abuse. One such example is "stealth marketing," in which bloggers who publish supposedly objective product reviews fail to disclose the free merchandise or cash payments they received for their flattering portrayals.

People need to be able to trust the information they receive. Furthermore, in workplace settings, coworkers need to have confidence in the discretion of their colleagues. As with email, any employee who discusses proprietary matters (see page 359) or who posts defamatory comments can face serious legal consequences—not to mention job termination. Also like email, social media create the potential for violations of copyright or privacy (see page 359). To avoid such problems, corporate blogs often have a moderator who screens any comment before it is posted.

Social media and privacy

To reinforce ethical, legal, and privacy standards, organizations such as IBM, the American Red Cross, Dell, and many others have created social media guidelines and policies. Recognizing the particular challenge of protecting patient privacy, the American Nurses Association and the National Council of State Boards of Nursing created special guidelines on social media and networking specific for nurses ("News Release").

Many companies view social media as an opportunity to reach thousands of potential customers—but not without risk. Employees assigned to work on social marketing may waste incredible amounts of time reading Facebook pages and looking at Twitter feeds. Also, if companies make a mistake (say, an inaccurate claim about a product) on a social network, those potential customers can turn the mistake into a public relations nightmare (Baker 48–50).

STRATEGIES for Social Media

▶ **Write with a friendly yet professional tone.** It's always nice to be friendly, but a professional tone will make your message more credible.

▶ **Keep ideas focused and specific.** Social media let you narrow your message down to a targeted audience (say, customers who use a specific model of laptop).

▶ **Be discreet about what you post.** When posting to your personal Facebook or other page, remember to omit private or potentially damaging information. It may be fun to tell your friends how many parties you've attended, but when you apply for a job, this information may come back to haunt you.

▶ **Keep global readers in mind.** Social media can typically be viewed by readers from across many countries and cultures. Keep the content accessible to a wide audience (see Chapter 1 for more on global audiences).

▶ **Have a social media policy.** No matter the size of your organization, having clear, accessible social media guidelines will ensure that social media communication is professional and consistent (both in content and in tone and style).

▶ **Choose the most appropriate format for your message.** A short tweet can reach thousands of readers quickly, but you'll need a link to another site (your Facebook page, say) for more information.

CHECKLIST
for Social Media

MyWritingLab™

☐ When creating a social media site for a company or organization, have I written content and used images that are professional and appropriate?

☐ When creating a social media site for myself, have I used the right site for the right purpose (e.g., *LinkedIn* for professional networking and job hunting)?

☐ For personal use, does the information I've posted portray me in a way that I would want a potential employer to see?

☐ For a workplace social media post, is my writing friendly yet professional in tone?

☐ Have I kept ideas focused and specific?

☐ For tweets that refer to a longer topic, have I included a link for more information?

☐ Have I used language and images that are appropriate for a global audience?

☐ Does my post or tweet adhere to the company's social media policy?

☐ Have I considered legal and ethical issues?

APPLICATIONS

GENERAL APPLICATION

MyWritingLab™

Explore several job-related social media sites (e.g., *LinkedIn*, Ryze, Spoke). What are the differences among these sites? For instance, all may offer to help you see your network of professional contacts, but does one of these sites offer a better visual display of connections? Do all of these sites let you upload your resume and provide a list of references? If you have an account with any of these, look at your profile to see how well it reflects your current experience and career goals. Make a list of five to six qualities that students should consider when writing and posting to professional networking sites.

TEAM APPLICATION

Work with a partner to look at your Facebook page and your partner's Facebook page. Imagine that you are managers interested in hiring new college students for a trainee position in your department. What do these Facebook pages tell you about these potential employees? What aspects of Facebook pages—pictures, text, connections—should college students consider during their transition from being a student to being a potential employee? Write a short summary of your thoughts, and share it with the class.

GLOBAL APPLICATION   MyWritingLab™

Customer review sites are written and read by people around the globe. If you are a social media director for a company, you'll need to read these reviews and write professional, thoughtful responses. Look up a service, restaurant, hotel, or other business using Yelp or TripAdvisor. Find one that has a mix of reviews (some good, some not so good). Did someone from the company write a response? If so, is it appropriate in tone and style for a global audience? Keeping a global audience in mind, write your own response to one or several of these (do not post it), and discuss it with a group of three to four students.

DIGITAL AND SOCIAL MEDIA APPLICATION   MyWritingLab™

Go to the Web site for the company or organization you used for the Global Application above. Does it have a published social media policy? If so, compare this with the posts you found on the customer review site. If not, draft a set of social media guidelines for this organization, and share it with your instructor. Search online for other social media guidelines and policies of similar organizations to help you think of topics that your guidelines should cover. Pay special attention to issues of word choice, tone, and privacy.

MyWritingLab™   Visit Chapter 20, *Social Media*, in MyWritingLab to complete this chapter's applications, to explore this chapter's overview, checklist, and flashcards, and to test your understanding of the chapter objectives.

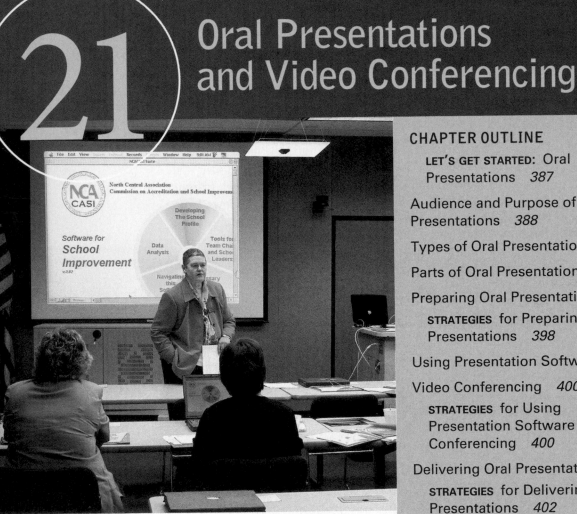

21

Oral Presentations and Video Conferencing

CHAPTER OUTLINE

LET'S GET STARTED: Oral Presentations *387*

Audience and Purpose of Oral Presentations *388*

Types of Oral Presentations *388*

Parts of Oral Presentations *391*

Preparing Oral Presentations *392*

STRATEGIES for Preparing Oral Presentations *398*

Using Presentation Software *399*

Video Conferencing *400*

STRATEGIES for Using Presentation Software and Video Conferencing *400*

Delivering Oral Presentations *401*

STRATEGIES for Delivering Oral Presentations *402*

CHECKLIST for Oral Presentations *402*

Applications *403*

LEARNING OBJECTIVES FOR THIS CHAPTER

► Analyze the audience and purpose of an oral presentation

► Organize an oral presentation logically

► Prepare for an oral presentation

► Use presentation software effectively

► Deliver a confident, professional oral presentation

LET'S GET STARTED
Oral Presentations

Most workplace professionals are required at some point to give an oral presentation. Before reading this chapter, take an informal report, formal report, or proposal that you have written, and use it as a basis for a presentation that you would give in class or at work. Create an outline for the oral presentation.

Questions to ask as you write the outline may include the following:

▸ Who is the audience, and how will my presentation make the content interesting and understandable for this audience?

▸ Do I need any additional research?

▸ What is the primary purpose of this presentation: informative, instructive, or persuasive? If persuasive, am I trying to persuade the audience to accept a point, take action, or buy something?

▸ Is the purpose of my presentation clear right from the start?

▸ Does my introduction create interest and provide an overview of the presentation?

▸ Are the transitions between sections clear?

▸ Have I created a clear, brief conclusion?

At the end of this chapter, review your initial Let's Get Started outline with your instructor or with a group of students to see how much you might change or modify the outline based on what you have learned from the chapter.

I n addition to being good writers and designers, technical communicators need to present their ideas effectively in person. The skills required to give an effective oral presentation include thorough research, strong organization, and stage presence. You may be asked to make oral presentations at meetings in your department or company (status reports, team meetings, and so on), at professional conferences or meetings, to your community, or in the classroom.

The importance of oral presentations in the workplace

Unlike written documents, oral presentations are interactive. Face-to-face communication is arguably the richest form of interaction because you can give and receive information via body language, vocal inflection, eye contact, and other physical

The interactive nature of oral presentations

means. Moreover, there is room for give and take, which does not happen with written documents. Oral presentations allow you to see how your audience reacts. You can get immediate feedback, and you can change or amend your ideas on the spot.

Presentations involve careful preparation

Most professionals use presentation software such as Microsoft PowerPoint or Apple Keynote when giving a presentation. But despite the visual appeal and easy-to-use templates such products offer, you still need to create a presentation that is well researched, clearly organized, and professionally delivered.

AUDIENCE AND PURPOSE OF ORAL PRESENTATIONS

Analyzing audience and purpose is a slightly different proposition when speaking rather than writing. Therefore, use the amended version of the Audience and Purpose Profile Sheet provided in Figure 21.1

Audience considerations

Do all you can to find out exactly who will be attending your presentation. Determine their roles within the organization. Learn about their attitudes and personal experiences regarding your subject. For example, managers may focus on the bottom line, while engineers may care more about the difficulties involved in the project you are proposing. Oral presentations are often delivered to a mixed group, so consider the attitudes of the group as a whole and speak to the needs of various factions. The group is also likely to consist of people from various cultural and linguistic backgrounds, so be sure to account for these differences.

Purpose considerations

Determine whether your purpose is to inform, instruct, or persuade. Does your audience simply need some vital information? If so, provide enough detail and explanation for people to understand the information clearly. Will they use your information to perform a task? If so, focus on the task itself and send background and other information via email after the presentation. Is your goal to influence your audience's thinking or sell something? If so, be sure to have all the specifications, costs, and other data that will help audience members make their decision. In short, knowing clearly what you wish to accomplish will help you formulate a definite plan for your presentation.

TYPES OF ORAL PRESENTATIONS

Five types of oral presentations

Your primary purpose will determine the type of presentation required: an informative presentation, a training presentation, a persuasive presentation, an action plan presentation, or a sales presentation.

Informative Presentations

Informative presentations provide facts and explanations

Informative presentations are often given at conferences, product update meetings, briefings, or class lectures. Your goal is to be as impartial as possible and to

FIGURE 21.1
Audience and purpose profile sheet for an oral presentation

AUDIENCE

Primary audience members: _____
(names, titles)

Secondary audience members: _____

_____

Are most attendees of this presentation members of the same team or group?
Y   N

Relationship with audience members: _____
(client, employer, other)

Technical background of audience: _____
(layperson, expert, other)

Cultural background of audience: _____

How many people will attend: 2–6   7–12   13–20   more than 20

PURPOSE

Primary purpose: _____ (informative, training,
persuasive, action plan, sales)

Secondary purpose(s): _____

Intended use of presentation: _____ (to inform or
educate; to persuade; to propose an action; to sell something)

ROOM or LOCATION for presentation

Conference tables, theater style, or other. Describe. _____

_____

EQUIPMENT AND TECHNOLOGY

Laptop or flash drive

Speakers or projector

Flip chart

Whiteboard or chalkboard

provide the best information you can locate. If your primary purpose is informative, observe these criteria:

- Keep the title of the presentation clear and factual.
- Stipulate at the outset that your purpose is simply to provide information.
- Be clear about your sources of information.

Training Presentations

Training presentations show how to perform a task

Training (or instructional) presentations can cover such topics as how to ensure on-the-job safety, how to use a specific software application, or how to exit a capsized kayak. Some technical communicators specialize in giving training presentations. If your primary purpose is instructional, follow these guidelines:

- Use a title that indicates the training purpose of the presentation.
- Provide an overview of the learning outcomes—what participants can expect to learn from the presentation.
- Create slides or a handout that participants can reference later when they are trying to perform the task(s) on their own.

Persuasive Presentations

Persuasive presentations attempt to gain support or change an opinion

To influence people's thinking, give a persuasive presentation. For example, an engineer at a nuclear power plant may wish to persuade her peers that a standard procedure is unsafe and should be changed. In a persuasive situation, be sure to perform adequate research so that you are well informed on all sides of the issue. If your primary purpose is persuasive, follow these guidelines:

- Be clear from the start that you are promoting a point of view.
- Use research and visual data (charts, graphs, etc.) to support your stance.
- Consider and address counterarguments in advance ("Some might say that this approach won't work, but here is why it will"), and be prepared to take questions that challenge your point of view.

Action Plan Presentations

Action plan presentations motivate people to take action

To get something done, give an action plan presentation. For example, if you wanted your company to address a design flaw in one of its products, you would give a presentation that outlined the problem, presented a specific solution, and encouraged listeners to implement the solution. If your primary purpose is to evoke action, follow these guidelines:

- Be clear up front about your purpose ("My primary purpose today is to ask you to act on this matter").
- Present the research to back up the need for your plan.
- Show that you have considered other plans but that yours is most effective.
- In closing, restate what you want your audience to do.

Sales Presentations

Technical sales presentations need to be well researched. (At many high-tech companies, technical sales representatives are often scientists or engineers who understand the product's complexities and also are good communicators). If your primary purpose is to sell something, observe these criteria:

Sales presentations inform and persuade

- Let the facts tell the story. Use examples to illustrate why your product or service is the right one.
- Know your product or service—and those of your competitors—inside and out. Thorough knowledge and a well-researched competitive analysis will make your presentation that much more persuasive.
- Display sincere interest in the needs and concerns of your customers.
- Provide plenty of time for questions. You may think you have made an airtight case, but you will need extra face-to-face time to field questions and convince skeptical audience members.

PARTS OF ORAL PRESENTATIONS

Like most technical documents, oral presentations should follow an introduction–body–conclusion structure.

Introduction

For introducing most presentations, pay attention to three main tasks:

Set the stage

1. Capture your audience's attention by telling a quick story, asking a question, or relating your topic to a current event or to something else the audience cares about.
2. Establish your credibility by stating your credentials or explaining where you obtained your information.
3. Preview your presentation by listing the main points and the overall conclusion.

An effective introduction might sound like this:

> How many times have you searched for medical information on the Web, only to find that after hours online you can't locate anything useful? If you're like most Americans polled in a recent survey, you may feel that you are wasting time when it comes to online medical information. My name is Travis Armstrong, and I've been researching this topic for some time. Today, I'd like to share my findings with you by covering three main points: how to search for medical information, how to separate good information from bad, and how to contribute to medical discussions online.

Body

Use small chunks and transitions in the body

Readers who get confused or want to know the scope of a print document can look back at the headings, table of contents, or previous pages. But oral presentations have no such features. To make your presentation easy to follow, structure the material into small chunks. To signal that you are moving from one main point to another, use transition statements such as, "Now that I've explained how to separate good information from bad, let me suggest how you can contribute to medical discussions on the Internet."

Conclusion

Tie everything together

Your conclusion should return full circle to your introduction. Remind your audience of the big picture, restate the main points you've just covered, and leave listeners with some final advice or tips for locating more information. You can also distribute handouts at this time.

PREPARING ORAL PRESENTATIONS

Preparing an oral presentation is a step-by-step process that requires research, planning, and rehearsal.

Research and Connect the Topic to Your Audience

Know your topic

Be prepared to support each assertion, opinion, conclusion, and recommendation with solid evidence. Begin gathering material well ahead of time. Use recognized sources, such as newspaper articles, peer-reviewed journals, industry fact sheets, government documents, and interviews. Check your facts for accuracy. If you will be using presentation software or handouts, you will need to indicate your information sources on the slides or handouts (typically as footnotes at the bottom of the slide or page). Keep track of your sources.

Relate the topic to your audience

Even the most well-researched presentation won't be effective unless the speaker connects the topic to the interests, backgrounds, and technical levels of the audience. Look back at your Audience and Purpose Profile Sheet and think about ways you can connect to ideas already familiar to your audience.

Create an Outline or Storyboard

If your presentation is a spoken version of a written report, you can use the outline from the written report. Otherwise, organize your ideas in terms of A- and B-level headings. Indicate on the outline any places where you want to use a visual. If you plan to use presentation software, go to "outline mode" or "outline view" to start laying out your presentation.

Use an outline to organize your thoughts

If your presentation includes multiple visuals, you might create a storyboard rather than an outline. Storyboards help you see how the visuals will complement the spoken content. A simple storyboard (Figure 21.3) for an oral presentation consists of a double-column format in which your discussion is outlined in the left column and the specific supporting visuals are described in the right column.

Use a storyboard to accommodate multiple visuals

Figure 21.2 is an outline for a short oral presentation with only a few slides and visuals, whereas Figure 21.3 is a partial storyboard for a longer oral presentation involving many visuals.

I. Introduction

   A. Introduce myself

   B. Open with a question ("How do students use social media in college?")

   C. Give audience overview of my presentation's organization

II. Body

   A. Discuss the types of social media used most frequently by today's college students

   B. Talk about social media and the college experience (e.g. meeting your roommate via Facebook; using LinkedIn for jobs and internships)

   C. Discuss several national surveys on social media and college students

   D. Present survey findings on social media and privacy

   E. Show some of the University's social media sites that students may not be familiar with

III. Conclusion

   A. Restate my main points

   B. Tell audience that I will take questions for the last 15 minutes

FIGURE 21.2
An outline for a short oral presentation

Pollution Threats to Local Groundwater

1.0   Introduce the Problem

    1.1   Do you know what you are drinking when you turn on the tap and fill the glass?

    1.2   The quality of our water is good but not guaranteed to last forever.

    1.3   Cape Cod's rapid population growth poses a serious threat to our freshwater supply.   (slide: *a line graph showing 20 year population growth*)

    1.4   Measurable pollution in some town water supplies has already occurred.   (slide: *two side-by-side tables showing 20 year increases in nitrate and chloride concentrations in three town wells*)

    1.5   What are the major causes and consequences of this problem, and what can we do about it?   (poster: *a multicolored list that previews my five subtopics*)

2.0   Describe the Aquifer

    2.1   The groundwater is collected and held in an aquifer.

        2.1.1.   This porous rock formation creates a broad, continuous arch beneath the entire Cape.   (slide: *a cutaway view of the aquifer's geology*)

FIGURE 21.3 A partial storyboard for a long oral presentation

Determine a Delivery Style

Use an appropriate delivery style

Your presentation's effectiveness will depend largely on how well it connects with listeners. Different styles of delivery (memorized, impromptu, scripted, and extemporaneous) create different connections.

Memorized delivery style

A memorized delivery takes a long time to prepare, offers no chance for revision during the presentation, and spells disaster if you lose your place. Avoid a memorized delivery style in workplace settings.

Impromptu delivery style

An impromptu (off-the-cuff) delivery style can be a natural way of connecting with listeners—but only when you really know your material, feel comfortable with your audience, and are in an informal speaking situation. Avoid an impromptu delivery style when making complex and formal presentations, no matter how well you know the material.

Scripted delivery style

In some formal settings (a speech, a keynote address, a conference paper), it may be appropriate for you to read your material verbatim from a prepared script. A scripted delivery can help you keep strict control over your material and meet time limits, but it offers little chance for audience interaction and can be boring. If you do plan to read aloud, rehearse until you are able to glance up from the script periodically without losing your place.

An extemporaneous delivery style is carefully planned, practiced, and based on notes that keep you on track. In this natural way of addressing an audience, you glance at your material and speak in a conversational manner. Extemporaneous delivery is based on key ideas in sentence or topic outline form, often projected as overhead transparencies or as slides generated from presentation software.

Extemporaneous delivery style

An extemporaneous delivery is typically the preferred method for oral presentations in the workplace: it provides somewhat of a script for the speaker and allows the speaker to interact with the audience while following along. However, there are dangers, such as losing track, skipping over a key point, or going over a time limit.

Table 21.1 summarizes the various uses and drawbacks of the latter three delivery styles (memorized style should always be avoided and is therefore not included). In many instances, some combination of methods can be effective. For example, in an orientation for new employees, you might prefer the flexibility of an extemporaneous format but also read a scripted passage aloud from time to time.

TABLE 21.1 Advantages and drawbacks of delivery styles

Delivery Method	* Main Uses *	• Main Drawbacks •
IMPROMPTU (inventing as you speak)	* in-house meetings * small, intimate groups * simple topics	• offers no chance to prepare • speaker might ramble • speaker might lose track
SCRIPTED (reading verbatim from a written work)	* formal speeches * large, unfamiliar groups * strict time limit * cross-cultural audiences * highly nervous speaker	• takes a long time to prepare • speaker can't move around • limits human contact • can appear stiff and unnatural • might bore listeners • makes working with visuals difficult
EXTEMPORANEOUS (speaking from an outline of key points)	* face-to-face presentations * medium-sized, familiar groups * moderately complex topics * somewhat flexible time limit * visually based presentations	• speaker might lose track • speaker might leave something out • speaker might exceed time limit • speaker might fumble with notes, visuals, or equipment

Choose Your Technology

Use the technology that suits your audience and purpose

Although presentation software is a helpful and popular tool (see the section on presentation software in this chapter), there are other options. For example, you might opt for a more natural, extemporaneous presentation in which you use handouts or flip charts. Or you might decide to sketch on a whiteboard or show a short video clip. Think about your audience: What would work best? What would keep people active, engaged, and listening?

Plan the Use of Visuals

Use visuals to enhance the presentation

Visuals not only add vigor and impact to a presentation, but they also summarize complex information and set a tone. Although visuals are an important component, they can also be overused or misused. A presentation that simply uses one visual after the other could bore or confuse an audience. Likewise, visuals that carry no real meaning or that are hard to see or decipher will frustrate the audience. Seek a balance of text/speech and visuals that enhance the presentation rather than distracting from it. Figure 21.4 uses one visual, a photograph of students using social media, to help break up the text on this slide and create visual interest.

**FIGURE 21.4
Four PowerPoint slides from a short oral presentation**
Note that for the full presentation, each bullet point on Slide 2 would have a corresponding slide as part of the body of the presentation.

Title page introduces the speaker and topic

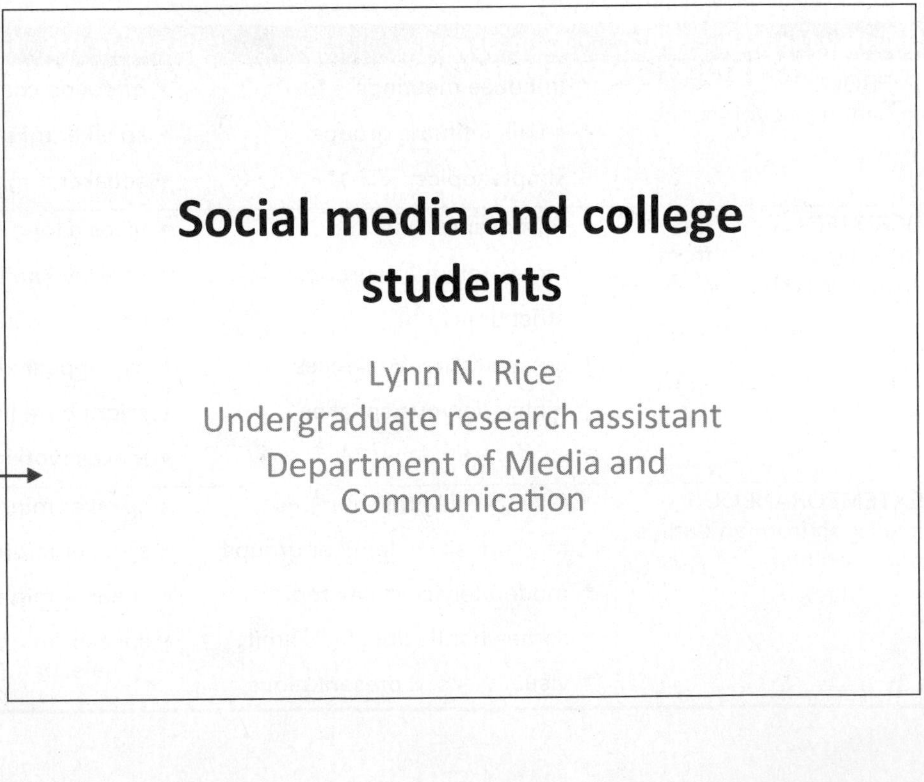

Social media and college students

Lynn N. Rice
Undergraduate research assistant
Department of Media and Communication

1.

Social media in college

- How do students use social media in college? ◄—— Overview slide previews the main points to be covered
  - Commonly used forms of social media
  - Connection of social media to the college experience
  - What we know from national surveys
  - Other social media sites at the University

2.

What do students use the most?

- Most commonly used sites by college students: ◄—— First slide from body of the presentation
  - Facebook
  - Twitter
  - LinkedIn

Source: Duggan, M., & Smith, A. (2013). Social media update 2013. Pew Internet & American Life Project.
Retrieved from http://www.pewinternet.org/2013/12/30/social-media-update-2013/. ◄—— Source information is set in smaller type at the bottom of the slide

3.

Conclusion slide
offers questions but
invites other input

Questions and discussion

- What are your experiences with social media on campus?
- How do you feel about privacy and social media?
- Other questions

4.

Practice the Presentation

Rehearse to fine-tune

On your own or with a volunteer viewer, practice your presentation. This process will give you an idea of how you sound and look while speaking; it will also reveal gaps or wordiness in your presentation and help you get the timing right. If possible, make an audio or video recording of yourself to see if you speak too fast or too slow or if you gesture too much or look stiff. Try to rehearse with the actual equipment you plan to use and in the actual setting.

STRATEGIES
for Preparing Oral Presentations

▶ **Determine your audience.** Fill out the audience portion of an Audience and Purpose Profile Sheet. Know exactly who your listeners are (primary and secondary), what their attitude is toward the topic, what they already know, and what they need to learn. If you anticipate that different audience members will have different needs, make sure you speak to the entire audience.

▸ **Determine your purpose.** Is the purpose of the presentation to inform, instruct, or persuade? Adjust your presentation to suit its particular purpose.

▸ **Do your research.** Make sure you understand your topic. Anticipate audience questions or objections, and prepare answers or responses.

▸ **Decide on your delivery style.** Avoid the memorized style, as you may lose your place. Choose an impromptu, scripted, or extemporaneous style, but recognize the pros and cons of each.

▸ **Organize your presentation.** Include an introduction, body, and conclusion. Prepare an outline (typical presentation) or storyboard (visually complex presentation) to work out what information to discuss and when.

▸ **Choose your technology.** You need not always use presentation software. Consider alternatives such as handouts, flip charts, or whiteboards.

▸ **Use visuals.** Whenever possible, enhance your presentation by using visuals, but only when they genuinely add to the discussion. Be sure that all your visuals are easy for the audience to see and understand.

▸ **Rehearse your presentation.** Practice, and correct any content or style problems based on your rehearsal.

USING PRESENTATION SOFTWARE

PowerPoint, a Microsoft product, is still the most widely used presentation software (Figure 21.4 was created using PowerPoint). Yet other software, such as Apple's Keynote or Open Office's Impress, is also used by students and professionals. These products run on a desktop or laptop computer; you can share files via email or a file-sharing site. Another approach is a program called Prezi that offers creative tools for animation and transitions. Google also has a presentation program, available through an Internet connection via Google Docs. Prezi, Google, and other such programs allow you to collaborate on a presentation because everyone on the team can access the same file without searching through old emails to find an attachment.

Overview of presentation software

Whatever software you choose, remember that good presentations are based on the qualities discussed previously in this chapter. They must be well researched, carefully planned, well organized, and correctly timed. Excessive material crammed on one slide might help you as you speak but will frustrate your audience. Also, while presentation software helps structure the speaker's story or argument, an overreliance on bulleted items can oversimplify complex issues and distract from the deeper message. In short, use the software as a tool, not as the brains of the operation. Don't let presentation software do the thinking for you.

For specific advice, see the Strategies for Using Presentation Software on pages 400–401.

VIDEO CONFERENCING

When audience members are at different job sites (around the country or in different countries), a face-to-face presentation may not be possible. Video conferencing allows team members to join the meeting but not be physically present. There are many kinds of video conferencing including the following:

- **Webinars** allow you to deliver a presentation via the Internet. Audience members are invited to connect to the Webinar via their computer and software such as WebEx, GoToMeeting, or Adobe Connect. Most Webinars display the presenter's slides on the screen while the presenter talks through each slide and controls when to change slides. You can also display video of the speaker and/or other conference participants. Audience questions are typically handled via video chat or a typed live chat feature.

- **Skype** allows people to connect via real-time audio and video from a computer, phone, or tablet. Skype software needs to be downloaded in advance, and each person needs to set up a user name and password. Skype has become quite popular, in part because it is free (and easy to use). But the sound and image quality may not always be adequate for complex technical and business presentations. Most companies prefer a Webinar or other secure in-house video conferencing approach.

- For video conferencing to work, everyone must be available at the same time. If you are on the east coast of the United States, for example, and some of your audience is in Europe, there could be anywhere from a five- to eight-hour time difference. Video conferencing with audiences in Asia requires even more careful time calculations. Depending on the location of team members, it may be impossible to get everyone to connect at the same time. In these cases, you may be able to record a session and allow people to view it, and your slides, later.

STRATEGIES
for Using Presentation Software and Video Conferencing

▸ **Don't let the software do the thinking.** Use your own research, sense of audience and purpose, and other original ideas to shape the presentation. Then use the software to help make the material accessible and interesting. The shape and content should come from you, not from the software.

▸ **Have a backup plan in case the technology fails.** Bring handouts to the presentation, and be prepared to give the presentation without the software. Don't distribute handouts until you are ready to discuss them; otherwise, people will start reading the handouts instead of paying attention to you.

➤

▸ **Start with an overview slide.** Orient your audience by showing an opening slide that indicates what you plan to cover and in what order.

▸ **Find a balance between text and visuals.** Excessive text is boring; excessive visuals can be confusing. Each visual should serve a purpose: to summarize information, to add emphasis, to set a tone, and so on. Avoid overcrowding the slides: Aim for no more than seven to nine lines per slide (including the heading) with no more than six to nine words per bulleted item.

▸ **Avoid using too many slides.** In general, aim for one slide per key point. If you are the kind of person who likes to embellish and enjoys speaking to a crowd, use fewer slides.

▸ **Don't simply read the slides.** The slides are there to keep you and your audience oriented and to highlight key points. But you should elaborate upon each slide, adding and analyzing details.

▸ **Avoid too much flash.** Don't allow the medium (animations, color, sound) to obscure your message.

▸ **Keep viewers oriented.** Don't show a slide until you are ready to discuss it. Present one topic per slide, bringing bullets (subtopics) on one at a time as you discuss them. Let your audience digest the slide data *while* you speak, not before or after.

▸ **End with a "conclusions" or "questions" slide.** Give your audience a sense of having come full circle. On a "conclusions" slide, summarize the key points. A "questions" slide can simply provide a heading and a visual. Allow time at the end of your presentation for questions and/or comments.

▸ **Use video conferencing when necessary.** If people can't be in the same place at the same time, use a video conferencing solution (a Webinar, for example) to allow all team members to participate in the presentation.

▸ **For video conferencing, keep international audience members in mind.** Remember that 9:00 A.M. your time may not work for people who live on the other side of the globe.

DELIVERING ORAL PRESENTATIONS

Many find that the actual delivery of an oral presentation is the most difficult hurdle. Most people experience anxiety when they must speak in public. If you are particularly nervous, seek additional advice about ways to calm your nerves, such as stretching beforehand and performing deep breathing exercises. You are likely to find that once you have actually spoken your first line, you will settle down quickly. The following Strategies offer further advice.

STRATEGIES
for Delivering Oral Presentations

▸ **Be rehearsed and prepared.** The best way to calm your nerves is to remind yourself of the preparation and research you have done. Practice your delivery so that it is professional and appropriate but natural for you. Also, know your material inside and out.

▸ **Memorize a brief introduction.** If you begin your presentation smoothly and confidently, you won't be as nervous going forward. Do not open by saying "I'm a little bit nervous today" or "I have a slight cold. Can everyone hear me in the back?" Just begin. A memorized introduction will help you avoid having to ad lib (potentially badly) when you are most anxious.

▸ **Dress for success.** Wear clothes that suggest professionalism and confidence.

▸ **Stand tall and use eye contact.** Good posture and frequent eye contact convey a sense of poise, balance, and confidence. Practice in front of a mirror. If looking people directly in the eye makes you nervous, aim just above people's heads. Or find a friendly face or two and look at those people first. As you gain confidence, be sure to cast your gaze around the entire room or conference table.

▸ **Take charge.** If you get interrupted but don't want to take questions until the end, remember that you are in control. Be polite but firm: "Thank you for that good question. I'll save it and other questions until the end of my presentation."

▸ **Gesture naturally.** Don't force yourself to move around or be theatrical if this is not your style. But do not stand like a robot, either. Unless you are speaking from a podium or lectern, move around just a bit. And when it's time to take questions, consider moving closer to the audience. In a conference room setting, if everyone else is seated, you should stand.

▸ **Allow time for questions, comments, and discussion.** Announce a time limit; listen carefully; ask for clarification if necessary; provide brief but well-considered replies (if time allows-otherwise continue later and in private). When the time isup, announce that you have time for one more question or comment, and conclude politely.

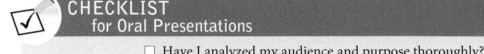

CHECKLIST
for Oral Presentations

☐ Have I analyzed my audience and purpose thoroughly?

☐ Have I done adequate research about the topic, looking into all sides of the problem or issue?

☐ Have I organized my material, using an outline or storyboard?

CHECKLIST *continued*

☐ Have I chosen a delivery style that best suits my skills and the needs of my audience?

☐ Have I decided to use presentation software (e.g., PowerPoint) or to use more basic technology or no technology at all?

☐ Am I using an appropriate number of visuals, and do the visuals serve a specific purpose?

☐ Have I rehearsed my presentation and ironed out problems with content and delivery?

☐ If using presentation software, have I followed the strategies given in this chapter?

☐ Have I calmed my nerves and gained confidence by following the strategies for delivering presentations in this chapter?

☐ Am I prepared to allow time for questions and comments and to interact with my audience effectively when doing so?

APPLICATIONS

GENERAL APPLICATIONS

MyWritingLab™

1. Prepare an oral presentation based on the formal report or proposal you wrote for this class. Develop an outline and a storyboard that includes at least three visuals. Ask your instructor for the time limit of the presentation (15 minutes? 20 minutes?), and practice so that you do not exceed the allotted time. Make note of places where you tend to struggle or places where you speak for too long.

2. At work, on an internship, or at a campus event, observe a lecture or speech, and evaluate it according to the Strategies boxes in this chapter. In a memo to your instructor (without naming the speaker), identify strong and weak areas and suggest improvements.

TEAM APPLICATION

In today's work world, presentations are often prepared by, and sometimes delivered by, more than one person. In groups of three to four people, come up with a simple presentation topic that everyone can work on. (You might want to base this topic on a group writing activity from the semester.) Discuss how, as a team, you will approach the research, planning, and creation of the presentation. For example, will one person be responsible for the research? Will another person put the slides together? Create a brief presentation for your instructor and classmates (using presentation software), describing the process you will take and the decisions that your team made.

GLOBAL APPLICATION   MyWritingLab™

You've been assigned to represent your company at an international conference or before international clients. As you plan and prepare your presentation, what can you do to remain sensitive to various cultural expectations? For example, some cultures might be offended by a presentation that gets right to the point without first observing formalities of politeness. Use the Internet to research issues about intercultural communication, then create a short presentation on this topic for the class.

SOCIAL AND DIGITAL MEDIA APPLICATION   MyWritingLab™

As noted in the Team Application above, presentations are often created collaboratively. What is the best way to share a presentation file and work on it as a group? Compare your options using PowerPoint, Prezi, Google drive, and other tools or sites. Create a short presentation for the class recommending what would work best for students on your campus.

MyWritingLab™   Visit Chapter 21, *Oral Presentations and Video Conferencing*, in MyWritingLab to complete this chapter's applications, to explore this chapter's overview, checklist, and flashcards, and to test your understanding of the chapter objectives.

A Documenting Sources*

WHAT IS PLAGIARISM?

When creating technical documents, especially more formal, longer documents such as reports, you will need to rely on outside research. To make your case credible, use outside sources wisely and avoid plagiarizing the work of others.

Plagiarism is using someone else's work—words, ideas, or illustrations, published or unpublished—without giving the creator of that work sufficient credit. A serious breach of scholarly ethics, plagiarism can have severe consequences. Students risk a failing grade or disciplinary action ranging from suspension to expulsion; a record of such action can adversely affect future professional opportunities. Scholars and teachers can face public disgrace and even be forced out of a position. Elsewhere in the workplace, plagiarism can lead to a lawsuit as well as permanent career damage.

Plagiarism violates three significant values: preserving intellectual honesty, giving credit to the work of others, and promoting intellectual growth. First, the academic community relies on the reciprocal exchange of ideas and information to advance knowledge and research. Using material without acknowledging its source violates this expectation and consequently makes it harder for researchers to verify and build on others' results. In addition, plagiarism cheats writers and researchers of the credit they deserve for their work and creativity. Even with the writer's permission, presenting another's work as one's own is equivalent to lying: it's a form of dishonesty. Finally, and perhaps most important for students, plagiarizing negates the very reason for attending college. A student who hands in a plagiarized paper has missed an opportunity for growth and learning.

---

*Portions of this appendix were written by Linda Stern, Publishing School of Continuing and Professional Studies, New York University, and adapted by the authors.

OUTLINE

What Is Plagiarism? *405*

Identifying Sources and Information to Be Documented *406*

Taking Effective and Accurate Notes *406*

   STRATEGIES for Taking Notes *407*

Quoting, Paraphrasing, and Summarizing Properly *408*

   STRATEGIES for Quoting the Work of Others *409*

   STRATEGIES for Paraphrasing the Work of Others *410*

   STRATEGIES for Summarizing the Work of Others *411*

Documentation: The Key to Avoiding Plagiarism *411*

MLA Documentation Style *413*

APA Documentation Style *425*

Other Documentation Styles *436*

Recognizing Copyright Issues *436*

Plagiarism is easy to Spot

Ethical considerations aside, it's hard to get away with plagiarism. Experienced professors can easily tell when a paper is not written in a student's own style or is more professionally prepared than they would expect. In addition, online services can now identify plagiarized papers, and academic institutions are subscribing to such services.

Most plagiarism is unintentional. To avoid plagiarism, you need to do all of the following:

Ways to avoid unintentional plagiarism

- Identify sources and information to be documented in your paper.
- Take effective and accurate notes.
- Understand how to quote, paraphrase, and summarize properly.
- Know how to document sources both in the text itself and at the end of your report.

IDENTIFYING SOURCES AND INFORMATION TO BE DOCUMENTED

The importance of documentation

Documentation is the key to avoiding plagiarism. The legal doctrine of *fair use* (see page 437) allows writers to quote or paraphrase a limited amount of another's work in their own papers and books. To make sure that they are not plagiarizing someone else's work, writers must therefore take care to document every source they consult accurately and clearly. Documentation involves providing readers with sufficient information about the sources you have consulted; consequently, readers may consult those sources themselves if they so desire. This sort of documentation ordinarily requires two elements: (1) an end-of-report list of sources used in the report (known as a Works Cited or References list) and (2) citations in the text of the report that link to the items in that end-of-report list.

What needs to be documented and what does not

Whenever you use information from an *outside source* (any source that isn't your own brain), you need to document that source. Some major outside sources that researchers often consult are discussed in Chapter 2 and include books, newspapers, magazines, government sources, radio or television programs, material from electronic databases, correspondence, films, plays, interviews, speeches, surveys, and Web sites. The one major exception to this rule is that you do not have to document *common knowledge*: widely known information about current events, famous people, geographical facts, or familiar history. When in doubt, the safest strategy is to provide documentation. (For more on what you should document, see page 412.)

TAKING EFFECTIVE AND ACCURATE NOTES

Why note-taking is important

Another key way to avoid unintentional plagiarism is to take notes systematically. Do not rely on your memory to keep track of the sources you consult and the information you want to use from those sources. Take detailed notes that identify the specific material and its sources; otherwise you may forget about a source you learned something from, thereby unintentionally plagiarizing.

Because most research today is done electronically, you need to be especially careful about taking notes if you cut and paste quotations or other material from an electronic source. Whether this source is a Web page, a blog or wiki, or a journal article available in electronic format, be sure to keep track of the author (individual or organizational), Web address, and date when you accessed the information. If the publication is a traditional one in e-format (such as the electronic version of the *New York Times*), record the title, page number, and other publication information needed for the citation.

Using old-fashioned notecards is one way to record your sources and the material you want to use. Figure A.1 shows a notecard entry for a bibliographic citation.

How to take notes

> Pinsky, Mark A. *The EMF Book: What You Should Know about Electromagnetic Fields, Electromagnetic Radiation, and Your Health.* Warner, 1995.

Record each bibliographic citation exactly as it will appear in your final report.

FIGURE A.1 A bibliographic citation

Researchers also take notes using citation software (such as Endnote, Zotero, and Mendeley). These programs allow you to search and retrieve your entries by author, title, topic, date, and other fields. You can also use these tools to generate in-text citations and references lists. Another option is to take notes in a word-processing file, then use the "Find" command to locate information quickly. Be careful when cutting and pasting direct quotes to mark these as such. Include all citation information.

Using citation software to take notes

STRATEGIES
for Taking Notes

▸ **Keep copies of your documentation information.** For all sources that you use, keep photocopies or accurate notes of the title and copyright pages and the pages with quotations you need. Highlight the relevant citation information in color. Keep these materials until you've completed your report.

▸ **Create the Works Cited or References list first.** Before you start writing your report, create a working bibliography, a list of possible sources to which you add entries as they emerge. When you finalize your list, you can delete entries for sources that you've decided not to use.

▸ **Record bibliographical information for each source you consult.** Use the citation format that will appear in your document. Record the information accurately so you won't have to track down a source at the last minute. When searching online, print out or save the full bibliographic record for each source or copy and paste the Web address into your document, thereby ensuring an accurate citation.

▸ **Determine whether to quote, paraphrase, or summarize.** When quoting others directly, be sure to record words and punctuation accurately. When restating material in your own words (paraphrasing and summarizing), preserve the original meaning and emphasis. Double-check if any portions of paraphrases or summaries are actually quotations, and insert the necessary quotation marks.

QUOTING, PARAPHRASING, AND SUMMARIZING PROPERLY

Three ways to use outside sources

To avoid plagiarism, you must use material from outside sources properly. You can integrate outside material into your paper in three ways: by quoting, paraphrasing, or summarizing. Each method must accurately convey the meaning expressed in the original source.

Quoting the Work of Others

Definition of a quotation

A *quotation* reproduces a portion of a source, using the exact words, for a purpose of your own: to support a statement or idea, to provide an example, to advance an argument, or to add interest or color to a discussion. A quotation can range in length from a word or phrase to several paragraphs. In general, quote the least amount that gets your point across.

In your notes, place quotation marks around all exact wording you borrow, whether the words were written or spoken (as in an interview or presentation) or appeared in electronic form. Even a single borrowed sentence or phrase or a single word used in a special way requires quotation marks, with the exact source properly cited. These sources include people with whom you collaborate. Figure A.2 shows notes for a quotation. Notes can be taken by typing your information in a word processing document.

**FIGURE A.2
Notes for a
quotation**

In your notes, place quotation marks around all directly quoted material.

> **Pinsky, Mark A. pp. 29–30**
>
> "Neither electromagnetic fields nor electromagnetic radiation causes cancer per se, most researchers agree. What they may do is promote cancer. Cancer is a multistage process that requires an 'initiator' that makes a cell or group of cells abnormal. Everyone has cancerous cells in his or her body. Cancer—the disease as we think of it—occurs when these cancerous cells grow uncontrollably."

STRATEGIES
for Quoting the Work of Others

▸ **Use a direct quotation only when absolutely necessary.** Sometimes a direct quotation is the only way to do justice to the author's words or thoughts. Use direct quotations to preserve the original line of reasoning, special phrasing or emphasis, precise meaning, or an especially striking or colorful example. Direct quotes convey the authority and complexity of expert opinion and can capture the original's voice, sincerity, or emotional intensity.

▸ **Copy the material from your source to your document exactly as it appears in the original.** Do not alter the original spelling, capitalization, or punctuation. If a quotation contains an obvious error, you may insert [*sic*], which is Latin for "so" or "thus," to show that the error appeared in the original. Record the exact page numbers, and double-check that you haven't altered the original expression in any way.

▸ **Use ellipses to keep quotations as brief as possible.** An ellipsis is three spaced periods (. . .) indicating that words have been omitted within a single sentence. Add a fourth period to indicate the end of a sentence or the omission of more than a sentence. The resulting passage must be grammatical and must not distort the original meaning. (For more on ellipses, see page 452.)

▸ **Use square brackets to insert your own clarifying comments or transitions.** To distinguish your words from those of your source, place them within brackets—for example, "This occupation [campus police officer] requires excellent judgment."

▸ **Integrate quoted material into your writing smoothly and grammatically.** Quotations must blend seamlessly into your text so that the resulting sentence is neither ungrammatical nor awkward, and punctuation must be handled properly. (For more on grammar and punctuation, see Appendix B.)

▸ **In your paper, set off long quotations as block quotations.** Avoid relying on long quotations except when you want to provide an extended example or definition or to analyze or discuss a particular idea or concept. Start on a separate line. Double-space and indent the entire block ten spaces. Do not indent the first line of the passage, and do not use quotation marks.

▸ **Cite the source of each quoted passage.** Immediately follow each quotation with a parenthetical reference (see pages 413 and 425) indicating the source.

Paraphrasing the Work of Others

Research is a process of independent thinking in which you work with the ideas of others to reach your own conclusions. Therefore, unless the author's exact wording is essential, try to paraphrase instead of quoting borrowed material. A *paraphrase* is a restatement, in your own words and your own sentence structure, of specific ideas or information from a source. The chief purpose of a

Definition of a
Paraphrase

paraphrase is to *maintain your own writing style* throughout your paper. A paraphrase can be about as long as the original passage.

Paraphrasing means more than changing or shuffling a few words; it means restating the original idea in your own words—sometimes in a clearer, more direct, and emphatic way—and giving full credit to the source. To offer as a paraphrase an original passage only slightly altered is plagiarism. Equally unethical is offering a paraphrase, though documented, that distorts the original meaning.

Figure A.3 shows notes in which the quotation in Figure A.2 has been paraphrased. Paraphrased material is not enclosed within quotation marks, but it is documented to acknowledge your debt to the source.

Signal the beginning of the paraphrase by identifying the source and the end by citing the location.

> According to Pinsky, most researchers doubt that cancer is caused by either electromagnetic fields or electromagnetic radiation. These electrical currents, however, may "promote" cancer by initiating the "multistage process" that leads to the proliferation of cancer cells that are otherwise present in small amounts in the healthy human body (29–30).

FIGURE A.3 Notes for a paraphrase

STRATEGIES
for Paraphrasing the Work of Others

- **Retain key words from the original to preserve its meaning.** Use quotation marks within your paraphrase to indicate quoted material.

- **Use your own words and sentence structure.** Do not duplicate the source's words (unless quoting briefly), and write the sentences in your own style.

- **Make sure your readers know when the paraphrase begins and ends.** Identify the source at the start of the paraphrase or as early into it as possible.

- **Be sure to preserve the author's original intent.** Check that your paraphrase is an accurate and objective restatement of the source's specific ideas.

- **Indicate the exact source of each paraphrased passage.** Immediately follow each paraphrase with a parenthetical reference (see pages 413 and 425) indicating the exact location of the material in the source.

Summarizing the Work of Others

Definition of a summary

Like a paraphrase, a *summary* is a restatement of the original in your own words. A summary, however, restates a large portion of the original text briefly, rather than restating a small portion of the original in about the same number of words. Figure A.4 shows notes in which the quotation in Figure A.2 has been summarized.

For more information on summarizing see Chapter 14.

Pinsky explains that electromagnetic waves probably do not directly cause cancer. However, they might contribute to the uncontrollable growth of cancer cells that are normally present—but controlled—in the human body (29–30).

Signal the beginning of the summary by identifying the source and the end by citing the location.

FIGURE A.4 Notes for a summary

STRATEGIES
for Summarizing the Work of Others

▶ **Use your own words and sentence structure.** If you must quote a crucial word or phrase directly, use quotation marks around the quoted words.

▶ **Make sure your readers know when the summary begins and ends.** As with a paraphrase, identify the source early in the summary.

▶ **Make sure your summary is an accurate restatement of the source's main ideas.** Do not add new details or remove essential details from the original.

▶ **Indicate the exact source of the summarized material.** Immediately follow each summary with a parenthetical reference (see pages 413 and 425) indicating the exact location of the material in the source.

DOCUMENTATION: THE KEY TO AVOIDING PLAGIARISM

Proper documentation satisfies professional requirements for ethics, efficiency, and authority.

Why You Should Document

Documentation is a matter of *ethics*, in that the originator of borrowed material deserves full credit and recognition. Moreover, all published material is protected by copyright law. Failure to credit a source could make you liable to legal action, even if your omission was unintentional. (For more on copyright, see page 436.)

Ethical reasons

Documentation is also a matter of *efficiency*. Accurate documentation provides a network for organizing and locating the world's recorded knowledge. If you cite a particular source correctly, your reference will enable interested readers to locate that source themselves.

Efficiency reasons

Finally, documentation is a matter of *authority*. In making any claim (say, "A Mercedes is more reliable than a Ford") you invite challenge: "Says who?" Data on road tests, frequency of repairs, resale value, workmanship, and owner comments can help validate your claim by showing its basis in *fact*. A claim's credibility

Authority reasons

increases in relation to the expert references supporting it. For a controversial topic, you may need to cite several authorities who hold various views. Readers of your research report expect the *complete picture.*

What You Should Document

Document any ideas or works that are not your own

Document any insight, assertion, fact, finding, interpretation, judgment, or other "appropriated material that readers might otherwise mistake for your own" (Gibaldi & Achtert, 3rd ed., 155)—whether the material appears in published form or not. Specifically, you must document these sources:

Sources that require documentation

- any source from which you use exact wording
- any source from which you adapt material in your own words
- any visual illustration: charts, graphs, drawings, or the like

How to document a confidential source

In some instances, you might have reason to preserve the anonymity of unpublished sources—say, to allow people to respond candidly without fear of reprisal (as with employee criticism of a company) or to protect their privacy (as with certain material from email inquiries or electronic newsgroups). You must still document the fact that you are not the originator of this material. Using MLA style (see page 413), you would provide a general acknowledgment in the text ("A number of employees expressed frustration with …"), along with a general citation in your list of Works Cited ("Interviews with department employees, May 2014"). Using APA style (see page 425), you would cite the confidential source in your text itself ("During interviews with department employees in May 2014 …").

Common knowledge need not be documented

As stated previously in this appendix, you don't need to document anything considered *common knowledge* (material that appears repeatedly in general sources). In medicine, for instance, it has become common knowledge that foods containing animal fat (meat, butter, cheese, whole milk) raise blood cholesterol levels. So in a research report on fatty diets and heart disease, you probably would not need to document that well-known fact. But you would document information about how the fat-cholesterol connection was discovered, what subsequent studies have found (say, on the role of saturated versus unsaturated fats), and any information for which some other person could claim specific credit. If the borrowed material can be found in only one specific source and not in multiple sources, document it. When in doubt, document the source.

How You Should Document

Document in text and at the end of the text

Cite borrowed material twice: at the exact place you use that material and at the end of your report. Documentation practices vary widely, but all systems work almost identically in the following respect: A brief in-text reference names the source and refers readers to the complete citation at the end of the report, which allows readers to consult the source if they so desire.

This appendix illustrates citations and entries for two styles that are widely used for documenting sources in professional writing:

- Modern Language Association (MLA) style for the humanities
- American Psychological Association (APA) style for social sciences

Unless your audience or your company has a preference, any style can be adapted to most research writing. Use one style consistently throughout your document.

MLA DOCUMENTATION STYLE

The *MLA Handbook*, 8th ed. (2016), requires that you cite a source briefly in your text (called parenthetical references or in-text citations) and fully at the end of the report (in a "Works Cited" list).

MLA Parenthetical References

For clear and informative parenthetical references, observe these guidelines:

- If you name the author in your discussion, do not repeat the name in your parenthetical reference; simply give the page or page range:

  Lederman points out that data provided by 796 colleges indicate that violent crime on campus began increasing rapidly around 1985 (31).

  Citing page numbers only

- If you cite two or more works in a single parenthetical reference, separate the citations with semicolons:

  (Gomez 293–94; Jones 32; Leduc 41)

  Three works in a single reference

- If you cite two or more authors with the same surname, include the first initial in your parenthetical reference to each author:

  (R. Jones 32)
  (S. Jones 14–15)

  Two authors with identical surnames

- If you cite two or more works by the same author, include the first significant word from each work's title or a shortened version of the title:

  (Lamont, *Biophysics* 100–01)
  (Lamont, *Diagnostic Tests* 81)

  Two works by one author

- If the work is by an institutional or corporate author or if it is unsigned (that is, if the author is unknown), use only the first few words of the institutional name or the work's title in your parenthetical reference:

Institutional, corporate, or anonymous author

(American Medical Association 2)

("Distribution Systems" 18)

Keep parenthetical references short

To avoid distracting the reader, keep each parenthetical reference as brief as possible. One method is to name the source in your discussion and to place only the page number in parentheses.

Where to place a parenthetical reference

For a paraphrase, place the parenthetical reference *before* the closing punctuation mark. For a quotation in the text, place the reference *between* the final quotation mark and the closing punctuation mark. For a quotation set off (indented) from the text, place the reference *after* the closing punctuation mark.

MLA Works Cited Entries

How to format the Works Cited list

The Works Cited list includes each source that you have paraphrased or quoted. Place your Works Cited list on a separate page at the end of the document. Arrange entries alphabetically by author's surname. When the author is unknown, list the title alphabetically according to its first word. For a title that begins with a numeral, alphabetize the entry as if the number were spelled out. Type the first line of each entry flush with the left margin. Indent the second and subsequent lines 1/2 inch. Double-space within and between entries.

How to cite individual items

Certain "core elements" of publication information, according to the *MLA Handbook*, 8th ed., should be included in every source citation, no matter what the delivery method (print or digital). These elements include the author and title of the source, the title of the larger entity (which MLA calls a *container*; for example, a journal, newspaper, website, or anthology where the source resides), the names of additional contributors when relevant, the publisher and publication date, and the page numbers or Web address (what MLA terms the *location*).

Table A.1 provides an overview of typical citation types; the rest of this section offers examples based on the MLA guidelines. The introductory section on digital sources (page 421) provides more detail on what the MLA calls the "core elements" of MLA citation style.

What to include in an MLA citation for a book

MLA Works Cited Entries for Books. Book citations should contain the information shown in the following examples. Note that unlike previous MLA handbooks, the 8th edition does not require city of publication unless that information is critical for your reader. (E-books are addressed later in this chapter.)

TABLE A.1 INDEX TO MLA WORKS CITED ENTRIES

BOOKS

1. Book, single author
2. Book, two authors
3. Book, three or more authors
4. Book, anonymous author
5. Multiple books, same author
6. Book, one or more editors
7. Book, indirect source
8. Anthology selection or book chapter

PERIODICALS

9. Article, magazine
10. Article, journal with new pagination each issue
11. Article, journal with continuous pagination
12. Article, newspaper

OTHER SOURCES

13. Encyclopedia, dictionary, other alphabetical reference
14. Report
15. Conference presentation
16. Interview, personally conducted
17. Interview, published
18. Letter, unpublished
19. Questionnaire
20. Brochure or pamphlet
21. Lecture
22. Government document
23. Document with corporate or foundation authorship
24. Map or other visual aid
25. Dissertation or thesis

DIGITAL SOURCES

26. Online abstract
27. Online article
28. Reference database
29. Online video (YouTube or other)
30. E-book
31. Personal email
32. Wiki
33. Blog
34. Podcast
35. Tweet
36. Web sites and other digital formats

1. Book, Single Author—MLA

Kerzin-Fontana, Jane B. *Technology Management: A Handbook.* 3rd ed.

American Management Assn., 2010.

Parenthetical reference: (Kerzin-Fontana 3-4)

2. Book, Two Authors—MLA

Vogel, Werner, and Henry Kalb. *Large-Scale Solar Thermal Power:*

Technologies, Costs and Development. Wiley-VCH, 2010.

Parenthetical reference: (Vogel and Kalb 71-88)

In general, use the publisher's name as it appears on the title page. For university presses, use the abbreviation *UP*. For page numbers with more than two digits, give only the final two digits for the second number when the first digit is identical.

3. Book, Three or More Authors—MLA

Santos, Ruth J., et al. *Environmental Crises in Developing Countries.*
Harper, 2009.

Parenthetical reference: (Santos et al. 9)

Et al. is the abbreviated form of the Latin *et alia*, meaning "and others."

4. Book, Anonymous Author—MLA

Structured Programming. Meredith, 2010.

Parenthetical reference: (*Structured* 67)

5. Multiple Books, Same Author—MLA

Chang, John W. *Biophysics.* Little Brown, 2009.

---. *Diagnostic Techniques.* Radon, 1999.

Parenthetical reference: (Chang, *Biophysics* 123-26) (Chang, *Diagnostic* 87)

When citing more than one work by the same author, do not repeat the author's name; simply type three hyphens followed by a period. List the works alphabetically by title.

6. Book, One or More Editors—MLA

Morris, A. J., and Louise B. Pardin-Walker, editors. *Handbook of New
Information Technology.* Harper, 2012.

Parenthetical reference: (Morris and Pardin-Walker 34)

For more than three editors, name only the first, followed by *et al.*

7. Book, Indirect Source—MLA

Kline, Thomas. *Automated Systems.* Rhodes, 1999.

Stubbs, John. *White-Collar Productivity.* Harris, 2002.

Parenthetical reference: (qtd. in Stubbs 116)

When your source (as in Stubbs, above) has quoted or cited another source, list each source in its appropriate alphabetical place in the Works Cited list. Use the name of the original source (here, Kline) in your text, and begin the parenthetical reference with *qtd. in* (or *cited in* for a paraphrase).

8. Anthology Selection or Book Chapter—MLA

Bowman, Joel P. "Electronic Conferencing." *Communication and
    Technology: Today and Tomorrow*, edited by Al Williams. Assn.
    for Business Communication, 1994, pp. 123-42.

Parenthetical reference: (Bowman 129)

The page numbers in the complete citation are for the selection cited from the anthology.

MLA Works Cited Entries for Periodicals.

Give all available information in this order: author, article title (in quotation marks), periodical title (in italics), volume and issue, date (day, month, year), and page numbers for the entire article—not just pages cited.

What to include in
an MLA citation for
a periodical

9. Article, Magazine—MLA

DesMarteau, Kathleen. "Study Links Sewing Machine Use to Alzheimer's
    Disease." *Bobbin*, Oct. 1994, pp. 36-38.

Parenthetical reference: (DesMarteau 36)

Use commas to separate the title of the magazine or journal and the date, and to separate the date and the page numbers. If no author is given, list all other information:

"Video Games for the Next Decade." *Power Technology Magazine*, 18 Oct.
    2009, p. 18+.

Parenthetical reference: ("Video Games" 18)

This article began on page 18 and continued on page 21. When an article does not appear on consecutive pages, give only the number of the first page, followed immediately by a plus sign. Use a three-letter abbreviation for all months except May, June, and July.

10. Article, Journal with New Pagination Each Issue—MLA

Thackman-White, Joan R. "Computer-Assisted Research." *American Library
    Journal*, vol. 51, no. 1, 2010, pp. 3-9.

Parenthetical reference: (Thackman-White 4-5)

Because each issue for that year will have page numbers beginning with 1, readers need the number of this issue: Here 51 is the volume number and 1 is the issue number. Omit *The, A,* or *An* from a journal or magazine title.

11. Article, Journal with Continuous Pagination—MLA

Barnstead, Marion H. "The Writing Crisis." *Journal of Writing Theory*,

vol. 12, 2009, pp. 415-33.

Parenthetical reference: (Barnstead 418)

When page numbers continue from issue to issue, readers won't need the issue number because no other issue in that year repeats the same page numbers. (Include the issue number, however, if you think it will help readers retrieve the article more easily.)

How to cite abstracts

If you are citing an abstract found in a bound collection of abstracts, and not the full article, include the information on the abstracting service right after the information on the original article.

Barnstead, Marion H. "The Writing Crisis." *Journal of Writing Theory*,

vol. 12, 2009, pp. 415-33. *Rhetoric Abstracts*, vol 67, 2010, p. 67.

If you are citing an abstract that appears before the printed article, add *Abstract*, followed by a period, immediately after the original work's page number or range.

12. Article, Newspaper—MLA

Baranski, Vida H. "Errors in Medical Diagnosis." *Boston Times*, 15 Jan.

2010, evening ed., Sec. B, p. 3+.

Parenthetical reference: (Baranski 3)

When a daily newspaper has more than one edition, cite the edition after the date. Include any introductory article in the newspaper's name. If no author is given, list all other information.

What to include in an MLA citation for a miscellaneous source

MLA Works Cited Entries for Other Sources.
Miscellaneous sources range from unsigned encyclopedia entries to conference presentations to government publications.

13. Encyclopedia, Dictionary, Other Alphabetical Reference—MLA

"Communication." *The Business Reference Book*. 2008 ed.

Parenthetical reference: ("Communication")

Begin a signed entry with the author's name. For any work arranged alphabetically, omit page numbers in the complete citation and the parenthetical reference.

For a well-known reference book, include only an edition (if stated) and a date. For other reference books, give the full publication information.

14. Report—MLA

Electrical Power Research Institute (EPRI). *Epidemiologic Studies of*
    Electric Utility Employees. Report No. RP2964.5, EPRI, Nov. 1994.

Parenthetical reference: (Electrical Power Research Institute [EPRI] 27)

If no author is given, begin with the organization that sponsored the report.

    For any report or other document with group authorship, include the group's abbreviated name in your first parenthetical reference and then use only that abbreviation in any subsequent reference.

15. Conference Presentation—MLA

Smith, Abelard A. "Multicultural Stereotypes in Elizabethan Prose
    Fiction." First British Symposium in Multicultural Studies,
    London, 11-13 Oct. 2012.

Parenthetical reference: (Smith)

For an unpublished presentation, include the presenter's name, the title of the presentation, and the conference title, location, and date. Do not italicize the conference information.

16. Interview, Personally Conducted—MLA

Nasson, Gamela. Personal interview, 2 Apr. 2010.

Parenthetical reference: (Nasson)

17. Interview, Published—MLA

Lescault, James. "The Future of Graphics." Interview by Carol Jable.
    Executive Views of Automation, edited by Karen Prell, Haber
    Press, 2013, pp. 216-31.

Parenthetical reference: (Lescault 218)

The interviewee's name is placed in the entry's author slot.

18. Letter, Unpublished—MLA

Rogers, Leonard. Letter to the author. 15 May 2010.

Parenthetical reference: (Rogers)

19. Questionnaire—MLA

Taynes, Lorraine. Questionnaire sent to 61 college administrators.

14 Feb. 2009.

Parenthetical reference: (Taynes)

20. Brochure or Pamphlet—MLA

Career Strategies for the 21st Century. Blount Economics Assn., 2010.

Parenthetical reference: (*Career*)

If the work is signed, begin with its author.

21. Lecture—MLA

Dumont, R. A. "Androgyny and the Rhetorical Tradition." University of

Massachusetts at Dartmouth, 15 Jan. 2010. Lecture.

Parenthetical reference: (Dumont)

If the lecture title is not known, write *Address, Lecture,* or *Reading* and do not use quotation marks. Include the sponsor and the location if they are available.

22. Government Document—MLA
If the author is unknown, begin with the name of the government, a comma, then the name of the agency:

Virginia, Highway Department. *Standards for Bridge Maintenance.*

Virginia Highway Standards Office, 2013.

Parenthetical reference: (Virginia Highway Dept. 49)

For any congressional document, identify the house of Congress (Senate or House of Representatives) before the title and the number and session of Congress after the title:

United States Congress, House Armed Service Committee. *Funding for the*

Military Academies. 108th Congress, 2nd session, U.S. Government

Printing Office, 2009.

Parenthetical reference: (U.S. Armed Services Committee 41)

For an entry from the *Congressional Record,* give only date and pages:

Cong. Rec. 10 Mar. 2006, pp. 2178-92.

Parenthetical reference: (*Cong. Rec.* 2184)

23. Document with Corporate or Foundation Authorship—MLA

Hermitage Foundation. *Global Warming Scenarios for the Year 2030.*
    National Research Council, 2009.

Parenthetical reference: (Hermitage Foundation 123)

24. Map or Other Visual Aid—MLA

Deaths Caused by Breast Cancer, by County. Map. *Scientific American,*
    Oct. 1995, p. 32D.

Parenthetical reference: (*Deaths Caused*)

If the creator of the visual is listed, list that name first. Identify the type of visual (*Map, Graph, Table, Diagram*) immediately following its title.

25. Dissertation or Thesis—MLA
Provide information in this order:

Rose, Jordan A. "Gravitational Waves as Represented in Online News
    Reporting." PhD dissertation, University of Minnesota, 2016.

MLA Works Cited Entries for Digital Sources.

MLA guidelines provide flexibility for citation formats based on the medium, but as with the print source examples shown above, they should include as much information as you think your reader will need to locate your original source.

What to include in an MLA citation for an electronic source

Digital sources include not only the ones listed here but also other media formats such as an Instagram posting; a discussion from a Facebook page; a YouTube or other online video; a posting to a user forum or discussion group. With so many new apps and formats coming into being every year, the following guidelines and examples provide you with a basis for creating source citations for new as well as existing media formats.

As described more generally on page 414 and illustrated in the previous examples, MLA guidelines suggest that Works Cited entries contain certain "core elements," including some or all of the following elements, as appropriate:

Author. Title of source. Title of container, other contributors,

version, number, publisher, publication date, location.

Two of these elements are especially important for documenting digital sources. *Container* refers to the place where the source resides, such as a book in a collection, a journal or magazine, a blog or Web page, or an e-book. *Location* refers to page numbers, Web address (URL), a digital library, or digital object identifier (DOI). So, for example, you might want to cite one of the Internal Revenue Services's Fact Sheets, located on their Web site. Following the core elements listed above, and the print example shown in item 22 (page 420), you would add information about the digital source in the "location" field. The citation would appears as follows (note that http:// is not required):

> Internal Revenue Service. "IRS Identity Theft Victim Assistance: How
> it Works." *IRS Fact Sheet FS-2016-3*, Jan. 2016, www.irs.gov/uac/
> Newsroom/IRS-Identity-Theft-Victim-Assistance-How-It-Works.

See the following examples for more illustrations of MLA style for digital sources; also, see style.mla.org for other examples.

26. Online Abstract—MLA

> Lane, Amanda D., et al. "The Promise of Microcircuits." *Journal of
> Nanotechnology*, vol. 10, no. 2, 2006, www.onlineabstracts.org/
> LaneA2006.

Parenthetical reference: (Lane et al.)

27. Online Article—MLA

> Jeffers, Anna D. "NAFTA's Effects on the U.S. Trade Deficit." *Sultana
> Business Quarterly*, vol. 3, no. 4, 2004, pp. 65-74, soltbizq.
> com/JeffersAD2004.

Parenthetical reference: (Jeffers 66)

28. Reference Database—MLA

> Sahl, J. D. "Power Lines, Viruses, and Childhood Leukemia."
> *Cancer Causes Control*, vol. 6, no. 1, Jan. 1995. PubMed
> Abstracts, PMID 7718739.

Parenthetical reference: (Sahl 83)

In the above example, the abstract was published as part of a journal called *Cancer Causes Control* but was accessed through a different "container," the PubMed database.

For abstracts or database entries that were not originally published in print, follow this example, providing enough information for readers to locate the source if necessary:

Argent, Roger R. "An Analysis of International Exchange Rates for
    2009." *Accu-Data*, Dow Jones News Service, 10 Jan. 2009, online.
    djnews.org/ID99783.

Parenthetical reference: (Argent)

If the author is not known, begin with the work's title. If the digital document has page numbers, include them in your entry and in your parenthetical reference.

29. Online Video—MLA

"How to Change Your Furnace Filter." *YouTube*, uploaded by USEnergy.
    gov, 28 Jan. 2016, www.youtube.com/watch?v=XCB234-v798s.

Parenthetical reference: (How to change)

Begin with the author's name, if known.

30. E-book—MLA

Duin, Ann Hill, et al. *Cultivating Change in the Academy*. University
    of Minnesota Digital Conservancy, 2012, purl.umn.edu/125273.

Parenthetical reference: (Duin et al. 2012)

A book that is published in both print and digital formats should be cited as a book, with no special mention of whether the book was read on paper or on a Kindle or other e-reader. (See items 1-8 earlier in this appendix for book citation examples in MLA format.) But books that are only available in digital formats should be cited per the example above. If possible, provide a Web address that is stable by looking for what is called a *permanent URL* or *permalink*. In the above example, this address is recognizable because it begins with "purl." Digital Object Identifiers (DOIs), discussed earlier, are another example of a stable Web address.

Another type of e-book you may encounter is a book that is either out of print or difficult to find and can best be located in a digital library, such as the HathiTrust, ProjectGuttenberg, or the Internet Archive. To help your readers understand how to access the book, cite it like a printed book but add the digital library information (location) at the very end:

Reiss, Ira L. *Family Systems in America*. Holt, Rinehart, and Winston,
    1980. HathiTrust Digital Library, catalog.hathitrust.org/
    Record/000711385.

31. Personal Email—MLA

Wallin, John Luther. "Frog Reveries." Received by Laura Gurak, 12 Oct.
   2009.

32. Wiki

"Printing Press." *Wikipedia.* Wikimedia Foundation, 2010.
   Accessed 1 June 2010.

Parenthetical reference: ("Printing")

Although you are not required to include the date that you accessed a source online, you may do so if you think that information might be useful to your reader.

33. Blog

Hecht, Jeff. "How Galveston Weathered the Storm." *New Scientist*
   Environment Blog, 15 Sept. 2008.

Parenthetical reference: (Hecht)

34. Podcast

"Countdown to Mars Touchdown." *NASA Solar System Audio Podcasts.* NASA,
   16 May 2008, www.nasa.gov/multimedia/podcasting/index.html.

Parenthetical reference: ("Countdown")

For wikis, blogs, and podcasts, decide whether your readers require a Web address (URL) or other information in order to locate the item you are citing. Wikipedia (item 32) is a well-known source that anyone can locate and does not need special location information. Since readers can easily locate with a quick online search the New Scientist Environment Blog (item 33), no Web address is given. But the NASA Solar System Audio Podcasts site (item 34) is not as easily found, so in that case, you would provide a Web address.

35. Tweet

Gurak, Laura (ProfGurak). "Here's a good article on accuracy and
   relevance of crowd sourced content: http://goo.gl/Bs2Ah."
   4 Dec. 2012, 6:48 p.m.

Parenthetical reference: (Gurak)

This tweet does not need a Web address (URL) or other location information; readers can go to the Twitter site for the author (ProfGurak) and search for the tweet by date posted.

36. Web sites and Other Digital Formats—MLA

For Web sites and other digital formats such as Facebook postings, Google maps, online discussion forums, and so forth, follow the "core elements" format shown on page 422, choosing items as appropriate to your citation. If the author is unknown, start with the title of source. If the source is easy to locate, omit the Web address.

> "Calcium." *University of Maryland Medical Center Medical Reference Guide*, University of Maryland, 26 June 2014.

> Samantha0212. "Taking Calcium Worked for Me." *WebMed Online Discussion Forum*, WebMed Online, 7 July 2016. webmed.org/forums/calcium/ posting 9934.

APA DOCUMENTATION STYLE

Another common citation style is detailed in the *Publication Manual of the American Psychological Association*, 6th ed. (2009). Because it emphasizes the publication date, APA style (or any similar author-date style) is preferred in the sciences and social sciences, where information quickly becomes outdated.

As in MLA style, APA style requires that you cite a source in text (parenthetical reference) as well as at the end of the report (where it is called a References list rather than a Works Cited list).

APA Parenthetical References

APA's parenthetical references (also called in-text reference citations) differ from MLA's as follows: the citation includes the publication date; a comma separates each item in the reference; and *p.* or *pp.* precedes the page number (which is optional in the APA system) or range, respectively. Here are specific guidelines:

How APA and MLA parenthetical references differ

- If your discussion names the author, do not repeat the name in your parenthetical reference; simply give the date and page number or range. When two authors of a work are named in your text, their names are connected by *and*, but in a parenthetical reference, their names are connected by an ampersand (&).

> Lederman (1995) cites recent data provided by 796 colleges indicating that violent crime on campus is increasing (p. 31).

Author named in the text

- If you cite two or more works in a single reference, list the authors in alphabetical order and separate the citations with semicolons:

Two or more works
in a single reference

| (Gomez, 2002; Jones, 2004; Leduc, 1998)

- If you cite a work with three to five authors, try to name them in your text to avoid an excessively long parenthetical reference. In any subsequent references to this work, name only the first author, followed by *et al.* (Latin abbreviation for "and others").

A work with three
to five authors

| Franks, Oblesky, Ryan, Jablar, and Perkins (2004) studied the role of
| electromagnetic fields in tumor formation.

- If you cite two or more works by the same author published in the same year, arrange the works alphabetically by title, and add a lowercase letter (a, b, c) to the year to differentiate them:

Two or more works
by the same author
in the same year

| (Lamont, 2005a, p. 135)
| (Lamont, 2005b, pp. 67–68)

- When a subsequent reference to a source follows closely after the initial reference, the date need not be included.

APA Reference Entries

How to format the
References list

The APA References list includes each source you have cited in your paper; it appears on a separate page at the end of the document. Arrange all entries alphabetically by the author's surname (when the author's name is unknown, alphabetize by the first word or numeral, as if the numeral were spelled out). Begin each entry flush with the left margin and indent second and subsequent lines 1/2 inch (or five spaces). Double-space within and between entries. In one notable difference from MLA style, APA style calls for only "retrievable" sources to appear in the reference list. Therefore, cite personal interviews, letters, and email messages in text only.

How to cite
nonretrievable
sources

How to cite
individual items

Following are examples of complete citations as they would appear in the References list. Shown immediately below each entry is its corresponding parenthetical reference as it would appear in the text. Note the capitalization, abbreviation, spacing, and punctuation in the sample entries.

Table A.2 provides an overview of the types of citations discussed in this section.

What to include in
an APA citation for
a book

APA Entries for Books. Any citation for a book should contain all applicable information in the following order: author, date, title, editor or translator, edition, volume number, and facts about publication—city, state (abbreviated), and publisher.

TABLE A.2 INDEX TO APA REFERENCES ENTRIES

BOOKS

1. Book, single author
2. Book, two to five authors
3. Book, six or more authors
4. Book, anonymous author
5. Multiple books, same author
6. Book, one to five editors
7. Book, indirect source
8. Anthology selection or book chapter

PERIODICALS

9. Article, magazine
10. Article, journal with new pagination for each issue
11. Article, journal with continuous pagination
12. Article, newspaper

OTHER SOURCES

13. Encyclopedia, dictionary, alphabetical reference
14. Report
15. Conference presentation
16. Interview, personally conducted

17. Interview, published
18. Personal correspondence
19. Brochure or pamphlet
20. Unpublished lecture
21. Government document
22. Miscellaneous items (unpublished manuscript, dissertation, and so on)

ELECTRONIC SOURCES

23. Online abstract
24. Print article posted online
25. Book or article available only online (no DOI)
26. CD-ROM abstract
27. Online encyclopedia, dictionary, handbook
28. Personal email
29. Blog posting
30. Newsgroup, discussion list, online forum
31. Wiki
32. Facebook and Twitter

GRAY LITERATURE

33. Press release
34. Technical or research report

1. Book, Single Author—APA

```
Kerzin-Fontana, J. B. (2010). Technology management: A handbook
      (3rd ed.). Delmar, NY: American Management Association.
```

Parenthetical reference: (Kerzin-Fontana, 2010, pp. 3-4)

Use only initials for an author's first and middle names. Capitalize only the first words of a book's title and subtitle and any proper names. Identify a later edition in parentheses between the title and the period. Omit the state abbreviation if the city is unambiguous.

2. Book, Two to Five Authors—APA

```
Vogel, W., & Kalb, H. (2010). Large-scale solar thermal power:
      technologies, costs and development. Weinheim: Wiley-VCH.
```

Parenthetical reference: (Vogel & Kalb, 2010)

Use an ampersand (&) before the name of the final author listed in an entry. As an alternative to a full parenthetical reference, name the authors in your text and include date (and page numbers, if appropriate) in parentheses. Give the publisher's name in full ("Yale University Press") but omit *Publisher, Company,* or *Inc.* If you are including the state (see item 1, on previous page), use the two-letter U.S. Postal Service abbreviations for states.

3. Book, Six or More Authors—APA

Fogle, S. T., et al. (2009). *Hyperspace technology.* Boston: Little, Brown.

Parenthetical reference: (Fogle et al., 2009, p. 34)

Et al. is the Latin abbreviation for *et alia,* meaning "and others."

4. Book, Anonymous Author—APA

Structured programming. (2010). Boston: Meredith Press.

Parenthetical reference: (*Structured Programming,* 2010, p. 67)

In your list of references, place an anonymous work alphabetically by the first key word in its title (ignoring *The, A,* or *An*). In your parenthetical reference, capitalize all key words in a book, article, or journal title.

5. Multiple Books, Same Author—APA

Chang, J. W. (2010a). *Biophysics.* Boston: Little, Brown.

Chang, J. W. (2010b). *MindQuest.* Chicago: Pressler.

Parenthetical reference: (Chang, 2010a) (Chang, 2010b)

Two or more works by the same author published in different years are distinguished by their dates alone, without the added letter.

6. Book, One to Five Editors—APA

Morris, A. J., & Pardin-Walker, L. B. (Eds.). (2012). *Handbook of new information technology.* New York: HarperCollins.

Parenthetical reference: (Morris & Pardin-Walker, 2012, p. 79)

For more than five editors, name only the first, followed by *et al.*

7. Book, Indirect Source—APA

Stubbs, J. (2010). *White-collar productivity.* Miami, FL: Harris.

Parenthetical reference: (cited in Stubbs, 2010, p. 47)

When your source has cited another source, list only this second source, but name the original source in your text: "Kline's study (cited in Stubbs, 2002, p. 47) supports this conclusion."

8. Anthology Selection or Book Chapter—APA

> Bowman, J. (1994). Electronic conferencing. In A. Williams (Ed.),
>
>   *Communication and technology: Today and tomorrow* (pp. 123-142).
>
>   Denton, TX: Association for Business Communication.

Parenthetical reference: (Bowman, 1994, p. 126)

The page numbers in the complete reference are for the entire selection cited from the anthology.

APA Entries for Periodicals.

A citation for an article should give this information (as available) in this order: author, date, article title (without quotation marks), publication, volume and (when necessary) issue number, and page numbers for the entire article, not just the portion cited.

What to include in an APA citation for a periodical

9. Article, Magazine—APA

> DesMarteau K. (1994, October). Study links sewing machine use to
>
>   Alzheimer's disease. *Bobbin, 36,* 36-38.

Parenthetical reference: (DesMarteau, 1994, p. 36)

If no author is given, provide all other information, placing the title in the author position. Capitalize only the first words in an article's title and subtitle as well as all proper nouns. Capitalize all key words in a periodical title. Italicize the periodical title and volume number.

10. Article, Journal with New Pagination for Each Issue—APA

> Thackman-White, J. R. (2010). Computer-assisted research. *American*
>
>   *Library Journal, 51*(1), 3-9.

Parenthetical reference: (Thackman-White, 2010, pp. 4-5)

Because each issue for a given year has page numbers that begin at "1," readers need the issue number (in this instance, 1). Here 51 is the volume number, which is italicized.

11. Article, Journal with Continuous Pagination—APA

> Barnstead, M. H. (2009). The writing crisis. *Journal of Writing*
>
>   *Theory, 12,* 415-433.

Parenthetical reference: (Barnstead, 2009, pp. 415-416)

In this example, 12 is the volume number. When page numbers continue from issue to issue for the full year, readers won't need the issue number because no other issue in that year repeats the same page numbers. (You can include the issue number if you think it will help readers retrieve the article more easily.)

12. Article, Newspaper — APA

> Baranski, V. H. (2010, January 15). Errors in medical diagnosis.
>
> *The Boston Times*, pp. B3,6.
>
> *Parenthetical reference:* (Baranski, 2010)

In addition to the year of publication, include the month and date. If the newspaper's name begins with *The,* include it in your citation. Include *p.* or *pp.* before page numbers. For an article on nonconsecutive pages, list each page, separated by a comma. If the entire article appeared on one page, no page number is necessary in the citation.

APA Entries for Other Sources. Miscellaneous sources range from unsigned encyclopedia entries to conference presentations to government documents. A full citation should give this information (as available): author, publication date, title of work, city, publisher (or volume and issue number), and page numbers (if applicable).

What to include in an APA citation for a miscellaneous source

13. Encyclopedia, Dictionary, Alphabetical Reference — APA

> Communication. (2008). In *The business reference book.* Upper Saddle
>
> River, NJ: Prentice Hall, p. 201.
>
> *Parenthetical reference:* (Communication, 2008)

For an entry that is signed, begin with the author's name and publication date.

14. Report — APA

> Electrical Power Research Institute. (1994). *Epidemiologic studies of*
>
> *electric utility employees* (Rep. No. RP2964.5). Palo Alto, CA:
>
> Author.
>
> *Parenthetical reference:* (Electrical Power Research Institute [EPRI], 1994,
> p. 12)

If authors are named, list them first, followed by the publication date. When citing a group author, as in example 14, include the group's abbreviated name in your first parenthetical reference, and use only that abbreviation in any subsequent reference. When the agency (or organization) and publisher are the same, list *Author* in the publisher's slot.

15. Conference Presentation—APA

Smith, A. A. (2012). Multicultural stereotypes in Elizabethan prose
  fiction. In A. Hodkins (Ed.), *First British Symposium on
  Multicultural Studies* (pp. 106-121). London: Harrison Press.

Parenthetical reference: (Smith, 2012, p. 109)

The date of the presentation is in parentheses. The name of the symposium is a proper name, so it is capitalized. For an unpublished presentation, include the presenter's name, year and month, title of the presentation (italicized), and all available information about the conference or meeting: "Symposium held at ..." Do not italicize this last information.

16. Interview, Personally Conducted—APA

This material is considered a nonrecoverable source, so it is cited only in the text, as a parenthetical reference:

Parenthetical reference: (G. Nasson, personal communication, April 2, 2010)

If you name the interviewee in your text, do not repeat the name in your citation.

17. Interview, Published—APA

Jable, C. K. (2013, June 7). The future of graphics [Interview with
  James Lescault]. In K. Prell (Ed.), *Executive views of automa-
  tion* (pp. 216-231). Miami: Haber Press.

Parenthetical reference: (Jable, 2013, p. 218)

Begin with the name of the interviewer, followed by the interview date and title (if available), the designation (in brackets), and the publication information.

18. Personal Correspondence—APA

This material is considered nonrecoverable data, so it is cited only in the text, as a parenthetical reference:

Parenthetical reference: (L. Rogers, personal communication, May 15, 2010)

If you name the correspondent in your text, do not repeat the name in your citation.

19. Brochure or Pamphlet—APA

This material follows the citation format for book entries (pages 426–429).

20. Unpublished Lecture—APA

Dumont, R. A. (2010, January 15). *Androgyny and the rhetorical tradition.* Lecture presented at the University of Massachusetts at Dartmouth.

Parenthetical reference: (Dumont, 2010)

If you name the lecturer in your text, do not repeat the name in your citation.

21. Government Document—APA

If the author is unknown, present the information in this order: name of the issuing agency, publication date, document title, place, and publisher.

Virginia Highway Department. (2013). *Standards for bridge maintenance.* Richmond, VA: Author.

Parenthetical reference: (Virginia Highway Department, 2009, p. 49)

When the issuing agency is both author and publisher, write *Author* in the publisher's slot. For any congressional document, identify the house of Congress (Senate or House of Representatives) before the date.

United States Congress. House. Armed Services Committee. (2010). *Funding for the military academies.* Washington, DC: U.S. Government Printing Office.

Parenthetical reference: (U.S. Congress, 2010, p. 41)

22. Miscellaneous Items (Unpublished Manuscript, Dissertation, and so on)—APA

Provide information in this order:

Author (if known). (Date of preparation). *Title of work* (italicized). Description (Unpublished manuscript, unpublished raw data, or the like).

For any work that has group authorship (corporation, committee, and so on), cite the name of the group or agency in place of the author's name.

What to include in an APA citation for an electronic source

APA Entries for Electronic Sources. In 2009, the APA published the *Publication Manual of the American Psychological Association,* 6th edition. This manual provides instructions for citation of print and electronic sources. For electronic sources in particular, the APA notes that "in general... include the same elements, in the same order, as you would for a reference to a fixed-media source and add as much electronic retrieval information as needed for others to locate the sources you cited" (187). Including the Web address is still recommended. However, one new feature is the use of digital object identifiers (DOIs). These are unique identifiers designed to last longer than Web addresses, which often disappear or get changed when Web pages are moved or renamed.

Identify the original source (printed or electronic) and give readers a path for retrieving the material. Provide all available information in the following order.

1. Author, editor, creator, or sponsoring organization.

2. Date the item was published or was created electronically. For magazines and newspapers, include the month and day as well as the year. If the date of an electronic publication is not available, use *n.d.* in place of the date.

3. Publication information of the original printed version (as in previous entries), if such a version exists. Follow this by designating the electronic medium [CD-ROM] or the type of work [Abstract], [Brochure]—unless this designation is named in the work's title (as in "Inpatient brochure").

4. Database names. Do not list database names (unless the database is obscure or the material hard to find), but do include the Web address (or DOI, discussed below).

5. Web addresses and DOIs. Provide the full electronic address. APA recommends only using home page Web address. For CD-ROM and database sources, give the document's retrieval number (see entry 23, below). Start the Web address with http://, but do not underline, italicize, use angle brackets, or add a period at the end of a Web address. When a Web address continues from one line to the next, break it only after a slash or other punctuation (except for http://, which should not be broken).

The APA now recommends using the DOI (Digital Object Identifier), when available, in place of a Web address in references to electronic texts. DOI numbers are found on some recent scholarly journals, especially in the sciences and social sciences. Here is a sample reference for a journal article with a DOI assigned:

Schmidt, D., et al. (2009). Advances in psychotropic medication. *Boston Journal of Psychotherapy, 81*(3), 398-413. doi: 10.1037/0555-9467.79.3.483

Parenthetical reference: (Schmidt, 2009)

23. Online Abstract—APA

Stevens, R. L. (2010). Cell phones and cancer rates. *Oncology Journal, 57*(2), 41-43. [Abstract]. Retrieved from the Dialog database. (MEDLINE Item: AY 24598).

Parenthetical reference: (Stevens, 2010)

Ordinarily an APA entry ends with a period. Entries that end with a Web address (or a DOI), however, omit the period at the end of the electronic address. If you are citing the entire article retrieved from a full-text database, delete [Abstract] from your citation.

24. Print Article Posted Online—APA

> Alley, R. A. (2009, January). Ergonomic influences on worker
>
> satisfaction. *Industrial Psychology, 5*(12), 672-678. Retrieved
>
> from http://www.psycharchives/index/indpsy/2009_1.html

Parenthetical reference: (Alley, 2009)

If you were confident that the document's electronic and print versions were identical, you could omit the Web address and insert "[Electronic version]" between the end of the article title and the period.

25. Book or Article Available Only Online (no DOI)—APA

> Kelly, W. (2009). *Early graveyards of New England.* Retrieved from
>
> http://www.onlinebooks.com/search/itemID=65321

Parenthetical reference: (Kelly, 2009)

This source exists only in electronic format.

26. CD-ROM Abstract—APA

> Cavanaugh, H. (1995). An EMF study: Good news and bad news [CD-ROM].
>
> *Electrical World, 209*(2), 8. Abstract retrieved from ProQuest
>
> File: ABI/INFORM database (62-1498).

Parenthetical reference: (Cavanaugh, 1995)

In this entry, 8 is the page number of this one-page article.

27. Online Encyclopedia, Dictionary, Handbook—APA

> Ecoterrorism. (2012). *Ecological encyclopedia.* Washington, DC: Redwood.
>
> Retrieved May 1, 2013, from http://www.eco.floridastate.edu/
>
> index.html

Parenthetical reference: ("Ecoterrorism," 2012)

Include the retrieval date for reference works that are routinely updated.

28. Personal Email—APA

Parenthetical reference: Fred Flynn (personal communication, May 9, 2013) provided these statistics.

Instead of being included in the list of references, personal email (considered a nonretrievable source) is cited fully in the text.

29. Blog Posting—APA

Owens, P. (2010, June 1). How to stabilize a large travel trailer.

> Message posted to http://rvblogs.com/comm/bilge

Parenthetical reference: (Owens, 2010)

30. Newsgroup, Discussion List, Online Forum—APA

LaBarge, V. S. (2009, October 20). A cure for computer viruses.

> Message posted to http://www.srb/forums/frwl/webZ/m2237.html

Parenthetical reference: (LaBarge, 2009)

Although email should not be included in the list of references, postings from blogs, newsgroups, and online forums, considered more retrievable, should be included.

31. Wiki—APA

Skull-base tumors. (n.d.). Retrieved June 10, 2009, from the Oncology

> wiki: http://oncology.wikia.com/wiki/Skull_base_tumors

Parenthetical reference: ("Skull-Base," n.d.)

Notice the "n.d." ("no date") designation for this collaborative Web page that can be written or edited by anyone with access.

32. Facebook and Twitter

NASA. (2013, January 8). Astronomers have made a 3D weather map of a

> brown dwarf using NASA)s Spitzer and Hubble Space telescopes!
> [Facebook update]. Retrieved from www.facebook.com/NASA/
> posts/128611970637320

Parenthetical reference: (NASA, 2013)

APA Entries for Gray Literature. The APA has new guidelines for citing so-called gray literature—material such as annual reports, fact sheets, consumer brochures, press releases, and technical reports (each type is so named in the title, in brackets, or elsewhere in the citation). In the *APA Style Guide to Electronic References*, gray literature is defined as "scientific information that falls outside the peer review process but is written by scholars or summarizes a body of scholarly work. Government departments, corporations and trade groups ... and other ... organizations produce gray literature" (p. 18). Much of this is written for the

What to include in an APA citation for gray literature

general public. In the sample citation in entry 33, the type of item is identified in brackets; in entry 34, it is part of the titling information.

33. Press Release—APA

American Natural Foods Association. (2009, January 20). *Newest food additive poses special threat to children, according to the upcoming issue of* Eating for Health [Press release]. Retrieved from http://www.anfha.org/releases/additives0620.html

Parenthetical reference: (American Natural Foods Association, 2009)

34. Technical or Research Report—APA

Gunderson, H., et al. (2007). *Declining birthrates in rural areas: Results from the 2005 National Census Bureau Survey* (Report No. 7864 NCB 2005-171). Retrieved from the National Center for Population Statistics: http://ncps.gov/pubs2007/pubs2007/2007171.pdf

Parenthetical reference: (Gunderson, 2007)

Notice that the report number, if available, is given after the title.

OTHER DOCUMENTATION STYLES

For class, on the job, or when writing for a specific publication, you may be required to use a documentation style different from the two described above. These other styles might include the Chicago Manual of Style, Council of Science Editors (CSE), Institute of Electrical and Electronics Engineers (IEEE), American Chemical Society (ACS), or others that are specific to a scientific, engineering, or professional field. Some of these styles use numbered citations within the text that appear almost like footnotes; references lists also have their own unique rules. You can learn more about these citation styles by searching online and at your college or university library.

RECOGNIZING COPYRIGHT ISSUES

Definition of copyright

Copyright is the legal system that gives authors and owners rights over their original works of authorship. These works can include books, musical recordings, photographs, drawings, letters, memos, email, Web pages, and any other expressions of ideas that are, as the law puts it, "fixed in a tangible medium." Copyright holders have the exclusive right to reproduce, distribute, perform, display, prepare derivative works, and publish their copyrighted material. Copyright holders also have the right to grant a license (essentially, to give permission) for others to use the material. In the United States, works created after 1978 are automatically copyrighted as soon as the material is fixed; that is, the moment the idea is recorded, written down, turned into an electronic document, or otherwise.

The purpose of copyright is to balance the reward for the intellectual labor of the author with the importance of making information freely available to the public. If all information were covered by copyright protection forever and ever, there would be no source of public information that authors and artists could use to create new ideas. But if all information were completely free of copyright protection, creators might not have any incentive to write songs or books, for example. This is why in the United States copyright is not forever, just for a limited time. This is also why there are some conditions under which you do not need to request copyright permission.

Works in the Public Domain

Many images, sounds, books, and other materials fall into what is called the *public domain*. In these cases, you do not need to request permission for use. Public domain works include works that were published in the United States 95 years before the current year. Most government documents are also public domain, and most commonplace information, such as height and weight charts or metric conversion tables, are also public domain. Many authors and artists publish work and expressly state that the work is in the public domain. Look on the Web site or document for more information. (If you are unsure about the work's status, you may want to request permission.)

Fair Use

Fair use is a legal doctrine that allows the use of some copyrighted material, under some circumstances, without permission. Congress established fair use as a way to balance creators' rights with public access. Fair use states that under certain conditions, it is legal to use copyrighted works without permission so long as the source is clearly identified. Courts tend to ask four questions about whether a use is considered fair:

- Is the material educational or commercial? (educational use is favored)
- Has the material been previously published? (use of published works is favored)
- How much of the material is being used? (less is favored)
- How will your use of the material affect the market value of the original? (if your use does not have an impact on the value of the original, this is favored)

Classroom and student use is almost always considered fair. Most use of small snippets of text, cited in a student or academic paper, is also considered fair use. Even commercial documents, such as annual reports, routinely cite information from publications such as the newspaper or research papers. These uses are all considered fair. However, if you are a consultant or employee of a for-profit organization and you wish to use a large amount of material or visuals such as photographs or graphics, fair use may not apply. In these cases, it is best to seek permission.

The Difference between Plagiarism and Copyright Infringement

If you receive permission to use someone else's material or if your use qualifies as fair use, you are probably covered when it comes to copyright. Most of the writing you will do for this class and in college generally will be situations where your use of outside material is considered educational and thus fair. But you still must document your source by providing an appropriate in-text citation as well as a reference; otherwise, you run the risk of plagiarism. Always provide a citation or caption, even if you didn't need copyright permission. Whether you use a direct quotation or a paraphrase, always include the source.

Copyright in a digital age

In our digital age, there is a tension between the openness of the Internet, which allows people to access music, text, and images easily on the one hand, and the restrictions on such items that copyright calls for on the other. It is easy to cut and paste material online but also easy to forget that this material is probably covered by copyright protection.

B) A Brief Handbook

The inside back cover of this book displays editing and revision symbols and corresponding page references. When your instructor marks a symbol on your paper, turn to the appropriate section here or in Chapters 5 and 6 for explanations, examples, and exercises. Chapter 5, which covers matters of structure, includes the following topics keyed to the editing and revision symbols:

- TS: the topic sentence (page 84)
- UN: paragraph unity (page 85)
- COH: paragraph coherence (page 85)

Chapter 6, which discusses matters of style, includes the following additional topics, also keyed to the editing and revision symbols:

- REF: avoiding ambiguous pronoun references (page 95)
- MOD: avoiding ambiguous modifiers (page 96)
- AV: using active voice whenever possible (page 96)
- PV: using passive voice selectively (page 97)
- NOM: avoiding nominalizations (page 98)
- ST MOD: unstacking modifying nouns (page 99)
- JARG: avoiding unnecessary jargon (page 100)
- W: avoiding wordiness (page 100)
- RED and REP: eliminating redundancy and repetition (page 102)
- COMB: combining related ideas (page 103)
- VAR: varying sentence construction and length (page 103)
- PAR: using parallel structure (page 104)
- TONE: adjusting your tone (page 105)
- SEXIST and BIAS: avoiding sexist and biased language (page 106).

OUTLINE

Grammar   440

Punctuation   445

Mechanics   453

Usage   456

Transitions   456

Lists   460

GRAMMAR

The following common grammatical errors are easy to repair.

frag

Sentence Fragments

A sentence fragment is a grammatically incomplete sentence. A grammatically complete sentence consists of at least one subject-verb combination and expresses a complete thought. It might include more than one subject-verb combination, and it might include other words or phrases as well.

Complete sentences

> This book summarizes recent criminal psychology research.
>
> The smudge tool creates soft effects.
>
> My dog, Zorro, ate my paper.

Even though the following example contains a subject-verb combination, it doesn't express a complete thought:

Sentence fragment

> Although the report was not yet complete.

Watch out for *although* and other words like it, including *because, if, as, while, since, when,* and *unless.* These are called subordinating conjunctions. Any of these words combined with a subject-verb combination produces a subordinate clause (a clause that expresses an incomplete idea). Subordinating conjunctions leave readers waiting for something to complete the thought. The thought can be completed only if another subject-verb combination that does express a complete idea is added:

Additional subject-verb completes the thought

> Although the report was not yet complete, I began editing.

This next group of words is a fragment because it contains no verb:

Fragment with no verb

> DesignPro, a brand-new desktop publishing program.

Simply add a verb to turn the fragment into a complete sentence:

Addition of verb corrects fragment

> DesignPro, a brand-new desktop publishing program, will be available soon.

> *or*

> DesignPro is a brand-new desktop publishing program.

Avoid sentences that seem to contain a subject-verb combination but actually do not. Gerunds (verb forms ending in *-ing* that act like nouns, such as *being* in the first sentence given) and participles (verb forms ending in -*ing* that act like adjectives, such as *barking* in the second sentence given) look like verbs but actually are not:

> Dale being a document design expert
> The barking dog

Gerund and participle fragments

These fragments can be turned into complete sentences by substituting a verb for the gerund or adding a verb:

> Dale is a document design expert.
> The barking dog finally stopped.

Verb substitution or new verb corrects fragment

Run-on Sentences

ro

A run-on sentence contains too many grammatically complete sentences joined together as one:

> For emergencies, we dial 911 for other questions, we dial 088.

Run-on sentence

This sentence can be repaired in various ways. One possibility is to divide it into two sentences:

> For emergencies, we dial 911. For other questions, we dial 088.

Division into two sentences corrects run-on

Another possibility is to use a semicolon to join the two sentences. This option indicates a break that is not quite as strong as the period and therefore signals to the reader that the two items are closely related:

> For emergencies, we dial 911; for other questions, we dial 088.

Added semicolon corrects run-on

Another possibility is to add a comma followed by a coordinating conjunction (*for, and, nor, but, or, yet, so*):

> For emergencies, we dial 911, but for other questions, we dial 088.

Coordinating conjunction corrects run-on

Comma Splices

cs

In a comma splice, two complete ideas (independent clauses) that should be *separated* by a period or a semicolon are incorrectly *joined* by a comma:

> Sarah did a great job, she was promoted.

Comma splice

There are a number of options for correcting comma splices. One option is to divide the splice into two separate sentences:

Division into two sentences corrects comma splice

| Sarah did a great job. She was promoted.

Another option is to use a semicolon to show a relationship between the two items:

Semicolon corrects comma splice

| Sarah did a great job; she was promoted.

A third option is to use a semicolon with a conjunctive adverb (an adverb, ending in *-ly*, that shows a relationship between the items, such as *consequently*):

Semicolon with conjunctive adverb corrects comma splice

| Sarah did a great job; consequently, she was promoted.

A fourth option is to use a coordinating conjunction. There are seven such conjunctions: *for, and, nor, but, or, yet, so*—you can remember them using the acronym "fanboys." Coordinating conjunctions create an equal relationship between the items:

Coordinating conjunction corrects comma splice

| Sarah did a great job and was promoted.

Finally, as on page 440, you can use a subordinating conjunction (a conjunction that creates an unequal relationship between the items):

Subordinating conjunction corrects comma splice

| Because Sarah did a great job, she was promoted.

Faulty Agreement—Subject and Verb

The subject of a sentence must agree in number with the verb. But when subject and verb are separated by other words, we sometimes lose track of the subject-verb relationship:

Faulty subject-verb agreement

| The lion's share of diesels are sold in Europe.

To correct the error, make the verb agree with its subject (*share*), not with a word that comes between the subject and the verb (in this case, the plural noun *diesels*):

Correct subject-verb agreement

| The lion's share of diesels is sold in Europe.

Some cases are trickier than others. For example, treat compound subjects connected by *and* as plural:

Compound subject takes plural verb

| Terry and Julie enjoy collaborating on writing projects.

In addition, with compound subjects connected by *or* or *nor*, the verb is singular if both subjects are singular and plural if both subjects are plural. If one subject is singular and one is plural, the verb agrees with the one closer to the verb. In the following example, the verb agrees with the closer subject, the plural *students*:

| Neither the professor nor the students were able to see what was going on.

Verb agrees with closer subject in compound subject

Also, treat most indefinite pronouns (*anybody, each, everybody*, etc.) as singular subjects:

| Almost everybody who registered for the class was there on the first day.

Indefinite pronoun agrees with singular verb

Additionally, treat collective subjects (*team, family, group, committee*, etc.) as singular unless the meaning is clearly plural. Both of the following sentences are correct. In the first sentence, the *group* is understood as a singular subject (the group is a single entity) and agrees with the singular verb *respects*, whereas in the second sentence, the *board* is understood as plural (as indicated by the plural word *authors*) and agrees with the plural verb *are*:

The group respects its leader.
The editorial board are all published authors.

Collective subjects agree with singular or plural verbs depending on meaning

Faulty Agreement—Pronoun and Referent

A pronoun must refer to a specific noun (its *referent* or *antecedent*), with which it must agree in gender and number. Faulty pronoun-referent agreement is easy to spot when the gender and number clearly don't match (e.g., "He should proceed at their own pace" should obviously read "He should proceed at his own pace"). However, when an indefinite pronoun such as *each, everyone, anybody, someone*, or *none* is the referent, the pronoun is always singular, as in the following examples:

`arg p`

Everybody should proceed at his or her own pace.
None of the candidates described her career plans in detail.

Indefinite referents agree with singular pronouns

Faulty Coordination and Subordination

Give equal emphasis to ideas of equal importance by joining them with one of the coordinating conjunctions: *for, and, nor, but, or, yet*, and *so* (you can memorize these by using the acronym "fanboys"). Likewise, show an unequal relationship between ideas (one idea dependent upon the other) by using a subordinating conjunction: *because, whereas, if, although, until*, and so on.

`coord`   `sub`

Coordination may be faulty when the ideas connected by a coordinating conjunction are not of equal importance or are not sensibly connected:

Faulty coordination

| I was late for work and wrecked my car.

To correct the problem, use a subordinating conjunction instead. Or express cause and effect or opinion in some other way, as in the following two examples:

Corrected versions

| Because I was late for work, I backed out of my driveway too quickly into oncoming traffic, wrecking my car.
or
| Late for work, I backed out of my driveway too quickly into oncoming traffic, wrecking my car.

Avoid subordinating ideas that should be of equal importance or that don't represent a genuine cause and effect relationship:

Faulty subordination

| Although John gets up early, he is never late for work.

To correct the problem and show a balanced relationship between the ideas, use a coordinating conjunction instead:

Corrected version

| John gets up early and is never late for work.

Avoid both excessive coordination and excessive subordination in complex sentences. Following are two versions of the same sentence, the first with excessive coordination and the second with excessive subordination:

Excessive coordination

| The climax in jogging comes after a few miles and I can no longer feel stride after stride and it seems as if I am floating and jogging becomes almost a reflex and my arms and legs continue to move and my mind no longer has control over my actions.

Excessive subordination

| The climax in jogging comes when after a few miles I can no longer feel stride after stride, yet it seems as if I am floating, because jogging becomes almost a reflex since my arms and legs continue to move while my mind no longer has control over my actions.

To repair either instance, blend coordination and subordination, deciding exactly which ideas should be balanced and which of the subordinated ideas is most important, as in the following revision. Here, the writer has decided to emphasize *jogging almost by reflex* as the most important idea (using the subordinating conjunction *when*) and to coordinate the four equally important sensations involved (*no longer able to feel every stride, nearly floating, my arms and legs still moving,* and *my mind no longer controlling my actions*) using commas and the coordinating conjunction *and*.

> The climax in jogging comes after a few miles, when I am jogging almost by reflex, no longer able to feel every stride, nearly floating, my arms and legs still moving, and my mind no longer controlling my actions.

Balance of coordination and subordination

Faulty Pronoun Case

ca

A pronoun's case (nominative, objective, or possessive) is determined by its role in the sentence: as subject, object, or indicator of possession.

If the pronoun serves as the subject of a sentence (*I, we, you, she, he, it, they, who*) or follows a version of the linking verb *to be*, its case is *nominative*:

> She completed her graduate program in record time.
> Who broke the chair?
> The chemist who perfected this distillation process is he.

Nominative pronoun case

If the pronoun serves as the object of a verb or a preposition (*me, us, you, her, him, it, them, whom*), its case is *objective*:

> The employees gave her a parting gift.
> To whom do you wish to complain?

Objective pronoun case

If a pronoun indicates possession (*my, mine, our, ours, your, yours, his, her, hers, its, their, whose*), its case is *possessive*:

> The brown briefcase is mine.
> Whose opinion do you value most?

Possessive pronoun case

The following sentences are incorrect and are followed by the corrected versions in parenthesis.

> Whom is responsible to who? (Who is responsible to whom?)
> The debate was between Marsha and I. (The debate was between Marsha and me.)

Faulty pronoun case

PUNCTUATION

pct

Punctuation marks are like road signs and traffic signals. They govern reading speed and provide clues for navigation through a network of ideas. The three marks of end punctuation—period, question mark, and exclamation point—work like a red traffic light by signaling a complete stop.

Period

A period ends a declarative sentence.

Period ends
declarative
statement

> | I see that you've all completed the essay.

It is also used as the final mark in some abbreviations, such as "Dr." and "Inc." and for certain numerical purposes ($18.43 and 26.2%).

Question Mark

A question mark follows a direct question:

Question mark ends
direct question

> | Have you all completed the essay?

A question mark should not be used to end an indirect question:

Incorrect

Period ends indirect
question

> | Professor Grim asked if all students had completed the essay?
> | Professor Grim asked if all students had completed the essay.

Exclamation Point

Use an exclamation point only when expression of strong feeling is appropriate:

Exclamation point
provides emphasis

> | I can't believe you finished the essay so fast!

Semicolon

Like a blinking red traffic light at an intersection, a semicolon signals a brief but definite stop. Semicolons have several uses.

A semicolon can be used to separate independent clauses (logically complete ideas) whose contents are closely related and are not already connected by a comma and a coordinating conjunction (*and, or, but,* etc.):

Semicolon separates
independent clauses

> | The project was finally completed; we had done a good week's work.

To Accompany Conjunctive Adverbs. A semicolon must accompany a conjunctive adverb such as *besides, otherwise, still, however, furthermore, moreover, consequently, therefore, on the other hand, in contrast,* or *in fact*:

Semicolon
accompanies
conjunctive adverbs

> | The job is filled; however, we will keep your résumé on file.
> | Your background is impressive; in fact, it is the best among our
> | applicants.

To Separate Items in a Series. When items in a series contain internal commas, semicolons provide clear separation between items.

> I am applying for summer jobs in Santa Fe, New Mexico; Albany, New York; Montgomery, Alabama; and Moscow, Idaho.

Semicolon separates items in a series

Colon

Like a flare in the road, a colon signals you to stop and then proceed, paying attention to the situation ahead. Colons have several uses.

:/

To Signal a Follow-Up Explanation. Use a colon when a complete introductory statement requires a follow-up explanation:

> She is an ideal colleague: honest, reliable, and competent.

Colon signals a follow-up explanation

Do not use a colon if the introductory statement is incomplete:

> My plans include: finishing college, traveling for two years, and settling down in Santa Fe.

Incorrect

To Replace a Semicolon. A colon can replace a semicolon between two related, complete statements when the second one explains or amplifies the first:

> Pam's reason for accepting the lowest-paying job offer was simple: She had always wanted to live in the Northwest.

Colon replaces a semicolon

To Introduce a Quotation. Colons can introduce quotations:

> The supervisor's message was clear enough: "You're fired."

Colon introduces a quotation

To Follow Salutations. Colons follow salutations in formal correspondence (e.g., Dear Ms. Jones:).

Comma

The comma is the most frequently used—and abused—punctuation mark. It works like a blinking yellow light, for which you slow down briefly without stopping. Never use a comma to signal a *break* between independent ideas, only a brief slow down. Use commas only in the following situations.

,/

To Pause Between Complete Ideas. In a compound sentence in which a coordinating conjunction (*and, or, nor, for, but*) connects equal (independent) statements, a comma usually precedes the conjunction.

> This is an excellent course, but the work is difficult.

Comma to pause between complete ideas

To Pause between an Incomplete and a Complete Idea. A comma is usually placed between a complete and an incomplete statement in a complex sentence when the incomplete statement comes first.

Comma between
an incomplete and
complete idea

| Because he is a fat cat, Jack diets often.

When the order is reversed (complete statement followed by an incomplete one), the comma is usually omitted:

No comma needed

| Jack diets often because he is a fat cat.

To Separate Items (Words, Phrases, or Clauses) in a Series. Use commas after items in a series, including the next-to-last item:

Comma separates
items in a series

Helen, Joe, Marsha, and John are joining us on the term project.
The new employee complained that the hours were long, the pay was low, the work was boring, and the supervisor was paranoid.

Use no commas if *or* or *and* appears between all items in a series:

No commas needed
if *or* or *and* appears
between all items

| She is willing to study in San Francisco or Seattle or even in Anchorage.

To Set Off Introductory Phrases. Introductory phrases include infinitive phrases (*to* plus a simple form of the verb), prepositional phrases (beginning with *at, of, in, on,* etc.), participial phrases (beginning with an *-ing* or *-ed* form of a verb), and interjections (emotional words that have no connection with the rest of the sentence). These phrases are set off from the remainder of the sentence by a comma:

Comma sets off
introductory phrases

To be or not to be, that is the question. (infinitive phrase)
In the event of an emergency, use the fire exit. (prepositional phrase)
Being an old cat, Jack was slow at catching mice. (participial phrase)
Oh, is that the verdict? (interjection)

To Set Off Nonrestrictive Phrases and Clauses. A *restrictive* phrase or clause modifies or defines the subject in such a way that deleting the modifier would change the meaning of the sentence. In the following sentence, "who have work experience" *restricts* the subject by limiting the category from all students to just those with work experience. Because this phrase is essential to the sentence's meaning, it is *not* set off by commas:

Restrictive phrase
(no comma)

| All students who have work experience will receive preference.

A *nonrestrictive* phrase or clause could be deleted without changing the sentence's meaning ("Our new manager is highly competent") and *is* therefore set off by commas:

> Our new manager, who has only six weeks' experience, is highly competent.

Nonrestrictive phrase (use comma)

To Set Off Parenthetical Elements.
Elements that interrupt the flow of a sentence (such as *of course, as a result, as I recall,* and *however*) are considered parenthetical and are enclosed by commas. These items may denote emphasis, afterthought, or clarification.

> This deluxe model, of course, is more expensive. (emphasis)
> Your essay, by the way, was excellent. (afterthought)
> The loss of my job was, in a way, a blessing. (clarification)

Commas to set off parenthetical elements

A direct address also interrupts a sentence and is set off by commas:

> Listen, my children, and you shall hear my story.

Commas to set off direct address

A parenthetical element at the beginning or the end of a sentence is also set off by a comma:

> Naturally, we will expect a full guarantee.
> You've done a good job, I think.

Commas to set off parenthetical elements at beginning and end

To Set Off Quoted Material.
Quoted items within a sentence are set off by commas:

> The customer said, "I'll take it," as soon as he laid eyes on our new model.

Comma to set off quoted material

To Set Off Appositives.
An *appositive*, a word or words explaining a noun and placed immediately after it, is set off by commas when the appositive is nonrestrictive:

> Martha Jones, our new president, is overhauling all personnel policies.
> Alpha waves, the most prominent of the brain waves, are typically recorded in a waking subject whose eyes are closed.

Comma to set off appositives

Other Uses.
Commas are used to set off the day of the month from the year in a date (May 10, 1989), to set off numbers in three-digit intervals (6,463,657), to

separate city and state in an address (Albany, Iowa), to set off parts of an address in a sentence (J. B. Smith, 18 Sea Street, Albany, Iowa, 51642), to set off day and year in a sentence (June 15, 2014, is my graduation date), and to set off degrees and titles from proper names (Roger P. Cayer, M.D., or Gordon Browne, Jr.).

Apostrophe

ap/

Apostrophes indicate the possessive, a contraction, and the plural of numbers, letters, and figures.

To Indicate the Possessive. At the end of a singular word or of a plural word that does not end in *-s*, add an apostrophe plus *-s* to indicate the possessive. Single-syllable nouns that end in *-s* take the apostrophe before an added *-s*:

Apostrophe to indicate possessives

> The people's candidate won.
> I borrowed Chris's book.

For words that already end in *-s* and have more than one syllable, add an *-s* after the apostrophe:

> Aristophanes's death

Do not use an apostrophe to indicate the possessive form of either singular or plural pronouns:

> The book was hers.
> Ours is the best school in the county.

At the end of a plural word that ends in *-s*, add an apostrophe only.

> the cows' water supply
> the Jacksons' wine cellar

At the end of a compound noun, add an apostrophe plus *-s*:

> my father-in-law's false teeth

At the end of the last word in nouns of joint possession, add an apostrophe plus *-s* if both own one item:

> Joe and Sam's lakefront cottage

Add an apostrophe plus *-s* to both nouns if each owns specific items:

> Joe's and Sam's passports

To Indicate a Contraction. An apostrophe shows that you have omitted one or more letters in a phrase that is usually a combination of a pronoun and a verb:

cont

> I'm
> they're
> you'd

Apostrophes to show contractions

Be careful with faulty contractions: For example, *they're* (short for "they are" and often confused with the possessive *their* and the adverb *there*); *it's* (short for "it is" and often confused with the possessive *its*); *who's* (short for "who is" and often confused with the possessive *whose*); and *you're* (short for "you are" and often confused with the possessive *your*). See Table B.1 (pages 457–459) for further examples.

To Indicate the Plurals of Numbers, Letters, and Figures. For example:

> The *6's* on this new printer look like smudged *G's*, *9's* are illegible, and the *%'s* are unclear.

Apostrophes to pluralize numbers, letters, and figures

Quotation Marks

Quotation marks have a variety of uses:

To Set Off the Exact Words Borrowed from Another Speaker or Writer. The period or comma at the end is placed within the quotation marks:

> "Hurry up," Jack whispered.
> Jack told Felicia, "I'm depressed."

Quotation marks to set off a speaker's exact words

A colon or semicolon is always placed outside quotation marks:

> Our student handbook clearly defines "core requirements"; however, it does not list all the courses that fulfill the requirements.

When a question mark or exclamation point is part of a quotation, it belongs within the quotation marks, replacing the comma or period.

> "Help!" he screamed.
> Marsha asked John, "Can't we agree about anything?"

But if the question mark or exclamation point pertains to the attitude of the person quoting instead of the person being quoted, it is placed outside the quotation mark:

> Why did Boris wink and whisper, "It's a big secret"?

To Indicate Titles. Use quotation marks around titles of articles, paintings, book chapters, and poems (but titles of books, journals, or newspapers should be underlined or italicized):

Quotation marks to
indicate titles

> The enclosed article, "The Job Market for College Graduates," should provide some helpful insights.

To Indicate Irony. Finally, use quotation marks (with restraint) to indicate irony.

Quotation marks to
indicate irony

> She is some "friend"!

 ## Ellipses

Three dots ... indicate that you have omitted material from a quotation. If the omitted words come at the end of the original sentence, a fourth dot indicates the period.

Ellipses to indicate
omitted material
from a quotation

> According to Beulah Montgomery, paper memorandums "... are now being ... replaced with email correspondence in most workplace situations. ..."

 ## Brackets

Brackets are used within quotations to set off material that was not in the original quotation but is needed for clarification:

Brackets to indicate
material added to
quotations

> "She [Amy] was the outstanding candidate for the scholarship."
> "It was in early spring [April 2, to be exact] that the tornado hit."

Use *sic* (Latin for "thus" or "so") in brackets when quoting an error from the original source:

Brackets to indicate
an error in a
quotation

> The assistant's comment was clear: "He don't [sic] want any."

 ## Italics

Use italics or underlining for titles of books, periodicals, films, newspapers, and plays; for the names of ships; and for foreign words or technical terms. Also, you may use italics *sparingly* for special emphasis.

Various uses of
italics

> The *Oxford English Dictionary* is a handy reference tool.
> My only advice is *caveat emptor.*
> *Bacillus anthracis* is a highly virulent organism.
> *Do not* inhale these fumes under any circumstances!

Parentheses

( )/

Material between parentheses, like all other parenthetical material discussed previously, can be deleted without harming the logical and grammatical structure of the sentence. Use parentheses to enclose material that defines or explains the statement that precedes it:

> An anaerobic (airless) environment must be maintained for the cultivation of this organism.
>
> The cost of running our college has increased by 15 percent in one year (see Appendix A for full cost breakdown).

Parentheses to define or explain preceding material

Dashes

--/

Dashes can be effective to set off parenthetical material if, like parentheses, they are not overused. Parentheses deemphasize the enclosed material, whereas dashes emphasize it:

> Have a good vacation—but watch out for sandfleas.
>
> Mary—a true friend—spent hours helping me rehearse.

Dashes to set off and emphasize material

On most word processing programs, a dash is created by two hyphens, which the software will typically convert to a dash.

MECHANICS

The mechanical aspects of writing a document include abbreviation, hyphenation, capitalization, use of numbers, and spelling. (Keep in mind that not all of these rules are hard and fast; some may depend on style guides used in your field.)

Abbreviation

The following should *always* be abbreviated:

- Titles such as *Ms.*, *Mr.*, *Dr.*, and *Jr.* when they are used before or after a proper name.
- Specific time designations (400 B.C.E., 5:15 A.M.).

Always abbreviate

The following should *never* be abbreviated:

- Military, religious, academic, or political titles (*Reverend, President*).
- Nonspecific time designations ("Sarah arrived early in the morning"—not "early in the A.M.").

Never abbreviate

Avoid abbreviations whose meanings might not be clear to all readers. Units of measurement can be abbreviated if they appear frequently in your document. However, a unit of measurement should be spelled out the first time it is used. Avoid abbreviations in visual aids unless saving space is absolutely necessary.

 ## Hyphenation

Hyphens divide words at line breaks and join two or more words used as a single adjective if they precede the noun (but not if they follow it):

Correct use of hyphens

> Com-puter (at a line break)
>
> An all-too-human error (but "The error was all too human")

Other commonly hyphenated words include the following:

Other uses of hyphens

- Most words that begin with the prefix *self-* (*self-reliance*, *self-discipline*—see your dictionary for exceptions).
- Combinations that might be ambiguous (*re-creation* versus *recreation*).
- Words that begin with *ex* when *ex* means "past" (*ex-faculty member* but *excommunicate*).
- All fractions, along with ratios that are used as adjectives and that precede the noun and compound numbers from twenty-one through ninety-nine (*a two-thirds majority, thirty-eight windows*).

cap ## Capitalization

Use capitalization in the following situations:

Uses of capitalization

- The first words of all sentences ("This is a good idea.").
- Titles of people if the title precedes the person's name, but not after (Senator Barbara Boxer but Barbara Boxer, U.S. senator).
- Titles of books, films, magazines, newspapers, operas, and other longer works. In addition to capitalizing the first word, also capitalize all other words within the title (*A Long Day's Journey into Night*) except articles, short prepositions, and coordinating conjunctions (*and, but, for, or, nor, yet*).
- Parts of a longer work (Chapter 25, Opus 23).
- Languages (French, Urdu).
- Days of the week (Saturday).
- Months (November).
- Holidays (Thanksgiving).

- Names of organizations or groups (World Health Organization).

- Races and nationalities (Asian American, Australian).

- Historical events (War of 1812).

- Important documents (Declaration of Independence).

- Names of structures or vehicles (Empire State Building, the *Queen Mary*).

- Adjectives derived from proper nouns (Chaucerian English).

- Words such as *street*, *road*, *corporation*, *university*, and *college* only when they accompany a proper noun (High Street, Rand Corporation, Stanford University).

- The words *north*, *south*, *east*, and *west* when they denote specific regions (*the South*, *the Northwest*) but not when they are simply directions (*turn east at the light*).

Do not capitalize the seasons (*spring*, *winter*) or general groups (*the younger generation*, *the leisure class*).

Numbers and Numerals

num

Numbers expressed in one or two words can be written out or written as numerals. Use numerals to express larger numbers, decimals, fractions, precise technical figures, or any other exact measurements:

> 543
> 2,800,357
> 3.25
> 15 pounds of pressure
> 50 kilowatts
> 4,000 rpm

Uses of numerals

Use numerals for dates, census figures, addresses, page numbers, exact units of measurement, percentages, times with A.M. or P.M. designations, and monetary and mileage figures.

> page 14
> 1:15 P.M.
> 18.4 pounds
> 9 feet
> 12 gallons
> $15

Additional uses of numerals

Do not begin a sentence with a numeral. If the figure needs more than two words, revise your word order:

> Six hundred students applied for the 102 available jobs.
> The 102 available jobs attracted 600 applicants.

Do not use numerals to express approximate figures, time not designated as A.M. or P.M., or streets named by numbers less than 100:

> Four fifteen
> 108 East Forty-Second Street

In contracts and other documents in which precision is vital, a number can be stated both in numerals and in words:

> The tenant agrees to pay a rental fee of eight hundred and seventy-five dollars ($875.00) monthly.

Spelling

Always use the spell-check or autocorrect function in your word processing or email software. However, don't rely on these tools exclusively. Take the time to use a dictionary for all writing assignments. If you are a poor speller, ask someone else to proofread every document before you present the final version.

USAGE

Be aware of the pairs of words (and sometimes groups of three words) that are often confused. Refer to Table B.1 for a list of the most commonly confused words.

TRANSITIONS

You can choose from three techniques to achieve smooth transitions within and between paragraphs.

Use Transitional Expressions

Use words such as *again, furthermore, in addition, meanwhile, however, also, although, for example, specifically, in particular, as a result, in other words, certainly, accordingly, because,* and *therefore.* Such words serve as bridges between ideas.

(*Text continues on page 459.*)

TABLE B.1 Commonly confused words

Similar Words	Used Correctly in a Sentence
Accept means "to receive willingly."	She *accepted* his business proposal.
Except means "otherwise than."	They all agreed, *except* Bob.
Affect means "to have an influence on."	Meditation *affects* concentration in a positive way.
Affect can also mean "to pretend."	Boris likes to *affect* a French accent.
Effect used as a noun means "a result."	Meditation has a positive *effect* on concentration.
Effect used as a verb means "to make happen" or "to bring about."	Meditation can *effect* an improvement in concentration.
Already means "before this time."	Our new laptops are *already* sold out.
All ready means "prepared."	We are *all ready* for the summer tourist season.
Among refers to three or more.	The prize was divided *among* the four winners.
Between refers to two.	The prize was divided *between* the two winners.
Cite means "to document."	You must always *cite* your sources in research.
Sight means "vision."	Margarita seems to have the gift of second *sight.*
Site means "a location."	Have the surveyors inspected the *site* yet?
Continual means "repeated at intervals."	Our lower field floods *continually* during the rainy season.
Continuous means "without interruption."	His headache has been *continuous* for three days.
Council means "a body of elected people."	I plan to run for student *council.*
Counsel means "to offer advice."	Because you have experience, I suggest you *counsel* Jim on the project as it moves along.
Differ from refers to unlike things.	This plan *differs* greatly *from* our previous one.
Differ with means "to disagree."	Mary *differs with* John about the plan.

(Continued)

TABLE B.1   Commonly confused words   (*Continued*)

Similar Words	Used Correctly in a Sentence
Disinterested means "unbiased" or "impartial."	Good science calls for *disinterested* analysis of research findings.
Uninterested means "not caring."	Boris is *uninterested* in science.
Eminent means "famous" or "distinguished."	Dr. Ostroff, the *eminent* physicist, is lecturing today.
Imminent means "about to happen."	A nuclear meltdown seemed *imminent.*
Farther refers to physical distance (a measurable quantity).	The station is 20 miles *farther.*
Further refers to extent (not measurable).	*Further* discussion of this issue is vital.
Fewer refers to things that can be counted.	*Fewer* than 50 students responded to our survey.
Less refers to things that can't be counted.	This survey had *less* of a response than our previous one.
Imply means "to insinuate."	This report *implies* that a crime occurred.
Infer means "to reason from evidence."	From this report, we can *infer* that a crime occurred.
It's stands for "it is."	*It's* a good time for a department meeting.
Its stands for "belonging to it."	The cost of the project has exceeded *its* budget.
Lay means "to set something down."	Please *lay* the blueprints on the desk.
Lie means "to recline." It takes no direct object.	This patient needs to *lie* on his right side all night.
(Note that the past tense of *lie* is *lay.*)	The patient *lay* on his right side all night.
Precede means "to come before."	Audience analysis should *precede* a written report.
Proceed means "to go forward."	If you must wake the cobra, *proceed* carefully.
Principle is always a noun that means "basic rule or standard."	Ethical *principles* should govern all our communications.
Principal, used as a noun, means "the major person(s)."	All *principals* in this purchase must sign the contract.

TABLE B.1 Commonly confused words (*Continued*)

Similar Words	Used Correctly in a Sentence
Principal, used as an adjective, means "leading."	Martha was the *principal* negotiator for this contract.
Stationary means "not moving."	The desk is *stationary*.
Stationery means "writing supplies."	The supply cabinet needs *stationery*.
Their means "belonging to them."	They all want to have *their* cake and eat it too.
There means "at that location."	The new copy machine is over *there*.
They're means "they are."	*They're* not the only ones who disagree.

(*Transitions, continued from page 456.*)

Repeat Key Words and Phrases

To help link ideas, repeat key words or phrases or rephrase them in different ways, as in this next paragraph (emphasis added):

> Whales are among the most *intelligent* of all mammals. Scientists rank whale *intelligence* with that of higher primates because of *whales' sophisticated* group behavior. These *bright creatures* have been seen teaching and disciplining *their* young, helping *their* wounded comrades, engaging in elaborate courtship rituals, and playing in definite *gamelike patterns. They* are able to coordinate such *complex cognitive activities* through *their* highly effective communication system of sonar clicks and pings. Such remarkable social organization apparently stems from the *humanlike* devotion that *whales* seem to display toward one another.

Repeated key words and phrases

The key word *intelligent* in the preceding topic statement reappears as *intelligence* in the second sentence. Synonyms describing intelligent behavior (*sophisticated, bright, humanlike*) reinforce and advance the main idea throughout.

Use Forecasting Statements

Forecasting statements tell your readers where you are going next:

> The next step is to further examine the costs of this plan.
> Of course, we can also consider other options.
> This plan should be reconsidered for several reasons.

Forecasting statements

If you encounter a situation in which you think you need a better transition but none of these methods seems appropriate, you may need to delete or move some information.

LISTS

Listed items can be presented in one of two ways: running in as part of the sentence (embedded lists) or displayed with each item on a new line (vertical lists).

Embedded Lists

An embedded list integrates a series of items into a sentence. To number an embedded list, use parentheses around the numerals and either commas or semicolons between the items, as in the following example:

Embedded list

> In order to complete express check-in for your outpatient surgery, you must (1) go to the registration office, (2) sign in and obtain your registration number, (3) receive and wear your red armband, and (4) give your check-in slip to the volunteer, who will escort you to your room.

Vertical Lists

Embedded lists are appropriate for listing only a few short items. Vertical lists are preferable for multiple items. If the items belong in a particular sequence, use numerals or letters; if the sequence of items is unimportant, use bullets.

There are a number of ways to introduce vertical lists. You can introduce a vertical list with a sentence that closes with "the following" or "as follows" and ends with a colon:

Vertical list using
following and a
colon

> All applicants for the design internship must submit the following:
>
> - Personal statement
> - Résumé
> - Three letters of reference
> - Portfolio

You can also introduce a vertical list with a sentence that closes with a noun and ends with a colon:

Vertical list using a
noun and a colon

> All applicants for the design internship must submit four items:
>
> 1. Personal statement
> 2. Résumé
> 3. Three letters of reference
> 4. Portfolio

Finally, you can introduce a vertical list with a sentence that is grammatically incomplete without the list items:

> To register as a new student:
> 1. Take the placement test at the Campus Test Center.
> 2. Attend a new student orientation.
> 3. Register for classes by Web or telephone.
> 4. Pay tuition and fees by the due date.

Vertical list using grammatical incompleteness

Do not use a colon with an introductory sentence that ends with a verb, a preposition, or an infinitive, as in the following incorrect examples:

> All applicants for the design internship must submit:
> - A personal statement
> - A résumé
> - Three letters of reference
> - A portfolio

Incorrect because the introductory sentence ends with a verb

> All applicants for the design internship need to:
> - Submit a personal statement and résumé
> - Forward three letters of reference
> - Provide a portfolio

Incorrect because the introductory sentence ends with a preposition

> All applicants for the design internship need to submit:
> - A personal statement
> - A résumé
> - Three letters of reference
> - A portfolio

Incorrect because the introductory sentence ends with an infinitive

If the sentence that introduces the list is followed by another sentence, use periods after both sentences. Do not use a colon to introduce the list:

> The next step is to configure the following fields. Consult Chapter 3 for more information on each field.
> - Serial port
> - Baud rate
> - Data bits
> - Stop bits

Vertical list without a colon

Note that some of the preceding examples use a period after each list item and some do not. As a general rule, use a period after each list item if any of the items contains a complete sentence. Do not use a period if none of the list items contains a complete sentence. Also note that items included in a list should be grammatically parallel. For more on parallelism, see page 104.

WORKS CITED

Carliner, Saul. "Demonstrating Effectiveness and Value: A Process for Evaluating Technical Communication Products and Services." *Technical Communication*, vol. 44, no. 3, 1997, pp. 252-65.

Centers for Disease Control and Prevention. *Social Media Guidelines and Best Practices*. United States Department of Health and Human Services, 16 May 2012, www.cdc.gov/SocialMedia/Tools/guidelines/pdf/FacebookGuidelines.pdf.

Coe, Marlana. *Human Factors for Technical Communicators*. Wiley, 1996.

Consumer Product Safety Commission. *Fact Sheet No. 65*. U.S. Government Printing Office, 1989.

Corbett, Edward P. J. *Classical Rhetoric for the Modern Student*. 3rd ed. Oxford UP, 1990.

Crosby, Olivia. *Employment Interviewing*. U.S. Department of Labor, 2000.

Daugherty, Shannon. "The Usability Evaluation: A Discount Approach to Usability Testing." *INTERCOM*, Dec. 1997, pp. 16–20.

Fisher, Anne. "Truth and Consequences." *Fortune*, 29 May 2000, p. 292.

Gartaganis, Arthur. "Lasers." *Occupational Outlook Quarterly*, Winter 1984, pp. 22–26.

Gibaldi, Joseph, and Walter S. Achtert. *MLA Handbook for Writers of Research Papers*. 3rd ed. Modern Language Assoc., 1988.

Girill, T. R. "Technical Communication and Law." *Technical Communication*, vol. 32, no. 3, 1985, p. 37.

Golen, Steven, et al. "How to Teach Ethics in a Basic Business Communications Class." *Journal of Business Communication*, vol. 22, no. 1, 1985, pp. 75-84.

Greenberg, Ilan. "Selling News Short." *Brill's Content*, Mar. 2000, pp. 64–65.

Hart, Geoff. "Accentuate the Negative: Obtaining Effective Reviews through Focused Questions." *Technical Communication*, vol. 44, no. 1, 1997, pp. 52-57.

Hein, Robert G. "Culture and Communication." *Technical Communication*, vol. 38, no. 1, 1991, pp. 125-26.

Hoft, Nancy L. *International Technical Communication: How to Export Information about High Technology*. Wiley, 1995.

Japikse, Catharina, "Lasagna in the Making." *EPA Journal*, vol. 20, no. 3, 1990, p. 27.

Kipnis, David, and Stuart Schmidt. "The Language of Persuasion." *Psychology Today*, Apr. 1985, pp. 40–46. Reprinted in *Understanding Persuasion*. 3rd ed. Edited by Raymond S. Ross, Prentice Hall, 1990.

Lavin, Michael R. *Business Information: How to Find it, How to Use It*. 2nd ed. Oryx, 1992.

MacKenzie, Nancy. Unpublished review of John M. Lannon's *Technical Writing*. 5th ed. Little Brown, 1991.

"Misconduct Scandal Shakes German Science." *Professional Ethics Report*. American Assoc. for the Advancement of Science, vol. 10, no. 3, 1997, www.aaas.org/sites/default/files/migrate/uploads/per10.pdf.

"News Release: ANA and NCSBN Unite to Provide Guidelines for Social Media and Networking for Nurses." *ANA/ American Nurses Association*, 19 Oct. 2011, www.nursingworld.org/FunctionalMenuCategories/AboutANA/Social-Media/ANA-NCSBN-Provide-Social-Media-Guidelines.html.

Office of Technology Assessment. *Harmful Non-Indigenous Species in the United States*. U.S. Government Printing Office, 1993.

"Performance Appraisal—Discrimination." *The Employee Problem Solver*. Alexander Hamilton Institute, 2000.

Ross, Raymond S. *Understanding Persuasion*. 3rd ed. Prentice Hall, 1990.

Rubin, J. *Handbook of Usability Testing: How to Plan, Design, and Conduct Effective Tests*. Wiley, 1994.

Ruiz, Rebecca. "How the Internet Is Changing Health Care." *Forbes*, 30 July 2009, www.forbes.com/2009/07/30/health-wellness-internet-lifestyle-health-online-facebook.html.

Spencer, SueAnn. "Use Self-Help to Improve Document Usability." *Technical Communication*, vol. 43, no. 1, 1996, pp. 73–77.

Stanton, Mike. "Fiber Optics." *Occupational Outlook Quarterly*, Winter 1984, pp. 27-30.

Vaughan, David K. "Abstracts and Summaries: Some Clarifying Distinctions." *Technical Writing Teacher*, vol. 18, no. 2, 1991, pp. 132-41.

Victor, David A. *International Business Communication*. Harper, 1992.

Weymouth, L. C. "Establishing Quality Standards and Trade Regulations for Technical Writing in World Trade." *Technical Communication*, vol. 37, no. 2, 1990, pp. 143-47.

Wojahn, Patricia G. "Computer-Mediated Communication: The Great Equalizer between Men and Women?" *Technical Communication*, vol. 41, no. 4, 1994, pp. 747–51.

"Writing for Social Media." *SFU Editorial Style Guide*, www.sfu.ca/clf/styleguide.html.

INDEX

Abbreviations, 453–454
About.com, 29
Abstracts
  descriptive, 275–276
  in formal proposals, 340
  in formal reports, 305, 310–311, 317
  as hard-copy research source, 36
  informative, 275
Academic web sites, 32
Academic writing, technical
    communication compared to, 4
Acceptance letters, 169–170
Accuracy
  ethics and, 72
  of summaries, 270
Acronyms, 211
Action plan presentations, 390–391
Active voice
  in instructions, 255
  readability and, 96–97
  in writing tone, 105
Adjustment letters, 200–202
Adobe Connect, 400
Agendas
  for meeting minutes, 292–293
  for meetings, 17
Almanacs, 36
Alphanumeric notations, 81
Ambiguous modifiers, 96
Ambiguous pronouns, 95–96
American Chemical Society (ACS), 426
American Psychological Association
    style. *See* APA (American
    Psychological Association) style,
    for documentation
Analysis of parts, in definitions, 212–213
Analytical reports
  feasibility reports, 293–295
  peer review reports, 298–299
  purpose of, 283
  recommendation reports, 296–298
APA (American Psychological
    Association) style, for
    documentation
  for books, 426–429
  for electronic sources, 432–435
  for gray literature, 435–436
  index to, 427
  for miscellaneous sources, 430–432
  for parenthetical references, 425–426
  for periodicals, 429–430
  for reference entries, 426
*APA Style Guide to Electronic
    References,* 435
Apostrophes, in punctuation, 450–451

Appendices
  in formal reports, 312, 323
  in proposals, 346
Application letters
  definition of, 158
  function of, 158
  sample, 160
  solicited, 159–160
  specificity in, 161
  tone in, 161
  unsolicited, 159
Aptitude, assessment of, 152–153
Arguable claim letters, 195, 197
Audiences
  analysis of, strategies for, 50
  for blogs, 371
  cultural backgrounds for, 47–48
  definitions by, 207–208
  for descriptions, 222, 235
  for emails, 352–353, 356
  for feasibility reports, 294
  for formal reports, 304–305
  global, for technical communication,
    12–13
  for instructions, 244
  for meeting minutes, 292
  for oral presentations, 388, 389
  for periodic activity reports, 287
  power connection approach to, 53
  primary, for documents, 45–46
  for procedures, 261
  for progress reports, 283–284
  for proposals, 328
  rational connection approach to, 54–55
  for recommendation reports, 296
  relationship connection approach to,
    54–55
  secondary, or documents, 45–46
  for social media, 377–379
  for specifications, 238
  for summaries, 268–269
  technical background for, 47
  for user-friendly documents, 132
  for web pages, 372
  for wikis, 371
  for workplace text messages, 357–358

Background information,
    in proposals, 334
Bar graphs
  multiple, 116–117
  simple, 117
Beaucoup!, directory of directories, 29
Bibliographic citations, 407

Bibliographic Index Plus, 35
Bibliographies, 35
Bing, search engine, 29
Block formats, of letters, 188, 189
Blogs
  advantages of, 363
  audience considerations for, 371
  corporate, 363–364
  general applications for, 374
  global applications for, 374
  as online research source, 32–33
  strategies for, 371–372
  team applications for, 374
  virtual teams use of, 21
  web-based applications for, 374
Boldface
  in document design, 138, 141, 144
  in web pages, 370
Books, as hard-copy research sources, 35
  APA documentation style for, 426–429
  MLA documentation style for, 414–417
Books in Print, 35
Brackets, 409, 452
Brochures
  instructional, 245–246
  purpose, 12
Budgets, usability of information and,
    59, 61
Bulleted items
  in document design, 132, 142, 144
  in memos, 185
  in web pages, 371

Calls for proposals (CFPs), 12
Capitalization, 454–455
Career objectives, in résumés, 154
Causal analysis, in formal reports,
    305–306
Cause and effect sequencing, 83, 314–323
Cautions, in instructions, 252–254
CFPs (calls for proposals), 12
Charts
  audience considerations, 129
  creation of, 121
  flowcharts, 119–121
  organization, 119, 121
  pie charts, 119–121
Chicago Manual of Style, 436
Chronological sequencing
  in complex product descriptions, 229
  explanation of, 83
  in general descriptions, 224
  in instruction forms, 83
  in progress reports, 286

Chunking
    outlining and, 83
    in web pages, 83, 368–369
Circular definitions, 217
Claim letters, 195–198
Claims
    exaggeration of, as ethical abuse, 70
    in persuasive documents, 52
    in proposals, 336
Clarity, in technical communication, 5,
        107–108
Closing summaries, 275
Coherence, of information
    in information structure, 77
    from paragraphing, 85–86
Collaboration
    team projects, 14, 20–21
    technical communication as, 14–22
Colons, in punctuation, 447
Color
    in document design, 141–142, 144
    in visuals, 127–128
    in web pages, 370
Commas, in punctuation, 447–450
Comma splices, 441–442
Commercial web sites, 32
Common knowledge, documentation
        from, 406
Commonly confused words, 457–459
Comparative analysis, in formal
        reports, 305
Completeness, of summaries, 270
Complex process descriptions
    conclusions in, 235
    definition in, 233
    headers in, 233
    labels in, 233–234
    language use in, 232
    outlines for, 232
    sequence in, 233
    titles in, 233
    visuals in, 233–234
Complex product description, 228–231
    conclusions in, 231
    labeling in, 230–231
    language use in, 228
    outlines for, 228
    sequence in, 229, 231
    titles in, 229
Computer-based instructions,
        247–250
Computer-supported cooperative work
        (CSCW), 21
Concise writing
    readability and, 108
    in summaries, 270
    wordiness, avoidance of, 100–102

Conclusions
    in complex process descriptions, 235
    in complex product descriptions, 231
    for formal reports, 307, 311, 321, 345
    in general descriptions, 224–225
    for instructions, 252
    in oral presentations, 392
    in presentation software, 398, 401
    in proposals, 334
Confidentiality
    documentation of sources and, 412
    in emails, 356
    ethics and, 67–68
    privacy rights, 358–359, 371
Conflict management, teamwork and
    constructive criticism in, 15–18
    cultural differences in, 17
    gender differences, 16
    interpersonal differences in, 15
    strategies, 18
Consistency
    in document design, 136, 145
    in specifications, 236–237
    in tone, 105
Constructive criticism
    in conflict management, 15–18
    in interviews, 171
    for peer review reports, 298
Contact information
    in inquiry letters, 195
    in résumés, 154
Copyrights
    definition of, 436
    in digital communication, 358–359
    documentation of sources and, 437
    fair use and, 406, 437
    infringement of, plagiarism and, 438
    for public domain material, 437
Corporate blogs
    external, 364–365
    internal, 363–364
Corporate wikis, 365
Costs, in proposals, 334, 343–344
Council of Science Editors style, 436
Counterfeiting, 74
Courtesy, in letters, 191
Cover letter. See Application letters
Credits, for sources
    in graphs, 119
    in photographs, 123
    in proposals, 335
    in tables, 116
Critical thinking, 26–27
Criticism. See Constructive criticism
Cross-referencing, in visuals, 127
CSCW (computer-supported cooperative
        work), 21

CSE (Council of Science Editors) style,
        for documentation, 436
Cultural bias, in personable writing
        style, 106
Culture or cultural differences
    conflict management and, 17
    ethical abuses and, 62, 70–71
    usability of information and, 62
Customer reviews, on social media,
        376, 379
Cut and paste, in summaries, 271
Cutaway diagrams, 123

Danger notices, in instructions, 252–254
Dashes, in punctuation, 453
Data, in formal reports, 307
Dates, in letters, 187
Decimal notations, 81–82
Definitions
    acronyms and, 211
    analysis of parts in, 212–213
    audience considerations for, 207–208
    circular, 217
    classification in, 217
    through comparison, 213
    in complex process descriptions, 233
    through contrast, 213
    detail level for, 217
    in dictionaries, 211
    in encyclopedias, 211
    ethical implications of, 208
    etymology in, 211
    examples in, 214
    expanded, 210, 215
    general applications of, 218
    global applications of, 219
    history sources for, 211–212
    item differentiation in, 217
    legal implications of, 208
    multiple expansion methods for,
        214–215
    negation in, 212
    nontechnical versions of, 207
    operating principles in, 212
    parenthetical, 209
    placement of, 216–217
    purpose of, 206–208
    required conditions for, 214
    for sentences, 209–210
    societal implications of, 208
    team applications of, 219
    technical versions of, 207
    through visuals, 213
    transitions in, 214
    web-based applications of, 219
Delivery, of oral presentations, 401–402

Delivery style, for oral presentations, 394–395
Descriptions
    audience considerations for, 222, 235
    conclusions in, 224–225
    general applications for, 240
    global applications for, 241
    introductions in, 223–224
    objectivity in, 222–223
    process, 225, 227
    product, 225–226
    in proposals, 334
    purpose of, 221–222
    sequence of topics in, 224
    specifications, 236–238
    strategies for, 235
    subjectivity in, 222–223
    team applications for, 240–241
    titles in, 223
    visuals in, 224, 225
    web-based applications for, 241
Descriptive abstracts, in summaries, 275–276
Design, in documents. *See also* Style
    boldface in, 138, 141, 144
    bulleted lists, 132, 142, 144
    for cohesiveness, 136, 145
    color in, 141–142, 144
    for consistency, 136, 145
    for emphasis, 140, 146
    fonts, 138–140
    footers in, 143, 145
    general applications for, 146
    global applications for, 147
    grid patterns, 136, 139
    headers in, 143, 145
    headings, 140–141, 144
    indentation in, 138
    indexes in, 144, 145
    ineffective, 133
    in instructions, 256–260
    italics in, 138, 141, 144
    justification of text in, 137, 139
    line spacing, 138, 140
    margins, 136, 139
    for navigation, 140, 146
    numbered lists, 142, 144
    for paragraphs, 136–137, 139
    for PDFs, 132, 134
    redesign, 134
    shading in, 141, 144
    software for, 135
    for table of contents, 144, 145
    team applications for, 146
    underlining in, 141, 144
    for usability of information, 61–62
    for user-friendly documents, 132

visual hierarchy in, 135
    web-based applications for, 147
    white space, 137–140
Details, in instructions, 254–255, 257
Diagrams
    audience considerations, 129
    creation of, 125
    importance of, 113
    purpose of, 122–123
    types of, 122–123
Dictionaries
    definitions in, 211
    as secondary source reference, 36
Digests, 278
Digital communication. *See also* Emails;
        Text messages, in workplace
    APA documentation style for, 432–435
    backup plans with, 360
    copyrights with, 358–359
    electronic résumés, 161–163
    Internet usage, 24
    MLA documentation style for, 421–425
    privacy protections in, 358–359
Digital Object Identifier (DOI), 34
Digital whiteboards, 21
Direct actions, in persuasive documents, 52
Directories, 36
Documentation, of sources. *See also*
        Credits, for sources; Plagiarism
    APA style, 425–436
    from common knowledge, 406
    confidential sources, 412
    copies of, 407
    copyright issues, 436–438
    efficiency of, 411
    for ethical reasons, 411
    function of, 406, 411–412
    as matter of authority, 411–412
    MLA style, 413–425
    from notes, 406–408
    from outside sources, 406
    paraphrasing others and, 409–410
    with quotes, 408–409
    by summarizing works of others, 410–411
    from works cited, 407
Documents. *See also* Design,
        in documents
    audience analysis for, 45–50
    budgets of, 59, 61
    editing of, 19–20
    informational, 5–7
    instructional, 5–6, 8
    intended use of, 51

mechanics of, 453–456
    persuasive, 9, 51–56
    plan development for, 59–61
    primary audiences for, 45–46
    purpose of, 50–51
    relationship with audiences with, 46–47
    secondary audiences for, 45–46
    task analysis for, 56–57
    transitions within, 456–460
DOI (Digital Object Identifier), 34
Dossiers, 163, 165–166

EBSCOHost, 34
Editing
    documents, 19
    strategies for, 19–20
    of summaries, 271
    symbols, 439
Editing software, 21
Education, in résumés, 156
Electronic information, misuse, 70
Electronic mailing lists, 33
Electronic résumés
    in emails, 161
    online, 161–162
    scanned, 162
Ellipses, 409, 452
Emails
    audience considerations for, 352–353, 356
    changing character of, 352
    components of, 353
    confidentiality in, 356
    formatting for, 356
    general applications of, 361
    global applications of, 361
    language use in, 356
    memos compared to, 178
    netiquette for, 353
    organization of, 353
    popularity of, 351
    proofreading of, 357
    purpose of, 352–353
    résumés in, 161
    signature blocks in, 356
    strategies for, 356–357
    style in, 353
    subject lines in, 356
    team applications of, 361
    text messages compared to, 358, 359
    in virtual meetings, 21
    web-based applications of, 361
    in workplace, 9, 353–355
Embedded lists, 460
Emergency notifications, 381–382

Employment, search for. *See also*
    Application letters; Dossiers;
    Portfolios; Résumés
  aptitude assessment in, 152–153
  industry-specific resources for, 153
  in job postings, 153–154, 380
  on LinkedIn, 161, 163, 165, 380
  research for, 153–154
  skills assessment for, 152–153
  through social networking, 161, 380
  Twitter, 380
Employment documents
  mission statement in, 165
  personal information in, 163, 166
Employment uses for social media, 380
Encyclopedias
  definitions in, 211
  as secondary source reference, 36
End matter
  in formal proposals, 332
  in formal reports, 311–312
E-portfolios
  copies in, 165
  item assembly in, 165
  mission statement in, 165
  personal information in, 166
Ethics
  abuse avoidance strategies, 72
  codes of, 71
  confidentiality and, 67–68
  cultural exploitation and, 70–71
  definitions and, 208
  in documentation of sources, 411
  for electronic information, 70
  exaggeration of claims, 70
  fabrication of information, 69–70
  general applications for, 73
  global applications for, 74
  in instructions, 251
  interpretation of, 72
  plagiarism and, 69, 405–406
  social media, 382–383
  stealing information, 70
  in summaries, 276, 278
  team applications for, 73
  in technical communication, 5, 67
  types of choices for, 67–98
  usability of information and, 62
  visual manipulation and, 70
  for visuals, use of, 128
  web-based applications, 74
  with web pages, 371
  workplace pressures and, 69
Exclamation points, in punctuation, 446
Executive summaries
  in formal reports, 310–311
  purpose of, 276
  sample of, 277

Expanded definitions
  hyperlinked, 216–217
  methods for, 210–214
  multiple methods, 214
  sample, 215
  usage of, 210
Experiments, as primary research
    source, 41
Experts, in informational interviews, 38
Explicit persuasiveness, 5
Exploded diagrams, 123
Extemporaneous delivery style, for oral
    presentations, 395
External corporate blogs, 364–365

Fabrication of information, as ethical
    abuse, 69–70
Facebook, 376, 380, 383
Face-to-face meetings, 15, 21
Fairness, 73
Fair use, copyrights and, 406, 437
Faulty coordination, in grammar,
    443–445
Feasibility analysis, in formal reports,
    306, 307
Feasibility reports
  audience considerations for, 294
  elements of, 295
  strategies for, 294
Feedback, on usability, of information, 62
Flowcharts, 119–121
Fluent writing, readability and
  importance of, 102
  parallel structure in, 104
  readability and, 108
  related ideas in, 103
  sentence construction in, 103–104
Follow-up letters
  acceptance letters, 169–170
  refusal letters, 169–170
  thank you letters, 168–169
Follow-up memos, 181, 183
Fonts
  in scanned résumés, 161
  size, 139, 140
  style, 138–140
  in web pages, 370
Footers, in document design, 143, 145
Forecasting statements, 459–460
Formal outlines
  with alphanumeric notations, 81
  with decimal notations, 81–82
Formal proposals
  abstracts in, 340
  appendices in, 346
  background information in, 334
  conclusions in, 334

costs in, 334, 343–344
  described, 329
  descriptions in, 334
  end matter in, 332
  front matter in, 332
  organization of, 332–334
  qualifications in, 334
  resolution in, 334
  samples of, 336–346
  statements in, 334
  strategies for, 335–336
  subject line in, 332
  table of contents in, 339
  timing in, 334
  titles in, 332, 338
  transmittal letter in, 337
Formal reports
  abstracts in, 305, 310–311, 317
  appendices in, 312, 323
  audience considerations for, 304–305
  causal analysis in, 305–306
  comparative analysis in, 305
  conclusions for, 307, 311, 321, 345
  data in, 307
  end matter in, 311–312
  executive summaries in, 310–311
  feasibility analysis in, 306, 307
  front matter in, 310–311
  general applications for, 325
  global applications for, 325
  glossary in, 312
  informal compared to, 303–304
  introductions in, 311, 318
  list of tables and figures, 310
  proofreading for, 313
  purpose of, 304–305
  purpose statement in, 307–308
  readability for, 308
  references in, 311–312, 322
  research for, 304
  sample, 313–324
  strategies for, 312–313
  structure of, 308
  table of contents in, 310, 316
  tables in, 309
  team applications for, 325
  text in, 311
  title page, 310, 315
  transmittal letters in, 309, 314
  user-friendly design in, 308
  visuals in, 308, 309
  web-based applications for, 325
  works cited list in, 311–312
Formal tone, in writing style, 105
Formatting
  for emails, 356
  of graphs, 121
  of headings, 87

of instructions, 244
of letters, 188
of memos, 178–179
of procedures, 244
for proposals, 335
in scanned résumés, 161
for usability of information, 59, 61
Front matter
in formal proposals, 332
in formal reports, 310–311
Functional résumés, 156–157
Functional sequences, in descriptions, 224, 233

Gender differences, 16
Global technical communication
effectiveness, 22
language issues in, 13, 24
research for, 13
Glossary, in formal reports, 312
Google, 29
Google+, 376, 380
Google Docs, 399
GoToMeeting, 400
Government standards, specifications and, 236
Government web sites, 32
Grammar. *See also* Punctuation; Sentences
comma splices, 441–442
faulty agreement, 442–443
faulty coordination, 443–445
faulty pronoun case, 445
pronouns, 443, 445
referent agreement, 443
sentence fragments, 440–441
subordination, 443–445
verb agreement, 442–443
Graphs
audience considerations, 129
bar, 116–117
creation of, 118–119
formatting of, 116
labels in, 112
line, 117–118
purpose of, 112
source credits in, 119
Gray literature
APA documentation for, 435–436
as hard-copy research source, 37
Grid patterns
in document design, 136, 139
in web pages, 370

Handbooks, 36
Hard-copy résumés, 161–163

Hard-copy sources, for research
abstracts as, 36
books, 35
gray literature, 37
in libraries, 35
online sources versus, 28
periodicals, 35
reference works, 35–37
Headers
in complex process descriptions, 233
in document design, 143, 145
Headings
in document design, 140–141, 144
formatting of, 87
in information structure, 86–87
in instructions, 258
in memos, 185
purpose of, 87
in web pages, 370
Honesty, 73
Hyperlinks
in e-portfolios, 166
expanded definitions, 216–217
formatting of, 370
in instructions, 134, 247–249
in online résumés, 166
Hyphenation, 454

Icons, 124–126
Idioms, 13
Illustrations, 122–123, 125, 129
IM (instant messaging)
text messages compared to, 357
virtual teams use of, 21
Imperative mood, in instructions, 255
Implicit persuasiveness, 5
Impromptu delivery style, for oral presentations, 394
Incoherent paragraphs, 85–86
Indentation, in document design, 138
Indexes
to APA reference entries, 427
in document design, 144, 145
to MLA reference entries, 415
as secondary source reference, 35–36
Inefficient style, in documents, 94–95
Informal proposals
background information in, 334
conclusions in, 334
described, 329
descriptions in, 334
end matter in, 332
front matter in, 332
organization of, 332–334
qualifications in, 334
resolution in, 334
statements in, 334

strategies for, 335–336
subject line in, 332
timing in, 334
titles in, 332
Informal reports
analytical, 293–299
definition of, 294
formal compared to, 303–304
general applications for, 300
global applications for, 301
informational, 283–293
team applications for, 300–301
web-based applications for, 301
Informal tone, in writing style, 105
Information
suppressing or downplaying, 70
theft, 70
Informational documents, 5–7
Informational interviews
expert opinions in, 38
follow-up to, 39
professionalism in, 39
strategies, 38–39
Informational memos, 182, 184
Informational reports
elements of, 285
meeting minutes, 292–293
periodic activity reports, 287
progress reports, 283–286
purpose of, 283–284
trip reports, 287–297
Information plans, for documents, 59–60
Informative abstracts, in summaries, 275
Informative oral presentations, 388, 390
InfoTrac, 34
Inquiry letters
contact information in, 195
research for, 195
solicited, 193
unsolicited, 193–194
Inside address, in letters, 187
Instant messaging (IM)
text messages compared to, 357
virtual teams use of, 21
Institute of Electrical and Electronics Engineers (IEEE), style guide for, 426
Instructional documents
clarity and relevance, 5
example, 8
purpose of, 6
sequencing in, 83–84
structure of, 77–80
Instructional videos
creation strategies for, 126
frames, 124
YouTube, 376, 382

Instructions
  active voice in, 255
  audience considerations for, 244
  body of, 252
  in brochures, 245–246
  cautions in, 252–254
  computers-based, 247–250
  conclusion of, 252
  content of, 254–255
  danger notices in, 252–254
  definition of, 243
  design in, 256–260
  details in, 254–255, 257
  ethical implications of, 251
  formatting of, 244
  general applications for, 265
  global applications for, 266
  headings in, 258
  hyperlinks in, 247–249
  imperative mood in, 255
  introductions in, 252
  legal implications of, 251
  notes in, 252–254
  numbered lists in, 258
  online, 250
  phrasing in, 256
  purpose of, 9, 244
  in quick reference materials, 246
  sample, 259–260
  sentence structure in, 256
  strategies for, 263
  style of, 255–256
  team applications for, 266
  technicalities in, 254–255, 257
  titles in, 251
  transitions in, 256
  types of, 245–250
  usability testing in, 263
  in user manuals, 246
  visuals in, 252
  warnings in, 252–254
  web-based applications for, 266
Intellectual property piracy, 74
Interactive web pages, 366
Internal corporate blogs, 363–364
International Standard Serial Number
  (ISSN), 34
Internet, as online research source,
  28–29
Internet forums, as research source, 33
Internet Public Library, 29, 34
Internet service providers (ISPs), 5
Interpersonal differences, 15
Interviews
  criticism in, 171
  follow-up for, 168–171
  informational, as hard-copy research
    source, 38–39

  personal attitude in, 170–171
  practice questions for, 168
  preparation for, 167
  purpose of, 167
  strategies for, 170–171
  types of, 167
Intranets, 21
Introductions
  in descriptions, 223–224
  in formal reports, 311, 318
  in instructions, 252
  in oral presentations, 391–392
ISPs (Internet service providers), 5
ISSN (International Standard Serial
  Number), 34
Italics
  in document design, 141, 144
  as punctuation, 452
  in web pages, 370

Jargon, readability and, 100
Job postings
  LinkedIn, 161, 163, 165, 380
  sources for, 153–154
  Twitter, 380
Justified text
  in document design, 137, 139

Labels
  in complex process descriptions,
    233–234
  in complex product description,
    230–231
  in graphs, 112
Language
  in complex process description, 232
  in complex product description, 228
  culturally-biased, 106
  in emails, 356
  in global technical communication, 13
  in letters, 191–192
  objectivity of, in descriptions, 223
  sexist, avoidance of, 106–107
  in specifications, 238
Legal factors
  for definitions, 208
  for instructions, 251
  for social media, 382–383
  for usability of information, 62
Letters. See also Emails; Memos
  acceptance, 169–170
  adjustment, 200–202
  application letters, 158–161
  body text in, 187
  claim, 195–198
  closing in, 187

  courtesy in, 191
  date in, 187
  direct approach in, 192
  follow-up, 168–170
  formatting of, 188
  function of, 185
  general applications for, 203
  global applications for, 204
  indirect approach in, 192
  inquiry, 193–195
  inside address in, 187
  for international readers, 192
  optional parts, 188
  overview of, 176–177
  purpose of, 9
  refusal, 169–170
  sales, 198–200
  sales proposals as, 333
  salutations in, 187
  sender's address, 187
  signature in, 187
  simple language in, 191–192
  solicited application, 159–160
  standard, 185–187
  strategies, 192–193
  tact in, 191
  team applications for, 204
  thank you, 168–169
  tone of, 188–192
  unsolicited application, 159
  web-based applications for, 204
  workplace, 186
  "you" perspective in, 188–191
Libraries, as hard-copy research
    source, 35
Library of Congress Gateway, 35
LibrarySpot, 35
Line graphs
  multiple, 118
  simple, 118
Line spacing, in document design,
  138, 140
LinkedIn
  job postings on, 161, 163, 165, 380
  professional networking, 376, 380–381
Links, in web pages, 370
Listed items
  embedded, 460
  vertical, 460–461

Manuals, 9–12. See also
  User manuals
Maps, 123
Margins, in document design, 136, 139
Media, in technical communication, 5
Medical procedures, 261
Meeting minutes, 292–293

Meetings. *See also* Virtual meetings
   agendas in, 17
   face-to-face, 15, 21
   purposes of, 15
   status cues in, 21
   team projects in, 15, 17
   teamwork in, 21
Memorized delivery style, for oral
   presentations, 394
Memos
   bullet items in, 185
   definition of, 177
   direct approach in, 178, 180, 185
   emails compared to, 178
   follow-up, 181–183
   formatting of, 178–179
   function of, 177
   general applications for, 203
   global applications for, 204
   headings in, 179
   indirect approach in, 180–181, 185
   informational, 182, 184
   information sequence in, 179
   main body of, 179
   overview of, 176
   purposes of, 9, 178
   strategies for, 185
   structure of, 178–179
   summary, 181–183
   team applications for, 204
   tone for, 178–181
   transmittal, 181–182
   web-based applications for, 204
   white space in, 185
Mission statement, in employment
   documents, 165
MLA Handbook, 413
MLA (Modern Language Association)
   style, for documentation
   for book entries, 414–417
   for digital sources, 421–425
   indexes to, 415
   for miscellaneous sources,
     418–421
   for parenthetical references, 413–414
   for periodicals, 417–418
   for works cited, 414
Modified block formats, of letters, 189
Modifiers, 96, 99
Monster.com, 161
Multiple bar graphs, 116–117
Multiple line graphs, 117–118

Negations, in definitions, 212
Negative adjustment letters, 200–202
Netiquette, for emails, 353
NewsBank, 34

Nominalizations, 98–99
Notations
   alphanumeric, 81
   decimal, 81–82
Notes
   bibliographic citation in, 407
   in instructions, 252–254
   for paraphrasing, 410
   for quotations, 408
   references in, 407
   for source documentation, 406–408
   for summaries, 411
Numbered lists
   in document design, 142, 144
   in instructions, 258
   in web pages, 371
Numbers and numerals, 455–456
Numeric data, in visuals, 113
Numeric tables, 114–115

Objectivity, in descriptions
   informative language in, 223
   maintenance of, 223
   purpose of, 222–223
Observation, as primary research
   source, 41
Online information. *See* Web pages
Online instructions, 250
Online magazines, 32
Online news outlets, 32
Online public access catalog (OPAC), 35
Online résumés, 161–163, 166
Online sources, for research
   academic, 32
   blogs as, 32–33
   commercial, 32
   downloading from, 30
   electronic mailing lists, 33
   e-libraries, 34
   forums as, 33
   government, 32
   magazine, 32
   news outlets, 32
   organizational, 32
   periodical databases as, 34
   search engines, 29
   secondary sources, 28–29
   strategies, 29–30
   subject directories, 29
   web sites as, 31–32
   wikis as, 33
OPAC (online public access catalog), 35
Operating principles, in definitions, 212
Oral presentations
   action plan, 390–391
   audience considerations for, 388, 389
   body of, 392

   conclusion in, 392
   delivery of, 401–402
   delivery style for, 394–395
   function of, 387
   general applications for, 403
   global applications for, 404
   informative, 388, 390
   as interactive, 387–388
   introductions in, 391–392
   outlining for, 393
   persuasive, 390
   practice for, 398
   preparation of, 388, 392–398
   purpose of, 388
   research for, 392–393
   for sales, 391
   with software, 399–401
   storyboarding for, 393–394
   strategies, 402
   team application for, 403–404
   technology for, 396
   for training, 390
   types of, 388–391
   visuals in, 396–398
   web-based applications for, 404
Organizational web sites, 32
Organization charts, 119, 121
Outlining. *See also* Storyboarding
   with alphanumeric notations, 81
   for complex process descriptions, 232
   for complex product descriptions, 228
   with decimal notations, 81–82
   formal, 81–82
   for oral presentations, 393
   organization of, 80–82
   short documents, 80
   strategies for, 82
   subtopics in, 81
   for web pages, 367–368
Outside sources, documentation from, 406

Paragraphs
   coherence from, 85–86
   design for, 136–137, 139
   incoherent, 85–86
   purpose of, 84
   sequences in, 86
   support, 84
   topic sentences in, 84
   unity from, 85
Paraphrasing, as documentation source,
   409–410
Parentheses, in punctuation, 453
Parenthetical definitions, 209
Parenthetical references
   APA style for, 425–426
   MLA style for, 413–414

Passive voice
  indirect, 98
  readability and, 97–98
PDF. *See* Portable Document
    Format (PDF)
Peer review
  reports, 298–299
  strategies for, 19–20, 298
  in teamwork, 19–20
Periodic activity reports, 287, 288
Periodical databases, 34
Periodicals
  APA documentation style for, 429–430
  as hard-copy research sources, 35
  MLA documentation style for, 417–418
Periods, in punctuation, 446
Personable writing style
  culturally-biased language and, 106
  sexist language and, 106–107
  tone in, 105–106
Personal data, in résumés, 156
Personal information, in employment
    documents, 163, 166
Persuasive documents
  audience connections with, 52–55
  claims for, 52
  constraints of, 55
  cultural context in, 55–56
  direct actions in, 52
  example of, 10–11
  purpose, 9
  strategies for, 55–56
  usability of information in, 51–56
Persuasiveness, of technical
    communication, 5–6
Persuasive oral presentations, 390
Photographs
  audience considerations, 129
  creation strategies of, 125
  purpose of, 123
  sharing, using social media, 376
Phrasing, in instructions, 256
Pie charts, 119–121
Plagiarism
  avoiding, 406
  copyright infringement and, 438
  definition of, 69, 405
  as ethical abuse, 69, 405–406
Planning proposals, 329, 330
Portable Document Format (PDF)
  in document design, 132, 134
  for memos, 185
  for résumés, 161–162
Portfolios
  copies in, 165
  item assembly in, 165
  mission statement in, 165
  personal information in, 166

Positive adjustment letters, 200–201
Power connection approach,
    to audiences, 53
PowerPoint, for oral presentations,
    399–401
Prepositional phrases, 101
Presentation software, 399–401
  conclusions in, 398, 401
  strategies for, 400–401
  video conferencing, 401
  visuals in, 401
Prezi program, for oral presentations, 399
Primary purpose, of documents, 51
Primary sources, for research
  definition of, 27
  experiments as, 41
  informational interviews, 38–39
  observations as, 41
  secondary versus, 27–28
  surveys, 39–41
  types of, 37–41
  unsolicited inquiries, 37
Print résumés, 161–163
Privacy rights
  in digital communication, 358–359
  with web pages, 371
Problem-solution sequencing, 83, 332, 369
Procedures
  audience considerations of, 261
  definition of, 243–244
  formatting of, 244
  general applications for, 265
  global applications for, 266
  medical, 261
  purpose of, 261
  safety, 261–262
  SOP, 9, 261
  strategies for, 263
  team applications for, 266
  types of, 261
  usability testing in, 263
  web-based applications for, 266
Process descriptions
  complex, 232–235
  regular, 225, 227
Product descriptions
  complex, 228–231
  regular, 225–226
Progress reports, 283–286
  audience considerations for, 283–284
  elements of, 284
  purpose of, 283
  strategies for, 284
Project management software, 21
Pronouns
  agreement, 443
  ambiguous references for, 95–96
  case for, 445

Proofreading
  of emails, 357
  for formal reports, 313
  of résumés, 158
  spelling, 456
  strategies for, 62–63
  for technical communication, 61–62
  for web pages, 372
Proposals
  appendices in, 346
  audience considerations for, 328
  background information in, 334
  CFPs, 12
  claims in, 336
  conclusions in, 334, 345
  costs in, 334, 343–344
  crediting sources in, 335
  descriptions in, 334
  formal (*See* Formal proposals)
  formatting for, 335
  general applications for, 347–348
  global applications for, 348
  to induce action, 336
  informal (*See* Informal proposals)
  objections to, anticipation of, 336
  planning, 329, 330
  purpose of, 328
  qualifications in, 334
  reports compared to, 327–328
  research, 329, 331, 335
  resolution in, 334
  RFPs, 12, 348
  sales, 332, 333
  solicited, 328
  statements in, 334
  strategies for, 335–336
  team applications for, 348
  timing in, 334
  types of, 328–332
  unsolicited, 328
  web-based applications for, 348
ProQuest, 34
*Publication Manual of the American
    Psychological Association*,
    425, 432
Public domain, works in, 437
Punctuation
  apostrophes, 450–451
  brackets, 409, 452
  colons, 447
  commas in, 447–450
  dashes, 453
  ellipses, 409, 452
  exclamation points, 446
  italics, 452
  parentheses, 453
  periods, 446
  question marks, 446

quotation marks, 451–452
semicolons, 446–447
Purpose of documents
intended use, 51
primary, 51
questions to ask, 50
secondary, 51
statements of, 51
Purpose statement, in formal reports,
307–308

Qualifications, in proposals, 334
Quality assurance, specifications for,
236–237
Question marks, in punctuation, 446
Questions
document usability, assessing, 61–62
headings, construction, 87
in presentation software, 401
in technical communication, 3
Quick reference materials, 246
Quotation marks, in punctuation,
451–452
Quotations, as documentation sources
brackets and, 409
citing sources for, 409
definition of, 408
ellipses in, 409
notes for, 408

Rational connection approach,
to audiences, 54–55
Readability
active voice and, 96–97
ambiguous modifiers and, 96
ambiguous pronoun references and,
95–96
clarity and, 95–100
conciseness and, 100–102
fluent writing and, 102–105
for formal reports, 308
general applications for, 108–109
global applications for, 109–110
jargon and, 100
nominalization and, 98–99
passive voice and, 97–98
personable style for, 105–107
purpose of, 94
redundancy and, 102
repetition and, 102
style and, 94–95
team applications for, 109
unstacking modifying nouns, 99
web-based applications for, 110
Reader-based communication, 4
Reader's Guide to Periodical Literature, 35

Really Simple Syndication (RSS) feeds,
364–365
Recommendation reports
audience considerations for, 296
elements of, 296–297
strategies for, 296
Redundancy, 102
References
APA style for, 426
in formal reports, 311–312, 322
in notes, 407
in résumés, 156
Reference works, as hard-copy research
sources, 35–37
Referent agreement, 443
Refusal letters, 169–170
Relationship connection approach, to
audiences, 54–55
Repetition, readability and, 102
Reports. See also Analytical reports;
Feasibility reports; Formal reports;
Informal reports; Progress reports
proposals compared to, 327–328
purpose, 12
Requests for proposals (RFPs), 12, 348
Research. See also Online sources, for
research
combination of sources in, 27
critical thinking in, 26–27
for employment, 153–154
for formal reports, 304
general applications of, 42
global applications of, 43
for global communication, 13, 43
hard-copy sources, 35–37
for oral presentations, 392–393
primary sources, 27–28, 37–41
purpose, 26
secondary sources, 27–37
team applications of, 42–43
for technical communication, 5–6
web-based applications of, 43
Research proposals
characteristics of, 329
need for, 335
structure of, 331
Resolution, in proposals, 334
Résumés
career objectives in, 154
contact information in, 154
credential distortion in, 158
education in, 156
electronic, 161–163
in emails, 161
functional, 156–157
general applications for, 173
global applications for, 174
interests as part of, 156

organization of, 156
personal data in, 156, 163
printed copy, 161–163
proofreading of, 158
purpose of, 154
references in, 156
reverse chronological, 156
sample, 164
scanning of, 162
standard, 155
team applications for, 174
web-based applications for, 174
work experience in, 156
Reverse chronological résumés, 156
Revision symbols, 439
RFPs (requests for proposals), 12, 348
Routine claim letters, 195–196, 198
RSS (Really Simple Syndication) feeds,
364–365
Run-on sentences, 441

Safety, specifications for, 236–237
Safety procedures, 261–262
Sales letters, 198–200
Sales presentations, 391
Sales proposals
characteristics of, 332
as letters, 333
Salutations, in letters, 187
Sample application letters, 160
Saving, scanned résumés, 162
Scanned résumés
fonts in, 161
formatting in, 162
Scripted delivery style, for oral
presentations, 394
Search engines, 29
Secondary purpose, of documents, 51
Secondary sources, for research
definition of, 27
hard-copy, 28, 34–37
online, 28–34
primary versus, 27–28
Semicolons, in punctuation, 446–447
Semiformal tone, in writing style, 105
Sender's address, in letters, 187
Sentence fragments, 440–441
Sentences
in fluent writing, 103–104
in instructions, 256
run-on, 441
Sequencing
cause and effect, 83, 314–323
chronological, 83, 224, 229, 286
in descriptions, 224
functional, in descriptions, 224
in paragraphs, 86

Sequencing (*Continued*)
problem-solution, 83, 332, 369
spatial, 83, 226
in web pages, 369
Setting, usability of information and, 57–58, 61
Sexist language, in writing style, 106–107
Shading
in document design, 141, 144
in web pages, 370
Signature, in letters, 187
Signature blocks, in emails, 356
Simple bar graphs, 117
Simple line graphs, 118
Skills, assessment of, 152–153
Skype, 400
Slang, 13. *See also* Jargon, readability and
Social media directors, 377
Social networking or media
advantages of, 363
audience considerations, 377–379
corporate uses, 377
customer reviews on, 376, 379
discretion in, 383
employment searches through, 161, 380
ethical concerns, 382–383
Facebook, 376, 380
general applications for, 384
global applications for, 385
Google+, 376, 380
legal concerns, 382–383
LinkedIn, 376, 380–381
organizations in, 377
policy, 378
purpose, 377–379
strategies for, 383
team applications for, 384–385
tone with, 383
Twitter, 381–382
types of, 376–377
web-based applications for, 385
workplace communication and, 377
YouTube, 382, 387
Software
for document design, 135
for editing, 21
for presentations (*See* Presentation software)
for project management, 21
Solicited application letters, 159–160
Solicited inquiry letters, 193
Solicited proposals, 328
SOP (Standard operating procedure), 9, 261
Spatial sequencing
in complex product descriptions, 229
in descriptions, 226
in outlining, 83

Specifications
audience considerations for, 238
consistency in, 236–237
definition of, 236
to ensure quality, 236–237
government standards and, 236
purpose of, 236
strategies for, 238
terminology in, 238
Spelling, 456
Standard operating procedure (SOP), 9, 261
Standard résumés, 155
Standard workplace letter, 186
Statements, in proposals, 334
Status cues, team meetings and, 21
Status reports, 283, 287
Stereotyping, 13. *See also* Culture or cultural differences
Storyboarding
for oral presentations, 393–394
of web pages, 367–368
Structure, of information
additional, 80
chunking, 83
coherence through, 77
general applications for, 92
global applications for, 92
headings, 86–87
in instructional documents, 77–80
nonstandard, 78–79
outlining, 80–82
overview of, 87–90
paragraphing, 84–86
parallel, in fluent writing, 104
purpose of, 77
sequencing, 83–84
standard, 77–78
team applications of, 92
unity through, 77
in user manuals, 91
web-based applications of, 92
Style
in emails, 353
inefficient, in documents, 94–95
of instructions, 255–256
personable, readability from, 105–107
readability and, 94–95
in summaries, 270
usability of information and, 62
in web pages, 370
Subject directories, 29
Subjectivity, in descriptions, 222–223
Subject lines
in emails, 356
in proposals, 332
Subordination, in grammar, 443–445
Subtropics, 81

Summaries
accuracy of, 270
audience considerations for, 268–269
closing, 275
completeness of, 270
conciseness of, 270
creation of, 270–273
cut and paste in, 271
definition of, 268
descriptive abstracts in, 275–276
as digests, 278
in documentation of sources, 410–411
editing of, 271
ethical considerations for, 276, 278
executive, 276–277
general applications for, 279–280
global applications for, 280
informative abstracts in, 275
nontechnical style in, 270
notes for, 411
original document comparisons, 271
purpose of, 269
strategies for, 278–279
team applications for, 280
types of, 273–276
web-based applications for, 280
Summary memos, 181, 183
Support paragraphs, 84
Surveys
methods of, 40
as primary research source, 39–41
questionnaires, 39
samples for, 39, 40
strategies, 40–41
target population for, 39, 40
usability, 264
Symbols, 124–126

Table of contents
in document design, 144, 145
in formal proposals, 339
in formal reports, 310, 316
in user manuals, 246, 247
Tables
audience considerations, 128
creation of, 116
in formal reports, 309
list of tables and figures, 310
numeric, 114–115
source credits in, 116
textual, 114–115
Tact, in letters, 191
Task analysis, for documents, 56–57
procedure sample, 57
for user-friendly documents, 132
worksheets, 58

Team projects
  CSCW and, 21
  meetings, 15, 17
  organizational strategies, 14–15
  planning forms for, 16
  progress report, 286
  technology in, 20–21
  virtual collaboration in, 20–21
Teamwork
  conflict management, 14–18
  digital application, 24
  editing documents and, 19–20
  in face-to-face meetings, 15, 21
  general applications for, 23
  global applications for, 24
  peer review in, 19–20
  project organization for, 14–15
  social media application, 24
  team applications for, 23
  virtual, 21
Technical communication
  academic writing compared to, 4
  accessibility of, 5
  clarity in, 5
  as collaborative, 14–21
  computer-based applications of, 24
  creation of, 4
  definition of, 3
  digital applications of, 20–21, 24
  efficiency of, 5
  ethics in, 5, 67
  features of, 4–6
  general applications of, 23
  global, strategies for, 13
  global applications of, 24
  global audience for, 3, 12–13
  global issues in, 13
  informational documents, 5–6
  instructional documents, 5–6, 8
  media usage in, 20–21
  online application of, 24
  persuasive documents, 9
  persuasiveness of, 5–6
  proofreading for, 61–62
  purposes of, 3, 6–9
  as reader-based, 4
  relevance of, 5
  as research-based, 5–6
  as task-oriented, 56
  team applications of, 14–15
  templates, 147
  types, 9, 12
  as user-centered, 4
  web-based application of, 24
  workplace questions in, 3
Technicalities, in instructions,
  254–255, 257
Teleconferencing, 21

Templates
  for résumés, 163
  for technical documents, 147
Text
  justified, 137
  unjustified, 137
  visual support for, 113
Text messages, in workplace
  advantages of, 357
  audience considerations for, 357–358
  emails compared to, 358, 359
  general applications of, 361
  global applications of, 361
  IMs compared to, 357
  length considerations for, 358
  purpose of, 357–358
  team applications of, 361
  web-based applications of, 361
Textual tables, 114–115
Thank you letters, 168–169
Timing
  in proposals, 334
  usability of information and, 59
Titles
  in complex process descriptions, 233
  in complex product description, 229
  in descriptions, 223
  in formal proposals, 338
  in formal reports, 310, 315
  in instructions, 251
  in proposals, 332
Tone, in documents
  active voice in, 105
  application letters, 161
  consistency in, 105
  formal, 105
  informal, 105
  letters, 188–192
  in memos, 178–181
  in personable writing style, 105–107
  readability and, 108
  semiformal, 105
  for social networking, 381
Topic sentences, 84
Training presentations, 390
Transitional expressions, 456, 459
Transitions, in instructions, 256
Transmittal letters, in formal proposals, 337
Transmittal letters, in formal reports,
  309, 314
Transmittal memos, 181–182
TripAdvisor, 387, 389
Trip reports, 287–291
Twitter
  emergency notifications, 381–382
  format, 381
  job postings on, 380
  purpose, 387

Underlining
  in document design, 141, 144
  in web pages, 370
Unjustified text, 137
Unsolicited application
  letters, 159
Unsolicited inquiries
  in letters, 193–194
  as primary source reference, 37
Unsolicited proposals, 328
Unstacking of modifying nouns, 99
Usability, of information
  assessment of, 45
  audience analysis in, 45–50
  budgets and, 59, 61
  content in, 61
  cultural considerations, 62
  definition of, 45
  design for, 61–62
  ethics for, 62
  feedback on, 62
  formatting for, 59, 61
  general applications of, 64
  global applications of, 65
  in instructions, 263
  legal factors for, 62
  length and, 59, 61
  organization for, 61
  persuasiveness in, 51–56
  plan development for, 59–61
  potential problems, anticipation of,
    58, 61
  in procedures, 263
  revisions of, 61–62
  setting for, 57–58, 61
  steps in preparing, 45
  style and, 62
  in surveys, 264
  task analysis in, 56–57
  team applications of, 64–65
  testing of, 61–62
  timing and, 59
  for user-friendly documents, 133
  visuals for, 62
  web-based applications, 65
  writing for, 61–62
Usability surveys, 264
User-centered communication, 4
User-friendly documents.
    See also Design, in
    documents
  audience analysis for, 133
  task analysis for, 132
  usability requirements for, 132
User manuals
  instructions in, 246
  structure of, 91
  table of contents in, 246, 247

Verb agreement, 442–443
Vertical lists, 460–461
Victor, David A., 17
Video. *See also* Instructional videos
   creation strategies for, 126
   frames in, 124
   YouTube, 382, 387
Video conferencing, 400–401
Virtual meetings
   emails for, 21
   project management software for, 21
   technology in, 20–21
Virtual teams
   collaboration in, 14, 20–21
   status cues and, 21
   technology used by, 21
Visual hierarchy, in document design, 135
Visuals
   audience considerations for, 126
   charts, 119–121, 129
   color in, 127–128
   in complex process descriptions,
      233–234
   in complex product descriptions, 230
   cross-referencing in, 127
   definition through, 213
   in descriptions, 224, 225
   diagrams, 113, 122–123, 125, 129
   ethical abuses with, 70
   ethical use of, 128
   in formal reports, 308
   general applications for, 129–130
   global applications for, 130
   graphs, 112, 116–119, 129
   with icons, 124–126
   illustrations, 122–123, 125, 129
   importance of, 112–113
   in instructions, 252, 253
   numeric data in, 113
   for oral presentations, 396–398
   photographs, 123, 125, 129
   placement of, 127
   presentation of, 127
   in presentation software, 399, 401
   purpose of, 112
   selection of, 126–127

with symbols, 124–126
   tables, 114–116, 128
   team applications for, 130
   technical data compared to, 112
   for text support, 113
   for usability of information, 62
   with video, 124, 126
   web-based applications for, 130
   in web pages, 370
   without text, 115

Warnings, in instructions, 252–254
Web-based instructions, 247–249
Web-based sources, for research.
      See Online sources, for research
Web conferencing, 21
WebEX, 400
Webinars, 400
Web logs. *See* Blogs
Web pages
   advantages of, 365–366
   audience considerations for, 366–367
   boldface in, 370
   bulleted items in, 371
   chunking in, 83, 368–369
   color in, 370
   copyright infringement with, 438
   design for, 370
   development of, 366
   ethical considerations for, 371
   font style in, 370
   general applications for, 374
   global applications for, 374
   grid patterns in, 370
   headings in, 370
   interactive, 366
   invasion of privacy issue with, 371
   italics in, 370
   links in, 370
   numbered lists in, 371
   outlining for, 367–368
   proofreading for, 372
   purpose of, 366–367
   sequencing in, 369
   shading in, 370

storyboarding, 367–368
   strategies, 372
   structure of, 367
   style in, 370
   team applications for, 374
   underlining in, 370
   user-friendly, 369
   visuals in, 370
   web-based applications for, 374
   white space in, 370
Web sites
   development process, 366
   as research source, 31–32
Whiteboards, 21
White space
   in document design, 133–134,
      137–140
   in memos, 185
   in web pages, 370
Wikis
   audience considerations for, 371
   corporate, 365
   external, 365
   general applications for, 374
   global applications for, 374
   as online research source, 33
   strategies for, 371–372
   team applications for, 374
   virtual teams use of, 21
   web-based applications for, 374
Wordiness, avoidance of, 100–102
Work experience, in résumés, 156
Workplace communication, social
      networking and, 377
Workplace emails, 353–355, 358
Works cited lists
   for documentation, 407
   in formal reports, 311–312
   MLA style for, 414

Yahoo! Directory, 29
Yahoo! Search, 29
Yelp, 379, 387
"You" perspective, in letters, 188–191
YouTube, 382, 387